MACROECONOMIC
AND
STABILISATION

MACROECONOMIC THEORY
AND
STABILISATION POLICY

ANDREW STEVENSON, VITANTONIO MUSCATELLI
University of Glasgow

MARY GREGORY
University of Oxford

Philip Allan/Barnes & Noble Books

First published 1988 by
PHILIP ALLAN PUBLISHERS LIMITED
MARKET PLACE
DEDDINGTON
OXFORD OX5 4SE

First published in the USA 1988 by
BARNES & NOBLE BOOKS
81 Adams Drive
Totowa
New Jersey 07512

British Library Cataloguing in Publication Data
Stevenson, Andrew
  Macroeconomic theory and stabilisation
  policy
  Macroeconomics   2. Great Britain —
  Economic policy — 1945–
  I. Title   II. Muscatelli, Vitantonio
  III. Gregory, Mary
  339'.0941   HC256.6

  ISBN 0–86003–048–2
  ISBN 0–86003–143–8 Pbk

Library of Congress Cataloging-in-Publication Data
Gregory, Mary.
  Macroeconomic theory and stabilisation
  policy.
  Includes index.
  1. Macroeconomics. 2. Economic Policy. 3. Economic stabilization.
  I. Muscatelli, Vitantonio.   II. Stevenson, Andrew.   III. Title
  HB172.5.G76   1988   339.5   87–33467

  ISBN 0–389–20781–1
  ISBN 0–389–20782–9 (pbk.)

Typeset by Dataset Marlborough Design, St Clements, Oxford
Printed and bound in Great Britain at
the Alden Press, Oxford

To Elaine, Mhairi and Norman

CONTENTS

PREFACE

The idea for this book emerged from our experience of teaching postgraduate and final-year undergraduate students in both Glasgow and Oxford. The principal purpose of the text is to provide an outline of what we consider to be the main debates and issues in modern macroeconomics as they relate to questions of macroeconomic policy. In using this book, two points need to be borne in mind. First, the focus in a text such as this is necessarily selective, and we have concentrated on key issues rather than attempting a comprehensive coverage of macroeconomic theory and policy as a whole. However, in those areas on which we have chosen not to dwell, we have provided some indications of where the interested student might read further. Second, in a book such as this, a knowledge and grasp of intermediate macroeconomics is an essential prerequisite for the reader. In this context, Chapters 1 and 2 are both to be regarded to a considerable extent as introductory to the remainder of the book.

In writing this book we have benefited greatly from discussions with colleagues at both Glasgow and Oxford. In particular, we would like to thank David Bell, John Foster, Terry Moody and Thomas Moutos for their helpful comments on earlier chapter drafts. In addition, we are grateful to Mark Partridge for the considerable technical assistance which he provided. We would also like to thank Professors Andrew Skinner and David Vines for their active encouragement during the writing of this book. Any errors and omissions in the text are entirely the responsibility of the authors.

Finally, we would like to pay tribute to the seemingly inexhaustible patience and good humour of Philip Allan, whose enthusiasm for this project survived in the face of a whole series of delays.

A.A.S.
V.M.
M.B.G.

NOTATION

We adopt the following mathematical notation in this book. For a function of a single variable, $y = f(x)$, the first derivative is denoted by one of the following alternative expressions: $f'(x)$, f_x, or dy/dx. Second derivatives are then denoted by $f''(x)$, f_{xx}, or d^2y/dx^2. Where multivariable functions of the type $y = f(x, z)$ are involved, the first (partial) derivative with respect to x is denoted by $\partial y/\partial x$ or f_x. Similarly, the second derivative with respect to x is given by $\partial^2 y/\partial x^2$ or f_{xx}, and the cross-partial derivative with respect to x and z is denoted by $\partial^2 y/\partial x \partial z$ or f_{xz}. Where variables are functions of time, their first derivatives with respect to time are indicated by dy/dt or $\dot{y}$, and their second derivatives by d^2y/dt^2 or $\ddot{y}$.

Variables which appear in logarithms or real terms are usually denoted by lower-case letters, whilst upper-case letters are reserved for variables in nominal terms. First differences of variables are denoted by Δy, so that $\Delta y = y_t - y_{t-1}$.

1
INTRODUCTION: THE THEORY
OF AGGREGATE DEMAND

The central concerns of this book are the role and conduct of macro-economic policy in general, and demand management in particular. We can define the latter as the manipulation of aggregate demand in a discretionary manner by the authorities with a view to attaining some final objectives in terms of real income or employment, the level of prices (or, more usually, inflation), or some combination of these.

This involves us in confronting three general questions. The most fundamental is whether demand management is indeed required at all. The central issue here is the extent to which we can expect price flexibility to generate market-clearing outcomes in the various sectors such that the economy can be seen as effectively self-stabilising, with no need for stabilisation policy on the part of the authorities. Many of the key issues involved in this question lie on what intermediate textbooks refer to as the 'aggregate supply' side of macroeconomics, and we focus on these in Chapters 2, 3 and 4.

The second general question concerns the channels through which monetary and fiscal policies influence aggregate demand, and the relative efficacy of these policies. These issues are confronted in the first instance in Chapters 5 and 6, and the discussion is then widened to an open economy context in Chapters 7 and 8.

The final set of questions concerns the design and conduct of monetary and fiscal policy. In Chapter 9 we examine the problems of policy design and the role of intermediate objectives, targets, indicators and techniques of optimal control. Finally, the conduct of policy in an open economy, with the recognition of international interdependence and the international transmission of policy, is discussed in Chapter 10.

In this chapter, as an introduction to these questions, we set out what

1

can be regarded as the mainstream textbook model of aggregate demand, the IS–LM model. In doing so, we lay the foundation for much of the analysis which follows in the remainder of the book.

Since the presentation of the IS–LM model has been honed through successive generations of textbooks, the presentation here will be relatively compact, and will assume familiarity with the general structure and functioning of the model. In the first section we set out the basic IS–LM relations under fixed prices. In the second section we introduce exogenous changes in the price level, but without confronting the issue of the form of the aggregate supply curve. In section 3 we introduce wealth effects into the product market and the asset market respectively, while in section 4 we preview further developments, including the implications of the budget identity for subsequent analysis.

1.1.   The IS–LM Model

In this section we set out the principal elements of the IS–LM system, which is to be regarded as laying the foundations for aggregate demand analysis. However, it should be noted at the outset that the IS–LM model is not to be regarded as a complete model of income determination since this requires the price level to be determined endogenously by integration of the aggregate supply side into the discussion, a task which is only begun in the course of this chapter and completed in the three chapters which follow. To facilitate the discussion in this section, however, we assume that aggregate supply is infinitely elastic at a given price level, so that section 1 in effect describes a fix-price Keynesian model of income determination.

The essence of the IS–LM model lies in the integration of real and monetary factors in the determination of aggregate demand. Whereas the circular flow and the 45° line model of elementary macroeconomics deals only with the flow of real output and expenditure, the crucial advance introduced in the IS–LM system is the incorporation of monetary factors as influences on aggregate expenditure. This integration of monetary with real factors is achieved through the conceptual division of the economy into two major macromarkets, the product market for the current flow of real output, and the money market for stocks of money and alternative financial assets. The central relationships in each market show that the key variable determined in one market also plays an important determining role in the other: the level of expenditure determined in the product market is a major determinant of the demand for money and so influences the outcome in the money market, while the rate of interest, determined in the money market, influences certain categories of expenditure on real output in the product market. Through these interrelationships, real factors impinge on monetary conditions, and vice versa.

1.1.1. The Product Market

Let us first turn to the product market to derive the IS curve. Output is considered as a single commodity, y, with a single price, P, sidestepping any aggregation and index number problems which may arise in such an aggregation. For the moment, only the flow dimensions of current expenditure and its equilibrium will be considered. Stocks of wealth will not affect expenditure, nor will flows of saving and investment affect wealth or stocks of fixed capital. In what follows, lower case symbols denote variables denominated in real terms.

Aggregate real expenditure, e, may be seen as comprising consumption (c), investment (i), government expenditure (g), and net exports (x):

$$e = c + i + g + x \tag{1.1}$$

where x is defined as exports minus imports.

This level of disaggregation of total expenditure e may be seen as having its origins in Keynes' *General Theory* (Keynes, 1936). The components of aggregate expenditure identified above have been the subject of extensive research since the publication of the *General Theory*. In what follows, we take a simplified view of the determinants of consumption, investment, government expenditure and net exports to facilitate our exposition of the product market. The individual functions used are (in a general, implicit, functional form):

$$c = c_0 + c(y - t) \qquad 0 < c_y < 1 \qquad 0 < \frac{dc}{dD} < 1$$

$$i = i_0 + i(r) \qquad i_r < 0 \qquad \frac{dI}{dr} < 0$$

$$g = g_0$$

$$t = t_0$$

$$x = x_0 + x(y) \qquad -1 < x_y < 0$$

Consumption is postulated to depend only on the current flow of real disposable income with the marginal propensity to consume out of disposable income positive and less than one. Furthermore, the consumption function also has an autonomous component, c_0, the 'intercept' term in the Keynesian consumption function. Investment depends partly on the interest rate, but also has an autonomous component i_0. Both government expenditure and tax revenue are treated as exogenous. A more common assumption would be to postulate a constant marginal rate of income tax. The apparently greater realism of this is, however, largely deceptive since in practice most tax systems are based on nominal rather than real income. Clearly, this treatment of the government sector is highly simplified, and fiscal influences on aggregate demand are discussed in greater detail in Chapter 6. Lastly, the determinants of net exports are usually subdivided into the determinants of exports and imports. For simplicity, we assume that net exports are a negative function of real income, due to the marginal propensity to import, which is usually assumed to be less than one (thus ensuring that $-1 < x_y < 0$). In addition, net exports have an autonomous component x_0, due to the fact that this simple model ignores other possible effects on net exports operating through changes in competitiveness and foreign income levels. These factors will enter our analysis once we examine more detailed models of the open economy from Chapter 7 onwards.

Substituting these expressions for the components of aggregate expenditure into (1.1), we have

$$e = c_0 + c(y - t_0) + i_0 + i(r) + g_0 + x_0 + x(y) \tag{1.2}$$

Since we are concerned primarily with the level of expenditure rather than its composition, we can simplify the notation of our subsequent analysis by aggregating individual components of (1.2) as follows:

$$e = e_0 + e(y, r, t_0) \qquad 0 < e_y < 1, e_r < 0, -1 < e_t < 0 \tag{1.2'}$$

where

$$e_0 = c_0 + i_0 + g_0 + x_0$$

and

$$e(y, r, t_0) = c(y - t_0) + i(r) + x(y)$$

We have therefore grouped together all autonomous elements of individual categories of expenditure into e_0, and all elements of these categories which depend on income and the interest rate into $e(y, r, t_0)$.

The product market is in equilibrium when the following condition holds:

$$y = e \tag{1.3}$$

This condition requires the equilibrium flow of real output (or income) to be equal to the flow of real expenditures. This is equivalent to the analysis represented in the 45° line model of elementary macroeconomics. In equilibrium, flows of output are such as to meet *ex ante* expenditures, and there are no unplanned changes in inventories. In other words, the product market is in equilibrium when all desired real expenditures are matched by an equivalent flow of real output. Substituting (1.2′) into (1.3):

$$y = e_0 + e(y, r, t_0) \tag{1.4}$$

Equation (1.4) defines the relationship between the level of real output and the rate of interest which is required for product market equilibrium. The locus of points of equilibrium in the product market may be drawn as the IS curve, which, assuming a linear form, is set out in Figure 1.1. The features of the IS curve can be summarised by inspecting the total differential of equation (1.4):

$$dy = \frac{(de_0 + e_r dr + e_t dt_0)}{(1 - e_y)}$$

where from our definition of e_0 and $e(y, r, t_0)$, it follows that

$$e_y = c_y + x_y$$

$$e_r = i_r$$

$$e_t = -c_y$$

and it is usually assumed that e_y, the sum of the marginal propensities to consume and import, is less than unity. The position, or intercept, of the IS curve is given by the autonomous elements of expenditure, e_0, and

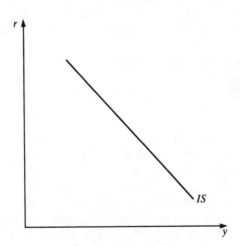

Figure 1.1 The IS Curve

hence the IS curve is shifted by a change in any of these. It is clear from the total differential of (1.4) that an increase in e_0 shifts the IS curve to the right. If we momentarily assume that the interest rate is exogenous and constant ($dr = 0$ in the total differential), the size of the shift may be immediately recognised as a reflection of the multiplier from the simple macromodel of income determination:

$$\frac{\partial y}{\partial e_0} = \frac{1}{(1 - e_y)} \qquad \frac{dy}{dK} = \frac{1}{\beta}$$

Expansionary fiscal policy, in the form of an increase in government expenditure or a reduction in taxation, is therefore expressed as a rightward shift in the IS curve, though it will be noted that an increase in government expenditure will shift the IS curve further to the right than will an equal cut in taxes. That is, from (1.4) and (1.2′) it follows that:

$$\frac{\partial y}{\partial g_0} = \frac{1}{(1 - e_y)}$$

and

$$\frac{\partial y}{\partial t_0} = \frac{-c_y}{(1 - e_y)} \qquad \frac{dy}{dT_0} = \frac{-\frac{dc}{dD}}{\beta}$$

We will return to this asymmetry between these two types of fiscal policy in the context of our discussion of the 'balanced budget multiplier' in Chapter 6. Similarly, an increase in autonomous net exports will shift the IS curve rightwards to the same degree as an increase in g_0. We will further extend our analysis of the open economy elements in the IS–LM system from Chapter 7 onwards.

The slope of the IS curve is given by:

$$\frac{dr}{dy} = \frac{(1 - e_y)}{e_r} < 0 \qquad \frac{dr}{dy} = \frac{\beta}{\frac{dI}{dr}}$$

The equilibrium level of expenditure varies inversely with the interest rate and the IS curve is therefore downward sloping. *Ceteris paribus*, at higher interest rates, the lower level of investment expenditures requires smaller saving flows to keep *ex ante* saving and investment flows equal (and hence maintain IS, or product market, equilibrium). As a result, higher interest rates must be matched by a lower level of income for IS equilibrium. The magnitude of the slope of the IS curve depends on the parameters e_y and e_r, respectively the income and interest sensitivity of expenditure:

$$\frac{\partial(dr/dy)}{\partial e_y} = \frac{-1}{e_r} > 0$$

$$\frac{\partial(dr/dy)}{\partial e_r} = \frac{-(1 - e_y)}{(e_r)^2} < 0$$

The greater is the income sensitivity of expenditure (and therefore the simple multiplier) the flatter is the IS curve. A given interest rate change and consequent change in investment expenditure will have a larger effect on income due to the larger multiplier. Alternatively, as the interest sensitivity of expenditure approaches zero, the IS curve becomes steeper. A given interest rate change will generate a smaller change in investment and therefore income. In the limiting cases, the IS curve approaches the horizontal as the marginal propensity to spend out of income approaches unity and/or the interest sensitivity of expenditure approaches infinity, while a vertical IS curve results from a zero interest sensitivity of expenditure.

The IS curve represents the locus of income and interest rate combinations which ensure that product market equilibrium (equation (1.3)) holds. However, it is an incomplete macroeconomic model, since it offers no explanation of how the interest rate is determined. In order to complete our model, we have to introduce the monetary sector.

1.1.2. The Money Market

In mainstream Keynesian theory, the determinants of the interest rate are to be found in the factors influencing demand and supply in the money market. Since both money and its substitutes, in the form of alternative financial assets in the Keynesian model, are held as stocks of wealth, the LM side is concerned with stock equilibrium rather than the flow equilibrium of the IS side.

In the streamlined treatment of the IS–LM model, the portfolio choice facing individual wealth holders is simplified to one between money and 'bonds', the latter to be taken as a collective term for assets which are not riskless, which bear a rate of return and which do not perform the function of a medium of exchange. We assume that these bonds have a fixed nominal value but a variable market price, and therefore a variable rate of interest. The current market value of the bond stock will vary inversely with the market interest rate, and in the case where the bonds have infinite lives (i.e. perpetuities), then $V = B/r$, where V is the market value of the bond stock, and B is the number of bonds outstanding paying one-unit coupon. Such interest rate valuation effects on the bond stock can be argued to have a certain macroeconomic significance. For example, they were cited as an important source of windfall gains/losses which could affect the consumption function in Keynes' original formulation. However, in the discussion presented here, such valuation effects have no crucial role to play, and for the remainder of this chapter, we shall assume, for simplicity, that the value of the bond stock is unaffected by interest rate changes, and can be measured by B, with the real value of the bond stock being given by B/P. In addition, since we are assuming a zero inflation rate, the nominal and real interest rates are identically given as r. ✳

The demand for real money balances, l, is postulated to be a function of real income and the rate of interest on bonds, and to be homogeneous of degree zero in the price level:

$$l = l(y, r) \qquad l_y > 0, l_r < 0 \tag{1.5}$$

This specification of the demand for money may be seen as following Keynes' original theory which distinguished three motives for liquidity preference — the transactions, precautionary and speculative motives — with the level of income as a key determinant of the first two, and the rate of interest being central to the speculative motive. However, subsequent work, particularly the development of the inventory-theoretic approach by Baumol (1952), has introduced the rate of interest as a determinant of transactions balances. In addition, an alternative rationale to Keynes' speculative motive underpinning the role of the interest rate in the asset demand for money has been introduced by Tobin (1958) in the form of the mean-variance approach to the analysis of portfolio diversification. (For a full exposition of the latter, see Chapter 5.) In a two-asset model such as IS–LM, however, these developments merely provide further micro-foundations for the specification of the demand for money function set out in (1.5).

On the supply side, we take the nominal money stock, M, to be exogenously determined by the monetary authorities, and we can write:

$$M = M_0 \tag{1.6}$$

We assume that all money is outside money (i.e. money to which there corresponds no private sector debt). By the same token, we assume that there is no banking system, and therefore that all money is high powered money. These are considerable simplifications, and the implications for monetary policy of removing them are discussed at length in Chapter 5.

The equilibrium condition for the money market is that the demand for real money balances should equal the outstanding real money stock:

$$l = \frac{M}{P}$$

Substituting the structural equations for money demand and supply, (1.5), (1.6), into this equilibrium condition gives the equation of the LM curve:

$$\frac{M_0}{P} = l(y, r) \tag{1.7}$$

defining the relationship between the level of income and the interest rate consistent with money market equilibrium. The equation of the LM curve can be rearranged as a relationship explicitly between y and r, as with the IS curve, and represented in Figure 1.2. At every point on the LM curve, the demand and supply of money are equal. For a given money stock, it shows the interest rate required at different income levels for money market equilibrium. Taking the total differential of (1.7):

$$d\left(\frac{M_0}{P}\right) = l_y dy + l_r dr \qquad \frac{\partial M}{\partial y} \cdot dy + \frac{\partial M}{\partial r} \cdot dr = 0$$

we may observe the main features of the LM curve.

The position of the curve is determined by the real money stock, an increase in the real money stock shifting the LM curve to the right. Thus, we have:

$$\frac{\partial y}{\partial (M_0/P)} = \frac{1}{l_y} > 0$$

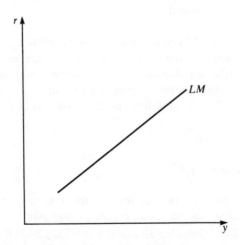

Figure 1.2 The LM Curve

It will be noted that the extent of the shift in LM for a given change in the real money stock depends inversely on l_y, the income sensitivity of the demand for money.

The slope of the LM curve is given by:

$$\frac{dr}{dy} = \frac{-l_y}{l_r} > 0$$

Since the demand for money responds positively to the level of real income and inversely to the rate of interest, the LM curve is upward sloping. *Ceteris paribus*, at higher levels of income, implying a higher transactions demand for money, equilibrium in the money market requires a higher interest rate to re-establish portfolio balance. The magnitude of the slope depends on the values of l_y and l_r, with the LM curve becoming steeper the higher the income sensitivity of the demand for money and the smaller is the absolute magnitude of its interest sensitivity. As income sensitivity aproaches zero, the LM curve tends to become horizontal. As is more frequently emphasised, when the interest sensitivity of the demand for money is zero, the LM curve is vertical, while when it is infinite, as in the Keynesian liquidity trap, the LM curve is horizontal.

The general formulation of the demand for money, $l = l(y, r)$, allows the various limiting cases to appear not as mutually exclusive but as alternative possibilities applicable perhaps over different ranges of values of y and r themselves. In this way the various Keynesian and monetarist positions, frequently stylised as the extreme cases above, may appear as zones of the curve rather than as alternative representations of the curve itself.

1.1.3.   IS–LM Equilibrium

Combining the IS and LM relationships, and continuing to assume a given price level, we can derive the values of income and the interest rate (y^* and r^*) consistent with equilibrium in the money and product markets simultaneously. These equilibrium values are functions of the exogenous variables (e_0, (M_0/P), which determine the positions of the two schedules:

$$y^* = y^*[e_0, (M_0/P), t_0] \tag{1.8}$$

$$r^* = r^*[e_0, (M_0/P), t_0] \tag{1.9}$$

The geometric representation of this equilibrium is given in Figure 1.3. Thus, the system is in full equilibrium at the point of intersection in Figure 1.3. We may regard the IS curve as showing what the level of output (and income) will be at alternative interest rate levels, ignoring the

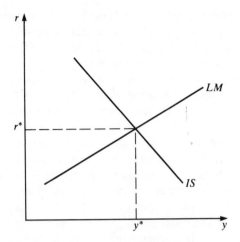

Figure 1.3 IS–LM Equilibrium

consequences for the money market (through the transactions demand for money). By the same token, we may interpret the LM curve as showing the interest rate required to clear the money market at different income levels (and therefore transactions demand), ignoring the consequences of the interest rate for demand in the product market. In full equilibrium, the income level which clears the product market is associated with an interest rate which clears the money market. The solution in terms of total differentials provides the basis for all the comparative static properties of IS–LM equilibrium:

$$\begin{bmatrix} 1 - e_y & -e_r \\ l_y & l_r \end{bmatrix} \begin{bmatrix} dy \\ dr \end{bmatrix} = \begin{bmatrix} de_0 - c_y dt_0 \\ d(M_0/P) \end{bmatrix} \qquad (1.10)$$

$$dy^* = \frac{l_r}{(1 - e_y)l_r + l_y e_r} [de_0 - c_y dt_0] + \frac{e_r}{(1 - e_y)l_r + l_y e_r} d(M_0/P)$$

$$dr^* = \frac{-l_y}{(1 - e_y)l_r + l_y e_r} [de_0 - c_y dt_0] + \frac{(1 - e_y)}{(1 - e_y)l_r + l_y e_r} d(M_0/P)$$

The signs for the composite parameters for e_0 and (M_0/P) are unambiguous. The equilibrium level of income is higher the higher is autonomous expenditure, whether in the form of consumption, investment, government expenditure or exports (rightward shifts in the IS curve), and the higher is the real money supply (a rightward shift in the LM curve). The equilibrium interest rate, on the other hand, also varies positively with exogenous expenditure, but inversely with the money supply. Moreover, it is easily shown that the responsiveness of income to a change in one of the autonomous components of expenditure, e_0, increases, *inter alia*, as e_y tends to unity, e_r tends to zero, and l_r tends to infinity, while its responsiveness to monetary impulses increases as l_r tends to zero, e_y tends to unity, and e_r tends to infinity. Geometrically, a given shift in the IS curve has a greater effect on income the flatter is the LM curve and the steeper is the IS curve, while a given shift in the LM curve has a greater effect on income the steeper is the LM curve and the flatter is the IS curve. These are familiar conclusions which lay at the heart of much of the debate between monetarists and Keynesians in the 1960s about the relative efficacy of monetary and fiscal policy, and they form the starting point for our discussion of demand management policies in Chapters 5 and 6.

The discussion so far has been set within a fixed-price framework. If this is interpreted as a perfectly elastic supply of output at a given price level, then the IS–LM model as set out above can be regarded as a model of income and output determination. In the next section, we examine how aggregate demand (and therefore income and output) responds to exogenous changes in the price level.

1.2. Aggregate Demand and the Price Level

In this section, we extend the analysis to take account of changes in the price level. However, since we are still concentrating on the aggregate demand side, we cannot yet integrate endogenously determined prices into the model. Rather, we merely allow for parametric changes in the price level which, if we wish to regard the following analysis as a theory of income determination, we may regard as shifts in a horizontal aggregate supply curve.

Since the expenditure and money demand functions are specified as homogeneous of degree zero in the price level, these relationships are invariant with respect to price level changes. The real money stock, however, varies inversely with the price level. This single point of entry for the price level in the IS–LM system is sufficient to ensure that, except under extreme assumptions, the equilibrium level of aggregate demand will vary inversely with respect to the price level. This is shown in Figure 1.4. As the price level falls from P_1 to P_2 to P_3 raising the real value of the nominal money stock M_0, the LM curve shifts from LM_1 to LM_2 to LM_3 and aggregate demand rises from y_1 to y_2 to y_3. This relationship between aggregate demand and the price level is shown in (y, P) space in Figure 1.5. Extending the IS–LM equilibrium analysis of (1.8), the equation of the aggregate demand curve with respect to the price level is:

$$y^* = y^*(P, e_0, M_0, t_0) \quad y_p^* < 0 \tag{1.11}$$

Aggregate demand is no longer uniquely determined by the exogenous components in the IS–LM system, namely the nominal money stock and

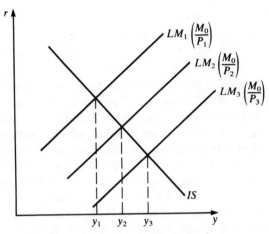

Figure 1.4   IS–LM and the Price Level

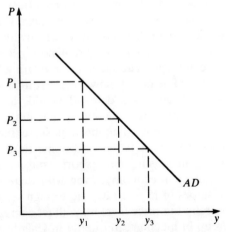

Figure 1.5   The Aggregate Demand Curve

exogenous expenditure, but it is also related to the price level. In differential form the IS and LM equations with a variable price level become:

IS: $(1 - e_y)dy - e_r dr = de_0 - c_y dt_0$

LM: $l_y dy + l_r dr = (1/P)dM_0 - (M_0/P^2)dP$ (1.12)

such that

$$\frac{dy}{dP} = \frac{- e_r}{(1 - e_y)\, l_r + l_y\, e_r}\,(M_0/P^2) < 0$$

The negative slope of the aggregate demand curve derives from what is familiarly known as the 'Keynes effect': the higher the price level the lower the real value of the nominal money stock, requiring a higher interest rate to preserve equilibrium in the money market, which in turn induces a lower level of interest-sensitive expenditure, an effect which is amplified via the multiplier. Thus, it is clear that the slope of the aggregate demand curve depends on all the structural parameters of the IS and LM functions. More specifically, the steeper is the LM curve and the flatter is the IS curve, the flatter is the aggregate demand curve. Thus, if the monetarist position is characterised as one where aggregate demand is highly responsive to changes in the price level, it is possible to derive this result for the aggregate demand curve by adopting the stylised monetarist case of a steep LM curve and a flat IS curve. Thus, the increase in the real money stock resulting from a given change in the aggregate price level will have a strong effect on the interest rate and, in turn, a strong effect on aggregate demand. On the other hand, in the stylised extreme Keynesian case (steep IS and flat LM), aggregate demand will be relatively insensitive to aggregate price level changes. A change in the real money stock has a weak effect on the interest rate and aggregate demand, rendering the aggregate demand curve steep. It should be noted, however, that the inclusion of net exports as a component of aggregate demand would, in a more fully specified model, tend to flatten the aggregate demand curve. This is because net exports can be expected to be a positive function of the country's competitiveness. Thus, a fall in the domestic price level will increase competitiveness, increasing net exports and hence aggregate demand. Therefore, in an open economy, even with extreme Keynesian assumptions about the slopes of IS and LM, the foreign sector provides a further mechanism whereby the price level may affect aggregate demand. This is a subject taken up in much greater detail in Chapters 7 and 8.

The position of the aggregate demand schedule is determined by the levels of autonomous components of expenditure e_0 (together with t_0) and the nominal money stock M_0. These are therefore the variables which will change the level of aggregate demand for any given price level. Thus, an increase in the nominal money stock or any autonomous component of expenditure, will shift the aggregate demand curve to the right by an amount dependent on the parameters determining the slopes of IS and LM. Ignoring the limiting cases mentioned above, expansionary monetary policy and expansionary fiscal policy will both shift the aggregate demand curve to the right, but their relative impact is determined within the IS–LM system.

The consequences of an increase in government expenditure on the one hand, and an increase in the money stock on the other, are illustrated in Figures 1.6 and 1.7 respectively. In Figure 1.6, the initial equilibrium is determined by IS_1 and LM_1, where LM_1 is associated with price level P_1. An increase in government expenditure (or indeed an increase in any autonomous component of expenditure) shifts the IS curve to IS_2, and aggregate demand increases from y_1 to y_2. In (y, P) space, the aggregate demand curve shifts to the right by the horizontal distance y_1y_2. In Figure 1.7, we again start from LM_1 and IS_1, and in this case we allow the nominal money stock to increase, shifting the LM curve to LM_2, raising aggregate demand from y_1 to y_2, and therefore shifting the aggregate demand function by that amount to the right.

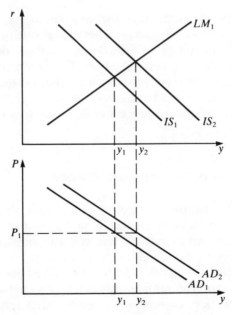

Figure 1.6 Fiscal Policy and Aggregate Demand

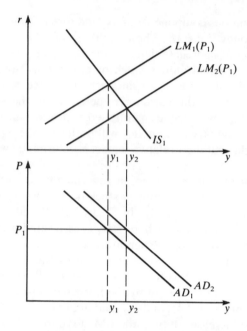

Figure 1.7   Monetary Policy and Aggregate Demand

The IS–LM system, then, lays the foundation for the analysis of aggregate demand. However, except in the special case of perfectly elastic supply at an exogenously given price level, it cannot be regarded as a complete theory of income determination. This is a matter to which we turn in Chapters 2, 3 and 4. For the remainder of this chapter, however, we examine some of the shortcomings of the simple IS–LM analysis of aggregate demand, and introduce some of the policy issues which are taken up in later chapters.

1.3.   The IS–LM Model and the Stock of Wealth

The analysis of the determination of aggregate expenditure through the IS–LM system has so far been conducted on the assumption of a constant stock of wealth, in terms of both financial and physical wealth. This assumption is generally defended on the grounds that the flows of saving and investment which, over time, can be expected to change these wealth stocks, are, in the short run, sufficiently small relative to the existing stocks that the effects of these current flows can be safely ignored. While we continue to adhere to the assumption of a constant stock of physical capital (since to do otherwise would move our discussion into the territory of growth theory which is beyond the scope of this book), in this section we examine the implications of relaxing the assumption of a constant stock of financial wealth. As we shall see, one justification for this approach is that, to the extent that financial wealth is denominated in nominal terms, as in the case of its monetary component, then its real value will be affected by changes in the price level. Thus, wealth effects may provide another mechanism whereby changes in the price level affect aggregate expenditure, and therefore influence the slope of the aggregate demand curve derived in the previous section. We begin by examining the role of wealth as a determinant of consumption and therefore of the position of the IS curve.

1.3.1. Wealth and the IS Curve

In introducing wealth as a determinant of expenditure, it is appropriate to depart for a moment from the Keynesian approach to the analysis of consumption, which focuses on the role of current disposable income as a determinant, and analyse the consumption decision in a neoclassical manner, focusing on the maximisation of utility through the intertemporal allocation of consumption subject to the constraint of total expected wealth, with time divided into two periods, the present and the future. In what follows, we assume that total financial wealth, W, comprises money, M, plus bonds, B. Thus, $W \equiv M + B$. In Figure 1.8, current real wealth, w_t, is the sum of currently owned assets, w_0, current real income, y_t, and expected future income, y_{t+1}, discounted at the rate r. Future wealth then follows as $w_{t+1} = (1 + r)w_t$, with the slope of the wealth constraint BB as

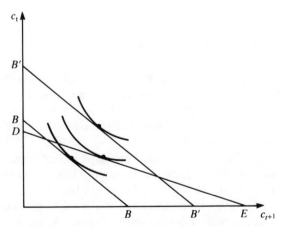

Figure 1.8 Wealth and the Consumption Decision

$-1/(1 + r)$. An increase in wealth, due to an increase in w_0, y_t or y_{t+1} shifts the constraint outwards with unchanged slope to $B'B'$, and provided that c_t is a normal good, consumption will rise. An increase in the interest rate, on the other hand, rotates the wealth constraint to DE as shown, the impact on c_t now incorporating a substitution effect as c_t becomes relatively more expensive in terms of foregone c_{t+1}, as well as a wealth effect. This analysis, while providing an additional reason for regarding private expenditure as likely to be interest-sensitive, is more significant in that it allows the IS curve to shift in response to a change in real wealth.

However, although the determinants of c_t can be expressed as only wealth and the interest rate, plus the factors shaping the indifference map, $c_t = c(w_t, r)$, imperfections in capital markets, especially those limiting individual households' ability to borrow against future income, suggest that current income, as well as wealth, should be retained as a determinant of aggregate consumption. This somewhat expanded form, as used in Patinkin (1965), makes a bridge between the Keynesian and neoclassical approaches:

$$c = c(y - t, r, W/P) \qquad c_y > 0, c_r < 0, 0 < c_{W/P} < 1 \qquad (1.13)$$

The restriction on c_r incorporates the assumption that the substitution effect of the interest rate on current consumption dominates its wealth effect, and the restriction $0 < c_{W/P} < 1$ follows from the assumption that both c_t and c_{t+1} are normal goods. Redefining the IS relationship to incorporate the influence of wealth on the level of real expenditure gives:

$$y = e_0 + e(y, r, W/P, t_0) \qquad e_y > 0, e_r < 0, 0 < e_{W/P} < 1, e_t = -c_y$$

and, totally differentiating:

$$(1 - e_y)dy = de_0 + e_r dr + e_{W/P}\, d(W/P) - c_y dt_0 \qquad (1.14)$$

As before, the slope of the IS curve varies inversely with both e_y and e_r. Its position, however, is now determined by the level of real wealth in addition to autonomous expenditure. Hence, the IS curve is shifted additionally by changes in the nominal stock of assets $(M + B)$ or by changes in the price level.

Wealth has now been denominated explicitly in real terms, $w = W/P$, to focus attention on the role of the nominal stock of financial assets in inducing changes in wealth through changes in the price level. Thus, a fall in the price level, for example, increases real wealth, generating a parallel outward shift in the wealth constraint in Figure 1.8, increasing aggregate consumption, and therefore shifting the IS curve to the right. This effect therefore provides an additional channel through which changes in the price level may affect aggregate demand, and this has the effect of rendering the aggregate demand curve flatter. As we shall see in Chapter 2, the possible existence of such wealth effects was to prove crucial in the debate between Keynesian and neoclassical economists, in the years after the publication of the *General Theory,* about the possibility of under-employment equilibrium under flexible prices. For the moment we may note that in the absence of wealth effects, it is possible for the aggregate demand curve to be vertical if we assume either a perfectly interest-elastic demand for money function (the liquidity trap) or perfectly interest-inelastic expenditure (putting to one side the question of the price sensitivity of net exports). In such cases, there is no channel through which price level changes can affect aggregate demand, in the absence of wealth effects, and flexible prices can do nothing on the demand side to alleviate unemployment. However, wealth effects on expenditure provide a new channel. Thus, even in the extreme case described above, where the IS curve is vertical and the LM curve is horizontal, rendering the 'Keynes effect' impotent, wealth effects on expenditure allow changes in the price level to shift the IS curve directly, restoring the negative slope of the aggregate demand curve.

While these matters will be discussed at greater length in the next chapter, we may note three additional points here. First, the above argument allows for <u>wealth effects to operate through changes in the real value of any nominally denominated form of wealth</u> (i.e. both money and bonds). A variant of this argument, associated particularly with Patinkin (1965), focuses solely on the monetary component of wealth. Thus, <u>changes in the price level change the real money stock which in turn affects aggregate demand direct</u>ly (rather than through any portfolio adjustment involving interest rates). This so-called '<u>real balance effect</u>' is perhaps more significant in that it focuses attention on a more direct transmission mechanism for monetary policy, whereby money stock increases feed directly into real expenditures, a mechanism developed by, and identified with, Milton Friedman and other monetarists, which we examine in Chapter 5.

Second, the fact that <u>changes in asset stocks, whether monetary or non-monetary, generate aggregate demand changes directly, provides another channel through which both the government and the foreign trade sectors may affect aggregate demand</u>. As we shall analyse more fully in Chapters 5, 6 and 7, changes in asset stocks, and therefore expenditure, may stem from the fiscal balance on the one hand, and the current account of the balance of payments on the other. Wealth effects play a leading role in the analysis of the transmission mechanism of fiscal and monetary policy and the adjustment to full equilibrium in the external balance.

Finally, for changes in asset stocks to exert wealth effects on expenditure, it is necessary for these assets to constitute 'outside' wealth. That is, they must be assets to which there corresponds no private sector liability (or debt). Consider, for example, the case of bonds issued by a private sector firm. Such bonds, while they are an asset to the holder, are a liability to the issuing firm. Thus, a fall in the price level, which increases the real value of the bond, may increase the wealth of the bond holder, but, by the same token, it increases the real value of the debt, and therefore reduces the net wealth, of the issuer. For the private sector as a whole, then, the bond does not represent net wealth, and price changes cannot affect aggregate expenditure through changing its real value. The precise definition of the assets which can be regarded as comprising outside or 'net' wealth to the private sector is not exactly a question which is free from controversy, as we shall see in Chapters 2 and 6.

1.3.2. Wealth and the LM Curve

In the same way as consumption may be affected by the stock of wealth, it can also be argued that wealth has a role to play in the demand for money function underlying the LM curve. In particular, much of the theoretical work on the demand for money subsequent to the *General Theory* has been built on the recognition that money is one of a range of assets in which individuals may seek to hold their wealth, and that, in general terms, the demand for money can be expected to be a positive function of its own rate of return, a negative function of the rates of return on alternative assets, and a positive function of the size of the overall portfolio i.e. wealth. Indeed, it could be argued that both monetarists and Keynesians share this general framework, and that many of the disagreements between them can be attributed to differences in the range of assets that are to be regarded as alternatives to money and therefore to be included in the portfolio allocation decision. While in the *General Theory* all money substitutes were aggregated into 'bonds', one of the contributions of Tobin's analysis has been to widen and disaggregate the range of alternative financial assets. (See, for example, Tobin 1969.) On the other hand, Friedman's approach (see, for example, Friedman 1956) is to include real as well as financial assets within the portfolio decision.

The full implications for monetary policy of these alternative theories are examined in Chapter 5. For the moment, we introduce the role of wealth in the demand for money in the simple money–bonds portfolio underlying the LM curve. Thus, the demand for money (assumed to be zero interest-bearing) is a function of the interest rate on bonds (i.e. *the* interest rate) and the stock of wealth (i.e. money plus bonds). Within this framework, we can retain the level of income as a determinant of the demand for money, on the grounds that, in allocating total wealth within the portfolio, the demand for money for transactions and precautionary purposes remains an important consideration for the wealth holder, and consequently, one might argue that the own rate of return on money lies in its uniqueness as a medium of exchange (or means of final payment), and that the inclusion of the level of income in the demand function is a reflection of this.

Thus, we can rewrite the LM curve as

CONSTANT

$$(M_0/P) = l(y, r) \qquad\qquad l_y > 0, l_r < 0, l_{W/P} > 0 \qquad\qquad (1.15)$$

DEMAND

The incorporation of the wealth effect on the LM curve, and therefore on the aggregate demand curve, has a number of important implications. First, the LM curve can now be shifted not only by a change in the money stock, but also by a change in the bond stock (assuming the bonds in question to be 'outside bonds'). Thus, an increase in the bond stock, as a consequence, for example, of bond-financed expenditure by the government, will tend to shift the LM curve to the left, as the increase in the wealth stock increases the demand for money. This effect becomes particularly important in the analysis of the effectiveness of fiscal policy under different financing regimes, as we shall see in Chapter 6.

Second, and leading on directly from the previous observation, the net effect of a change in the bond stock on the position of the aggregate demand curve depends on the relative strength of the wealth effects in the two sectors. An increase in the bond stock will tend to shift the IS curve to the right, through the wealth effect on expenditure analysed in the previous subsection, while simultaneously shifting the LM curve to the left for reasons set out above. If the wealth effect on expenditure is smaller than the wealth effect on the demand for money, then an increase in the real stock of wealth is contractionary, shifting the aggregate demand curve to the left. This is illustrated in Figure 1.9.

The wealth effect on expenditure shifts the IS curve to the right, to IS_1, while the wealth effect on the demand for money shifts the LM curve to the left, to LM_1. In this case, the net outcome for y in Figure 1.9(a), and therefore for the position of the aggregate demand curve in Figure 1.9(b), is contractionary but it is clearly possible for the relative strength of the two wealth effects to be reversed, such that an increase in the bond stock would be expansionary, shifting the aggregate demand curve to the right.

Finally, it should also be noted that, in the context of this analysis, the impact of changes in the price level on the position of the LM curve depends on the precise specification of the role of wealth in the demand for money function. For example, if we assume that the demand for money is homogeneous in wealth, that is, an increase in wealth increases the demand for money in the same proportion, then an increase in the price level reduces the demand for money and the supply of money in the same

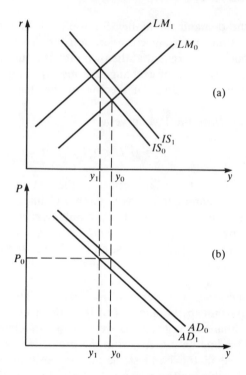

Figure 1.9   The Bond Stock and Aggregate Demand

proportion, leaving interest rates unaffected, apart from the Keynes effect noted earlier.

1.4.   Aggregate Demand: Further Considerations

The model of aggregate demand set out in this chapter forms the basis of much of the analysis of macroeconomic policy in the remainder of the book. In general terms, fiscal policy is seen as operating on the IS curve and monetary policy on the LM curve, the relative slopes of these schedules determining how far these policies shift the aggregate demand curve. However, as we have begun to see in the previous section, the introduction of wealth into the analysis begins to complicate the picture. We complete this chapter by introducing two further sets of considerations which have a considerable bearing on the later analysis in this book. The first of these concerns the treatment of the monetary sector.

So far, our treatment of the asset demand for money has followed the simple money–bonds portfolio introduced by Keynes. As we noted above, subsequent developments in the portfolio approach treat money as one of a number of alternative forms of wealth. An important early insight in this respect was that of Metzler (1951) who recognised that in the Hicksian IS–LM system, where the interest elasticity of expenditure derives from the declining marginal efficiency of capital, bonds and real capital are treated as perfect substitutes, in so far as in equilibrium the interest rate on bonds is equal to the marginal efficiency of capital. The replacement of this assumption with that of imperfect substitutability, where the money–bonds portfolio is in effect replaced by a money–bonds–real capital portfolio, has far-reaching implications for the analysis of the transmission mechanism of monetary policy, as Tobin has elegantly pointed out (Tobin 1961 and 1969). This analysis can be easily extended to the case where money has a whole range of substitutes, as we shall see in Chapter 5.

Second, our simplified version of the money supply can be adapted to allow for the existence of banking system. This has two important implications. First, if we include bank deposits in the definition of money, the supply of money is no longer necessarily uniquely determined by the monetary authorities. The behaviour of the banking system must be taken into account. This raises the question of whether the money stock is exogenous, as has been implied in the discussion in this chapter, or whether it is partly or wholly endogenous. The second implication of including the banking system in the analysis is that the money stock is no longer entirely to be regarded as outside wealth, since at least some bank deposits have corresponding private sector debt, in the form of bank loans to the private sector. The implications of this for the role of wealth effects are discussed in Chapter 2.

Finally, we should note that the existence of financial institutions other than banks (non-bank financial intermediaries) may also have important implications for the analysis. Their liabilities may represent near-money substitutes, with implications for the process of portfolio adjustment, and therefore their behaviour, unless controlled by the authorities, may have profound implications for the implementation of monetary policy and the relevance of money stock control.

The second main complication to the analysis set out in previous sections is the existence of the so-called budget identity. This refers to the accounting relationship between the public sector deficit, the balance of payments and the private sector's holdings of wealth. Assuming no banking sector, the general form of the budget identity can be set out as follows:

$$PSD = \Delta H + OMO - BP$$

where H is high powered money, PSD is the public sector deficit, OMO is open market bond sales (and therefore measures increased bond holdings by the private sector), and *BP* is the balance of payments surplus. The budget identity expresses the fact that the excess of government expenditure over fiscal revenue must be financed, and that this finance may take a number of forms. In the simplified version set out above, sources of finance to the government, other than taxation, are divided into three general categories. As we shall see in Chapters 5 and 6, different forms of the budget identity may be adopted, depending on the degree of financial disaggregation, but the simple version above is sufficient for our present purposes. In this case, the government is seen as financing its fiscal deficit by a combination of monetary and non-monetary means. The former refers to government borrowing by the issue of assets which fall within the definition of high powered money. In the absence of a banking system, this would consist of increasing the supply of cash and could accurately be described as 'printing money'. However, in the more realistic case where a banking system exists, whose liabilities are included within the definition of money, then ΔH could include various forms of government borrowing from the central bank.

The government may also borrow from the private sector by selling non-monetary assets, which accounts for the other two terms in the budget identity. Government bond sales (*OMO*) serve to finance the fiscal deficit and do not increase the money stock so long as the bonds are held by the non-bank private sector. (In the case where a banking system is allowed for, bond purchases by the banking system are not included in *OMO*, as we shall explain in Chapter 5.) The inclusion of the balance of payments in the budget identity requires an additional word of explanation. It is assumed for simplicity that when the balance of payments is non-zero (that is, exchange rates are not perfectly flexible), the surplus/deficit is financed by purchases/sales of foreign exchange by the domestic authorities. Thus, when the balance of payments is in deficit, the government can be seen as selling non-monetary assets in the form of foreign currency, and therefore a balance of payments deficit can, in this way, be viewed as financing a fiscal deficit. Similarly, a balance of payments surplus involves net purchases of foreign exchange by the government, and this must be financed from the other items in the budget identity. In the case where the exchange rate is perfectly flexible (i.e. where the authorities do not intervene in the foreign exchange market) the balance of payments term becomes zero (see Chapter 8).

The key point to bear in mind in the above discussion is that the budget identity is precisely that — an identity. One can infer no causal interconnection between the four items, and the identity may be arranged in any way. Instead of presenting the identity as a description of the financial implications of fiscal policy (as indeed we shall in Chapter 6), one can place ΔH on the lefthand side, and frame the discussion in terms of sources of monetary expansion/contraction (as in Chapter 5). Alternatively, we can set *BP* on the lefthand side and analyse it in terms of its monetary consequences (as in Chapter 7).

The budget identity will, then, be of recurring importance throughout this book. For the moment, however, we make one key point in the context of the IS–LM model as the basis of the analysis of aggregate demand. Given that the fiscal deficit is included in the IS curve, then once we include wealth as an argument in the expenditure function and the demand for money function, the IS and LM curves become interdependent. For example, a fiscal deficit, unless it is exactly matched by a trade deficit, must necessarily increase either the stock of money or of bonds, with ongoing consequences for the position of both the IS and LM curves. Thus, the IS–LM model must be regarded as a short-run model focusing on flow equilibrium. As soon as wealth effects and the budget identity are introduced, the question of long-run stock equilibrium becomes paramount, and much of the analysis of macroeconomic policy, particularly when dealing with fiscal policy and open economy questions, has been dominated by precisely this issue.

1.5. Conclusion

In this chapter we have set out what can still be regarded as the mainstream model of aggregate demand, starting from the narrow Keynesian IS–LM model and extending it to take account of price level changes and wealth effects. Much of the debate on the relative roles of monetary and fiscal policy carried on intermittently through the 1950s and the 1960s, and culminating in the early 1970s in Friedman's debate with the critics (see Gordon 1974), was conducted largely in terms of the slopes and relative stability of the IS and LM curves. More recent developments in these debates have been centred on the budget identity, the role of wealth (in terms of both its size and its composition) and the considerations introduced by the open economy. These are questions to which we devote considerable attention later in this book.

However, before that discussion can be set properly in context, the consequences of shifts in aggregate demand, and hence the objectives of aggregate demand policy, must be identified. So far we have assumed, for didactic reasons only, that the supply of output is perfectly elastic at an exogenously given price level. In seeking to replace this assumption with a theory of aggregate supply, we enter the arena for what has become the central, and fiercest, debate in modern macroeconomics; this is the subject matter of the next three chapters.

2
CLASSICAL VERSUS KEYNESIAN ECONOMICS: THE DEBATE ON UNDEREMPLOYMENT EQUILIBRIUM

The analysis of the previous chapter centred on establishing the determinants of aggregate demand, with the price level taken as given exogenously. In the next three chapters, the focus shifts to the supply side of the economy and to the relationship between output and the price level. The representation of the supply side of the economy, however, produces fundamental differences between the various schools of macroeconomic analysis, regarding the self-equilibrating or full employment properties of the macrosystem and the role of demand changes in this. These divergent views underlie the debates on the role of stabilisation policy, the channels and efficacy of monetary and fiscal measures, and the appropriate design of macroeconomic policy which form the material of the latter part of this book.

A highly simplified representation of the essence of these debates can be given in terms of the nature and slope of the aggregate supply schedule (AS) in (y, P) space in Figure 2.1. Figure 2.1 (a) illustrates the framework adopted in Chapter 1, with aggregate supply perfectly elastic at a given price level. Output responds one for one to changes in aggregate demand, and the 'multiplier' effects of, for example, a monetary expansion on aggregate demand (a shift of AD_0 to AD_1) are identical in their effect on output. For any given price level, output is demand-determined. This is sometimes presented as the extreme Keynesian view of the economics of depression, when output can be expanded at constant costs, overriding diminishing returns. However, casual empiricism suggests that the relevance of this view is limited. The opposite view is shown in Figure 2.1(b), where the aggregate supply curve is vertical. Any shift in aggregate demand does not alter the level of real output, but only the price level. This is the familiar representation of 'classical aggregate supply', under which the level of output is supply-determined, with variations in demand serving merely to alter the price level. If, however, the aggregate supply schedule is upward sloping, as in Figure 2.1 (c), then both output and the price level vary with changes in aggregate demand, the relative extent of the change in each depending on the slope of the *AS* schedule.

The analytical stances summarised in these stylised representations are the subject matter of the next three chapters. In this chapter the view represented as classical aggregate supply will be treated at some length as it plays a central role in much of the analysis of this and the following chapters. In the first instance this representation may be traced back to the classical economists whom Keynes sought to rebut, and serves as the starting point of the debate on stabilisation policy between Keynes and the classical economists, and their respective successors, regarding the possibility of macroeconomic equilibrium at less than full employment. This debate was resolved at a conceptual level some thirty years after the publication of the *General Theory* (Keynes 1936) in the neoclassical synthesis developed by Patinkin (1965), in which the classical properties were confirmed for the long-run equilibrium of the macrosystem even with the incorporation of the (mainly demand-side) innovations pioneered in the *General Theory*. Patinkin's analysis, however, coexisted comfortably with the Keynesian view on the role for stabilisation policy in the context of equilibrating forces seen as weak and slow acting. Divergences of stance on the role and effectiveness of stabilisation policy were accepted as reflecting differing judgements as to the empirical magnitudes of the various parameters of the adjustment process rather than fundamental disagreements on the functioning of the macrosystem.

Indeed, attempts by Keynesians to establish an analytical stance outside the neoclassical synthesis were essentially unsuccessful. Two variants will be discussed. The traditional approach, the so-called Keynesian 'fixedwage' model, postulates downward rigidity in the money wage, and hence the failure of the labour market to clear. While this generates involuntary unemployment, no convincing rationale for wage stickiness and the

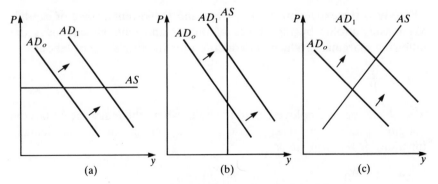

Figure 2.1 The Aggregate Supply Schedule

consequent market failure was offered. The more comprehensive attempt from the Keynesian side to resist the classical or neoclassical conclusions at a theoretical rather than empirical level came from the so-called 'disequilibrium' theorists, who invoked the distinction between actual and 'notional' demand and supply. A discussion of these views concludes the present chapter.

2.1.   Classical Aggregate Supply and the Neoclassical Synthesis

2.1.1.   *Classical Aggregate Supply*

Although normally referred to as the classical aggregate supply schedule, the derivation of this is most straightforwardly presented in neoclassical terms. We adopt the Marshallian short-run context in which capital stock and technology are fixed, and the output of the economy's single good depends only on the input of the variable factor, labour, assumed to be homogeneous and perfectly divisible. The labour market thus becomes central to the analysis of the supply of output.

The short-run production function for the ith firm incorporates diminishing returns to the variable factor, labour:

$$q_i = q(N_i, \bar{K}_i), \qquad q_N > 0, \, q_{NN} < 0$$

where q denotes the supply of output (distinguished from y, the demand for output), N is the number of units of labour employed and K the flow of capital services into the production process, assumed proportional to the capital stock in place (which is assumed fixed). For the competitive firm which is a price-taker in both product and factor markets, profits are given by:

$$\pi_i = Pq(N_i, \bar{K}_i) - WN_i - R\bar{K}_i$$

where W is the exogenous money wage and R the rental price of capital. Maximising profits by the choice of output and employment gives the following marginal productivity condition for the firm's use of labour:

$$q_N = \frac{W}{P}$$

whereby labour is employed up to the point where the real wage equals the marginal product of labour. Reformulating this as the labour demand function for the firm yields:

$$N_i^d = N^d\left(\frac{W}{P}\right) \qquad\qquad dN^d/d\left(\frac{W}{P}\right) < 0$$

where the negative slope incorporates the Marshallian assumption of diminishing returns.

Turning to labour supply, for the jth household maximising utility under a budget constraint we have:

$$N_j^s = N^s\left(\frac{W}{P}\right) \qquad\qquad dN^s/d\left(\frac{W}{P}\right) > 0$$

where the upward slope of the household's labour supply schedule is established by imposing the assumption that the substitution effect of a change in the real wage on the household's demand for leisure dominates the income effect when both income and leisure are normal goods.

Aggregating labour demands across all firms and labour supply across all households in the economy, and combining these with a market-clearing condition, gives the simplest classical representation of the labour market:

$$N^d = N^d\left(\frac{W}{P}\right) \tag{2.1a}$$

$$N^s = N^s\left(\frac{W}{P}\right) \tag{2.1b}$$

$$N^d = N^s \tag{2.1c}$$

The labour market clears at a unique equilibrium level of the real wage $(W/P)^*$ and level of employment N^* (see Figure 2.2a). With each firm adhering to the marginal productivity condition for the use of labour, given its capital stock, an aggregate production function for the economy's output, q, can be derived in the same form as for the firm to give the level of aggregate output corresponding to the market-clearing level of employment:

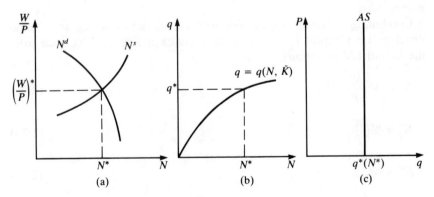

Figure 2.2 'Classical' Aggregate Supply

$$q^* = q(N^*\left(\frac{W}{P}\right)^*, \bar{K})$$

as in Figure 2.2b.

Totally differentiating equations (2.1a)–(2.1c) shows that retaining equilibrium requires equiproportional changes in the money wage and the price level: $dW/W = dP/P$. Consequently $d(W/P)^*/dP = dN^*/dP = 0$. The market-clearing levels of employment and the real wage are invariant with respect to the price level, the money wage adjusting in the same proportion as the price level. Since the equilibrium level of output q^* depends only on N^*, it too is invariant with respect to the price level: $dq^*/dP = 0$. The classical aggregate supply schedule in (q, P) space is therefore vertical (see Figure 2.2c).

2.1.2. *Properties of the Classical Model*

The properties of a macromodel incorporating the classical aggregate supply schedule may be briefly summarised. First, by the market-clearing condition in (2.1), full employment in the labour market holds by assumption. All those seeking employment at the going real wage will find an employer demanding their services. Second, the actual level of employment which is generated depends only on the factors determining the positions of the labour demand and supply schedules: the size of the capital stock, and the state of technology on the one side, and income–leisure preferences of households on the other. In particular the level of aggregate demand plays no role in determining employment and output. Consequently, any macromodel incorporating the classical aggregate supply schedule is at least partially recursive, the supply-side variables being independent of outcomes in the expenditure and monetary sectors. Finally, the classical view is essentially Walrasian in its equilibrium perspective and in the necessary role played by flexibility in prices and the money wage.

Combining a classical supply side with the model of aggregate demand developed in Chapter 1, but for the moment excluding wealth effects from the IS and LM equations, we have:

$$N^d = N^d\left(\frac{W}{P}, \bar{K}\right) \tag{2.2a}$$

$$N^s = N^s\left(\frac{W}{P}\right) \tag{2.2b}$$

$$N^d = N^s \tag{2.2c}$$

$$q = q(N, \bar{K}) \tag{2.2d}$$

$$y = q \tag{2.2e}$$

$$y = e(y, r) \tag{2.2f}$$

$$l(y, r) = \frac{M}{P} \tag{2.2g}$$

The recursive structure is clear. Equations (2.2a), (2.2b) and (2.2c) jointly determine N^* and $(W/P)^*$. The short-run production function (2.2d) then determines aggregate output, which must equal aggregate demand (2.2e). With y determined through equilibrium with aggregate supply, the IS curve (2.2f) determines the equilibrium real interest rate, while the role of the monetary sector, encapsulated in the LM curve (2.2g), is to determine the price level. Finally, flexibility in the money wage, W, ensures that, for a given price level, the equilibrium level of the real wage can be established.

The model can also be illustrated geometrically using a four-quadrant diagram (Figure 2.3). Quadrant (iii) contains the labour market relationships (2.2a)–(2.2c), establishing N^* and $(W/P)^*$. The production function in quadrant (iv) shows the level of output q^* (aggregate supply) associated with the level of employment N^*. To bring aggregate expenditure y^* into

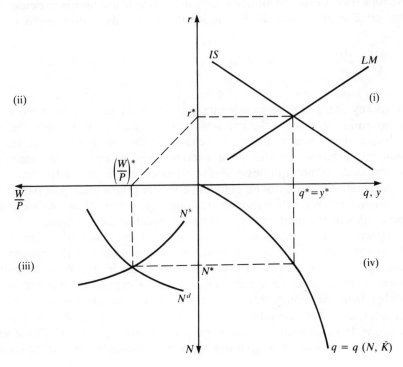

Figure 2.3 The 'Classical' Model

equilibrium with aggregate supply q^* requires a particular interest rate r^* as shown in quadrant (i). A flexible price level ensures, through movements of the LM curve, that the IS–LM system yields the required (y^*, r^*) combination. Quadrant (ii) summarises the relative factor prices which the model implies.

The fundamental feature of the classical model is therefore that the equilibrium level of output (q^*) is determined exclusively on the supply side, from the condition of full employment in the labour market. The role of aggregate demand is the purely passive one of adapting to this. In the model outlined in equations (2.2), the (real) interest rate plays its strictly classical role of equating savings and investment i.e. of adjusting the level of interest-sensitive expenditure such that real aggregate demand equates to real supply. The flexible price level then equilibrates the nominal relationships.

The model of equations (2.2) incorporates three major classical properties, namely the classical dichotomy, the strict quantity theory, and the neutrality of money. The equilibrium values of the real variables of the system (N, y, q, W/P, and r) are established through the subset of equations (2.2a)–(2.2f), independent of the monetary sector introduced in (2.2g). The classical system 'dichotomises' into separate real and monetary sectors. The role of the money supply in the classical system is to determine the price level. Totally differentiating (2.2g) with dy = dr = 0 gives:

$$\frac{dM}{M} = \frac{dP}{P}$$

Thus any change in the money supply changes the price level in the same proportion, replicating the prediction of the traditional quantity theory. Also, money is neutral in that any change in the money stock changes all nominal variables in the same proportion, leaving all real variables unchanged. While quintessentially classical, these properties are not equivalent, and each can be eliminated by the reformulation of particular relationships. We will return to this question below when analysing the properties of the model presented by the neoclassical synthesis.

However, the fundamental characteristic of the classical system is the invariance of equilibrium output and employment with respect to aggregate demand and the price level. This stems from two assumptions. First, both labour demand and labour supply depend on the real wage rather than the money wage. We return to this assumption later in this chapter, when we consider the Keynesian fixed-wage model, and again more widely in considering the wage determination process in Chapters 3 and 4. The second, and even more important, assumption is that the labour market clears. All unemployment is therefore voluntary, by definition. The possibility of underemployment equilibrium or the persistence of Keynesian involuntary unemployment, where individuals are rationed in the quantity of labour which they can supply, cannot be a macroeconomic issue under the classical view of the labour market.

2.1.3. The Neoclassical Synthesis

It was the view that involuntary unemployment could not persist as an intrinsic feature of the labour market, but only as a friction, or temporary malfunctioning, which Keynes sought to refute in the *General Theory*. The determination to explain unemployment not in the narrow context of the labour market but in terms of the functioning of the macroeconomy as a whole motivated the entire approach of the work. Yet the debates which followed from its publication through until the mid-1960s progressively suggested that, in spite of its many major and durable innovative features, the *General Theory* had failed in its central purpose of establishing the theoretical possibility of underemployment equilibrium and the persistence of involuntary unemployment.

To look at these debates we will accept the Hicksian IS–LM model of aggregate demand as encapsulating the innovations of the *General Theory*: the principle of effective demand, the consumption function, the multiplier, the marginal efficiency of investment, and liquidity preference. This view has Keynes' own endorsement (see Keynes 1986), although subsequently Hicks himself and others have sought, from differing standpoints, to cast doubt on its adequacy, and even its basic suitability as a vehicle for representing the ideas of the *General Theory* (Hicks 1967; see also Solow 1984). In the first instance we combine the IS–LM model with the classical postulate of flexible prices which function to clear markets. The central question can then be posed: can effective demand be insufficient, so as to give rise to a situation of excess aggregate supply, which is not self-correcting, such that involuntary unemployment persists? Within the framework of the model set out in equations (2.2) the only possibilities for a failure of market clearing rest with one or other of the so-called Keynesian limiting cases, the liquidity trap, or the interest insensitivity of expenditure.

The general case is illustrated in Figure 2.4. Suppose that initially the economy is at point E in quadrant (i), at an income y_1 below full employment income y^*. With a 'classical' labour market, this must imply that employment is below full employment, and therefore that real wages are above the full employment (equilibrium) real wage, $(W/P)^*$, at $(W/P)_1$. The classical postulate that prices adjust to clear markets means that nominal wages, W, will fall as workers attempt to return into employment. This will in turn cause a fall in prices as firms' marginal (labour) costs are falling. The downward pressure on the price level will raise the real value of the money stock pushing the LM curve to the right (the 'Keynes effect') until full employment is restored. Thus, provided prices and wages are perfectly flexible, the economy has a self-equilibrating nature.

However the 'Keynes effect' may fail in two special cases. First, in Figure 2.5, the infinite interest elasticity of the demand for money at r_1 (the 'liquidity trap') prevents any further reduction in the interest rate, precluding the stimulus to expenditure and the consequent reduction of excess supply. Second, if the IS curve is interest-inelastic, although the increase in real money balances through the Keynes effect brings a fall in the interest rate, expenditure does not respond, again leaving aggregate demand insufficient (see Figure 2.6).

Thus the outcome of the first major round of the debate between the followers of Keynes and economists of a classical or neoclassical persuasion, as encapsulated in equations (2.2), was to attenuate the view on the possibility of underemployment equilibrium from a 'general' theory to a theoretical stance applicable only in two highly special cases. Both of

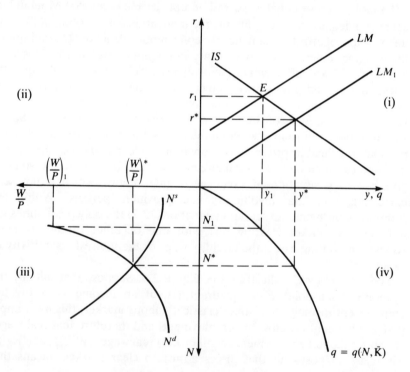

Figure 2.4 The 'Keynes Effect'

these cases, moreover, could be argued to involve an element of failure in the price system: in the case of the liquidity trap due to a lack of downward flexibility in the interest rate, and in the vertical IS curve case due to a lack of price sensitivity in terms of the responsiveness of investment expenditure to the interest rate.

The *coup de grâce* in this debate on the possibility of underemployment equilibrium when prices function to clear markets came with the incorporation of real wealth as a determinant of expenditure (the Pigou or real-balance effect; see Patinkin 1965). This ensures that even in the two Keynesian limiting cases, given flexible prices and money wages, the macrosystem will attain full employment equilibrium. We now turn to analysing the role of these wealth effects in the neoclassical synthesis.

2.1.4. *Wealth Effects and the Neoclassical Synthesis*

The origins of the debate on wealth effects culminating in the neoclassical synthesis can be found in the writings of Haberler (1941) and Pigou (1941, 1943, 1947). In what subsequently became known as the 'Pigou effect', it

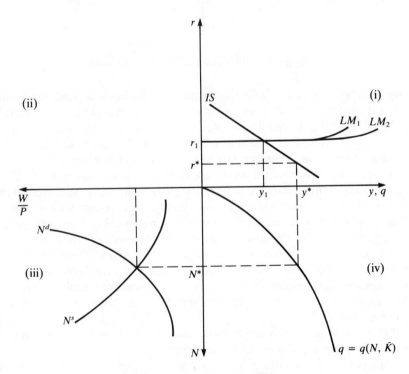

Figure 2.5 The Liquidity Trap

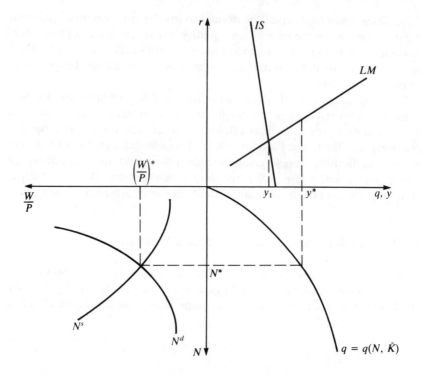

Figure 2.6   The Interest-Inelastic IS Curve

was postulated that aggregate consumption expenditure depended not only on real income, but also on private sector net wealth. Later, Patinkin (1965) argued that if wealth consisted of real money balances, expenditure may depend on wealth, and thus real balances. This particular version of wealth effects is sometimes referred to as the 'real-balance' effect. What constitutes net wealth in a monetary economy is an issue to which we return later in this section. For the moment we direct our attention to the way in which we expect a change in wealth to affect consumer expenditure. It may be noted at the outset that the following model of consumption has strong affinities with the classical theory of saving as a function of the rate of interest, a feature which Keynes himself (1936, Book III) preserved in a minor role, alongside the emphasis on current disposable income as the principal determinant of consumption, which subsequently became the Keynesian 'absolute income hypothesis'. Developments in the theory of consumption since Keynes (e.g. Friedman 1957, Modigliani and Brumberg 1954) must be seen as a move back towards the theory of consumption based on intertemporal utility optimisation.

To examine the wealth effects on consumer expenditure we recall the analysis of Figure 1.8. In Figure 2.7 we again illustrate the choice facing an individual between current consumption, c_t, and future (next period) consumption, c_{t+1}. The slope of the budget line, as discussed in Chapter 1, is given by $-P_{t+1}/P_t$ $(1 + r)$, where r is the interest rate at which the individual can freely borrow and lend on the basis of current and expected future real income, Y_t/P_t and Y_{t+1}/P_{t+1}, where P_t and P_{t+1} are respectively the current and future expected price level. Let the budget line initially be *AB*, with equilibrium at point *E*, with a given existing wealth stock V_0. Suppose P_t and P_{t+1} fall in equal measure, increasing the value of real wealth, and shifting the budget line rightwards to $A'B'$. Equilibrium is now at E', the increase in consumption from c_1 to c_2 representing the Pigou effect.

It is important to realise that the effect is potentially ambiguous, with an alternative possible equilibrium at E'', but only if c_t is an inferior good with respect to wealth. Early in the debate, however, Pigou (1947) argued that it was unlikely that an equilibrium such as E'' would be relevant, referring to Keynes' theory of consumption which was largely independent of the level of the interest rate, with a marginal propensity to consume less than one, implying that individuals would still save, even at a zero rate of interest. This, Pigou argued, implies that individuals attach utility to the accumulation of wealth (either because they appreciate wealth for its own sake, or because they wish to leave bequests), and thus one can assume that individuals will experience diminishing marginal utility from additions to their real wealth. As a result, an increase in real wealth is likely to increase consumer expenditure.

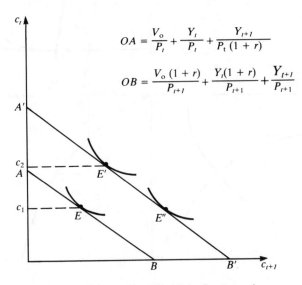

$$OA = \frac{V_o}{P_t} + \frac{Y_t}{P_t} + \frac{Y_{t+1}}{P_t(1 + r)}$$

$$OB = \frac{V_o(1 + r)}{P_{t+1}} + \frac{Y_t(1 + r)}{P_{t+1}} + \frac{Y_{t+1}}{P_{t+1}}$$

Figure 2.7 Wealth Effects on Consumption

Thus the Pigou or wealth effect on expenditure provided an additional mechanism whereby the economy could return to full employment following a fall in aggregate demand. This is shown in Figure 2.8. If the economy is initially in underemployment in the liquidity trap or with a steep IS curve, a fall in prices will not only shift the LM curve to the right, as M/P increases, but the IS curve will also shift from IS_1 to IS_2 as the increase in real wealth increases expenditure through the Pigou effect. Thus the economy cannot settle in underemployment equilibrium, even in the two Keynesian special cases. In terms of our aggregate demand and supply analysis, the liquidity trap and steep IS curve render expenditure insensitive to changes in the price level in the absence of the Pigou effect. Thus, in these special cases the aggregate demand curve will be vertical, and full employment will not be achieved even if prices and wages are fully flexible. However, the incorporation of the Pigou effect causes expenditure to respond to changes in the price level thus ensuring that the aggregate demand curve is downward sloping. With a vertical aggregate supply curve this ensures that the economy will settle at full employment.

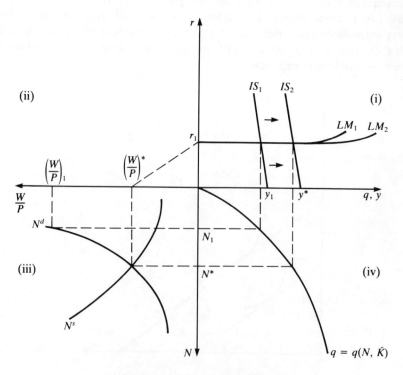

Figure 2.8 The 'Pigou' Effect

2.1.5. Some Doubts on the Neoclassical Synthesis

A number of reservations may be expressed as to how far the neoclassical synthesis is an effective characterisation of self-equilibrating forces in the economy. First, and counter to the spirit of much of Keynes' analysis, the methodology of the neoclassical synthesis is strictly that of comparative statics, where any change, such as a fall in the price level, takes place *ceteris paribus*, and in particular without inducing the expectation of either a further change or a reversal. But it is apparent that if individuals, following a fall in current prices, expect a *further fall* in prices in the next period, this is more likely to cause current consumption to fall, as individuals postpone consumption in the anticipation of future price falls. Then initial underemployment may cause price falls which in turn drive the economy away from full employment equilibrium. Keynes' (1936, 1937) own account of how expectations are formed does indeed suggest that households and firms put much weight on past experience when forming their expectations. If expectations of price changes are extrapolative, this may cause expenditures to be postponed. Furthermore, firms may postpone investment plans if they expect a recession to continue, affecting investment expenditure in a similar way to consumer expenditure. For both these reasons, falling prices may cause the IS curve to shift back to the left, which would weaken the argument for a self-equilibrating economy. This line of criticism has wider applicability since it centres on the appropriate modelling of the formation of expectations. We return to this issue in Chapters 3 and 4.

Furthermore, in our argument so far we have not discussed what constitutes 'net wealth'. Clearly the significance of the Pigou effect depends in part on the size of the nominal wealth base on which it is operating. Which assets form net wealth has been the subject of considerable debate. So far we have suggested that financial assets enter the definition of wealth, but the status of some assets as private sector net wealth has been challenged. First, let us examine money, which is generally seen as comprising currency plus bank deposits. At the level of the individual's balance sheet, holdings of money certainly constitute an asset, providing they are not offset by a matching liability (i.e. an equivalent private sector debt). For an economy as a whole, therefore, currency may be clearly seen as net wealth, as it constitutes a net asset to the private sector with no matching liability. However, bank deposits are generally matched by bank loans, except to the extent that banks hold cash reserves, or reserves at the central bank. To the extent that bank deposits are matched by banks' holdings of such reserves, these must be seen as net wealth (effectively it is as if the bank stored individuals' money holdings for safe keeping). Currency plus bank deposits matched by reserves are therefore net wealth and are known as *outside money*. However, those bank deposits which are lent to the private sector involve a matching liability to the latter. This type of money is known as *inside money*, and it has been argued by Gurley and Shaw (1960) that it cannot be regarded as net wealth, unlike outside money, which clearly is. The simple argument which they advance is that, for the private sector in aggregate, holdings of inside money (assets) are matched by an equivalent amount of loans (liabilities) from the banking sector. Thus, adopting Gurley and Shaw's argument, it follows that the wealth effect on expenditure is diluted considerably, reducing the economic system's ability to restore full employment equilibrium.

The argument that inside money does not constitute net wealth was challenged by Pesek and Saving (1967), and Johnson (1969). Pesek and Saving do not dispute the fact that bank deposits are to a large extent matched by bank loans and that *in this sense* inside money does not constitute net wealth to the private sector. However, Pesek and Saving pointed out that bank liabilities perform a medium of exchange function in the economy, and therefore may be seen as yielding a stream of future returns in terms of their services. Providing that the bank pays no interest on its deposits, or that the interest paid on bank deposits does not match the utility yield from the services money provides, then inside money must constitute net wealth. Johnson (1969) takes a similar approach by arguing that to the extent that money may be costlessly created through a process of financial intermediation such as that described above, in the sense that its return (interest on bank deposits) is below that of alternative private sector assets (e.g. real capital), money may be regarded as net wealth. This is because, given a demand function for real money balances which is negatively related to the yield on alternative assets, some individuals would have been willing to hold money balances even at a higher return on alternative assets than the one prevailing in the market. This existence of a *consumer surplus*, Johnson argues, confirms that money (of both an outside and inside type) constitutes net wealth.

The arguments advanced by Pesek and Saving and Johnson challenge the usefulness of the distinction between outside and inside money, focusing more on the services which money provides as a medium of exchange. On the other hand, a similar distinction has been drawn between 'outside' and 'inside' bonds. The former consist of bonds issued by agents outside the domestic private sector (the domestic government, foreign governments or foreign firms), while the latter typically imply corresponding liabilities to other individuals in the domestic private sector (for example, bonds issued by domestic private firms). Inside bonds are therefore not normally regarded as net wealth. Since there are no corresponding private sector liabilities, it follows that foreign bonds are net wealth, and we shall use this result in Chapters 7 and 8. However, whether outside bonds issued by the domestic government can be regarded as net wealth is a more contentious matter. It has been argued, notably by Barro (1974), that they do not, on the grounds that ultimately government debts have to be financed out of future taxation or the issue of high powered money, as implied by the budget identity introduced in Chapter 1. If individuals take into account future taxes, they will recognise a claim against the private sector equivalent to the value of the government debt, which is thus not regarded as net wealth. If the government services the debt not by increases in taxation, but by issuing more high powered money, it still does not follow that government bonds are net wealth. To the extent that such a monetary expansion is expected to cause inflation, real wealth will not increase as a result of the increase in high powered money, and thus again bonds will not be considered as net wealth. We will return to this issue in Chapter 6.

The equilibrating role of wealth effects may be further questioned on rather different grounds. Macroeconomics typically ignores distributional considerations in aggregating to economy-wide magnitudes; but in the case of wealth effects the neglect of possible differences of behaviour *within* the private sector may be particularly serious. If falling prices have a stronger effect on the expenditures of net debtors in the private sector than on the spending of net creditors, the rising real value of inside assets may actually reduce expenditure. In addition, if the economy enters a severe depression, this may cause bankruptcies which instantly reduce expenditures, and even the greater risk of bankruptcy may be sufficient to cause further deflation. Minsky (1963, 1972) argues that such a debt and bankruptcy spiral may be the primary driving force in an economy below full employment, and that such a spiral contributed considerably to the depression of the 1930s. It is certainly arguable that such adverse effects on expenditure more than outweigh the possible effects from the increased net worth of the stream of services from money balances following a fall in the price level.

Ultimately, the significance of wealth effects, and their role as a stabilising force in the economy, is an empirical matter, albeit one on which the evidence remains unsatisfactory. The arguments advanced above provide grounds for suggesting that although wealth effects preclude underemployment equilibrium as a theoretical possibility, in practice the economic system may return to full employment only very slowly.

Quite separately from their role in returning the economy to full employment, wealth effects have the additional consequences of weakening some of the properties of the classical model. When wealth in the form of real outside money balances, M/P, is included as a determinant of expenditure in (2.2f), the classical dichotomy no longer holds. Equations (2.2f) and (2.2g) must be solved jointly for the interest rate and the price level, the equilibrium value of the interest rate (a real variable) thus depending upon monetary conditions. This is Patinkin's (1965) integration of monetary and value theory, through the 'real-balance effect'.

When non-money financial assets, such as bonds of fixed nominal value, are introduced, both the strict quantity theory and neutrality no longer hold. This can be seen intuitively from the fact that in the presence of bonds a monetary change does not lead to an equiproportionate change in wealth: the interest rate is no longer invariant to money supply changes, and the price level likewise changes non-proportionally. Thus, introducing real wealth as an influence on expenditure in (2.2f) (without, for simplicity, also incorporating it on the LM side) we have:

$$y = e(y, r, \frac{(M + B)}{P})$$

Consider the effects on a monetary expansion, keeping constant the level of output and the stock of bonds ($dy = dB = 0$):

$$\frac{dr}{dM} = \frac{-e_v\left(\frac{M}{P}\right) + e_v \frac{(M + B)}{P}}{P[e_r\left(\frac{M}{P}\right) + l_r e_v \frac{(M + B)}{P}]} \tag{2.3a}$$

$$\frac{dP}{dM} = \frac{e_r + l_r e_v}{e_r\left(\frac{M}{P}\right) + l_r e_v \frac{(M + B)}{P}} \tag{2.3b}$$

where e_v is the effect on expenditure of a change in real wealth $v = (M + B)/P$. It is clear from (2.3a) that the interest rate will be invariant to money supply changes ($dr/dM = 0$) only if $B = 0$. Thus, in the presence of a nominal stock of bonds an increase in the money stock is no longer neutral. In addition, from (2.3b) it is apparent that the quantity theory proposition $dP/P = dM/M$ (i.e. $dP/dM = P/M$) holds only for $B = 0$.

However, this modification to the neoclassical synthesis raises other issues. First, once we acknowledge the inclusion of bonds in the definition of wealth, invoking a monetary change is no longer straightforward. There are different ways in which the government may increase the money stock: they may either implement an unaccompanied increase in the money stock, or engage in a monetary expansion through open-market operations. A purchase of bonds on the open market by the monetary authorities implies the simultaneous changes $dM = -dB$, which generate different results from an unaccompanied increase in the money stock illustrated in (2.3). Second, as mentioned above, Barro (1974) argued that government bonds may not be considered net wealth. A full discussion of these issues is held over until Chapters 5 and 6.

A final feature of the neoclassical synthesis model which may be modified is the household's labour supply decision. Until now, we have regarded wealth effects as operating solely through the expenditure side of the model. A much more dramatic change to the structure of the classical system emerges, however, if the household's labour supply decision is integrated with its consumption plan, so that labour supply varies with household wealth (Deaton and Muellbauer 1980, Blundell and Walker 1982). Then the recursiveness of the classical system disappears altogether, and the equilibrium level of aggregate supply becomes dependent upon monetary conditions.

2.1.6. The Neoclassical Synthesis: Conclusions

As long as the classical rules of the game are observed, with prices functioning flexibly and efficiently to clear markets, Keynes' central proposition of underemployment equilibrium cannot be sustained, in spite of the many contributions to macroeconomic theory pioneered in the *General Theory*. This aggregate demand analysis developed by Keynes was merged with the fundamental conclusions of classical economics to constitute the 'neoclassical synthesis' (Johnson 1961). However, in order for the model to generate the central classical prediction that the economy is self-stabilising at full employment, wealth effects are vital; but these have been shown to operate at the expense of some of the properties of the classical model, notably the neutrality of money. Thus, Keynes' innovations on the aggregate demand side, although not successful in arguing for the existence of underemployment equilibrium, lead eventually to the undermining of the classical dichotomy, the independence of all 'real' variables from monetary conditions, which underpinned the traditional quantity theory.

While Keynesians could be argued to have lost the intellectual debate, they certainly regarded themselves as having the more relevant stance at the practical level. Their pragmatic view was that the forces ensuring the self-equilibrating properties of the classical system were in practice weak and slow acting. If the interest sensitivity of the demand for money was high, and of expenditure low, while the wealth effects were weak, this could cause the economy to move very slowly towards full employment. In addition, expectations of a continuing recession and a bankruptcy spiral might well outweigh those self-stabilising forces. In these circumstances, government fiscal and monetary policy might ensure a more rapid return to full employment.

The most important divide, however, centred on the functioning of the price system itself. The classical world of perfectly flexible prices was not the world with which Keynes was concerned. Limited flexibility, approximating to rigidity, was the empirically relevant characterisation of the price system, with perfect flexibility as the limiting, or special, case (Johnson 1961, Tobin 1977). Stabilisation policy, manipulating aggregate demand towards the full employment level, was then not an adjunct to price flexibility but the dominant partner in the equilibrating process. This conclusion was emphasised by the 'non-market-clearing' models developed by some Keynesians in the 1960s and 1970s, to which we now turn.

2.2. Keynesian Non-Market-Clearing Models

2.2.1. *The Keynesian Fixed-Wage Model*

The first sustained Keynesian attempt to re-establish underemployment equilibrium in the face of the neoclassical synthesis was the 'fixed-wage' model. There are two variants of this model. The first introduces rigidity of the nominal wage, and the second adds to this money illusion in labour markets. Both of these two new assumptions were directly invoked by Keynes.

Turning first to the assumption of wage rigidity, Keynes suggested that even in the presence of unemployment there might be a downward rigidity in the money wage: 'workers will usually resist a reduction in money wages' (Keynes 1936, p. 8) and 'every trade union will put up some resistance to a cut in money wages, however small' (*ibid.*, p. 15).

Taking the money wage as set exogenously essentially introduces two changes simultaneously. The more important is that the market-clearing condition for the labour market must be dropped. Only by accident will this exogenous money wage imply the level of real wage consistent with market clearing. In the absence of a market-clearing condition, the determinants of the actual level of employment must be specified. In the Keynesian approach it is assumed that employment is determined by demand up to full employment, i.e. the market typically displays excess supply, with employment determined by the 'short' side of the market (labour demand). The second implied change is that the labour supply equation becomes redundant, at least as far as the determination of the actual wage and employment are concerned. The role of the 'long' side of the market is confined to completing the disequilibrium properties, by determining the level of unemployment or excess supply. A further implication is that the real wage varies inversely with the price level throughout, and therefore as long as employment is demand-determined, employment (and hence output) rises with the price level. The aggregate supply schedule is therefore upward sloping until the full employment level. It should be stressed that fixed-wage models concentrate on rigidity in the money wage, and continue to regard the price level as flexible.

This can be illustrated with the aid of the four-sector diagram in Figure 2.9. The nominal wage is assumed fixed at W_0 throughout. Quadrant (ii) shows the different levels of the real wage implied by W_0 for different price levels. We start from a position of full employment, with

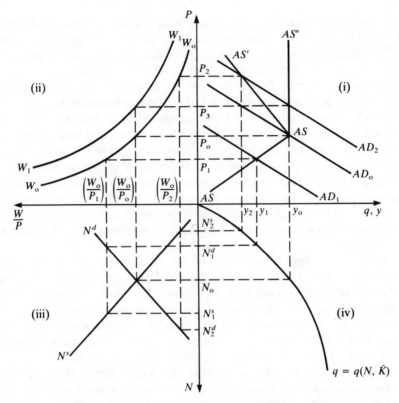

Figure 2.9 The Keynesian Fixed-Wage Model

aggregate demand AD_0 in quadrant (i) giving price level P_0 which, in conjunction with the given nominal wage generates the real wage (W_0/P_0) which clears the labour market (quadrant (iii)). Next consider a fall in aggregate demand to AD_1. Firms reduce prices, but given the nominal wage W_0, the real wage must rise. This produces excess supply in the labour market. The short side of the market (labour demand) determines actual employment and output. Thus a fall in aggregate demand serves to reduce both prices and output (to P_1 and y_1), tracing out a movement along AS–AS in quadrant (i), associated with a rise in the real wage to (W_0/P_1) and generating unemployment, $(N_1^s - N_1^d)$. Of this unemployment $(N_0 - N_1^d)$, is considered *involuntary*, or demand-deficient, as this would be the amount of unemployment eliminated if the government were to expand aggregate demand back to AD_0, restoring the market-clearing real wage.

This version of the fixed-wage model, however, runs into difficulties when there is *excess demand* for labour. Suppose aggregate demand were expanded beyond AD_0 to AD_2, reducing the real wage to (W_0/P_2). At this lower wage there is excess demand in the labour market (quadrant (iii)), and actual employment is determined by labour supply (the short side of the market), at N_2^s. If wages remain fixed at W_0, the aggregate supply curve becomes backward bending beyond full employment output y_0, as shown by the AS' schedule in quadrant (i). The prediction that output and employment fall once the economy is expanded beyond its full employment output level is generally rejected as counter-intuitive. It is therefore more common to assume that a 'wage-floor' only operates below full employment, and that once full employment is reached workers will not accept real wage cuts, but will bid up nominal wages in line with increases in the price level. If we allow upward flexibility of the money wage an increase in aggregate demand from AD_0 to AD_2 in quadrant (i) will bid up wages to W_1, so as to restore the full employment real wage $(W_0/P_0) = (W_1/P_3)$. This implies that beyond y_0, the aggregate supply curve has classical properties: it is vertical, as depicted in the schedule AS'' in quadrant (i).

Nevertheless, this first variant of the fixed-wage model has certain drawbacks. First, it is not entirely clear why workers only resist real wage cuts once full employment N_0 has been reached, while allowing their real wage to be eroded when aggregate demand is expanded below full employment. Second, it is arguable that if workers strike their wage bargain in money terms, they may be subject to some extent to *money illusion*. As Keynes observed in the early pages of the *General Theory*, 'Ordinary experience tells us, beyond any doubt, that a situation where labour stipulates (within limits) for a money wage rather than a real wage, so far from being a mere possibility, is the normal case' (Keynes 1936, p. 9). Indeed, in imposing a 'wage-floor' only below full employment, while allowing upward flexibility of nominal wages beyond N_0 in Figure 2.9, we are effectively assuming that workers only suffer from money illusion below full employment. To avoid this asymmetry, we examine the effect of introducing money illusion in our fixed-wage model over all ranges of output and employment. First of all let us consider the implications of assuming money illusion for labour supply behaviour in the labour market. When labour supply depends on the money and not the real wage, then the supply curve for labour will shift with every movement in the price level. The implications of this are shown in Figure 2.10, where labour supply, N^s, is assumed to vary positively with the *nominal* wage, W. A rise in the price level from P_0 to P_1 will lower the real wage, but this will not be perceived by workers suffering from money illusion. They will therefore be prepared to supply the same labour as before at a lower real wage, causing a rightward shift in the labour supply schedule, from N_0^s to N_1^s.

Consider introducing the assumption of money illusion in the model described in Figure 2.9. An expansion in aggregate demand from AD_0 to AD_2 will cause prices to increase. With money illusion, however, this will

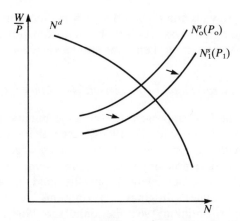

Figure 2.10   Money Illusion in the Labour Market

invoke an increase in labour supply, for every level of the real wage, in the manner shown in Figure 2.10. The rightward shift in the labour supply function (Figure 2.10) will bid down the real wage, increasing employment. The introduction of money illusion is therefore sufficient to ensure that output and employment can be expanded beyond their full employment levels (y_0 and N_0 in Figure 2.9). As a result, the aggregate supply schedule will be upward sloping over all ranges of output in this second variant of the fixed-wage model, as depicted in Figure 2.1(c).

To summarise our results so far, the first variant of the fixed-wage model produces an upward sloping aggregate supply curve below full employment. The aggregate supply curve becomes backward bending or vertical beyond full employment, depending on whether we assume that the nominal wage remains fixed or is flexible upwards beyond full employment. Our second variant of the fixed-wage model, which adds the assumption of money illusion to that of a fixed nominal wage, can produce an upward sloping aggregate supply curve over all ranges of output.

Although producing the prediction of underemployment equilibrium which may be remedied by the manipulation of aggregate demand, the Keynesian fixed-wage model is unsatisfactory as a piece of theorising. The money wage, one of the major variables of the system and the key determinant of involuntary unemployment, is left exogenous (i.e. unexplained). How does it come to be at its current level rather than some other level? More importantly, is it absolutely rigid, or merely 'sticky'? Under what circumstances will it change, and how far? The Keynesian answer to these points proceeded no further than some suggestive remarks on, for example, the importance of wage relativities. If market forces prevailed in the long run, and nominal wages began to fall to eliminate the excess supply of labour, prices would fall and the results of the neoclassical synthesis would again apply, with full employment attained via the Keynes and Pigou effects. A justification for the existence of nominal wage rigidity was required, but unfortunately a theory of sticky prices, or non-Walrasian markets, was still lacking.

2.2.2. The Reinterpretation of Keynesian Non-Market-Clearing Models

A second 'Keynesian' approach to the determination of output and employment has its roots in the 1960s, when there was already some dissatisfaction with the assumption of fixed money wages in explaining the phenomenon of underemployment equilibrium. Some economists believed that the IS–LM and aggregate supply–demand paradigms seriously misrepresented Keynes' original contributions to economic theory (see, for example, Patinkin 1965, Leijonhufvud 1968). But quite apart from the exegetical issues which were raised, a substantial literature attacked the market-clearing, semi-Walrasian foundations of conventional aggregate supply and demand models, and proposed alternative models which displayed some *non-market-clearing* (or *disequilibrium*) characteristics (see, for example, Clower 1965, Barro and Grossman 1971, Grandmont and Laroque 1974, Benassy 1975, Malinvaud 1977, and Muellbauer and Portes 1978).

We have already noted the Walrasian market-clearing nature of the macroeconomy when a classical aggregate supply curve is assumed. This aspect of the aggregate demand and supply model is relatively easy to see when prices, wages, and the interest rate are perfectly flexible, and the economy is in full employment equilibrium, as depicted in Figure 2.11.

In this case all the markets under consideration are in equilibrium, as the

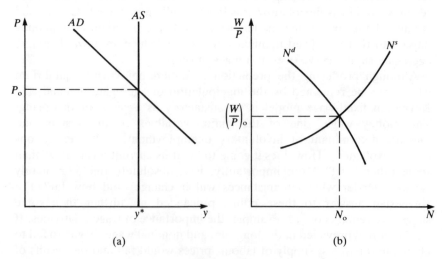

(a)   (b)

Figure 2.11

real wage is such that the demand and supply of labour coincide, and given that the economy is on both the IS and LM curves, the goods, money, and bonds markets are in equilibrium. However, in situations of less than full employment, it seems more difficult to cast the Keynesian model in Walrasian terms. Consider a fall in aggregate demand with fixed money wages such that output falls below the full employment level (Figure 2.12(a)). Given that the money wage is fixed, and prices have fallen, the real wage has risen above its equilibrium level (W/P_0) to (W/P_1) (Figure 2.12(b)), and there is an excess supply of labour, as the actual amount of labour employed, N^e, is less than the amount households are willing to supply at the higher real wage, N^s_1. However, given that the economy is still at the intersection of the aggregate demand and supply curves, it appears that all the other markets under consideration are still in equilibrium. This seems to contradict Walras' Law, which states that the excess demands in all markets must sum to zero. (For a full statement of Walras' Law, see Harris 1981.)

One way in which the model may be reconciled to Walras' Law is by redefining our demand for goods and money equations so that the *planned* demand for goods and money would be that which prevailed when income was at the full employment level, i.e. y^* in Figures 2.11 and 2.12. Thus, an excess planned supply in the labour market would be matched by excess demand somewhere else in the economy. However, this reinterpretation is not without its difficulties. While it may be argued that Keynes built his model of underemployment equilibrium on the assumption of a fixed money wage, it is difficult to argue that the theory of liquidity preference or the consumption function was cast in terms of households' planned income (i.e. full employment income). This illustrates the semi-Walrasian nature of the aggregate supply and demand paradigm. While it is essentially built on the classical model of the labour market where labour supply is derived from the theory of choice between income and leisure, and labour demand from the theory of production, it grafts this on to a model of aggregate demand which is built on, among other things, the Keynesian consumption function and the theory of liquidity preference. These latter concepts are distinctly *not* derived from a classical theory of consumer choice, and hence it is not surprising that it becomes difficult to interpret a situation where the real wage is too high (Figure 2.12) in terms of Walras' Law.

At this point, different approaches have been sought for the resolution of this problem. In section 1 we have seen that economists of a classical and neoclassical persuasion have sought to emphasise the self-stabilising role of economic systems. These models may be interpreted as an attempt to emphasise the Walrasian nature of the aggregate demand and supply model by concentrating on full employment states, where Walras' Law unambiguously holds. Indeed, recent attempts to develop the micro-economic foundations of the consumption and investment functions

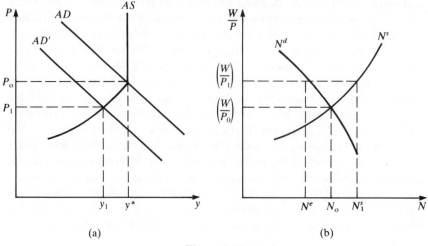

(a)   (b)

Figure 2.12

(see Hall 1978, Begg 1982) in line with the development of 'new classical' macroeconomics (to which we shall return in Chapter 3) may be interpreted as moves away from the distinctly non-Walrasian nature of the Keynesian theory of aggregate demand. These theories of aggregate demand place greater emphasis on the maximisation of utility and profits by households and firms, and hence are distinctly classical in nature, in contrast, for instance, to Keynes' absolute income hypothesis which was not derived from an explicit optimisation exercise on the part of households. A second approach is to continue with the use of the aggregate supply and demand paradigm, even in analysing situations of under-employment, implicitly accepting the non-Walrasian nature of the model as presented. The Keynesian fixed-wage model analysed in subsection 2.2.1 fits this category, as do several of the models which are analysed in Chapters 3 and 4. The third broad group, whose work we examine in this section, have developed the non-Walrasian nature of the simple aggregate demand and supply model, first by emphasising the non-classical nature of Keynesian aggregate demand (see Clower 1965, Leijonhufvud 1968), and second by developing a theory of the labour market which departs from classical concepts (see Patinkin 1965, Barro and Grossman 1971). In this sense the Keynesian literature on 'non-market-clearing' or 'disequilibrium' models may be seen as offering a new perspective on both the aggregate supply and aggregate demand sides.

2.2.3. A Model of 'General Disequilibrium'

In a model with flexible wages and prices as outlined in section 1 (Figure 2.11), a fall in aggregate demand will cause an excess supply in both goods and labour markets which causes an instantaneous fall in prices and wages, such that the system is restored to full employment equilibrium. The self-equilibrating nature of the system derives from the down-ward slope of the aggregate demand curve. Wages and prices fall equiproportionately, so that the real wage remains unchanged at the level which clears the labour market $(W/P)^*$. As we saw in Chapter 1, and emphasised in subsection 2.1.3, the various determinants of the slope of the aggregate demand curve are important links in this self-stabilising mechanism.

However, consider the case where prices and wages do not adjust instantaneously. Most simple 'disequilibrium' models, including the one presented here, assume that in the short run prices and wages are entirely fixed. However, as will become apparent, the results of these models are not dependent upon the existence of totally fixed wages and prices. Even if prices and wages are partially flexible, yet do not move quickly enough so as to clear markets, disequilibrium models will still be relevant to macroeconomic analysis. If prices and wages do not adjust following a downward aggregate demand shock, as AD shifts to AD', there will be excess supply in both goods and labour markets (Figure 2.13(i)). As firms find that they cannot sell their previous (full employment) output y^* in goods markets at price P^*, but only sell y_1, they will reduce the amount of labour employed from N^* to N_1 (see Figure 2.13(iii)). Note that the economy has now moved off the labour supply schedule N^s in Figure 2.13(ii), as the real wage is still $(W/P)^*$, the full employment real wage (given that neither prices or wages have changed), and less labour is employed. It is useful at this point to distinguish between *notional* and *effective* concepts of demand and supply. The demand curve for labour, N^d, (Figure 2.13(ii)) derived from classical production theory (the notional demand curve) has become irrelevant for the determination of employ-ment where prices and wages do not adjust. Instead, *quantities* of output and employment are deemed to adjust faster in this model in response to excess demand/supply situations. The relevant, or *effective* demand for labour in this model, is the schedule ABC in Figure 2.13(ii). However, the system does not settle permanently at points E and E' of Figures 2.13(i) and 2.13(ii) respectively, as the analysis does not yet allow for any response on the part of the households.

Consider the household's choice between income and leisure, illustrated in Figure 2.13(v). To simplify the diagrammatic exposition we assume that all households are identical. The indifference map then represents households' aggregate preferences with regard to the choice between income and leisure. Households derive their income exclusively from work as $(W/P)N^s$. The slope of the budget line OS is then given by (W/P). As we saw from Figure 2.13(ii), before the initial shock to aggregate demand, households supplied N^* of labour at the equilibrium real wage $(W/P)^*$, and

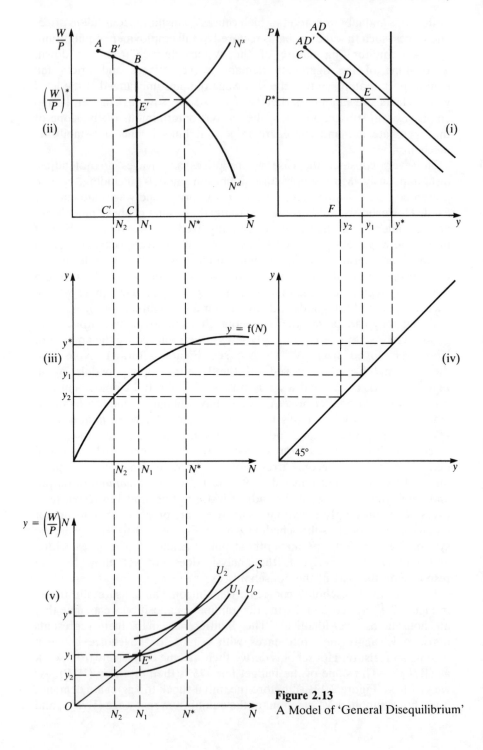

Figure 2.13
A Model of 'General Disequilibrium'

received an income of y^*, equivalent to the full employment output level in Figure 2.13(i). After the shock to aggregate demand, given that the real wage remains constant, the slope of the budget line remains fixed at $(W/P)^*$. However, firms' effective demand for labour has now fallen to N_1, as we saw from Figure 2.13(ii), and therefore households find that they are constrained to operate at a suboptimal position E'' on their indifference map in Figure 2.13(v). This is merely another way of representing what we have already shown in Figures 2.13(i) and 2.13(ii). Households are forced to supply labour off their *notional* supply curve N^s, and hence their income falls to y_1. However, given that the Keynesian consumption function has a marginal propensity to consume, c, which is less than unity, households will only purchase cy_1 worth of goods in the next time period. As a result, firms will find that they cannot sell output y_1, and that effective demand has fallen to CDF in Figure 2.13(i), corresponding to income level y_2. This, in turn, forces firms to reduce their employment levels further to N_2 in Figure 2.13(iii), and from Figure 2.13(ii) we see that this represents a fall in the effective demand for labour schedule to $AB'C'$. This will in turn lower households' income and consumption to y_2 and cy_2 respectively. Thus, the initial demand shock has a quantity adjustment corresponding to the original Keynesian multiplier, assuming fixed wages and prices. Final equilibrium will be at an underemployment position because wages and prices fail to adjust. The multiplier process will be stable because the marginal propensity to consume is assumed to be less than one.

Clearly, the above analysis is valid even if prices and wages adjust in part, providing that they fail to adjust immediately to the level required to cause a sufficient rise in aggregate demand to secure full employment. If wages and prices adjust in part, there will still be a multiplier process, but this will cause a smaller deviation from y^* than the case described above. Whether Figure 2.11 or Figure 2.13 is a closer representation of reality following a fall in aggregate demand depends on the speed of adjustment of prices and wages.

2.2.4. *A Critique of 'Disequilibrium' Models*

The fixed-money wage Keynesian model can be seen as a special case of the more general 'disequilibrium' models. While in the latter both prices and wages fail to adjust, in the former, prices are flexible, and nominal wages are fixed. In the fixed-wage model, consider a fall in aggregate demand from an initial position of full employment. As we saw in Figure 2.12, Walras' Law does not hold. Only the labour market has an excess supply, as the price level falls sufficiently fast to eliminate the excess supply in the goods market. Thus, the fixed-wage model does not produce the full Keynesian multiplier effect of our 'disequilibrium' model of the previous section (Figure 2.13), as the goods market remains in equilibrium throughout in the former. Whether the disequilibrium model represents a better approximation to reality than our upward sloping aggregate supply curve model with fixed money wages and flexible prices depends on our views regarding relative wage and price rigidities in the labour and goods markets. However, given the tractable nature of the simple upward sloping aggregate supply curve model, it is not surprising that the aggregate demand and supply paradigm has been retained. Provided we wish to focus on labour market rigidities, the aggregate demand and supply paradigm provides an effective vehicle for macroeconomic analysis.

Furthermore, while the fixed-money wages model with money illusion may explain why output and employment rise above 'full employment' following an expansion in aggregate demand through the assumption of money illusion, the same result cannot be obtained using a general disequilibrium model. In the disequilibrium model above (see Figure 2.14) an increase in aggregate demand from an initial position of full employment equilibrium causes excess demand for both goods and labour when prices and wages do not adjust. As households are unwilling to supply more labour at the unchanged real wage, notional labour supply falls short of firms' effective demand for labour. Employment cannot increase as firms are rationed in the labour market, and as a result output cannot increase. To restore the result that output may rise above its full employment level, we need to reintroduce the assumption of money illusion advanced in subsection 2.2.1.

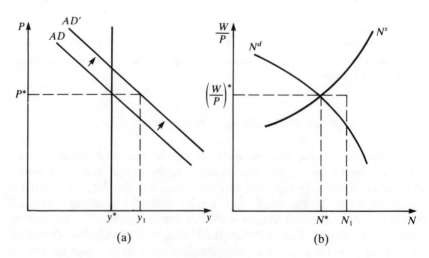

Figure 2.14

In that they allow underemployment equilibria, disequilibrium models tend to be seen as constituting 'theories of depression', modifying and enriching some of the ideas already present in Keynes and in the neoclassical synthesis. However, given the fact that disequilibrium models cannot explain why employment and output should rise above their classical equilibrium levels, (without assuming money illusion on the part of the workers), they do not seem to be particularly appropriate for describing the economics of inflation.

However, the most fundamental criticism of these models of disequilibrium is that, although they offer an interesting description of the multiplier process while wages and prices are fixed, or at the very least 'sticky', they do not explain why disequilibrium should persist in the long run, provided wages and prices eventually adjust to eliminate market disequilibria. Then the Keynes effect and the Pigou effect will increase effective demand until full employment is restored. The only way in which disequilibrium models can ensure a long-run underemployment equilibrium is by a continued reliance on sticky prices and wages. Furthermore, while disequilibrium theorists build on the assumption that there is no instantaneous price adjustment to clear markets, they do not offer an alternative theory of how prices are determined in non-clearing markets. As Arrow (1959) and Grandmont and Laroque (1974) point out, if we abandon the theory of general equilibrium, we have to abandon much of microeconomic theory which regards economic agents as making choices, *given* prices determined in the market as a whole. Thus Keynesian disequilibrium models lack the secure microfoundations on which the Walrasian approach is based.

Nevertheless, in spite of these failures the Keynesian revolution has exerted a powerful and lasting influence. It focused the debate on the forces which tend to restore the economy to full employment from a position of underemployment. Keynes' aggregate demand framework, with its departure from classical consumption (saving) and money demand theory shifted the burden of macroeconomic adjustment from the direct classical link where the interest rate equated saving and investment to the indirect link of the Keynes and Pigou effects. These, as we have seen, may be weak links on which to build a self-stabilising economic system. Furthermore, greater attention was focused on the workings of the labour market, whose flexibility became the main issue on which the main macroeconomic debates of the post-war period have been focused (see Chapters 3 and 4). In addition to this, the neutrality of money stock changes under the old quantity theory was challenged, leading to a whole literature on the effects on an economy's growth path and composition of output under different monetary conditions (the so-called 'superneutrality' debate; see, for example, Tobin 1965, Sidrauski 1967, Johnson 1967, Stein 1970 and Rose 1966).

However, these debates were in a sense overtaken by events, as the problem of inflation (and subsequently stagflation) began to dominate the course of economic research. A theory of stabilisation policies in an inflationary environment was needed, and in a sense began with the empirical work of Phillips (1958) on wage inflation and unemployment. A parallel debate to the one outlined in this chapter ensued, as Keynesians and monetarists argued over the scope and desirability of stabilisation policies. The theory of aggregate supply surveyed here allowed for inflationary situations only in the sense that the price level was assumed to rise with expansions in aggregate demand. In the next chapter we consider a dynamic version of the price and wage formation process surveyed here, and in so doing we develop the framework within which the modern debate on stabilisation policy has been conducted.

3

AGGREGATE SUPPLY: MONETARISM AND NEW CLASSICAL MACROECONOMICS

In Chapter 2, we outlined the debate between Keynesian and pre-Keynesian 'classical' economics on the possibility of underemployment equilibrium. However, the post-war period has been characterised by both variable employment levels and recurring inflation, and in this chapter, and in Chapter 4, we examine the alternative theories which have sought to explain these developments.

In section 1, we examine the way in which inflation was analysed within the early post-war Keynesian framework, as provided by the Phillips curve, and how this theoretical structure came under attack from the monetarist school. In section 2, we outline the development of new classical macroeconomics and the role of rational expectations. Finally, in section 3, we review the ways in which empirical studies have sought to validate the principal new classical propositions. In an appendix to this chapter, we present a formal account of the methods of solution of rational expectations models.

3.1. The Phillips Curve and Stabilisation Policy

3.1.1. The Phillips Curve and its Theoretical Foundations

The dilemma for the simple Keynesian model set out in Chapter 2 was how to explain inflation, given that changes in aggregate demand could only change output and employment on the assumption of fixed money wages. This was apparently resolved by the discovery by Phillips (1958) of an inverse non-linear relation between the level of unemployment and the rate of growth of money wages (see Figure 3.1) for the United Kingdom over the period 1861–1957. This relationship became known as the 'Phillips

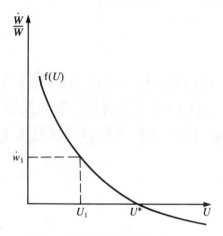

Figure 3.1   The Phillips Curve

curve', and was seen as completing the Keynesian model, by suggesting a trade-off between wage inflation and unemployment. However, it was initially presented as an empirical relationship without theoretical foundations. Lipsey (1960) attempted to rectify this by formulating the Phillips curve as a labour market adjustment process, where the rate of growth in money wages reflects the degree of excess supply or excess demand in the labour market as proxied by the level of unemployment. More formally we may write, in logarithms:

$$\dot{w} = f(n^s - n) \qquad f'(.) < 0, f(0) = 0 \qquad\qquad (3.1)$$

where $\dot{w}$ is the rate of growth of nominal wages, n is the actual employment level, and n^s is the labour supply. When the labour market is in equilibrium, $n = n^s$, and hence the money wage stops adjusting ($\dot{w} = 0$). In terms of Figure 3.1 this would imply that U^* is the point where $n = n^s$. The Phillips curve is then interpreted as showing the way in which wage inflation reflects excess demand in the labour market.

The Phillips curve may be readily incorporated within a more complete macroeconomic model of inflation (see, for example, Samuelson and Solow 1960), where a rise in aggregate demand increases output and hence employment, thus generating wage inflation. However, such a model founders on the same difficulty as the Keynesian models of Chapter 2: output and employment cannot exceed the neoclassical equilibrium levels. This is demonstrated with the aid of Figure 3.2(a), illustrating the neoclassical labour market introduced in Chapter 2. Suppose that the labour market is initially in equilibrium at point E. An aggregate demand expansion forces up prices. Assuming that nominal wages are initially fixed, the resulting fall in real wages leads to excess demand of E_1–E_2 in the labour market. The Phillips curve suggests that this excess demand generates wage inflation, but for the mechanism of equation (3.1) to operate we require actual employment, n, to be greater than labour supply, n^s. This cannot be achieved in a neoclassical labour market, given that the short side of the market determines the actual amount of labour services bought and sold, and the level of employment cannot rise above n^*. In other words, with a neoclassical labour market, it is impossible to reach a situation where $n > n^s$, thus rendering the theoretical rationale for the Phillips curve invalid.

Thus the incorporation of Lipsey's theoretical concept of the 'Phillips curve' in our macroeconomic model is incompatible with the neoclassical theory of labour supply. This is another way of stating the point made in Chapter 2, that to draw an upward sloping aggregate supply curve beyond the point of labour market equilibrium requires money illusion on the part of workers. The only difference here is that we have moved to a dynamic setting by introducing a theory of wage inflation through equation (3.1). While the Phillips curve and the upward sloping aggregate supply curve differ in that the former explains the way in which money wages adjust in the presence of excess demand in the labour market, and the latter keeps money wages fixed in the presence of such excess demand, they nevertheless share common ground in that the existence of both is conditional on a repudiation of the neoclassical theory of labour supply.

As will be recalled from Chapter 2, one possible escape from this problem is to assume money illusion on the part of workers such that they are willing to supply the additional labour E_1–E_2 in Figure 3.2(a). In terms of Figure 3.2(b), following an expansion in aggregate demand, prices and nominal wages rise. If workers misinterpret this rise in nominal wages as a

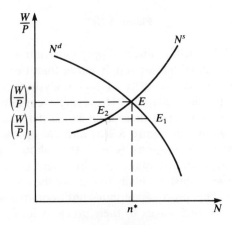

Figure 3.2(a)

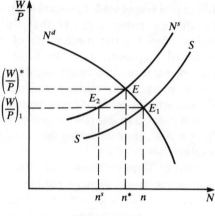

Figure 3.2(b)

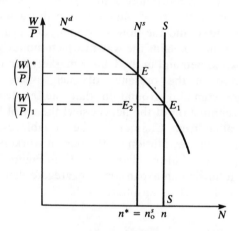

Figure 3.2(c)

rise in *real* wages, they will in effect supply more labour at every level of the real wage. The actual labour supply curve then becomes curve SS in Figure 3.2(b). (Note the similarity of this analysis to that provided in Figure 2.10 of the previous chapter.) However, eventually we may expect workers to perceive that in fact there is an excess demand of E_1-E_2 in the labour market as shown in Figure 3.2(b) and bid up the nominal wage. What the Phillips curve suggests is that the labour market does not instantly clear through an instantaneous adjustment of the nominal wage, but that money wages adjust gradually to remove the excess demand E_1-E_2 via equation (3.1). This process continues until nominal wages have risen sufficiently to restore real wages to their previous level, and n equals n^s once more. This would therefore cause output to return to its equilibrium 'full employment' level. Note, however, that it is implicitly assumed in the Phillips curve model that workers, even once they perceive an excess demand for labour E_1–E_2 and a lower real wage, will not relinquish their jobs, but instead exert upward pressure on nominal wages.

The above analysis illustrates the Phillips curve account of how the labour market adjusts to a one-off change in aggregate demand. We will now show how a simple Keynesian macroeconomic model augmented by a Phillips curve may be used to describe inflation. While up till now we have dealt with once-and-for-all increases in aggregate demand which caused increases in the price *level*, it follows that to describe ongoing inflation, we have to consider a *sustained* aggregate demand expansion, modelled, for example, through a growth process in the money stock. The model may be formally stated as follows (in a log-linear form):

$$y = \alpha_0 - \alpha_1 r \qquad\qquad \alpha_0, \alpha_1 > 0 \qquad\qquad\qquad (3.2a)$$

$$y = (m - p)/\beta_0 + \beta_1 r \qquad \beta_0, \beta_1 > 0 \qquad\qquad\qquad (3.2b)$$

$$\dot{m} = k \qquad\qquad\qquad\qquad\qquad\qquad\qquad\qquad\qquad (3.2c)$$

$$\dot{w} = -\phi(n^s - n) \qquad\qquad \phi > 0 \qquad\qquad\qquad\qquad (3.2d)$$

$$n^s = n_0^s \qquad\qquad\qquad\qquad\qquad\qquad\qquad\qquad\qquad (3.2e)$$

$$y = \gamma n \qquad\qquad\qquad\qquad 0 < \gamma < 1 \qquad\qquad\qquad (3.2f)$$

$$p = \delta + (1 - \gamma) n + w \qquad \delta < 0 \qquad\qquad\qquad\qquad (3.2g)$$

Equations (3.2a) and (3.2b) are IS and LM curves, omitting wealth effects. Equation (3.2c) states that monetary growth is exogenously fixed by the monetary authorities at some rate k. Equation (3.2d) is a linear version of the Phillips curve introduced in (3.1), with the labour supply fixed exogenously at a level n_0^s as shown in (3.2e). It is assumed, in line with our argument above, that employment is demand-determined but the nominal wage adjustment process in equation (3.2d) attempts to close the gap between n and n^s. Taking n^s as exogenously fixed and not dependent upon the real wage implies that the N^s and SS curves from Figure 3.2(b) are vertical, as in Figure 3.2(c). This is merely a simplifying assumption: making n^s more elastic with respect to the real wage would not change the essential properties of the model. The production function is short-run in character, with a fixed capital stock and technology, so that in (3.2f) only the labour variable is present, and we assume diminishing returns to the variable factor. Equation (3.2g) represents the labour demand function, with the marginal product of labour equal to the real wage. Note that the model implies an upward sloping aggregate supply schedule which can be derived by substituting for n from (3.2f) into (3.2g), and keeping the nominal wage (w) fixed at a given value.

This model may be solved by substituting equations (3.2a), (3.2b), (3.2f), and (3.2g) into (3.2d) to yield the following system of two dynamic equations:

$$\dot{w} = (\phi/\Delta)(m - w) - \phi n_0^s - (\phi/\Delta)\frac{(\delta - \beta_0\beta_1\alpha_0)}{\alpha_1} \tag{3.3}$$

$$\dot{m} = k \tag{3.2c}$$

where $\Delta = \gamma\beta_0(1 + \beta_1/\alpha_1) + (1 - \gamma)$.

This model may be easily interpreted in terms of our simple aggregate supply and demand model of Chapter 2. The IS–LM system gives the aggregate demand curve, which continuously shifts rightwards as the money stock grows (equation (3.2c)). The aggregate supply curve is upward sloping, due to the assumption of money illusion, and shifts leftwards as the nominal wage increases to eliminate the excess demand in the labour market (equation (3.3)). First, let us consider the response of this model to a once-and-for-all increase in the money stock, ignoring the growth process assumed in (3.2c). This is shown in Figure 3.3(b). The initial increase in aggregate demand from AD to AD' causes an increase in the price level and a fall in the real wage and results in excess demand in the labour market. The Phillips curve suggests that nominal wages will adjust gradually until they have removed the excess demand, and AS has shifted to AS'. Thus, the Phillips curve cannot explain *sustained inflation*, nor a *permanent fall* in unemployment with a once-and-for-all increase in the money stock. To obtain these results, we have to allow continuous aggregate demand expansion, as assumed in (3.2c).

Suppose that the system is initially at full employment equilibrium income y^*, corresponding to $n = n^s$. The instant after the money stock begins to grow, the aggregate demand curve will have shifted to the right to AD' in Figure 3.3(a), thus causing the price level to rise. As in the case of a once-and-for-all increase in the money stock, this increases labour demand (3.2g) and actual employment, since workers are assumed to be willing to supply the additional labour $n - n^s$ at the lower real wage. The excess demand for labour causes the money wage to rise (3.2d), and the AS schedule shifts upward according to the speed of adjustment, ϕ, incorporated in the Phillips curve. With monetary growth continually shifting the AD schedule rightwards over time, we have an inflationary process of rising prices and wages. There are therefore two offsetting influences in this model: monetary growth which increases excess demand in the labour market, and the wage adjustment process embodied in the

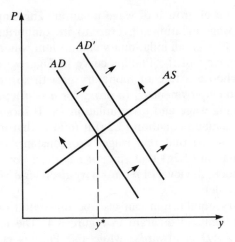

Figure 3.3 (a)

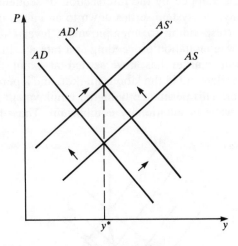

Figure 3.3 (b)

Phillips curve which tends to remove it. These forces are illustrated by the arrows in Figure 3.3(a).

The interesting feature of this model, in contrast to our aggregate demand and supply model, is that it can explain convergence to an inflationary equilibrium. This may be illustrated by differentiating equation (3.3) with respect to time:

$$\ddot{w} = \left(\frac{\phi}{\Delta}\right)(\dot{m} - \dot{w}) \qquad\qquad (3.4)$$

where $\ddot{w}$ is the rate of growth of wage inflation. This implies that, if the system is stable, wage inflation converges to an equilibrium where $\ddot{w} = 0$, and hence where $\dot{w} = \dot{m}$, an inflationary equilibrium, where $n > n^s$ even in the long run. In terms of the Phillips curve of Figure 3.1, the monetary authorities can choose a rate of monetary growth so as to achieve the desired level of unemployment U_1 (a proxy for $n - n^s$), and trade this off against the resulting wage and price inflation $\dot{w}_1$. It should be noted that from the labour demand equation (3.2g) it follows that in an inflationary equilibrium $\dot{p} = \dot{w}$, so that real wages are constant. However, it also follows from equation (3.2g) that since n has risen above n^s due to the initial demand shock, the level of p must have risen *vis-à-vis* w, i.e. the real wage must have fallen.

This inflationary equilibrium can also be illustrated on the aggregate supply–aggregate demand diagram in Figure 3.4. The monetary growth continually shifts AD rightwards, while the Phillips curve adjustment mechanism continuously shifts the AS curve leftwards. The dynamic path of the economy is mapped by the intersection of sequential AS and AD curves. Eventually, the system settles down to an inflationary steady state at output y_1, corresponding to unemployment level U_1 on the Phillips curve, and with wage inflation proceeding at a rate $\dot{w}_1$. In terms of Figure 3.2(c), the labour market has now settled at point like E_1, with a continuous excess demand in the labour market, and a permanently higher employment level. This permanently higher employment level is 'bought' by a lower real wage in inflationary equilibrium. The adjustment of the

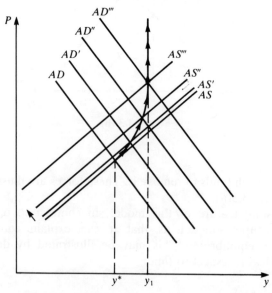

Figure 3.4 The Dynamic Path of the Economy with a Simple Phillips Curve

nominal wage is in response to excess demand, and, although in the long run wages and prices rise at the same rate, the real wage is not restored to its initial level. Therefore, our inflationary equilibrium involves money illusion on the part of workers even in the long run, and is therefore incompatible with the neoclassical theory of labour supply.

The upward sloping aggregate supply schedule introduced in Chapter 2 was derived by assuming money illusion, and its slope depends on the labour demand schedule. In contrast, the slope of the Phillips curve depends upon the speed of adjustment to excess demand, ϕ, but movements along this curve also rely on the assumption of money illusion, as workers, even in the long run, do not recognise the fall in their real wages. Only in the special case of a once-and-for-all aggregate demand expansion does the Phillips curve ensure a return to full employment and a full employment real wage (Figure 3.3(b)). It is this reliance of Keynesian fixed-wage and Phillips curve models on money illusion which was to prove the focus of sweeping criticism by economists of a neoclassical persuasion.

3.1.2. *Monetarism and the Phillips Curve: Long-Run Equilibrium*

The main monetarist attack on the Phillips curve came with Milton Friedman's (1968) presidential address to the American Economic Association, where Friedman countered the Keynesian model of the labour market by convincingly arguing that optimising workers will not exhibit money illusion and will base their labour supply decision on the level of the real wage, as postulated in the neoclassical model of the labour market. Thus, according to Friedman, the Phillips curve was fundamentally misspecified, and should be cast in terms of the rate of growth of the real wage instead of the rate of growth of the money wage. Thus, the correct specification of the Phillips curve would be:

$$\dot{w} - \dot{p} = f(U)$$

where U is the unemployment rate. Or, alternatively, if we argue again that unemployment is a proxy for excess demand in the labour market, we have:

$$\dot{w} - \dot{p} = f(n^s - n) \qquad f'(.) < 0, f(0) = 0 \tag{3.5}$$

However, in practice workers in the labour market will negotiate their wages in money terms, on the basis of the expected inflation rate in the economy, so that $\dot{p}$ in (3.5) should be replaced by $\dot{p}^e$, the expected inflation rate. Thus, equation (3.5) implies that, instead of the unique Phillips curve of Figure 3.1, we should have a series of Phillips curves, each corresponding to a particular level of expected inflation, $\dot{p}^e$, as illustrated in Figure 3.5. Along each Phillips curve, nominal wages adjust in exactly the

Macroeconomic Theory & Stabilisation Policy

way described in the previous subsection, except that workers now take
into account the expected inflation rate.

In order to see the effect of allowing for inflationary expectations in the
Phillips curve in terms of the simple macroeconomic model described in
equations (3.2), we replace the Phillips curve in (3.2d) with a linear version
of the 'expectations-augmented' Phillips curve of equation (3.5):

$$\dot{w} = -\phi(n^s - n) + \dot{p}^e \tag{3.2d'}$$

However, in order to complete the expectations-augmented model, we
need to specify the way in which workers form their inflationary
expectations. A general approach is to assume that workers look at past
inflation rates in forming their expectations. One such mechanistic model
assumes that workers take expected inflation to be a geometrically
weighted average of past actual inflation rates. In discrete time this can be
written as:

$$\Delta p_t^e = \lambda \Sigma_{i=0}^\infty (1 - \lambda)^i \Delta p_{t-i} \qquad 1 > \lambda > 0$$

where λ is the weight attached to last period's inflation rate. When λ is
close to zero, more weight is placed on recent, relative to distant,
experience of inflation, while a value of λ closer to unity implies that
workers take greater account of inflation rates from further back in the
past. Because our model is in continuous time, we can write down a
continuous time approximation to this expectations formation mechanism:

$$\ddot{p}^e = \omega(\dot{p} - \dot{p}^e) \qquad \omega > 0 \tag{3.6}$$

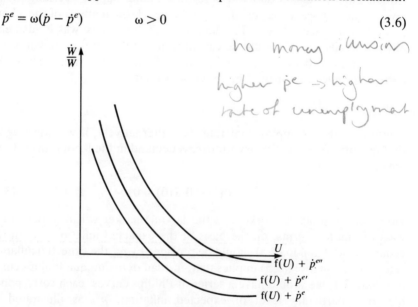

no money illusion

higher pe → higher rate of unemployment

Figure 3.5 The Expectations-Augmented Phillips Curve

Equation (3.6) states that in any given time period, workers' inflationary expectations are adjusted by a proportion of the difference between actual inflation and expected inflation. This is merely another way of stating the proposition that expected inflation is a geometrically weighted average of past actual inflation rates. Expectations are therefore *backward looking* in this model, and are known as *adaptive expectations* (see Cagan 1956, Friedman 1957).

Incorporating (3.6) and (3.2d') into our model alters its properties substantially. In the previous subsection we saw that in the absence of inflationary expectations, the monetary authorities could permanently increase output and employment in the economy by raising monetary growth, trading this off against a higher rate of wage and price inflation. However, the introduction of inflationary expectations suggests that such real output gains can be only temporary. In our inflationary equilibrium of Figure 3.4, wages and prices are rising at the same rate. Equation (3.6) implies that in such an equilibrium $\dot{p} = \dot{p}^e$. In the long run under adaptive expectations, a steady-state inflation tends to become fully anticipated, as individuals' expectations slowly converge on the actual inflation rate.

This can be illustrated in terms of our aggregate demand and supply diagram (see Figure 3.6). The initial rise in monetary growth leads to increasing output and employment, as the initial price rise depresses real wages in the economy. However, as wage and price inflation approaches its equilibrium rate, expected inflation begins to approach actual price inflation, the adjustments to nominal wages raising real wages back to the level prevailing before the onset of monetary growth. As a result, in full equilibrium, wage and price inflation is equal to the rate of monetary growth, with output back to its 'full employment' or 'natural' level, y^*, following the path shown by the arrows in Figure 3.6. Immediately after the increase in monetary growth, rightward shifts in the aggregate demand function outweigh leftward shifts in the aggregate supply function as the backward looking inflationary expectations, and hence nominal wages, adjust only partially to the rising inflation. Eventually, inflationary expectations catch up and restore the economy to y^*, where the AD and AS curves are shifting in opposite directions at the same time.

This process can also be illustrated on an 'expectations-augmented' Phillips curve (see Figure 3.7). Initially the economy is assumed to be at its 'natural' or 'full employment' unemployment level U^*. An increase in monetary growth pushes the economy along the downward sloping (or short-run) Phillips curve XX to a point such as A. As inflationary expectations rise, however, the short-run Phillips curve XX begins to shift upwards reflecting the $\dot{p}^e$ term in (3.2d'). Eventually, the economy returns to its 'natural' unemployment rate, U^*, at a point such as B, but with a higher equilibrium price and wage inflation rate, reflected in X_1X_1.

This, in Friedman's view, emphasises the fallacy of the Phillips curve,

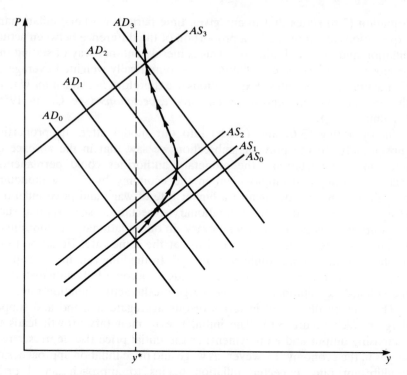

Figure 3.6 The Dynamic Path of the Economy with an
Expectations-Augmented Phillips Curve

except as a short-run phenomenon. A government attempting to trade off
a higher inflation rate against lower unemployment will merely obtain a
short-term reduction in unemployment and a *permanently* higher inflation
rate. If the authorities attempt to keep unemployment permanently below
U^*, this will require accelerating monetary growth, and will lead inevitably
to *accelerating* inflation. Conversely, raising the level of unemployment
permanently above U^*, will lead to accelerating deflation.

  This view of U^* as a 'knife edge' led Friedman to the policy prescription
that monetary policy should concentrate purely on setting monetary
growth on a constant growth path, in accordance with the trend real growth
rate of the economy. It also seemed to provide a simple cure for inflation.
An economy at point B in Figure 3.7 can achieve a zero inflation rate by
reversing the process which took it to B. A reduction in monetary growth
would lower inflation, *temporarily* increasing unemployment until finally
point U^* is reached once more. There is no long-run trade-off between
inflation and unemployment: the Phillips curve is a short-run phenomenon.

  Friedman's critique of the Phillips curve leads to two monetarist
prescriptions for monetary policy. First, an economy which suffers from a
constant rate of inflation can achieve a reduction in the inflation rate by

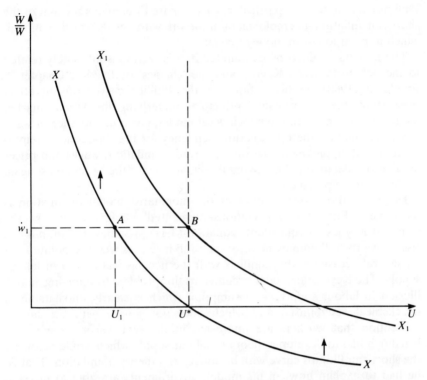

Figure 3.7 Inflation in a Model with an Expectations-Augmented Phillips Curve

lowering the rate of monetary growth. Though this may lead to lower output and higher unemployment in the short run, in the long run the economy will settle down at the natural level of output and unemployment, with a lower inflation rate. Second, Friedman argued that governments' ignorance regarding the level of 'full employment' output and their political urge to seek low levels of unemployment provided an important reason for refraining from fine-tuning demand management policies. This seemed to be confirmed by the accelerating inflation in the world economy in the late 1960s and 1970s, which monetarists ascribed to excessively expansionary monetary policies on the part of individual countries.

3.1.3. Monetarism and the Phillips Curve: Short-Run Labour Market Adjustment

We have examined the way in which Friedman's reinterpretation of the Phillips curve leads to a model with markedly different long-run properties compared to those of the Keynesian model of inflation. We now examine in more detail the behaviour of workers in the short run in the augmented

Phillips curve model. In particular, we compare Friedman's account of the short-run inflation–unemployment trade-off with the Keynesian model, which implied long-run money illusion.

The monetarist doctrine expounded in this section is intimately related to the debate between Keynes and the 'classics' outlined in Chapter 2. Friedman (1968), in his critique of the Phillips curve, was in effect reasserting those neoclassical principles underlying the labour market model of Chapter 2. In the neoclassical model, given the absence of wage and price rigidity, there is a natural tendency for the economic system to settle at full employment. During a period of inflation, wages and prices are likewise deemed to be moving freely, and hence the system must again settle at full employment.

However, the above account of the monetarist model of inflation is incomplete. First, the 'expectations-augmented' Phillips curve, like the standard Keynesian equivalent (equation (3.1)), assumes that output can rise above its 'full employment' or 'natural' level. As we have pointed out on several occasions, this conflicts with the neoclassical theory of labour supply. The Keynesian model circumvents this problem by implying money illusion in labour supply, an assumption which is clearly unpalatable to neoclassical economists, and which does not square with Friedman's contention that workers are interested in the real wage. As a result, Friedman had to develop a theory of labour supply which would reconcile the short-run Phillips curve with his longer-run theory of inflation. That is, he had to explain how, in his model, governments are able to increase output above y^* and lower unemployment below U^* in the short run. To complete Friedman's account of the short- and long-run trade-off between inflation and unemployment, therefore, we must add a theory of labour supply to replace equation (3.2e).

Friedman's account relies on the temporary misperception of the real wage level by rational economic agents in the labour market. Workers base their labour supply decisions on the *expected* real wage $(w - p^e)$, so that equation (3.2e) is replaced by:

$$n^s = f(w - p^e) \qquad\qquad\qquad\qquad (3.2e')$$

Following an aggregate demand expansion, there will be an increase in prices and nominal wages caused by the resulting excess demand in goods and labour markets. However, workers have adaptive expectations with regard to the general price level, and only partially revise their inflationary expectations in line with actual inflation. Hence they initially perceive the rise in nominal wages to be an increase in real wages. This is exactly the argument illustrated in Figure 3.2(b): the actual labour supply schedule shifts to SS, and the increased labour supply depresses the real wage and increases the firms' demand for labour, thus increasing employment. As workers' expectations of inflation approach the actual inflation rate, they will realise that though nominal wages have risen, their real wage has fallen. They then withdraw their additional labour supply, thus removing the initial short-run output gains and gradually shifting the SS curve back to N^s. In the long run the labour market settles at point E once more, and there is no long-run money illusion. This illustrates the difference between the monetarist and Keynesian views of the labour market. In the Keynesian model, the growth in aggregate demand is sufficient to offset the Phillips curve wage adjustment in (3.2d), thus keeping the labour market at a point such as E_1 in Figure 3.2(b), implying that workers must suffer from money illusion even in the long run. On the other hand, the expectations-augmented Phillips curve (3.2d') and the labour supply function (3.2e') ensure that in the monetarist model, workers slowly perceive that their real wage has fallen, and respond to this by raising their nominal wages sufficiently so as to reverse the initial fall in the real wage rate, taking the economy back to full employment. The arrowed path in Figure 3.6 shows the short-run adjustment path of the economy in the monetarist model.

It should be noted that workers in Friedman's model are at an informational disadvantage with respect to firms. While the firm is assumed to know the price for its own product and knows its factor costs (wage costs) with certainty, the worker is assumed to have only an imperfect knowledge of the general price level. It would be possible, however, to generalise the model to one in which the firm is likewise not certain of the current price for its product relative to the general price level, and the real cost of its inputs, and has to form some view about these variables, which it revises through time. However, this would not radically alter the conclusions of Friedman's basic 'natural rate' model.

To complete this section, we now turn our attention briefly to models of unemployment which were developed alongside Friedman's account of the short-run Phillips curve. These *search models* explain the short-run trade-off between inflation and unemployment in a rather different manner in that they focus on the flows in and out of frictional unemployment. Nevertheless, they have a central point in common with Friedman: that a fall in unemployment below the natural rate is due to mistaken perceptions by workers regarding their wage.

3.1.4. Search Theory and Unemployment

The search approach to unemployment (see Phelps 1970a, 1970b, Mortensen 1970a, 1970b) takes as its starting point the individual worker who is assumed, at any given time, to face a variety of job opportunities, each with its own wage offer. Although each worker has his own idea of the probability distribution of wage offers available, he does not know without approaching each particular firm what offer it would make to him. Furthermore, it is assumed that workers must relinquish their existing jobs if they wish to participate in the job search process. The search process is therefore costly, involving both foregone earnings and explicit search costs; but further search costs may be rewarded by a better job. Balancing the costs of further search against the expected return defines the worker's 'acceptance wage', the minimum level at which he will accept any particular job offer. The search process implies unemployment, with inflows as workers decide to seek a better job and outflows when acceptance wages are met. In steady state, unemployment persists but inflows are equal to outflows. The stock of unemployed is of constant size, but changing composition. This type of unemployment may be seen as voluntary and *frictional*, in that optimising workers are attempting to obtain the best possible wage offer under the circumstances, subject to search costs.

The relevance of job search in the present context is that it can be used to explain a fall in unemployment during a demand expansion. As demand increases, firms in general will wish to increase their workforce, and will raise their wage offers, both to ensure that they retain their current workers, and in an attempt to attract new workers. To begin with, these increased wage offers are *perceived* individually as improved offers relative to offers in competing firms. The rate of acceptances will increase, the numbers of those leaving employment decrease, and unemployment will fall. However, once it is recognised that the whole distribution of wage offers has moved upwards, acceptance wages will be revised upwards, and some workers, realising that the offer from their present employer is not exceptional in relative terms, will reverse their decision and resume search. *Search*, or *frictional*, unemployment will then return to its previous level.

Search theorists and Friedman share the common central idea that the short-run Phillips curve is explicable in terms of workers' temporary misperceptions of the real wage. However, while Friedman argues in terms of a reduction in total unemployment due to temporary money illusion in a competitive labour market, search theory is couched in terms of a labour market with monopsonistic elements, and where workers may be heterogeneous.

According to both these accounts, deviations from the natural rate of unemployment must be seen as temporary aberrations. Providing that the labour market can be described in market-clearing, neoclassical terms, a long-run trade-off between unemployment and inflation cannot logically exist. Following Friedman's critique of the Phillips curve, much time and energy was spent in estimating empirical expectations-augmented Phillips curves of the type described in equation (3.2d′). Empirical studies centred on testing whether a coefficient of unity could be found in the inflationary expectations term, thereby confirming the absence of a long-run trade-off between inflation and unemployment. The results obtained were less than conclusive (see for instance Gordon 1970, Lucas 1972b), and even if Keynesian attempts at discovering such a trade-off had succeeded, one would still have to provide a theoretical justification for this result. Furthermore, a Keynesian argument for short-run interventionist stabilisation policy can still be made even if the *long-run* aggregate supply and/or Phillips curve is vertical. As Phelps (1972) and Hall (1976) point out, providing a short-run trade-off exists, a government may adopt stabilisation policies in the face of both aggregate demand and aggregate supply disturbances, if it can correctly identify such shocks and act on them swiftly.

In this context, the debate about the possible role for stabilisation policy involves two general questions. First, governments may apply *feedback policy rules* to reduce fluctuations in the economy only if they can identify the nature of the short-run disturbances correctly and implement policy measures efficiently. Friedman's argument in favour of a *fixed money supply* rule may only hold if governments have such imperfect information about the underlying economic structure and the nature of disturbances to it that intervention is likely to make matters worse rather than better. Thus the argument between monetarists and Keynesians reduces partly to one about whether policy-makers 'may be trusted' to execute counter-cyclical policy efficiently.

The other issue determining the scope for stabilisation policy concerns the speed of adjustment of the system to long-run equilibrium. The key factor in this is the nature of the expectations formation mechanism in general, and the speed of adjustment of expectations in particular. The assumption of adaptive expectations (equation (3.6)) is an *ad hoc* way of modelling expectations with no theoretical rationale. It could be argued that individuals' expectations should be treated as endogenous rather than derived from an arbitrary (and mechanistic) formula. The development of the so-called 'new classical' macroeconomics centres on the application of the concept of *rational expectations*, which has revolutionised the theory of how economic agents form expectations, and which has consequently had profound implications for the theory of stabilisation policy.

3.2. Rational Expectations and the New Classical Macroeconomics

3.2.1. *The Concept of Rational Expectations*

The modelling of economic agents' expectations has always been regarded as an awkward issue in economics, albeit a crucial one. Moreover, the way in which expectations are analysed can be fundamental to the behaviour of the economic model in which expectations are embedded. For instance, in the expectations-augmented Phillips curve model of the previous section, if we were to replace the assumption of adaptive expectations with the assumption that workers could accurately predict the future actual path of inflation, we would expect them to behave differently. As workers observe that the inflation rate has increased permanently, they will revise their wage claims upwards, thus causing the economy to return to its 'natural' rate of unemployment far sooner than under the assumption of adaptive expectations.

One of the most disturbing aspects of the assumption of adaptive expectations is that they are entirely backward looking. Suppose, for example, that previous experience has suggested a strong link between monetary expansion and price increases. If economic agents were to observe an increase in the rate of monetary growth, it might be plausible to assume that they will recognise this as a source of a future increase in the inflation rate. In other words, in forming their inflationary expectations, economic agents may be expected to take into account what they perceive to be the underlying model of inflation in the economy. However, in contrast, under adaptive expectations, workers will ignore the increase in monetary growth and merely look at past inflation — surely not the most efficient way for rational agents to form expectations. In practice, agents will form their view of the future with regard to a variety of relevant information variables available at the present time.

A related problem is that the assumption of adaptive expectations allows economic agents to commit a series of systematic forecast errors following a change in the rate of inflation: surely a rational agent would not *consistently* underpredict the permanently increased inflation rate following the rise in monetary growth? However, it is not entirely apparent what expectations formation mechanism economists should employ in place of the adaptive expectations hypothesis. If agents are to avoid such systematic expectational errors, it is apparent that no fixed mechanistic formula of the type described in equation (3.6) will do. The appropriate expectations generating mechanism must take account of the underlying economic model. That is, we would expect a 'rational' economic agent's expectations of future economic events to be *endogenous* to the economic model.

One way of implementing the notion of 'endogenous expectations' was originally suggested in the context of microeconomics by Muth (1961), and later applied in a macroeconomic context by the new classical school of macroeconomics. Muth's rational expectations hypothesis (REH) assumed that economic agents do not make systematic forecasting errors. This implies that individuals' perceptions of the underlying economic model coincide with the *best model* of the economy (i.e. that model of the economy which appears to give the best account of the actual behaviour of economic variables). To state this property of the REH more formally, agents' *subjective* expectations of economic variables are assumed to coincide with the objective mathematical conditional expectations of those variables. Or, to put this another way, under the REH economic agents' expectations of economic variables X_t^e equal on average their true value, X_t:

$$X_t^e = X_t + \varepsilon_t$$

where ε_t is a zero-mean error term which is uncorrelated with the information set available when expectations are formed (this is usually assumed to be at time $t - 1$). If X_t^e and X_t were to differ, by a term which was in some sense predictable, from information at the disposal of economic agents, then agents could improve their forecasts by taking such information into account. The REH therefore assumes that economic agents fully exploit all available information in arriving at their forecasts.

At one extreme this assumption has some startling implications: where the underlying model is deterministic and there is no uncertainty relating to the value of particular variables, the REH reduces to the assumption of *perfect foresight*. Agents are then able to predict exactly the values of variables. More typically, there will be random influences on the economy (often due to unquantifiable economic or non-economic factors), and hence X_t^e and X_t will diverge, but it will remain true that $X_t^e = E(X_t | \Omega_{t-1})$, where $E(. | \Omega_{t-1})$ denotes the expected value of the variable X, conditional on the information set Ω_{t-1} available to economic agents at time $t-1$. The error term ε will be present because economic agents cannot have complete knowledge of the economic system. Nevertheless, it should be apparent that the ε_t should be white noise, and that it should be uncorrelated with Ω_{t-1} because otherwise economic agents would not be exploiting their information to their full advantage.

There are two criticisms which may be made of this view of agents' expectations formation. First, it is argued that the REH offers no explanation of the process whereby economic agents discover the underlying economic model, and that it is therefore of relevance only in situations where the economic structure has been invariant over long periods of time (see Buiter 1980). If initially agents have no knowledge of the underlying economic structure we could expect them to make systematic forecasting errors in the short run. The issue of 'learning' in RE models has been extensively researched (see, for example, Frydman and Phelps 1983, Bray and Savin 1984, DeCanio 1979, B. M. Friedman 1979), and we return to this issue in Chapter 4. In general, it has been shown that 'learning' by individuals need not necessarily cause expectations to converge in the manner postulated in RE models.

Second, the REH does not recognise that, in practice, the collection of information involves costs (including time), and that economic agents may not have the economic incentive to acquire a *detailed* knowledge of the economic structure. In such cases, though expectations may be unbiased, the variance of ε may be quite large because large parts of the economic system remain unexplained.

Nevertheless, neither of these criticisms is directed at the basic purpose of the REH, which is to generate expectations which are endogenous to the economic model. They merely suggest that the process of learning and information gathering by agents should be further studied, to examine whether the REH could be improved. Furthermore, as we shall see below, many new classical results do not require individuals to have a full information set, but only that policy-makers do not have an information advantage relative to the private sector. That is, that Ω_{t-1} is the information set for all economic agents, including the government.

3.2.2. New Classical Macroeconomics and Monetary Policy: the Strong Invariance Proposition

We now turn to the application of the REH to a simple macroeconomic model, concentrating on monetary policy as this has been the subject of most attention in the recent literature and in any case the results obtained may be extended to include fiscal policy. Furthermore, to avoid complicated wage–price dynamics, we shall employ the aggregate demand–aggregate supply paradigm rather than a model incorporating an expectations-augmented Phillips curve, since it will be apparent from the argument in section 1 that the two concepts are intimately related. In doing so, we follow Sargent (1973), and Sargent and Wallace (1976).

The new classical view of aggregate supply as embodied in the work of Lucas (1973), Sargent (1973), and Sargent and Wallace (1976) is similar to that which may be deduced from the arguments presented by Friedman (1968) and the search theorists. We begin by recalling the short-run production function, and labour demand and supply functions used in subsections 3.1.1 and 3.1.3 (where again all variables are in logarithms):

$$y = \gamma n \tag{3.2f}$$

$$n^s = \theta(w - p^e) \tag{3.2e''}$$

$$p = \delta + (1 - \gamma)n + w \tag{3.2g}$$

where (3.2e″) is a log-linear version of (3.2e′). We may obtain the aggregate supply function by first of all substituting for w from (3.2g) into (3.2e″). This yields the following expression for employment:

$$n = \frac{-\delta\theta}{(1 + \theta(1 - \gamma))} + \frac{\theta(p - p^e)}{(1 + \theta(1 - \gamma))}$$

Substituting for n into (3.2f), this yields the so-called 'surprise' aggregate supply function:

$$y_t = y^* + \beta(p_t - p_t^e) + u_t \tag{3.7}$$

where $y^* = -\delta\gamma\theta/(1 + \theta(1 - \gamma))$, and $\beta = \theta\gamma/(1 + \theta(1 - \gamma))$. Note that we have added time subscripts for convenience, and a stochastic term u_t, which is assumed to be white noise, to capture any random effects on aggregate supply. The 'natural' level of output is given by y^*, (i.e. the level at which output settles if the price level equals its expected value), and output deviates from its natural level only in response to an unexpected rise in the price level. Equation (3.7) follows directly from the account of the labour market described in subsection 3.1.3: following an expansion in aggregate demand, excess demand in the goods and labour markets causes prices and wages to rise. If workers do not initially recognise the increase in the price level, the real wage will fall (Figure 3.2(b)), and output and employment will rise. However, this output response will only take place if workers mistake the nominal wage rise for a real wage rise, because they base their labour supply decision on the expected real wage (equation (3.2e″)).

The 'surprise' supply function is the static aggregate supply equivalent of the expectations-augmented Phillips curve. As we noted in subsection 3.1.3, an output and employment response to price increases relies on an asymmetry of information, where firms base their labour demand decision on full knowledge of the price for the product they sell, p, and the input they buy, w, but workers only know with certainty the nominal value of the labour they sell, but have to form an expectation of the general price level.

In the spirit of Lucas (1973), we can generalise the theory underlying the 'surprise' supply function, by considering a number of individual economic agents, who can be seen as selling a good (which may be a consumption good or a factor input), and purchasing the goods produced by all other economic agents. Each agent–producer will therefore decide on his output plan on the basis of his *expected real product price*, just as a worker bases his labour supply decision on his expected *real* wage. The real product price, like the real wage, is a measure of the price of the individual's product *relative* to the general price level. Following an aggregate demand expansion, the prices of all goods will increase, and if individual agents perceive this to be a rise in the price for their product *relative* to the prices of all other goods, they will believe that their *real product price* has risen. They will therefore expand their output. Thus, Lucas' (1973) account of the 'surprise' supply function need not rely on any asymmetry of information between firms and workers: output and employment react to price 'surprises' as suppliers of both goods and factors of production formulate a view regarding their real product price. This leads to an

aggregate supply function of the type detailed in (3.7). We shall outline
Lucas' account of producers' supply decisions in more detail in
subsection 3.2.4.

We may now illustrate diagrammatically the effects of adopting such
an aggregate supply function. In Figure 3.8(a) we show an expansion in
aggregate demand. Let us assume that it is fully *anticipated* by all economic
agents. The upward sloping aggregate supply curve is drawn for a given
expected price level. Because economic agents are assumed to anticipate
the consequent rise in prices from P_0 to P_1, the rightward shift in the
aggregate demand curve is matched by an equal leftward shift in the

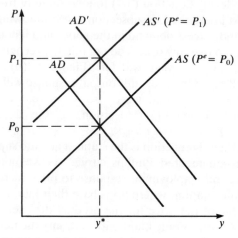

Figure 3.8(a)   An Anticipated Aggregate Demand Expansion

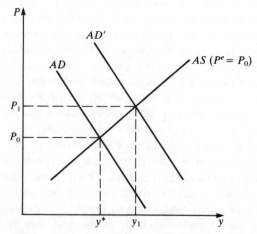

Figure 3.8(b)   An Unanticipated Aggregate Demand Expansion

aggregate supply curve, since wages and prices are adjusted upwards as workers and firms seek to protect their real wages and relative (or real) product prices. In contrast, an *unanticipated* rightward shift in the aggregate demand function (see Figure 3.8(b)) is not matched by a shift in the aggregate supply function and leads to an increase in output and employment.

The fact that in this analysis real income responds only to unanticipated demand changes has profound implications for the effectiveness of stabilisation policies. Let us assume that the authorities seek to stabilise real income through monetary policy and that the LM curve is interest-insensitive, which enables us to regard the IS curve as irrelevant to the determination of aggregate demand. Though this may appear restrictive, the conclusions which we derive for monetary policy carry over to the case of fiscal policy in a more general IS–LM model. The LM equation which we adopt is (in logarithms):

$$m_t + k + v_t = p_t + y_t \qquad (3.8)$$

where k is a constant, and v_t is a stochastic term, which captures random aggregate demand shocks, and is assumed to be white noise. In addition, we assume that the government wishes to stabilise the economy at its natural level in the face of exogenous aggregate demand and supply shocks, such as u_t, and v_t, and that it seeks to do this by adopting a 'feedback' monetary policy of the type:

$$m_t = -\gamma y_{t-1} \qquad \gamma > 0 \qquad (3.9)$$

where the authorities decrease the money stock whenever output rises, and increase it when it falls. (We examine this type of policy rule in more detail in Chapter 9, when we also discuss more formally the rationale behind such stabilisation policies. For the moment, we focus our attention on the government's *ability* to influence the path of output and employment.) To complete the model, we are required to make some assumption regarding the formation of price expectations. In the case where expectations are formed adaptively, as we saw in the previous subsection, systematic government policy of the type described in (3.9) can influence output and employment in the short run. However, let us now assume that individuals form their expectations at time $t - 1$ according to the REH. In other words, we assume that expectations of the price level at time t, p_t^e, are formed conditional on the information set Ω_{t-1}, where Ω_{t-1} contains information on all the economic variables of the model at time $t - 1$. In this case, substituting for y_t from (3.7) into (3.8), we obtain:

$$m_t + k - p_t = y^* + \beta(p_t - p_t^e) + u_t - v_t$$

substituting for m_t into the above expression using (3.9):

$$-\gamma y_{t-1} + k - p_t = y^* + \beta(p_t - p_t^e) + u_t - v_t \tag{3.10}$$

Taking expectations of (3.10) conditional on time $t - 1$ (and noting that $E(p_t \mid \Omega_{t-1}) = p_t^e$, $E(u_t \mid \Omega_{t-1}) = 0$, and $E(v_t \mid \Omega_{t-1}) = 0$), we obtain:

$$p_t^e = -\gamma y_{t-1} + k - y^* \tag{3.11}$$

which implies that economic agents form their expectations of the price level at time t by taking into account the government's money supply rule. Notice, however, that they expect aggregate demand and supply shocks to be on average equal to zero, and that therefore these do not enter (3.11). By substituting (3.11) into (3.10), we can obtain an expression for the price level:

$$p_t = -\gamma y_{t-1} + k - y^* + \frac{(v_t - u_t)}{(1 + \beta)} \tag{3.12}$$

By comparing (3.11) and (3.12) we note that in this model with random disturbances to aggregate demand and supply, the price level and its expected value diverge by a white noise error term, $(v_t - u_t)/(1 + \beta)$. Substituting (3.11) and (3.12) into (3.7), we obtain:

$$y_t = y^* + \frac{\beta}{(1 + \beta)}(v_t - u_t) + u_t \tag{3.13}$$

Thus from (3.13) it follows that, by adopting the REH, y_t and y^* diverge by a purely random term: output never *systematically* deviates from its 'natural' level. Furthermore, the dramatic result for the debate about stabilisation strategies is that systematic government policy cannot affect real output or employment as the policy parameter γ does not appear in (3.13).

This strong *policy invariance* or *policy neutrality* result follows because the REH assumes that economic agents know the underlying economic model, and hence can correctly anticipate any systematic aggregate demand fluctuations such as those implied by the government policy rule. As a corollary to this, it is apparent that only unsystematic or unanticipated disturbances, such as v_t and u_t, can have real effects in the economy. As shown in Figure 3.8(a), an *anticipated* increase in the money stock will merely raise the price level without any effect on output. Only *unanticipated* changes in the money stock (which must be random given that economic agents are assumed to observe the government's policy rule) can affect output. In models with the REH, forward looking variables (like the price level in this model) are therefore assumed to 'jump' so as to carry the model to its new equilibrium. This analysis may be extended to dynamic models with more than one dynamic endogenous variable and which contain RE variables. This is illustrated in the appendix to this chapter.

This invariance result has major implications for the effectiveness and conduct of counter-cyclical stabilisation policy. Anticipated shocks have no real effects, and hence the role of stabilisation policy is limited to offsetting unanticipated shocks. However, unless governments have some degree of information advantage over the private sector in being able to predict such shocks, these may not be offset. The natural conclusion which follows from this result is that stabilisation policy is at best not superior to a fixed money supply rule (i.e. setting $\gamma = 0$). Furthermore, if the government does not have total control over the money stock, but is liable to commit policy errors, then stabilisation policy may actually make matters worse, by rendering the price and output levels more volatile. This may be illustrated by adding a policy error term to (3.9):

$$m_t = -\gamma y_{t-1} + \varepsilon_t \qquad\qquad \gamma > 0 \qquad\qquad (3.9')$$

where ε_t is a white noise stochastic disturbance, and represents any random deviations from the authorities' desired policy setting, due, for example, to the authorities' inability to achieve total control over the money stock. In this case, following the argument set out in equations (3.10)–(3.12) and noting that $E(\varepsilon_t \mid \Omega_{t-1}) = 0$, it follows that:

$$y_t = y^* + \frac{\beta}{(1 + \beta)}(v_t + \varepsilon_t - u_t) + u_t \qquad\qquad (3.13')$$

Output again deviates from its 'natural' level by a random term, which now includes the policy error, ε_t. It follows, by comparing (3.13) and (3.13'), that the variance of output around its 'natural' level has increased due to the presence of ε_t, as has the variance of the price level. We will return to a more detailed analysis of optimal policy in Chapter 9, but it is worthwhile to note here that if we believe that counter-cyclical monetary policy involves an additional element of uncertainty due to the presence of policy errors, fixed money supply rules (setting $\gamma = 0$ in (3.9) and (3.9')) will definitely dominate counter-cyclical policies (setting $\gamma > 0$).

However, even in the absence of policy errors, the arguments for stabilisation policy are considerably weakened by the REH, given that counter-cyclical aggregate demand policy is *at best* ineffective in stabilising output at full employment. These results represent a more damaging attack on Keynesian stabilisation policies than that of Friedman (1968). While the latter severely questioned the efficiency of stabilisation policy, given imperfect information and policy lags, the simple addition of the

REH to the natural rate hypothesis implies that, even in the short run, counter-cyclical policy has nothing to contribute to the stabilisation of the economy, and may actually be detrimental if 'policy errors' are commonplace.

3.2.3.   *Keynesian Objections to the REH and the Policy Neutrality Result*

Keynesian objections to the implications of the REH may be divided into a number of categories. First, we consider those objections to the concept of rational expectations itself. Some economists object to the idea that economic agents can possibly 'know the correct underlying economic model'. Surely the individual's thought process when making economic decisions does not involve considerations of this type? However, this is not a significant criticism. The relevant question is not whether 'taking objective conditional mathematical expectations' is a correct description of individual behaviour, but whether the implications of the REH can be verified empirically. In practice, economic agents may behave 'as if' their expectations were 'rational', even though their thought processes do not correspond to the theoretical description of the REH. We can provide an analogy from sport to illustrate this argument. Though the game of billiards may be described in terms of the complex physics of mechanics, professional players of billiards may achieve their playing objectives without explicit recourse to the laws of physics to calculate the trajectories of the billiard balls. Similarly, economic agents may behave according to the predictions of the REH without knowing the economics behind it.

As we mentioned in subsection 3.2.1, some economists have objected to the fact that the REH provides no description of the way in which economic agents learn about policy rules and the economic structure. As we shall see in Chapter 4, in some circumstances this may lead to modifications of the strong invariance proposition. Others again have noted that if governments have an informational advantage, the strong invariance proposition will not hold. While acceptable in itself, this *a priori* critique of the REH is a weak peg on which to hang the argument in favour of stabilisation policies, especially in times when good communications ensure the rapid spread of economic intelligence, and government economic statements are accurately scrutinised.

Overall, criticisms such as these merely call for a modification to the REH, not its total rejection. A more promising line of argument attacks not the REH itself, but the model to which it has been applied. The new classical view involves the joint hypothesis of a market-clearing neo-classical model of the labour market and the REH, and thus the strong invariance result proposed by the new classical school depends essentially on the 'natural rate' hypothesis. In an attempt to justify stabilisation policies, Keynesians have developed a number of non-market-clearing models, and we examine these in Chapter 4.

In addition, some economists have alleged that 'neutrality' and 'superneutrality' results hold only within highly restrictive model specifications (see Buiter 1980, Tobin and Buiter 1980). For example, government expenditure directed at increasing productive capacity will have real effects not captured in models where the 'natural rate' is exogenously given. Such effects can also be ascribed to monetary policy, through interest rate effects on capital accumulation.

Finally, and perhaps most importantly, the model outlined above, which follows Sargent and Wallace (1976), cannot explain sustained deviations of the economy from the 'natural rate', which, as Modigliani (1977) argues, is a serious shortcoming of new classical models, given that the 'persistence' of the business cycle is an empirical phenomenon which macroeconomic theory has to explain. Furthermore, Modigliani also draws attention to other macroeconomic phenomena which the simple model outlined above fails to explain. First, there is the observation made already in the 1930s, and reiterated in the later 1960s, that real wages move pro-cyclically with output and employment (see Dunlop 1938, Tarshis 1939, Kuh 1966 and Bodkin 1969), in contrast to the prediction of the 'surprise' supply function. To be fair, however, this criticism may also be levelled against the standard short-run upward sloping Keynesian aggregate supply curve, where any increases in output and employment are combined with falling real wages. However, as we shall see in the next subsection, new classical models can be constructed to generate pro-cyclical movements in the real wage.

Second, the observed pro-cyclical movement of labour productivity, which seems to contradict the law of diminishing returns to a variable factor, must also be explained. Any model which insists on a static downward sloping demand for labour function contradicts this observation. Again, as we shall see in the next subsection, some new classical models have also attempted to come to terms with this observation.

3.2.4. New Classical Models of the Business Cycle

An early new classical account of the business cycle is provided by Lucas (1973), and relies heavily on his account of the 'surprise' supply function. Lucas' model describes suppliers of a single good located in a number of separate sectors (or markets). In each sector, the price of a good can be seen as the sum of the average (economy-wide) price index, p_t, and an additional element, z_t, which depends on relative demand conditions in that particular sector:

$$p_t = \rho_t + z_t \tag{3.14}$$

The price for the good produced in any sector, p_t, therefore depends on z_t, a relative demand shock which is random and is distributed with zero mean and finite variance σ_z^2. In each sector, the economic agent's supply decision depends in part on supply (output) in the last period, y_{t-1}, and partly on projected increases in the *relative* price for his product. They are assumed not to respond to increases in the *general* price level, as this would imply money illusion. Thus, supply in any sector, y_t, depends on:

$$y_t = \beta(p_t - E_t\rho_t) + \lambda y_{t-1} \tag{3.15}$$

This is similar to the 'surprise' supply function for a single sector, except for the λy_{t-1} term which has replaced y^* and to which we shall return later. Expectations are assumed to be formed according to the REH, where economic agents observe current and past prices for their products, as well as past output and past relative demand shocks. Note that E_t denotes expectations formed conditional on the information set Ω_t available at time t:

$$\Omega_t = (p_t, p_{t-1}, \ldots, \rho_{t-1}, \rho_{t-2} \ldots, y_{t-1}, y_{t-2}, \ldots)$$

It should be stressed that, in contrast to the model of subsection 3.2.2 (where expectations were conditioned on information at $t - 1$), the information set here also contains one variable (p) which is observed at time t. This is because we assume that economic agents know the price of the commodity they are selling with certainty. This serves to emphasise that one should carefully consider the information set on which expectations are conditioned before applying the REH to a model. We note that the average price index ρ_t has a variance σ_ρ^2. Unfortunately, because the separate components of p_t in (3.14) are unobservable in the time period when the supply decision has to be made, the economic agent faces a *signal extraction* problem. Following a rise in p_t, suppliers have to decide whether this reflects a rise in the general price level, ρ_t (which agents do not know, i.e. it does not enter the information vector Ω_t) or a rise in the relative demand component, z_t. Lucas then derives the following expression for $E_t\rho_t$:

$$E_t\rho_t = \theta E_{t-1}\rho_t + (1 - \theta)p_t \tag{3.16}$$

where the information set Ω_{t-1} is the same as Ω_t, but excludes p_t. Current expectations of the average price level $E_t\rho_t$ depend partly on last period's expectations of ρ_t, $(E_{t-1}\rho_t)$, and partly on the current price for the firm's good, p_t. We may now substitute for $E_t\rho_t$ from (3.16) into (3.15):

$$y_t = \beta\theta(p_t - E_{t-1}\rho_t) + \lambda y_{t-1} \qquad\qquad (3.15')$$

The factor of proportionality θ is given by $(\sigma_z^2 + \sigma_\rho^2)/\sigma_z^2$. Thus, as the variance of relative price shocks, σ_z^2, decreases with respect to the variance of absolute price shocks, σ_ρ^2, θ tends to zero and the firm in this sector will not increase supply in response to price increases, because in this case the firm perceives price variability to be due in the main to absolute rather than relative price changes.

Lucas' account of the business cycle is then simple: suppose, to begin with, that agents are accustomed to stability in the overall price level, and perceive price changes in their market as relative price changes, i.e. θ is close to unity. An increase in aggregate demand generates price increases which are seen as relative price rises, and real incomes rise. However, as people learn about the relatively higher variability of the aggregate price level, the value of θ will fall, and they will be less likely to increase output, even in the short run. In terms of Figure 3.8, as economic agents perceive a higher variability in the general price level, the slope of the short-run aggregate supply curve will become steeper.

Lucas also examined empirical evidence on the relationship between output and price (inflation) volatility between countries. In general, he found that in countries which had had recent experience of volatile prices (e.g. Argentina), output was less responsive to aggregate demand changes, compared to countries where prices had been less volatile (e.g. the USA, West Germany). This aspect of Lucas' model illustrates the problems which inflation may cause to the allocative mechanism. In the presence of high price variability any relative price changes will be less easily perceived by economic agents, thus causing inefficiencies in the allocation of resources. However, despite its intuitive appeal, Lucas' evidence is less convincing when we compare countries with similar inflation experiences.

Furthermore, any serial correlation in output in the Lucas model, which is necessary to explain the phenomenon of 'persistence', depends on the term λy_{t-1}, which introduces output dynamics into Lucas' aggregate supply relation. This can be seen by noting that, if we sum across all sectors, the total output in the economy, y_t, depends on the forecast error in the aggregate price level:

$$y_t = \beta\theta(\rho_t - E_{t-1}\rho_t) + \lambda y_{t-1} \qquad\qquad (3.15'')$$

From the assumption of RE, the forecast error $(\rho_t - E_{t-1}\rho_t)$ must be random, and hence any serial correlation is merely *assumed*, through the introduction of the dynamic term λy_{t-1}. This term ensures that any unexpected shock to the price level will initiate cycles in the output level, even if such shocks are random (due to the randomness of the forecast error in the general price level). The procedure of including λy_{t-1} is *ad hoc*, and not based on any theory. Thus, in itself Lucas' model does not satisfactorily answer Modigliani's critique.

Nevertheless, as Sargent (1979) suggests, serial correlation in output may be obtained in this model if agents cannot observe lagged aggregate prices (ρ) for recent past time periods i.e. the ρ_{t-i} are removed from the information set Ω. However, this is also an *ad hoc* procedure, as it offers the authorities an information advantage, which we criticised on *a priori* grounds above. Lucas (1975) also modifies his earlier model by allowing agents to observe only the variance of nominal aggregate demand, rather than the actual aggregate price level. This also rescues the theory by predicting serial correlation in output, but again at the price of an *ad hoc* assumption regarding the information set on which expectations are conditioned. This is subject to the charge raised by Buiter (1980) that:

> By suitable redefinition of the information set conditioning the forecast, any pattern of serial correlation in the endogenous variables of a model can be rationalised as consistent with Muth-rational expectations. By becoming irrefutable, the hypothesis would cease to belong to the realm of scientific (i.e. positive or empirical) theory, as defined by Popper (1959). (Buiter 1980, p. 38)

However, there are alternative new classical models which can account for business cycles as well as for the cyclical behaviour of the real wage and productivity referred to above. For example, Lucas and Rapping (1969) develop a dynamic model of intertemporal labour supply and consumption decisions by the household. They provide a classical theory of the business cycle in the sense that output and employment fluctuations are not generated by fluctuations in the money stock, but by real factors. Though the model is complex and will not be described in detail here, we can indicate the basis for its results. As the individual's labour supply decision is not now a static one, as in the simple neoclassical model of labour supply, but a dynamic *intertemporal* one, he considers all *future* real wage levels in deciding his *current* labour supply. Assuming that households maximise their intertemporal utility, Lucas and Rapping then derive a labour supply function which has the general functional form:

$$n_t^s = f(r_t, r_{t+j}, (A/P)_t, (W/P)_t, (W/P)_{t+j}) \tag{3.17}$$

where r represents the real interest rate and A represents the household's nominal non-human assets. These two variables enter the function because households are making a joint labour supply and consumption decision (in accordance with the 'classical' theory of consumption). This current labour supply depends on current and future real wages. Lucas and Rapping predict that if the household is faced with a temporary increase in the real wage, it will increase its labour supply temporarily, while labour supply is more inelastic with respect to permanent increases in the real wage. This prediction is derived on the basis of a cost-of-leisure argument. If workers observe a temporary increase in their wage today, why not work harder now, and take more holidays later? Households essentially behave like intertemporal speculators with regard to their leisure time. Sargent (1979) combines this model of labour supply with a model of dynamic labour demand by firms to obtain a full dynamic model of the labour market (see also Sargent 1978a). On the other side of the labour market in this model, the firm is also assumed to engage in intertemporal optimisation by maximising the sum of expected future (discounted) profits. In a similar fashion to Lucas and Rapping (1969), Sargent derives the firm's dynamic labour demand schedule:

$$n_t^d = g\left(\left(\frac{W}{P}\right)_t, \ \left(\frac{W}{P}\right)_{t+j}\right) \tag{3.18}$$

The labour demand schedule is dynamic because firms cannot smoothly reallocate factors of production among their production functions, but face costs of adjustment in changing their level of labour input rapidly. (A similar costs-of-adjustment argument was made in the case of capital goods by Lucas and Prescott (1971)). Equations (3.17) and (3.18) together yield a dynamic labour market, in which employment and the real wage display cycles. To drive the dynamic system, Sargent introduces random shocks to households' preferences and to firms' technology (i.e. the production function). The result is that random shocks to real factors (technology) cause cycles in employment and real wages. The precise shape of such cycles depends on the specification of the exogenous shocks to the system. If we assume that shocks to households' preferences, ε_t, and to technology, α_t, are white noise processes, then employment will follow a difference equation of the type:

$$n_t = a_0 n_{t-1} + a_1(\varepsilon_t - a_2\alpha_t) + a_3 \tag{3.19}$$

What this equation in effect describes is what we may regard as cyclical variations in the *natural* level of employment: aggregate demand management techniques can do nothing to reduce the amplitude or frequency of such cycles. In fact, in so far as aggregate demand policy causes 'signal extraction problems' of the type described by Lucas (1973), feedback stabilisation policies of the type described in (3.9) may actually accentuate the cycles in the economy and hence prove to be counter-productive. The only type of policies which may attenuate such cycles, as Sargent (1979) suggests, are supply-side taxation policies which by affecting the households' labour supply decision are designed to smooth out such cycles.

A further feature of this model of the business cycle is that it can explain the empirical evidence on real wages and productivity. As the Lucas and Rapping model shows, households will *increase* their supply of labour in response to a temporary real wage increase, thus accounting for the pro-cyclical movement of real wages. Labour productivity will also move pro-cyclically, as firms adjust labour inputs only gradually in upswings, and output will rise faster than employment. Thus, not only do such dynamic new classical models have the merit of explaining the problem of persistence, but they also offer an explanation for phenomena which the simple static neoclassical synthesis and Keynesian models could not explain. However, these empirical observations cannot be regarded as evidence which may help us to choose between alternative Keynesian and new classical views of the business cycle, as Keynesian models may be similarly modified to account for these phenomena. For instance, Solow and Stiglitz (1968) suggest that the observed pro-cyclical movement of the real wage and labour productivity leads us away from equilibrium models of the labour market to a disequilibrium approach. A general disequilibrium model, as we saw in Chapter 2, can reconcile a number of real wage levels with a given output level. Furthermore, Phelps (1969) explains these phenomena by introducing a production lag in his model: labour demand also depends on the *expected* real wage, in a similar fashion to labour supply. Lastly, Scarth and Myatt (1980) obtain pro-cyclical movements in the real wage by introducing partial adjustment in the demand for labour, in a similar fashion to Sargent (1979).

In conclusion, therefore, we may note that there are two new classical explanations of the business cycle: the first explains the business cycle in terms of problems of *signal extraction* faced by economic agents (see Lucas 1973, 1975). This approach to the business cycle can explain how monetary expansions may affect real output, but cannot explain serial correlation in deviations from the natural rate. The second approach constitutes a supply-side explanation of the business cycle (see Lucas and Rapping 1969, Sargent 1978a, 1979), and sees fluctuations in output as serially correlated movements in the natural rate.

These two approaches are, of course, not mutually exclusive. A complete new classical account of the business cycle could involve elements of both approaches: for instance, aggregate demand shocks may cause actual output changes which in turn set off supply-side adjustments in a dynamic labour market, with cycles in the 'natural' level of output. The new classical theory of the business cycle therefore implies that movements in the actual level of output can cause movements in its 'natural' level, and hence that the observation of a positive correlation between movements in the money stock and real output does not offer casual empirical support for the Keynesian case. Thus, overall, casual empirical evidence does not enable us to discriminate between new classical and Keynesian accounts of real output determination. To test new classical models meaningfully, more formal empirical models had to be developed, as we shall see in the next section.

3.3. Empirical Evidence on the New Classical Models

3.3.1. Tests on the Real Effects of Anticipated and Unanticipated Money

The empirical literature on new classical models is vast. In practice, the REH has been applied to many economic relationships. For example, the implications of the REH for the consumption function have received attention in recent years (see Hall 1978, Sargent 1978b, Flavin 1981, Davidson and Hendry 1981). Similarly, Sargent (1978a) estimated dynamic labour demand schedules along the lines described in section 2, and Sargent (1977) examines the demand for money during periods of hyperinflation. In Chapter 8 of this book we will also examine the application of the REH to foreign exchange markets. Nevertheless, the most striking implications of the REH for the stabilisation policy debate remain the strong neutrality results obtained by models such as the one by Sargent and Wallace (1976) cited in section 2. As a result, the main attention of empirical research has been focused on testing the strong policy invariance proposition, resulting in what has become known as the 'anticipated–unanticipated money debate'. We recall from the previous section that new classical models predict that it is only unanticipated money supply shocks which will have real output effects.

Early empirical evidence on the new classical invariance proposition was provided by Barro in a series of papers (see Barro 1977b, 1978, 1979, Barro and Rush 1980). The approach followed consists first of all of finding an appropriate measure of anticipated changes in the money stock. That is, the researcher seeks an optimal forecasting regression equation for the money stock, given a past information set which may include any relevant economic variables which help to forecast the money stock. Essentially, the representative economic agent is assumed to behave *as if* he can observe such an optimal forecasting equation. This assumption is not totally unjustified, as the REH implies that economic agents estimate the expected value of an unobserved variable, given a past information set, in a manner which is optimal. Linear regression may, in certain circumstances, be seen as an optimal expectations generating mechanism (see Sargent 1979). For instance, Barro and Rush (1980) estimate the following forecasting equation for the (logarithm of the) money stock:

$$\Delta_1 m_t = \alpha_0 + \alpha_1 \Delta_1 m_{t-1} + \alpha_2 \Delta_1 m_{t-2} + \alpha_3 g_t$$
$$+ \alpha_4 (U_{t-1}/1 - U_{t-1}) + u_t \tag{3.20}$$

where Δ_i denotes the difference operator such that $\Delta_i X_t = (X_t - X_{t-i})$, m_t denotes the money stock, g_t the deviation of government expenditure from its trend level, and U_t represents unemployment. Using (3.20), the anticipated money series may be obtained by using the fitted values of the forecasting equation, while the residuals offer a series for unanticipated monetary growth. These unanticipated and anticipated money series are then used to test whether they can explain movements in real output or unemployment. Barro (1977b) and Barro and Rush (1980) provide evidence on US annual data over the 1946–73 and 1949–77 periods respectively. In general, they find that lagged monetary innovations (unanticipated money) are significant in explaining unemployment fluctuations, while anticipated money does not offer any additional explanatory power. Similar results have been obtained for the United Kingdom by Attfield, Demery and Duck (1981a, 1981b) with an approach broadly equivalent to that of Barro.

A related approach to testing the invariance propositions was provided by Sargent (1976a), whose evidence in support of the natural rate hypothesis is based on the Granger–Sims concept of econometric causality (see Granger 1969, Sims 1972). Considering Z_t as a policy variable, Sargent proposes the following dynamic regression for a real variable such as unemployment, U_t:

$$U_t = \Sigma_{i=1}^{m} \alpha_i U_{t-i} + \Sigma_{i=1}^{n} \beta_i Z_{t-i} \tag{3.21}$$

If the neutrality proposition holds, it is arguable that lagged values of policy variables, Z_{t-i}, will not affect current unemployment. The natural rate hypothesis may then be tested by testing the null hypothesis that all the β_i are equal to zero. If the null hypothesis holds, then unemployment can only be explained by lagged values of unemployment itself. This implies that unemployment fluctuations are due to fluctuations in the 'natural rate', or alternatively some other real factors, in line with new classical accounts of the business cycle. In terms of Granger–Sims causality, the hypothesis to be tested is that policy variables do not 'Granger-cause' unemployment. Sargent provides causality tests for a variety of different policy variables, Z. He uses the logarithm of the money supply, real budget deficits (federal, state, and local government), the GNP deflator, a manufacturing wage index, and various measures of government expenditure. The tests provide encouraging *prima facie* evidence for the neutrality proposition, by indicating only a small effect of policy variables on unemployment.

Nevertheless, despite such encouraging evidence, these empirical tests of new classical invariance models all ignore a potentially serious *identification* problem: the problem of *observational equivalence*. It is to this issue that we now turn.

3.3.2. Observational Equivalence in Policy Invariance Models

Early in the empirical debate on the invariance proposition, it was realised that there were problems in discriminating between new classical and Keynesian predictions in empirical models of the type described above, as both types of model yield a similar reduced form. In practice this phenomenon of 'observational equivalence' is a statistical identification problem peculiar to econometric models which embody the REH. (Readers not familiar with the conventional identification problem in estimating simultaneous equation econometric models with jointly dependent variables should note that a survey of such issues is offered by numerous econometric textbooks e.g. Johnston 1984, Harvey 1981).

The first account of the phenomenon of observational equivalence was offered by Sargent (1976b), who noted that dynamic models of the type illustrated in (3.21) were unable to discriminate between new classical and Keynesian explanations of fluctuations in unemployment. In the case of tests of the type applied to (3.21), this identification problem is particularly simple to illustrate, adopting a simpler model than that discussed in Sargent (1976b), without loss of generality.

As discussed above, the causality tests of Sargent (1976a) purport to discriminate between Keynesian models and models of a new classical type in which only unanticipated money affects unemployment (or output), U_t:

$$U_t = \alpha(m_t - E_{t-1}(m_t)) + \beta U_{t-1} \qquad (3.22)$$

In addition, unemployment is likely to display cycles due to real factors, thus explaining the inclusion of lagged values of U_t. For simplicity we assume that such lagged unemployment effects are adequately captured by a single lag of unemployment. A 'Keynesian' model of the business cycle, however, would have the contrasting implication that lagged anticipated values of the money stock do affect unemployment, thus yielding a reduced form of the type:

$$U_t = \gamma_0 m_t + \gamma_1 m_{t-1} + \delta U_{t-1} \qquad (3.23)$$

Though these two models have different policy implications, their reduced forms turn out to be identical. Suppose that the government's policy rule is such that the current money stock depends on last period's money stock:

$$m_t = \rho m_{t-1} \qquad (3.24)$$

If economic agents form their expectations according to the REH and have full information about the money supply generating process (3.24), then the reduced form for the new classical model may be obtained by substituting (3.24) into (3.22):

$$U_t = \alpha m_t - \alpha \rho m_{t-1} + \beta U_{t-1} \qquad (3.25)$$

It should be apparent that (3.25) and (3.23) are identical *in structure*: the fact that the lagged money stock enters a regression equation for unemployment neither proves nor disproves the 'Keynesian' model. Therefore, models of the type used by Sargent (1976a) (see equation (3.21)) are useless in discriminating between the two views on policy effectiveness.

Nor does the 'proper modelling' of anticipated and unanticipated money through the use of a forecasting equation like (3.22), following Barro, necessarily resolve the observational equivalence problem. Consider the above 'Keynesian' model (equation 3.23)) in which anticipated money matters. If we adopt a forecasting equation such as (3.24) to obtain a series for anticipated and unanticipated money, then the fitted equation will be:

$$m_t = \hat{\rho} m_{t-1} + \hat{\varepsilon}_t \qquad (3.24')$$

where $\hat{\rho}$ is the estimated parameter, and $\hat{\varepsilon}$ is the residual of the model which gives us the unanticipated money series. Applying the chain rule of forecasting to (3.24'), we can note that:

$$m_t = \hat{\rho}(\hat{\rho} m_{t-2} + \hat{\varepsilon}_{t-1}) + \hat{\varepsilon}_t$$

and by substituting sequentially for further lags of m_{t-i}, we can obtain:

$$m_t = \hat{\varepsilon}_t + \hat{\rho}\hat{\varepsilon}_{t-1} + \hat{\rho}^2\hat{\varepsilon}_{t-2} + \ldots.$$

In other words, the current actual money supply may be expressed as a geometric sum of past unanticipated values of the money stock. As a result, it follows that the m_t and m_{t-1} terms in equation (3.23) can be expressed in terms of past values of the unanticipated money stock. Thus, a Keynesian model of unemployment cycles can generate the result that only past *unanticipated* money matters. It is therefore not surprising that models of the Barro type do not escape the problem of observational equivalence. While Sargent's model involves direct estimation of a reduced form such as (3.25), Barro considers a two-stage estimation of the forecasting model (3.24), which is then substituted into (3.22). Yet the overall result is the same: the reduced form for the new classical model is the same as one which may be obtained from an appropriate Keynesian model.

The observational equivalence problem may be overcome in a variety of ways, all of which involve finding a number of identifying restrictions. This was pointed out by McCallum (1979a) and Buiter (1983), who suggested that such identifying restrictions could be testable. As Buiter points out, one type of identifying restriction involves finding a variable, X, which enters the forecasting equation (3.24) but not the unemployment equation (3.22). This would then enable us to identify the parameters in the reduced form (3.25). It can be easily shown that if we have a forecasting equation of the type:

$$m_t = \rho m_{t-1} + \eta X_{t-1} \tag{3.24''}$$

then the reduced form for the new classical model becomes (3.25') instead of (3.25):

$$U_t = \alpha m_t - \alpha \rho m_{t-1} + \beta U_{t-1} - \alpha \eta X_{t-1} \tag{3.25'}$$

which now differs from the reduced form for the Keynesian model (3.23). The identification problem is therefore resolved in the conventional way by finding a variable which enters one structural equation, but not the other, thus enabling us to identify the structural parameters.

A second type of identifying restriction noted by Buiter (1983) and Abel and Mishkin (1983) relies on imposing *a priori* restrictions on the lag structure of the new classical model. This is more applicable in a more complex new classical model in which current unemployment depends not only on lagged unemployment and *current* values of unanticipated money, but also on *lagged* values of unanticipated money. In other words, past, as well as current, errors in forecasting the money stock affect unemployment. Despite objections that such models are not truly new classical in spirit (see McCallum 1979b), as they involve persistent forecasting errors, it is possible that such lagged effects reflect prolonged problems of signal extraction. Furthermore, it is not impossible that such lagged forecast errors may be present due to adjustment costs in labour markets along the lines described in the new classical accounts of the business cycles. A more complex new classical model along these lines, as considered by Buiter (1983) or Abel and Mishkin (1983), would therefore have a structure like:

$$U_t = \Sigma_{i=0}^n \alpha_i (m_{t-i} - E_{t-i-1}(m_{t-i})) + \beta U_{t-1} \tag{3.22'}$$

In this case, it is apparent that one could identify restrictions on the lag length n. In particular, if we know *a priori* that $n = 0$, we could discriminate between the new classical model and a more general Keynesian reduced form, as this would generate testable restrictions on the reduced form.

In addition to such identifying restrictions on structural parameters and lag lengths, it is apparent by simple analogy with the general concept of econometric identification that appropriate restrictions on the covariance matrix may also identify the structural parameters of the reduced form. Nevertheless, it will be clear to the reader that the problem of observational equivalence cannot be dismissed out of hand. It is by no means certain that variables can be found which enter the forecasting equation but which are excluded from (3.22), especially given that (3.22) is in itself probably a semi-reduced form of a complex structural model. Similarly, it is not entirely obvious whether we can impose any *a priori* restrictions on the lag structure of (3.22′). Only in cases where we are sure that the REH implies that past forecast errors do not enter the reduced form can we impose such identifying restrictions with confidence. In practice, this involves accurate knowledge of the structural model underlying (3.22′). One case where we could restrict $n = 0$ is when testing for efficient financial markets, since to assume otherwise would imply unexploited profit opportunities due to the persistence of past forecast errors (see Mishkin 1983).

Overall, therefore, we can see that the problems of observational equivalence render these empirical tests for the policy invariance proposition less clear. Evidence in favour of new classical models may be interpreted as inconclusive, unless a powerful case can be made to support the presence of identifying restrictions. In the absence of the latter, tests of models embodying the REH are not feasible. At present, the evidence still appears inconclusive.

3.3.3. The 'Lucas Critique' of Econometric Policy Evaluation

Another suggestion offered by Sargent (1976b) to resolve the problem of observational equivalence may be outlined here. Sargent suggested that if economic policy should change so that the feedback rule governing the money supply process (e.g. equation (3.24)) altered, this would offer one way of discriminating between new classical models and their Keynesian counterparts. This can be easily demonstrated in the context of our simple models of equations (3.22)–(3.25). Recall that the reduced form for the Keynesian model is:

$$U_t = \gamma_0 m_t + \gamma_1 m_{t-1} + \delta U_{t-1} \tag{3.23}$$

If the money supply policy rule changes from (3.24) to the following slightly different rule:

$$m_t = \rho' m_{t-1} \tag{3.26}$$

where the policy rule parameter ρ has changed to ρ', then the reduced form for the new classical model would become:

$$U_t = \alpha m_t - \alpha \rho' m_{t-1} + \beta U_{t-1} \qquad (3.27)$$

In other words, following the change in policy rule, we should observe a change in one of the parameters of the reduced form. Thus, Sargent suggests, one way to discriminate between new classical and Keynesian models is to examine data across different policy periods, as models of the former kind will predict shifts in the parameters of the reduced form, while Keynesian models will not. Though it is certainly true that in models with RE such parameter changes can be expected, Sargent's proposition cannot be seen as a complete resolution to the observational equivalence problem. It is perfectly plausible, as we shall see in Chapter 4, to construct models which, while incorporating the REH, still allow scope for stabilisation policies. Parameter shifts following policy changes must also be expected in such models, and hence this property (which follows naturally from the REH) cannot be seen as exclusive to new classical models. This merely goes to emphasise that new classical policy invariance propositions result not from the REH alone, but from the market-clearing models to which the REH is applied.

Nevertheless, the implications of the REH for parameter stability in the estimated reduced forms illustrated above has important consequences for the policy evaluation of econometric models, as Lucas (1976) has forcefully argued. The argument above shows that the parameters of an economic model may not remain constant in the face of policy changes in the presence of RE. This proposition has become popularly known as the 'Lucas critique', and has potentially devastating implications for the formulation of economic policy. As Lucas points out, under RE, simulation of existing models cannot provide any guidance as to the actual consequences of alternative economic policies, as the policy-maker cannot predict the effects of such policies on the parameters of his model. For example, a conventional dynamic consumption function may not correctly predict the effects of an income tax cut because its dynamic structure will change following the tax cut. It is therefore wrong to base policy on such estimated econometric relationships, as they are a poor guide to the future path of the economy. In a similar way, as we shall see in Chapter 5, the Lucas critique may also explain sudden shifts in the demand for money relationship following policy changes.

Despite the wide applicability of Lucas' critique, a more pragmatic approach to the use of econometric relationships for policy evaluation may still be valid. Sims (1980), for instance, argues that unless policy changes are major and wide-ranging, the effects of the Lucas critique may be limited, as the dynamics of the model will still in part be determined by non-policy parameters. Furthermore, provided that the econometric relationship is modelled by taking into account the REH expectations generating equation (i.e. the forecasting equation in our above examples), the Lucas critique may to some extent be circumvented, as the policy-maker can then take into account the effects of policy changes on the reduced form's parameters when designing economic policy.

Nevertheless, the Lucas critique is important in that it shows the way in which our conventional wisdom on policy-making is altered once we take into account the fact that economic agents' expectations are likely to be endogenous to the model. For far too long economists have ignored the fact that economic agents' reactions to policies have been inappropriately modelled (as in the case of the adaptive expectations hypothesis).

3.3.4.   The REH and Policy Invariance: a Joint Hypothesis

We have so far laid great emphasis on the fact that the new classical models' policy invariance results derive from a combination of the REH and neoclassical market-clearing models. As a result, many of the empirical tests of policy invariance are actually *joint empirical tests* of the REH and the underlying economic model. Given the possibility of incorporating the REH in alternative structural models, it would be interesting to evaluate the REH separately from the model to which it is applied.

In practice, separate tests of the REH are rare, with some examples provided recently by Mishkin (1982, 1983) and Abel and Mishkin (1983). The procedure differs from that employed in the Barro-type model in that in the latter case the researcher first estimates the forecasting equation to generate values for anticipated and unanticipated money and then uses these series to estimate a model such as (3.22). This two-step procedure has been criticised on the grounds that it leads to inconsistent estimates of the model's standard errors, and hence possibly to invalid statistical inference (see Pagan 1984, Sargan 1986). Furthermore, as Mishkin (1983) points out, the *joint* estimation of forecasting equations and reduced forms such as (3.24) and (3.25) enables us to devise a separate test for 'rationality'. One may test, for instance, whether the estimated value for ρ in the reduced form (3.25) is equal to its estimated value in the forecasting equation (3.24). This tests whether the policy parameters implicit in the reduced form correspond to those in the money supply generating process. Therefore, such a test of the cross-equation restrictions represents a test of 'rationality'. Using these methods, Mishkin (1982) shows some empirical support for 'rationality', while support was lacking for the strong policy invariance proposition (though it should be noted that Mishkin's model is still subject to the same identification problems discussed in subsection 3.3.2).

3.3.5. Conclusions

In this section we have examined the empirical evidence in favour of the new classical invariance proposition. In general, as we have seen, the evidence is somewhat mixed. This is due in no small part to the additional complications in econometric methods implied by the REH (for a survey see Wickens 1982, Wallis 1980). Despite the methodological difficulties in testing RE, as a concept it now occupies a central position in modern macroeconomics, and has presented a challenge to the essence of Keynesian economics by arguing that under RE stabilisation policy is totally ineffective. As we shall see in Chapter 4, the Keynesian response to this challenge may be subdivided into two categories. In one category we place those models which take on board many of the features of new classical models, but are modified so as to relax the strong invariance propositions of the latter. Second, we consider those models which attack the neoclassical market-clearing nature of markets in general (and labour markets in particular) in new classical models.

Appendix: Solving Dynamic Rational Expectations Models

As we explained in subsection 3.2.2, in simple rational expectations models of aggregate demand and supply, the forward looking price level will 'jump' in response to anticipated shocks so as to return the economy to its 'natural rate' equilibrium. In this appendix we examine the reactions of forward looking expectations variables in more complicated dynamic models. Some of the techniques outlined here will be used to some extent in Chapter 8 when analysing open economy models which adopt the REH. Although the discussion will be conducted in terms of an abstract economic model, these techniques have found numerous applications in macroeconomics. For a fuller survey of the mathematical methods outlined here the reader is referred to Blanchard and Kahn (1980), Dixit (1980), Begg (1982), and Currie and Levine (1984b).

Consider an economic model with two dynamic endogenous variables, X and Y. Suppose that X is a forward looking expectational variable, for example the price of a financial asset. In general, such variables can move freely at any instant in time, and are said to be 'free' or 'non-predetermined'. In contrast, Y is a variable whose value at any time t is given by the past behaviour of the economic model. For instance, one can think of variables like the capital stock, real income, certain inflexible prices, etc., whose very nature does not allow them to be subject to discrete jumps at any point in time. Variables such as Y are said to be 'predetermined'. Suppose that X and Y are linked via the following dynamic system:

$$\begin{bmatrix} \dot{X} \\ \dot{Y} \end{bmatrix} = \begin{bmatrix} \alpha_{11} & \alpha_{12} \\ \alpha_{21} & \alpha_{22} \end{bmatrix} \begin{bmatrix} X \\ Y \end{bmatrix} + \begin{bmatrix} \beta_1 \\ \beta_2 \end{bmatrix} \qquad\qquad (A3.1)$$

M

Consider the following alternative possibilities for the stability of this dynamic system. First, as shown in the phase diagram in Figure 3.9(a), the system could be *globally stable* (see Gandolfo 1972, Chiang 1984). Alternatively, as shown in Figure 3.9(b), the system could be *saddlepoint stable*. In the former case, conventional economic and mathematical analysis tells us that the system will converge to equilibrium no matter

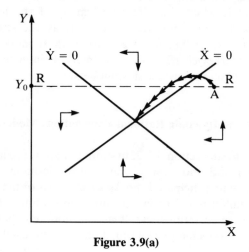

Figure 3.9(a)

Figure 3.9(b)

where it starts off. On the other hand, in the case of a saddlepoint equilibrium, we know that the variables will converge to equilibrium only if the system starts off on the *saddlepath SS*. Starting off at a point such as *A*, for instance, will set the economy off on a divergent path. As a consequence, such saddlepoint equilibria are usually seen as unstable in conventional economic models, while global stability is seen as a desirable property.

The same does not hold in the case of models where one or more variables are expectational variables, and we apply the REH. In this case, economic agents are assumed to solve the best available economic model, and, as in the case of Figure 3.9(b), identify the only convergent path to equilibrium. Supposing that the system is initially at point *A*, the 'free' forward looking variable, *X*, is assumed to 'jump' so as to carry the economy to point *B*, on the saddlepath to equilibrium, with the 'predetermined' variable fixed initially at Y_0. Furthermore, the property of global stability is now actually undesirable, since starting at point *A* in Figure 3.9(a), and for a given predetermined value of *Y*, Y_0, any value of *X* will enable the economy to converge to equilibrium. In terms of Figure 3.9(a) any starting point along the line *RR* will permit convergence to equilibrium. Thus, in a globally stable model, there is a degree of indeterminacy in agents' expectations of *X*, and hence in the actual realisation of *X* (see McCallum 1983, Scarth 1985). In contrast, in a model which is saddlepoint stable, only one value of *X* will enable convergence to equilibrium, and hence forward looking agents can agree on which value *X* should take (and will take) under the assumption of perfect foresight.

Thus, to summarise the above argument, in dynamic models with rational expectations variables, it is optimal for the dynamic system to have a saddlepoint structure. The forward looking variable will then take on the initial value (i.e. 'jumps' to that value) which ensures that the system converges to equilibrium. In algebraic terms, the simultaneous system of differential equations shown in (A3.1) will in general have the following solution (for real and distinct characteristic roots):

$$X(t) = \bar{X} + A_{11}\exp(\lambda_1 t) + A_{12}\exp(\lambda_2 t) \tag{A3.2}$$

$$Y(t) = \bar{Y} + A_{21}\exp(\lambda_1 t) + A_{22}\exp(\lambda_2 t) \tag{A3.3}$$

where $\bar{X}$ and $\bar{Y}$ are the equilibrium values of *X* and *Y*, the λ_i are the characteristic roots of the dynamic matrix **M** in (A3.1), and the A_{ij} are arbitrary coefficients dependent upon the initial conditions of the system. Assuming that the system is saddlepoint stable, one of the characteristic roots will be positive and the other one will be negative. Let us assume, say, that $\lambda_1 > 0$. To ensure that *X* 'jumps' so as to put the system on to its saddlepath effectively means setting the arbitrary coefficients on the unstable root (A_{11} and A_{21}) equal to zero. We then solve for the initial conditions for X which are consistent with this restriction. Note that the initial value of Y is predetermined, as Y is not free to 'jump'.

Solving the system in this manner, so that the initial values of the free variables are set so as to make the system 'jump' on to the saddlepath is sometimes known as imposing the *transversality condition*. As has been pointed out on numerous occasions by critics of the REH, imposing this condition involves making the implicit assumption that economic agents will choose that rational expectations path which converges to equilibrium, i.e. economic agents choose equilibrium behaviour. Though the 'transversality assumption' has been defended on the grounds that there is no reason why economic agents should act so as to set the economy off on an explosive path, a more credible defence would be to point out that models of intertemporal optimisation also often involve imposing such transversality conditions (see Hadley and Kemp 1971, Brock 1975, Sargent 1979). However, recently there have been some suggestions that divergent paths from equilibrium in saddlepoint models may help to explain short-run instability in asset markets (see Blanchard 1979). The economy may, in the short run, follow a divergent path thus displaying what has sometimes been called a 'speculative bubble'.

To conclude this appendix it should be pointed out that the techniques described above can be applied to models with more than two dynamic endogenous variables. In general a dynamic system with n dynamic equations will satisfy the required saddlepoint property if the number of unstable (positive) characteristic roots of the transition matrix equals the number of forward looking 'free' variables.

4
AGGREGATE SUPPLY AND STABILISATION POLICIES: THE KEYNESIAN PERSPECTIVE

In the previous chapter we have seen how the upward sloping Keynesian aggregate supply schedule and the related Phillips curve relationship came under attack in the first instance by Friedman (1968), and latterly by the new classical school. In this chapter we examine the Keynesian riposte to this neoclassical challenge.

Keynesians face two related problems in the debate about the role and effectiveness of stabilisation policy. The first is that the economy will not settle at a point other than the 'natural rate' in the long run, if we retain the assumption that both labour and goods markets are essentially neoclassical in nature, with wages and prices not totally rigid. As we saw in Chapter 2, the need for government intervention arises only if the self-stabilising forces on the aggregate demand side act slowly.

Second, as we have seen from Chapter 3, a trade-off between inflation and unemployment must rely on workers accepting real wage cuts. In other words, the existence of even a *short-run* trade-off between inflation and unemployment must rely on some short-run stickiness in nominal wages, or a misperception of short-run price movements on the part of workers. The scope for stabilisation policies will be limited to the short run, to offset unwanted fluctuations in output and employment around their 'natural' levels.

In this chapter we examine some alternative explanations which have been advanced to explain why output and employment fluctuations may be greater than the new classical macroeconomics suggests. In section 1 we demonstrate that rational expectations models do not necessarily preclude a role for stabilisation policies. In sections 2 and 3 we examine some fundamental critiques of the aggregate demand and supply paradigm, based as it is on neoclassical labour and goods markets. These different strands of the literature should not be treated as mutually exclusive, or

101

fully integrated. As we shall see, one of the major problems facing Keynesian models is that in attempting to depict the complexity of the determination of employment, output, wages and prices 'in the real world', they soon become intractable. As a result, most models examine only some aspects of the wage and price formation process, and represent only a partial answer to new classical macroeconomics.

4.1.   Policy Non-Neutrality under Rational Expectations

4.1.1.   *Explicit Contracts and the Role for Stabilisation Policies*

Following the development of the new classical invariance proposition, and in particular the work of Sargent and Wallace (1976), interest centred on the extent to which the policy ineffectiveness result would hold if some of the basic features of the underlying macroeconomic model were altered, even if the assumption of rational expectations was retained. Some of the strong policy invariance conclusions have been found to be dependent not only on the adoption of rational expectations, but also on a particular model structure.

We will first analyse the way in which policy is non-neutral in the presence of multiperiod labour contracts. In particular, Fischer (1977a) and Taylor (1980) examine models with rational expectations in labour markets, but where nominal wage setting is subject to contractual practices. In this section we will analyse one version of these models, a simplified version of the one presented by Fischer (1977a), and relate it to the model used by Sargent and Wallace (1976). Later in this section we will examine some alternative modifications to the new classical models which likewise allow a role for stabilisation policies.

Fischer (1977a) examines the consequences of introducing explicit nominal wage contracts in a simple macroeconomic model. In contrast to the continuous auction market implicit in the neoclassical labour market model, he assumes that workers fix their nominal wages by contract at discrete time intervals. We can consider two types of contract: the first is a single-period contract, where nominal wages are altered after every time period, and the second is a multiperiod contract, where nominal wages negotiated at any given time remain in force over several time periods. We follow Fischer in first outlining a model in which there are single-period contracts, and where the invariance proposition holds, and then show that when multiperiod contracts are introduced, government policy becomes effective. We make the conventional assumption that firms' supply of output is negatively related to the real wage:

$$y_t^s = \alpha + \beta(p_t - w_t) + u_t \tag{4.1}$$

where y^s represents firms' supply of output, p represents the price level, and w the nominal wage, with all variables expressed in logarithms, and u_t representing a white noise disturbance term. If we then assume that wage contracts are set in terms of nominal wages, and are negotiated at the end of each time period, then nominal wages are set before agents know what the outcome will be for the price level during the period in which the contract is in force. In other words, the wage rate is set at time $t - 1$ based on workers' expectations of the price level at time t. Wage-setting behaviour then follows the rule:

$$w_t = \delta_t + E_{t-1}(p_t) \tag{4.2}$$

where $E_{t-1}(.)$ denotes expectations formed at time $t - 1$, and δ_t denotes the target real wage pursued by workers for time t (which in a neoclassical market for homogeneous labour will be the real wage which clears the labour market). In what follows we can, without loss of generality, scale the variables such that $\delta_t = 0$. This simplifies the notation without affecting the results. Note also that in this model expectations are formed rationally.

Substituting (4.2) into (4.1), we obtain the familiar Lucas 'surprise' aggregate supply function, already outlined in Chapter 3:

$$y_t^s = \alpha + \beta(p_t - E_{t-1}(p_t)) + u_t \tag{4.3}$$

where α may be seen as the 'natural level' of income. Again, in what follows, for simplicity we scale such that $\alpha = 0$, and $\beta = 1$. Neither of these assumptions affects the model's results. Thus:

$$y_t^s = (p_t - E_{t-1}(p_t)) + u_t \tag{4.3'}$$

Suppose that aggregate demand is determined by a simple 'quantity theory of money' relationship:

$$y_t^d = m_t - p_t - v_t \tag{4.4}$$

where y^d represents aggregate demand, m represents the money stock, both expressed in logarithms, and v_t is a white noise disturbance term. For simplicity velocity has been set equal to 1 (when v_t is zero).

Suppose next that the monetary authorities attempt to offset all past disturbances to the economy through their operation of a feedback monetary rule of the type:

$$m_t = \Sigma_{i=1}^{\infty} a_i u_{t-i} + \Sigma_{i=1}^{\infty} b_i v_{t-i} \tag{4.5}$$

where the a_i and b_i are policy parameters. The values of these policy parameters will depend on the authorities' objectives. If, for example, we assume that the authorities attempt to minimise the variance of output around its 'natural' or equilibrium value, then we solve for the implied values of these parameters. These issues will be addressed in detail in Chapter 9.

It should be noted, however, that in this model the shocks impinging on the economic system are assumed to be totally random, v_t and u_t being white noise disturbances. Under these circumstances, the rationale for stabilisation policy, namely to attempt to offset totally random shocks, is clearly questionable. However, in this chapter we will devote our attention primarily to the government's *ability* to affect the real economy through its policies rather than on the optimal choice of stabilisation strategy. In Chapter 9 we will analyse the optimal policy choice in detail. It will then become clear that even though governments may be *able* to affect the real economy, it may not be optimal for them to do so. In other words, the policy neutrality debate and the optimal policy debate should be treated as distinct.

Given the government's assumed stabilisation strategy, as embodied in (4.5), it is obvious that workers can correctly calculate the value of m_t at time $t - 1$, since m is set with reference to past disturbances alone. Thus,

$$E_{t-1}(m_t) = m_t \tag{4.6}$$

Given these equations, the Sargent–Wallace result follows quite naturally. Equating aggregate supply and demand in (4.3) and (4.4) we obtain:

$$2p_t = m_t + E_{t-1}(p_t) - (u_t + v_t) \tag{4.7}$$

Taking expectations at time $t - 1$ of (4.7), and substituting back into (4.7), it is easy to show that:

$$p_t - E_{t-1}(p_t) = -\left(\frac{1}{2}\right)(u_t + v_t) \tag{4.8}$$

Finally, substituting back into equation (4.3):

$$y_t^s = \left(\frac{1}{2}\right)(u_t - v_t) \tag{4.9}$$

This shows that any deviations from natural output are purely random, depending on current exogenous aggregate demand and supply shocks, and do not depend on government policy, as a_i and b_i do not appear in (4.9). This is the much cited Sargent–Wallace policy neutrality result, which holds when labour contracts are renegotiated every time period. ✗

Suppose, however, that labour contracts cannot be renegotiated every time period, but are valid, say, over two time periods. In this case, wage-setting behaviour no longer follows the pattern described in (4.2), but instead:

$$w_t^1 = E_{t-1}(p_t) \text{ and } w_t^2 = E_{t-2}(p_t) \tag{4.2'}$$

where w^1 represents wage contracts negotiated at time $t - 1$ and are therefore based on price expectations at that particular time, and w^2 represents wage contracts negotiated at time $t - 2$, and thus are based on price expectations at time $t - 2$. If we assume that half of all wage contracts in the economy are negotiated in alternate years, then at time t, the average real wage is given by:

$$\left(\frac{1}{2}\right) \Sigma_{i=1}^2 (w_t^i - p_t)$$

Thus the aggregate supply function now becomes:

$$y_t^s = \left(\frac{1}{2}\right) \Sigma_{i=1}^2 (p_t - w_t^i) \tag{4.10}$$

By following the same argument of the single-period contract model, we obtain an equation for the determination of output in a rational expectations model with two-period contracts:

$$y_t^s = \left(\frac{1}{2}\right) (u_t - v_t) + \left(\frac{1}{3}\right) (a_1 u_{t-1} + b_1 v_{t-1}) \tag{4.11}$$

Contrast (4.11) with (4.9), its equivalent in the single-period contracts model. With two-period contracts, monetary policy can affect real output, due to the presence of a_1 and b_1 in (4.11). The policy ineffectiveness result disappears because of an increased amount of rigidity in the wage-setting process. At any given time, half of the contracts in the economy still have one additional period to run. Thus government intervention at time t can affect the real wage of those workers who are bound by contract to a given nominal wage until time $t + 1$. Policy has time to work because the authorities are free to react to exogenous shocks at every time period, while workers, in the aggregate, are not. To summarise, therefore, contracts introduce an asymmetry in the relative ability of workers and governments to affect the economy, thereby undermining the original Sargent–Wallace invariance proposition.

One implication of the Fischer model is that a policy aimed at reducing the rate of inflation through tight money might incur a cost in terms of increased unemployment. Early statements on this matter by adherents of the new classical school were remarkably sanguine (see, for instance Sargent 1981). However, Taylor (1983), using the actual distribution of contract lengths for the United States, suggested that the increase in unemployment may be sufficiently high and of sufficiently long duration to jeopardise the political feasibility of the policy.

However, the contractual approach described above has been criticised by Barro (1977a) on the grounds that nominal wage contracts of the type described by Fischer lead to an inefficient allocation of resources. Barro argues that there are advantages to both firms and workers in revising contracts if these lead to divergences between the marginal product of labour and the marginal value of leisure (i.e. to disequilibrium in the neoclassical labour market). Thus, efficient contracts should not only set the nominal wage rate, but also the level of output, so that employment and output would always be determined independently of monetary factors (see Barro 1977a, Hall and Lillien 1979). However, while the Barro-type contract may be efficient, and while simple nominal wage contracts of the Fischer type may seem irrational, Fischer (1977b) points out that the former rarely occur in practice while the latter do. The reason for this, Fischer argues, is that contracts of the type envisaged by Barro must include contingency clauses to allow for different possible outcomes or 'states of the world'. Thus 'efficient' contracts must allow for all possible outcomes for the price level, and only then would the invariance result hold once more. At the other extreme, the invariance proposition would follow if there was a spot auction market in labour, and a complete absence of contracts. Fischer rejects both of these cases as unrealistic. The costs of administering contracts of the type proposed by Barro would be high, and the reliance on a spot auction market, with the increased uncertainty which it would entail, would be resisted by both firms and workers. We take up some of these issues below.

The main conclusion from the Fischer model is that there is a possible role for stabilisation policy in offsetting aggregate demand and supply shocks. Furthermore, even if, in an inflationary environment, workers demand wage contracts which are not set in nominal terms but are indexed to the price level, this will not totally invalidate the effectiveness of stabilisation policy in the Fischer model unless a highly specific indexing formula is used (see Fischer 1977a).

However, as Taylor (1979) points out, though models with contracts afford policy-makers some power in stabilising the economy, they do not allow for sustained deviations from the natural rate of output. A further feature of nominal contract models is that they imply a trade-off between the variability of output around the natural rate and the variability of inflation. Suppose in the model above that the system is subjected to both aggregate demand and aggregate supply shocks, v_t and u_t. In the absence of government stabilisation policy these will impinge on output in the short run. Given the structure of these shocks, stabilisation policy may reduce the variance of output around the natural rate. However, given that monetary policy eventually feeds through to price changes, output stabilisation must generate greater price variability.

We will return to discuss labour market contracts in section 2, where we examine further the microeconomic nature of contracts, and consider the view that the contractual relationship between workers and firms may extend well beyond explicit agreements on wages. However, before discussing such *implicit contracts*, we briefly turn to examine some other examples whereby the adoption of RE does not necessarily produce strong invariance results.

4.1.2. Other Cases of Policy Non-Neutrality

The introduction of multiperiod contracts undermined the strong policy invariance result by introducing an element of stickiness in the adjustment of wages to prices. A plethora of results similarly undermining the Sargent–Wallace proposition may be obtained by other modifications to the underlying model (for a useful survey see Pesaran 1984). In what follows we restrict our discussion to three examples.

First, following Buiter (1980), non-clearing markets can be introduced into the basic new classical model, via the assumption that prices are sticky. This is a direct parallel of the explicit contract model of Fischer outlined in subsection 4.1.1, in that the source of non-neutrality lies in an imperfect pricing mechanism, but now in the goods rather than the labour market. Assume that the 'surprise' aggregate supply function in (4.3) is defined with respect to equilibrium prices, $\bar{p}_t$:

$$y_t^s = \alpha + \beta(\bar{p}_t - E_{t-1}(p_t)) + u_t \tag{4.3''}$$

Again, we set $\alpha = 0$ and $\beta = 1$, as in subsection 4.1.1. It is logical to redefine (4.3) in terms of equilibrium prices, because in determining production levels, firms will compare equilibrium prices to wage rates, which are given by (4.2). Suppose that firms adjust their prices slowly, due to the existence of contracts between buyers and sellers in goods markets. The adjustment process in prices may be described, for simplicity, by a simple partial adjustment process:

$$p_t - p_{t-1} = \lambda(\bar{p}_t - p_{t-1}) \tag{4.12}$$

where λ can be thought of as the fraction of price contracts renegotiated each time period. Substituting (4.12) into (4.3″) to eliminate $\bar{p}$, we obtain a new version of the 'surprise' aggregate supply function:

$$y_t^s = (p_t - E_{t-1}(p_t)) + ((1/\lambda) - 1)(p_t - p_{t-1}) + u_t \qquad (4.13)$$

If we now adopt the same aggregate demand function and monetary policy rule as in subsection 4.1.1 (equations (4.4)–(4.6)), equation (4.7) becomes:

$$2p_t = m_t + E_{t-1}(p_t) - (u_t + v_t) + \left(1 - \frac{1}{\lambda}\right)(p_t - p_{t-1}) \qquad (4.7')$$

Taking expectations of (4.7′), and substituting back into (4.7′):

$$p_t - E_{t-1}(p_t) = -\frac{(u_t + v_t)}{\left(1 + \dfrac{1}{\lambda}\right)} \qquad (4.14)$$

Substituting this expression back into (4.13), we find that:

$$y_t^s = \frac{\left(\dfrac{u_t}{\lambda}\right) - v_t}{1 + \dfrac{1}{\lambda}} + \left(\frac{1}{\lambda} - 1\right)(p_t - p_{t-1}) \qquad (4.15)$$

Output now depends not only on a random term, as was the case in (4.9), but also on current prices, and therefore on current government policy. Thus, the existence of price stickiness ensures that the strong invariance proposition does not hold.

However, this type of sluggish price adjustment is open to the same charges of *ad hoc* theorising as the explicit contract models outlined in subsection 4.1.1. Such models inevitably have to appeal to the 'real world' observation that prices do not always adjust flexibly to produce a market-clearing solution (see Okun 1981). The debate then has to focus on the reasons why wages and prices do not adjust flexibly. In this sense, such 'Keynesian' models, though not without intuitive appeal, still lack sound microfoundations explaining the nature of price adjustment in imperfect markets. We return to this issue below.

As our second example, consider an alternative policy rule to the one in (4.5). Suppose that the authorities apply a simple *feedback policy rule*:

$$m_t = ay_{t-1} + z_t \qquad (4.16)$$

where z_t is a white noise error term. The government attempts to stabilise the economy by setting its policy on the basis of past income. We again retain the aggregate demand and supply relationships outlined in sub-section 4.1.1 (equations (4.3) and (4.4)). As we have already seen in Chapter 3, this policy rule will not invalidate the invariance proposition, as the disturbance z_t is *additive*. Suppose, however, that instead of (4.16) we adopted a policy rule with a *multiplicative* error term, i.e.:

$$m_t = az_t y_{t-1} \tag{4.16'}$$

where z_t now has a mean value of unity, a constant variance, and is uncorrelated with any aggregate demand or supply disturbances, u_t and v_t. As a result, there will be a random policy error in setting the money supply, whose magnitude depends on the value taken by z_t each period. By adopting an identical procedure to the one followed above, we can obtain the following expression for output:

$$y_t^s = \left(\frac{1}{2}\right)(u_t - v_t) + \left(\frac{1}{2}\right)(ay_{t-1})(z_t - 1) \tag{4.17}$$

Thus we can see that deviations of output from the 'natural level' are dependent upon the policy rule, and that (4.9) can only be reobtained from (4.17) by making z_t constant and equal to unity, which would be the case in the simple feedback rule with additive disturbances (4.16). The reason for this result can be seen by comparing the expressions for the actual and expected money stock for the two policy rules in (4.16) and (4.16'), given respectively in equations (4.18) and (4.18'):

$$m_t - E_{t-1}(m_t) = z_t \tag{4.18}$$

$$m_t - E_{t-1}(m_t) = ay_{t-1}(z_t - 1) \tag{4.18'}$$

As can be noted from (4.18'), the policy rule with multiplicative disturbances can produce a divergence between the actual and expected money stock which is dependent upon the policy parameter a. It should be noted that economic agents are not making systematic errors in predicting the money stock in either (4.18) or (4.18'). However, the variance of the prediction errors is independent of a in the case of (4.18), while this is not the case for (4.18'). Thus, it is natural that a should explicitly appear in the aggregate supply equation (4.17), as it will affect the variance of income about its equilibrium level. The effects of multiplicative disturbances on the invariance propositions are discussed in further detail by Snower (1981) and Pesaran (1984).

Third, all the examples so far have assumed that economic agents (in the form of wage setters) accurately observe the parameters of the authorities' policy rule. In the previous two examples the assumption of rational expectations has been retained, while some of the other assumptions of the underlying structural model have been modified. We now turn to the question of whether it is reasonable to assume that agents always know the 'true' model of the economy, given that knowledge about the economic system has to be acquired over time. New classical models have rarely given much space to the issue of the way in which knowledge is acquired about such structural parameters in the economy, but recently a great deal of attention has been devoted to the process of 'learning' which agents face when forming expectations (see, for example, Taylor 1975, Blanchard 1976, B. M. Friedman 1979, Bray 1982, Frydman and Phelps 1983, and Bray and Savin 1984). The main conclusion of these studies is that, provided that agents know the correct specification of the 'true' economic model, a 'rational' learning process will ensure that agents' expectations converge to the rational expectations solution. These 'rational' learning procedures essentially assume that economic agents do perceive the correct model structure and estimate its unknown parameters by progressively incorporating new observations into the data set. In this way they learn the true values of the structural parameters — but only gradually. Their learning process is therefore 'rational' in the sense that their expectations converge to the rational expectations solution. (This, however, will not be the case if agents do not know the correct specification of the model *a priori* (see Blume and Easley 1982), a possibility which we will not pursue here.)

We retain our aggregate demand and supply functions of subsection 4.1.1 (equations (4.3) and (4.4)), and assume that the *true* current government policy feedback rule is given by (4.16). However, agents initially misperceive the value of the policy parameter, due, say, to the fact that the policy rule has only been introduced recently. Thus agents initially still observe the 'old' policy rule given by (4.19):

$$E_{t-1}(m_t) = dy_{t-1} \qquad\qquad (4.19)$$

However, as soon as the policy rule changes, agents' money stock expectations will converge from (4.19) to the expected value of (4.16) through the 'rational' learning process:

$$E_{t-1}(m_t) = (dy_{t-1})e^{-\mu t} + (ay_{t-1})(1 - e^{-\mu t}) \qquad\qquad (4.20)$$

As time passes, expectations converge to the rational expectations solution, and μ represents the rate at which individuals learn about the new policy rule. Equation (4.20) may be seen as approximating some of the properties of a 'learning curve' as analysed by Arrow (1962), (see also Gapinski 1982). Solving the model for output:

$$y_t^s = \left(\frac{1}{2}\right)(u_t + z_t - v_t) - \left(\frac{1}{2}\right)[(d - a)y_{t-1}]e^{-\mu t} \qquad\qquad (4.21)$$

equation (4.21) shows that government policy can affect real output in a measure given by the bias present in agents' expectations of the policy rule parameter:

$$- \left(\frac{1}{2}\right)[(d - a)y_{t-1}]e^{-\mu t}$$

Thus, these models may be regarded as introducing a gradual learning process such that this affords the government an information advantage.

To summarise the results of this section, we have shown that the strong invariance proposition of the new classical school stems from the two main assumptions underlying these models. First, they assume that the underlying model is a market-clearing one, with no price or wage rigidity. Second, they assume that expectations are formed rationally. These should be treated as totally independent when considering models of this type. We have shown that if we relax either the market-clearing assumption (as in the case of the Fischer (1977) contract model, or the Buiter (1980) sticky prices model), or the information structure built into the simple new classical models (as in the case of 'multiplicative disturbances' or the 'learning' model), the strong invariance propositions do not hold. In these cases stabilisation policies are feasible (though whether they are desirable is a matter which we will return to in Chapter 9).

The type of stabilisation policies which are required are, however, different from those which may be needed in models without rational expectations (for instance, the underemployment equilibrium models of Chapter 2). In all the models considered above leading to policy non-neutralities, policy may not be seen as causing *lasting* deviations from the 'natural' level of output. Ultimately the economic system is self-stabilising and any shock impinging on it will not have a lasting effect. This differs in an essential way from early Keynesian models which were designed to explain underemployment equilibria and required sustained expansions to restore the economy to full employment. In the models outlined so far in this chapter stabilisation policies have to be aimed at minimising the fluctuations of the economy (e.g. the variance of income) around the 'natural' income level, as the long-run self-stabilising nature of the economic system renders any other type of stabilisation policy redundant.

4.2. Implicit Contracts and Stabilisation Policies

4.2.1. *Implicit Contracts: Definitions and Models*

So far we have been concerned with Keynesian counter-positions to new classical macroeconomics which may be regarded as lying within the standard aggregate supply–aggregate demand paradigm. In this section we depart from this framework by turning to a detailed examination of the nature of contracts in the form of 'implicit contract' theory, which has been seen by some Keynesians as providing an alternative vindication of the need for stabilisation policies. In looking at these models we will concentrate on two main questions. First, do such models suggest a role for stabilisation policies? Second, do they suggest that the economy may not settle at the 'natural' levels of income and employment, thus calling for rather different stabilisation policies from the ones discussed in section 1?

Implicit contract theory takes as its point of departure certain observations about the nature of the labour market which set it apart from other markets, and which, it is argued, simple neoclassical models neglect. For instance, given that labour supply and demand involve the sale and purchase of very heterogeneous and industry-specific skills, it is arguable that decisions by firms on whether to employ or dismiss labour will not be taken lightly. The typical firm will probably attach considerable value to maintaining a long-term firm-specific workforce. Similarly, the worker with specific job skills may have to face a lengthy search process if looking for a new job. The worker engaged in a search process may also be interested not only in the pecuniary aspect, but also in the other dimensions of a job, like security, hours of work, etc.

As a result of the costly nature of the process of matching firms and workers, the labour market will not behave like a spot auction market: labour becomes a quasi-fixed factor of production for the firm, and on the supply side, workers will not leave their present job for alternative employment unless the wage advantage is sufficient to offset the costs of changing jobs. In contrast to the neoclassical model, they may not move if wages rise only marginally above the wage offered by the present employer. Empirical findings confirm this tendency for workers to spend a major part of their working lives with one employer (see, for example, Hall 1980, 1982 for the United States, and Main 1982 for the United Kingdom). Furthermore, Feldstein (1975) and Lillien (1980) found that most lay-offs are of a temporary nature, as the majority of workers dismissed during a recession ultimately returned to their original employers.

Given that the fixed-cost nature of labour employment leads to a certain degree of immobility in the labour market, it is natural for the relationship between a firm and its employees to be characterised by some explicit contractual arrangement, confirming each side's desire to obtain some guarantee about the other's commitment to the relationship. However, while explicit contracts will typically deal with issues such as wage rates, hours of work, conditions of work, etc., they will not usually deal with questions of total amounts of labour employed. The reason for this is that if a firm finds itself faced with a fall in demand for its product, it will need the freedom to alter total levels of employment, given that wage rates are predetermined by previous contractual arrangements. Therefore, the firm's employment decisions will not be completely bound by an explicit contract. As we saw in subsection 4.1.1 in the context of the debate between Barro (1977a) and Fischer (1977b), such contracts would have to cover all contingencies and could not possibly be administered successfully. Similarly, explicit contracts only cover the setting of wages over a short period, typically a year or two. In this regard, Rosen (1985) highlights an interesting similarity between the economics of labour and the economics of marriage. While some aspects of each partner's rights and duties in marriage are governed by explicit laws, many other 'unwritten rules' are required to ensure that the partnership is successful and acceptable to both parties.

What happens to the behaviour of firms and workers with regard to those variables which are not covered by explicit contracts? Provided that firms and workers engage in a consistent pattern of behaviour *vis-à-vis* issues which are not covered by legally binding agreements, some type of contractual arrangement clearly still exists. Firms and workers may reach a mutual understanding about what actions will be taken in relation to employment and wage decisions, and provided that there is mutual trust between the two parties, such *implicit* agreements may have as much force as written explicit ones. Implicit contract models focus more on this particular aspect of the relationship between workers and firms because these may shed some light on the determination of employment, on which explicit contracts usually have little to say. In addition, implicit contract theory can also offer new insights into the process of wage determination beyond the duration of the explicit contract.

It should be emphasised that the implicit contracts introduced in this section are fundamentally different from explicit contracts of the type analysed by Fischer (1977a). While in the latter the nominal wage is sticky in the short run due to a contractual commitment, the wage rate is still essentially determined in a neoclassical labour market. In contrast, implicit contracts imply a labour market which is fundamentally different from the spot auction market of the neoclassical model. As Okun (1981) points out, the labour market behaves according to the laws of the 'invisible handshake' rather than the 'invisible hand'.

Typically, implicit contract theory uses the tools of choice under uncertainty. Firms and workers face uncertain future economic conditions, and have to agree on the optimal decision with regard to employment and wage setting given a variety of possible future states of the world. It should be stressed that implicit contract models should not be interpreted as descriptions of *actual* bargaining or contracting behaviour by the two parties. As Rosen (1985) points out, an implicit contract must be treated *as if* it were an explicit one, and may be interpreted as the result of a mutual understanding between workers and firms.

We now present a representative model of implicit contracts, which is a simplified version of a model set out by Rosen (1985), and which builds on the original work by Azariadis (1975). Consider a firm which produces a perishable output. The employees are assumed, for simplicity, to be all identical in terms of preferences and work skills, and the size of the potential workforce can be assumed fixed, by the available supply of the relevant industry- or firm-specific skills. Suppose that the firm and its workers are uncertain as to the price which will prevail in the market for the good the firm produces. We therefore denote the price for the firm's good as $p(\theta)$, where p depends on the state of the world, θ. Let us assume for simplicity that only two states of the world are possible, i.e. $\theta = 1, 2$, so that when $\theta = 1$ ('good times') the firm is able to sell its product at a more favourable price in the market than when $\theta = 2$ ('bad times'). Let us also assume that each of these two states of the world may occur with respective probabilities $\pi(1)$ and $\pi(2)$, and that both firms and workers agree on these probabilities. The type of random shock which we consider is one where $p(\theta)$ has a fixed mean, $\bar{p}(\theta)$, which is given by:

$$\bar{p}(\theta) = p(1)\pi(1) + p(2)\pi(2)$$

That is, we are considering a *relative demand* shock for the firm's particular product, where firms and workers agree both on the *ex ante* probability of each state of the world θ occurring, and on the *ex post* realisation in terms of product price of a particular θ. This symmetry of information turns out to be of particular importance.

The contract which firms and workers agree on takes into account all possible states of the world, and specifies the following terms:

(a)   the wage rate, $w(\theta)$, which the firm offers its employed workers in each state of the world;

(b)   the proportion, $\lambda(\theta)$, of the labour force under contract, N, which will be employed in each state of the world;

(c)   the unemployment insurance payments, $r(\theta)$, (if any) which the firm will pay to workers who are laid off in each state of the world.

Note that this model could be easily generalised to the case where the firm does not make such unemployment compensation payments directly to workers, but where it pays insurance contributions to a central government agency or private insurance company, and the latter compensate unemployed workers.

We now consider the aims of both the firm and its workers in constructing such a contract. The firm has a production function where output, Q, depends entirely on labour input, ignoring all other factors of production:

$$Q = f(\lambda(\theta)N) \tag{4.22}$$

where $\lambda(\theta)$ is the proportion of the total workforce N employed under state of the world θ. The firm sells the output it produces at price $p(\theta)$.

Next suppose that workers have the following utility function with regard to the choice between income and leisure:

$$U = U(y(\theta) + mL) \tag{4.23}$$

where y is the payment which the worker receives in state of the world θ, either wage payments, $w(\theta)$, or insurance payments, $r(\theta)$, and L represents the proportion of the worker's normal working time dedicated to leisure, such that $L = 1$ denotes that the worker is unemployed, and $L = 0$ denotes that the worker is employed. Note that this special type of utility function assumes, for simplicity, that w and L are perfect substitutes, where m is a constant and represents the marginal rate of substitution between w and L. The advantage of this formulation is that workers will either choose to be fully employed ($L = 0$) or will choose to be unemployed ($L = 1$) given w and r. That is, the labour supply problem does not permit any intermediate solutions where workers are employed for part of their available working time. This formulation originally adopted by Azariadis (1975) may be relaxed (see Sargent 1979, Rosen 1985), without drastically altering the conclusion of the simple model. As a result, if a worker is unemployed, he has a utility level $U(r(\theta) + m)$, and if he is employed he has utility $U(w(\theta))$. Note that given that all workers are identical, each faces an equal probability of being laid off, should 'bad times' occur and the firm decide not to employ the whole of the contracted labour force. This has come to be referred to as the assumption of 'lay-offs by random draw'. Given that $\lambda(\theta)$ represents the proportion of the total labour force employed in state of the world θ, for each state of the world, λ represents the probability of an individual worker being employed, and $(1 - \lambda)$ the probability of him being laid off. Given that the probabilities of each of the two states of the world $\theta = 1, 2$ occurring are $\pi(1)$ and $\pi(2)$ respectively, the *ex ante* expected utility of a worker in this firm is:

$$E(U) = \pi(1)\{U(w(1))\lambda(1) + U(r(1) + m)(1 - \lambda(1))\}$$
$$+ \pi(2)\{U(w(2))\lambda(2) + U(r(2) + m)(1 - \lambda(2))\} \tag{4.24}$$

Similarly, the profits, $R(\theta)$, of the firm for each state of the world can be calculated as follows:

$$R(1) = p(1)f(\lambda(1)N) - \lambda(1)Nw(1) - (1 - \lambda(1))Nr(1) \tag{4.25a}$$

$$R(2) = p(2)f(\lambda(2)N) - \lambda(2)Nw(2) - (1 - \lambda(2))Nr(2) \tag{4.25b}$$

Next, assume that the firm has a utility function, V, defined over expected profits, $R(\theta)$, such that:

$$V = V(R(\theta)) \tag{4.26}$$

Having introduced the utility functions for both workers and the firm, we must now make some assumption about the attitude towards risk of both parties. The usual assumption in implicit contract models is that workers are risk averse, so that $dU/d(y(\theta) + mL) > 0$, and $d^2U/d(y(\theta) + mL)^2 < 0$. The attitude of the firm towards uncertain profits is usually regarded as risk neutral, so that $dV/dR(\theta) = 1$, in which case we could dispose of equation (4.26) and merely assume that the firm maximises expected profits:

$$E(R) = \pi(1)R(1) + \pi(2)R(2) \tag{4.26'}$$

The usual justification for this assumed asymmetry in attitudes towards risk by workers and firms is based on the firm's superior access to capital markets. Initially, however, we retain the more general assumption that firms attempt to maximise (4.26), and that they too are risk averse, so that $dV/dR(\theta) > 0$, $d^2V/dR(\theta)^2 < 0$.

Given the preferences of the firm and workers, the contract has to specify, for each state of the world, the wage rate, insurance payments and the firm's employment decision, i.e. $w(1)$, $w(2)$, $r(1)$, $r(2)$, $\lambda(1)$, and $\lambda(2)$. The optimal contract must lie on the 'contract plane' or Pareto frontier between the functions $U(.)$ and $V(.)$, and therefore the problem may be cast in terms of constrained (or Lagrangean) optimisation. There will obviously be a large number of such possible contracts, each corresponding to particular levels of utility U, and V. To observe the nature of these contracts we focus on one such point, corresponding to some fixed utility level $\bar{u}$ or $\bar{v}$. We may either consider the problem as one of the firm maximising (4.26) subject to the constraint of (4.24) (see Sargent 1979), or alternatively as workers maximising (4.24) subject to (4.26) (see Rosen 1985). We adopt the latter approach in what follows, and therefore consider the problem as one of workers finding their optimal contingency plan for wages and employment *given* that the firm has to achieve some utility level $\bar{v}$ given by, say, the normal profit rate in the industry. We set up the Lagrangean function, K:

$$
\begin{aligned}
K = \ &\pi(1)\{U(w(1))\lambda(1) + U(r(1) + m)(1 - \lambda(1))\} \\
&+ \pi(2)\{U(w(2))\lambda(2) + U(r(2) + m)(1 - \lambda(2))\} \\
&+ \mu\{\bar{v} - V(\pi(1)R(1) + \pi(2)R(2))\} \tag{4.27}
\end{aligned}
$$

where μ represents the Lagrange multiplier. If workers maximise K with respect to $w(\theta)$, $r(\theta)$, and $\lambda(\theta)$, for $\theta = 1, 2$, we obtain the following first-order conditions:

$$\partial K/\partial w(1) = \partial U(w(1))/\partial w(1) + \mu N(\partial V(.)/\partial R(1)) = 0 \tag{4.28a}$$

$$\partial K/\partial w(2) = \partial U(w(2))/\partial w(2) + \mu N(\partial V(.)/\partial R(2)) = 0 \tag{4.28b}$$

$$\partial K/\partial r(1) = \partial U(r(1) + m)/\partial r(1) + \mu N(\partial V(.)/\partial R(1)) = 0 \tag{4.28c}$$

$$\partial K/\partial r(2) = \partial U(r(2) + m)/\partial r(2) + \mu N(\partial V(.)/\partial R(2)) = 0 \tag{4.28d}$$

$$\partial K/\partial \lambda(1) = U(w(1)) - U(r(1) + m)$$
$$- \mu N(\partial V(.)/\partial R(1))[p(1)(\partial f(.)/\partial \lambda(1)) - w(1) + r(1)] = 0 \tag{4.28e}$$

$$\partial K/\partial \lambda(2) = U(w(2)) - U(r(2) + m)$$
$$- \mu N(\partial V(.)/\partial R(2))[p(2)(\partial f(.)/\partial \lambda(2)) - w(2) + r(2)] = 0 \tag{4.28f}$$

$$\partial K/\partial \mu = \bar{v} - V(\pi(1)R(1) + \pi(2)R(2)) = 0 \tag{4.28g}$$

These conditions are somewhat complicated, but they summarise the main results which may be derived from this model.

The key result is that workers will be equally well off whether they are laid off, or whether they are retained in employment in each state of the world. This may be seen by comparing (4.28a) and (4.28c) and also (4.28b) and (4.28d), from which it follows that, for any state of the world θ:

$$\frac{\partial U(w(\theta))}{\partial w(\theta)} = \frac{\partial U(r(\theta) + m)}{\partial r(\theta)} \tag{4.29}$$

Given that we assumed above that $d^2U/d(y(\theta) + mL)^2 < 0$, from the assumption that workers are risk averse, it follows that the function $dU/d(y(\theta) + mL)$ is monotonic. We can then deduce from (4.29) that $w(\theta) = r(\theta) + m$ and also $U(w(\theta)) = U(r(\theta) + m)$ for any state of the world θ. Thus, workers are equally well off whether in employment or unemployment in each state of the world.

The reader familiar with the microeconomics of insurance markets should note the similarity with the result obtained from this model. Workers negotiate contracts such that they insure against the risk of being laid off. If they are fully insured when 'bad times' arrive, each individual worker will be equally well off if he becomes unemployed or if he is retained in work. Workers and firms agree to insurance payments to ensure that this is the case, and this means that workers are indifferent to the outcome of the 'random draw' for lay-offs. Note, however, that this does *not* imply that workers are indifferent between states of the world, as they

118 Macroeconomic Theory & Stabilisation Policy

are unambiguously worse off during 'bad times' compared to 'good times'. This can be readily seen from equations (4.28a)–(4.28d) where it is apparent that the actual values for w and r depend on the firm's utility function, $V(.)$, which in turn depends on the price the firm gets for its product. When the firm faces 'bad times' it will lower both wages and insurance payments to its unemployed workers. Thus both firms and workers will prefer 'good times' to 'bad'; but within a given state of the world workers will be indifferent between being laid off and remaining in employment.

The model has even stronger conclusions if we make the additional assumption that firms are risk neutral. As we saw above, this involves setting $dV/dR(\theta) = 1$, for any state of the world θ. Imposing this restriction on equations (4.28a)–(4.28d), we obtain the following result:

$$\frac{\partial U(w(1))}{\partial w(1)} = \frac{\partial U(w(2))}{\partial w(2)} = \frac{\partial U(r(1) + m)}{\partial r(1)} = \frac{\partial U(r(2) + m)}{\partial r(2)} = -\mu N$$

This shows not only that workers are indifferent between being laid off or remaining employed *within a given state of the world*, but that they are *indifferent between different states of the world*. Thus, unlike the case where firms are risk averse, now workers are indifferent between 'good' and 'bad' times, as their wages or insurance payments are invariant across different states of the world.

This result has two key implications. First, firms are effectively totally insuring workers against 'bad times', and all risk is shifted from risk averse workers on to risk neutral firms. Again this may be seen in terms of an insurance contract. The firm acts as an actuarially fair insurance company who is willing to take any fair bets which the workers are willing to offer it. If 'good times' occur the firm gains in terms of lower real wages, which may be interpreted as workers paying an insurance premium to insure themselves against the possibility of 'bad times'. When 'bad times' occur, firms pay out wages which are higher than they otherwise would have been, which may be interpreted as an insurance pay-out, and workers are no worse off as a result. Thus, when we make this particular asymmetric assumption about the firm's and worker's attitudes towards risk, it seems that wages are rigid across different states of the world. Thus, demand shocks which create 'good' and 'bad' times for the firm do not affect real wages, provided that firms bear all the risks.

Second, instead of wage adjustments, price shocks cause changes in employment, which varies between different states of the world, as can be seen from equations (4.28e) and (4.28f). In general, when the firm enters 'good times' it increases its employment, and the converse applies during 'bad times'. The supply and demand for labour in an industry with implicit contracts may then be illustrated as in Figure 4.1.

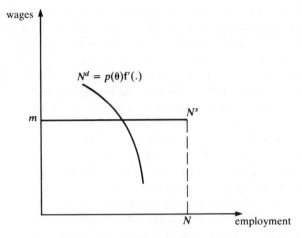

Figure 4.1

The labour supply curve, N^s, is horizontal because of our results which indicate that labour supply is perfectly elastic at a given wage rate. From (4.28e), (4.28f), and (4.29) we can see that given that $\overline{U}(w(\theta)) = U(r(\theta) + m)$, and that $w(\theta) = r(\theta) + m$, then (4.28e) and (4.28f) simplify to:

$$p(1)(\partial f(.)/\partial\lambda(1)) = w(1) - r(1) = m \qquad (4.28e')$$

$$p(2)(\partial f(.)/\partial\lambda(2)) = w(2) - r(2) = m \qquad (4.28f')$$

This can be interpreted as the standard efficiency condition for the labour market which equates marginal revenue product with the marginal rate of substitution between work and leisure, and ensures that the outcome of the contract does not involve any 'inefficiencies', whatever the state of the world. Thus the labour supply curve will be flat up till the point where all N workers under contract are employed. Beyond N, the firm is quantity-constrained, and the N^s curve is discontinuous, as all labour is fully employed and wages are fixed. The labour demand curve, N^d, is represented by the marginal revenue product curve which is downward sloping (due to the usual assumptions of diminishing returns in the production function f(.)), and whose exact position in Figure 4.1 depends on the value of $p(\theta)$. Thus, as p varies across states of the world, N^d shifts rightward or leftward. If we generalise our model so as to allow a whole range of states of the world instead of the two considered so far, this will allow a variety of possible employment levels, all in combinations with a constant wage of $(r(\theta) + m)$ across the states of the world, provided, of course, that firms are risk neutral.

One problem with this model is the peculiar nature of the labour supply curve, which is discontinuous beyond N. This difficulty may be overcome by abandoning the assumption that labour considers work and leisure to be perfect substitutes, and by allowing workers to negotiate the number of hours worked, rather than employment status (where L is restricted to be equal to 0 or 1). Rosen (1985) shows that under these circumstances, wages will rise once employment reaches N, and the N^s curve will acquire a conventional upward slope beyond this level. This is shown in Figure 4.2. Thus, only below N are wages inflexible downwards, and if the labour demand curve stays above N, wages adjust and all workers are employed. Only once the firm hits very bad times, and N^d falls below N, are some workers laid off and wages remain constant.

These results have often been presented as a vindication of the Keynesian claim that *nominal wages* are 'sticky' in the presence of aggregate demand shocks. However, there are a number of problems in adopting this interpretation. First, our simple model has dealt with a single firm, and does not discuss movements in the aggregate price level. However, if the aggregate price level were not constant across states of the world, it would have to enter the utility functions of both firms and workers, and the implicit contract would be struck in terms of *real wages*.

Second, as Rosen (1985) points out, the model does not even imply *real wage rigidity* across different levels of *aggregate demand*. We noted above that the 'good' and 'bad' times which the firm faced were due to shifts in demand (and therefore price) for the firm's product around a *given mean*, $\bar{p}(\theta)$. An increase in aggregate demand in the economy will cause an improvement in the mean value of $p(\theta)$, and change the whole basis of the contract, raising the real wage. In terms of our above model, this rise in

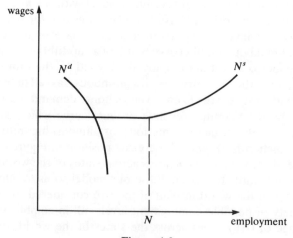

Figure 4.2

$\bar{p}(\theta)$ may be represented as a rise in both $p(1)$ and $p(2)$. Shifts in $\bar{p}(\theta)$ are known as 'uninsurable risks' and these have a simple analogy in the market for insurance. If households insure their home against fire, and they contract an actuarially fair insurance, they will be no worse off whether their hourse burns down or not, as they receive adequate compensation should the worse happen. However, if the probability of a fire occurring increases, then households will be worse off given that their (actuarially fair) premiums will increase. Implicit contracts are similar in that if times are 'generally better', and $\bar{p}(\theta)$ rises, then both the firm and its workers will be better off. Thus the contract market described above cannot explain either nominal or real wage rigidity in the face of aggregate demand shocks.

Furthermore, one feature of the model outlined above which would not be readily acceptable to Keynesians is that workers are no worse off if they are laid off or retained in employment. Since they are indifferent between employment and unemployment when totally insured against the risk of the latter, any unemployment may be regarded as *voluntary*. *Involuntary* unemployment will occur if firms offer incomplete insurance to workers. As Rosen (1985) points out, there are two possible reasons why this may be the case, and these may be illustrated with reference to the analogy of house insurance. Generally, households are incompletely insured in the sense that they will feel worse off if their house burns down. There are two possible reasons for this. First, asymmetric information between the insurer and the insured on the probability of the fire occurring will lead to non-actuarial (excessive) premiums. Second, complete insurance may imply moral hazard, in that households may be particularly careless with regard to fire if they are completely insured, thus affecting the probability of a fire occurring.

These two factors may also be present in the case of an implicit contract. First, asymmetric information in implicit contracts is introduced in models where the firm observes the realisation of different states of the world but workers do not (see, for example, Calvo and Phelps 1977, Hall and Lillien 1979, Grossman and Hart 1983, Azariadis 1983, and Green and Kahn 1983). These models generally lead to inefficient employment decisions which may give rise to involuntary unemployment. Second, the problem of moral hazard will be relevant if workers are completely insured, in that workers may well opt for unemployment if they are indifferent between the two states of the world. The costs implied by moral hazard, together with the running costs of an insurance scheme for unemployed workers, may well induce the firm not to offer complete insurance cover. Azariadis (1975), for example, makes the extreme assumption that no unemployment insurance is offered by the firm (i.e. $r(\theta) = 0$ in the above model). In this case, unemployed workers are definitely worse off than their employed colleagues, and unemployment is involuntary.

It should also be noted that there are alternative types of microeconomic model which, like implicit contract models, attack the neoclassical view of the labour market. First, some models of the labour market have paid less attention to the contractual aspect of these markets and more to the wage bargaining process involving trade unions (see, for example, MacDonald and Solow 1981). These models are also able to predict that real wages are 'sticky' and that employment and output fluctuations will be commonplace in an economy where workers reach wage settlements through trade union bargaining, but where firms retain the freedom to hire and lay off workers. Second, *efficiency wage* models take as their point of departure the hypothesis that workers' productivity is dependent upon their wage levels. Under these circumstances, it may be optimal for firms to fix wages above their market-clearing levels (for a survey see Akerlof and Yellen 1987). These models will not be analysed here, but it should be stressed that they are similar to implicit contract models in that they attack the market-clearing labour market which lies at the heart of neoclassical macroeconomic models.

4.2.2.   *Implicit Contracts and the Role for Stabilisation Policies*

To consider some of the implications of implicit contract models for stabilisation policies, let us first summarise some of the conclusions of the preceding section. Contract markets generally build on the assumption that the firm deals with a workforce which has a fixed size, N, due to the fact that there are fixed cost elements involved in employment decisions. As described above, workers may have industry- or firm-specific skills, and the empirical evidence on re-employment ratios may be seen as supportive of this type of model. Rational firms and workers will, if faced with uncertainty over the firm's performance, seek to negotiate wage rates, unemployment insurance payments, and employment levels for all possible states of the world. The result of such a contract will be that unemployment may or may not be voluntary (depending on whether workers receive complete insurance cover by their firm), and that some real wage rigidity may be observed as the firm enters relatively 'good' and 'bad' times, that is as the firm's product price falls and rises around some fixed mean value $\bar{p}(\theta)$. These models do not by themselves explain nominal wage rigidity, nor fixed real wages when aggregate demand goes up *permanently*. Provided that a firm's performance improves 'on average', that is the mean price which a firm gets for its product, $\bar{p}(\theta)$, rises, then real wages will rise. What these models *can* explain is the way in which *temporary* shocks to aggregate demand may cause employment, rather than price and wage, fluctuations.

One of the main problems in assessing the macroeconomic implications of the above analysis is that these models are distinctly microeconomic in character. As Rosen points out, a contract market for labour is not necessarily less efficient than a spot auction market, but merely different. Inefficient labour usage and involuntary unemployment may only enter these models through market imperfections. This should be readily apparent from the construction of such models. Neoclassical labour demand and supply functions are independently derived on the basis of firm and worker preferences, given perfect knowledge about market conditions on the part of both parties. Real wages then provide the signals whereby labour is efficiently allocated to its use in production. In contrast, in a contract model price uncertainty is introduced, and the two sides in the market are assumed to come together in an attempt to share risks. Thus real wages no longer provide a conventional price signal in the face of limited fluctuations in labour demand, and the shocks are reflected in employment changes (see Stiglitz 1984).

The implication of this model seems to be, therefore, that in the vicinity of current labour market equilibrium for the industry under consideration, random demand shifts lead to employment rather than wage responses, providing that the demand shifts do not appear to be persistent. However, this only holds provided that the workforce is sufficiently large to cope with 'good times' for the particular firm. It is not inconceivable that during 'good times' the whole workforce N will be fully employed. At that point the firm can only expand output by attempting to attract labour from other industries, or hiring less skilled (less productive) labour which may currently be unemployed.

To draw some macroeconomic conclusions from these microeconomic models requires us to extend the discussion by considering the aggregation of individual contract markets for labour. Suppose that there exist T industries in the economy, each of which behaves as if it were a contract market of the type described in the previous subsection. Each industry will therefore have a workforce of N_i (for $i = 1, \ldots, T$), containing labour which has certain industry-specific skills. Starting from a position of 'full employment', where there is no involuntary unemployment among either skilled or unskilled labour, consider an exogenous fall in demand for the product of some of the T industries in the economy. Given the presence of implicit contracts in these industries, if the demand shock is initially seen as temporary, there will probably be a rise in involuntary unemployment in each of these industries (if we assume that unemployment insurance is not complete), initially detected in a rise in unemployment among less productive, unskilled labour, and to a lesser extent in skilled labour.

We would expect the economic system be self-stabilising in the long run however, because, if the fall in expenditure turns out to be permanent, two countervailing forces will be set in motion. First, as described above, the permanent fall in demand will be interpreted in the affected industries as non-insurable risks, and implicit contracts will be 'renegotiated' so as to bring about a fall in wages so that unemployment will fall. Second, as Grossman (1977, 1978) points out, if firms and employed workers choose not to 'renegotiate' contracts during persistent slumps, then there will be an incentive among those workers who are unemployed (and incompletely insured) to 'break ranks' by reneging on their contract and by bidding for a job in an alternative industry, causing a general downward movement in wages. This again will tend to restore the economy to full employment, though this adjustment may be slow if interindustry mobility is low. It is during these times that any unemployed unskilled workers may play an 'arbitraging' role, as they represent that section of the labour force that is not bound by contracts and is therefore more mobile, albeit less productive (see Azariadis 1976, Rosen 1983). How fast the economy returns to full employment depends on the speed with which implicit contracts are 'renegotiated'.

However, given that in the short run some industries experience quantity rather than price adjustments, is there scope for governments to attempt to reverse the initial fall in demand, thus avoiding an unnecessary period of involuntary unemployment? At first sight, the answer would seem to be 'yes', but there are two caveats. First, as pointed out above, employment insurance must be incomplete otherwise all unemployment is voluntary. In this case there is no reason for governments to offset output and unemployment fluctuations, as these may be seen as 'efficient'.

Second, and perhaps more important, the disaggregated nature of the model presents some difficulties for a government which attempts to offset any exogenous demand shocks. If the government increases aggregate demand in response to a fall in employment in some, but not all, industries, given scarce mobility of labour across skill-specific jobs in the short run, this is likely to cause upward wage pressure as fully employed firms which experience an expansion attempt to attract more labour into their industry, and the policy may not significantly reduce involuntary unemployment in the short run. This scenario shows the complicated nature of designing aggregate demand stabilisation policies when contract markets exist and labour markets are effectively 'segmented' between industries, with slow mobility of labour between industries due to the presence of industry-specific skills.

In conclusion, then, the main drawback in using implicit contract theory to assess the effectiveness of stabilisation policies is that it deals with individual firms or industries in isolation. In this section we have briefly sketched some of the possible implications of aggregating different contract markets, and have suggested that aggregate demand stabilisation policies become difficult to use at positions near to full employment in the economy as a whole. This theme has been taken up by some Keynesians who have considered the main flaw of simple Keynesian models based on money illusion or explicit (fixed money wage) contracts to be their lack of proper microfoundations. While an upward sloping short-run aggregate supply curve suggests an important role for aggregate demand policy, it seemed to paint an inaccurate picture of what aggregate demand policy could and could not do in the vicinity of full employment, due to the restrictive assumption of homogeneous product and labour markets in the aggregate demand–supply paradigm. One way of departing from this restrictive assumption of homogeneous markets is to incorporate some aspects of implicit contract theory, in particular the existence of firm-specific skills and slow wage adjustment, into a full *macroeconomic* model. The theory of 'bottlenecks' which we shall examine in section 3 incorporates these features, but, unlike implicit contract theory, it pays less attention to the equilibrium of the individual firm and worker and the price and quantity adjustment mechanism of contract markets, and concentrates more on the resulting properties of the aggregate economy.

4.2.3. 'Customer' Markets and Price Inflexibility

So far we have concentrated on the labour market as a source of wage rigidity. However, similar arguments may be applied to the behaviour of firms in goods markets in order to explain why prices may not be as responsive to demand shocks as would be predicted from a 'spot auction' market. Okun (1975, 1981) has suggested that product markets for heterogeneous goods should be seen instead as 'customer' markets, where sellers set their prices and buyers have to incur search costs in finding their preferred product and supplier. Such search and information costs imply that each seller has some monopoly power, even where different sellers' products have many features in common. Once buyers build up a relationship with a particular supplier, they will be averse to breaking this link on the basis of small price differentials in the market. Such monopoly power ensures that 'arbitrage' in goods markets is by no means perfect.

Furthermore, Okun (1981) suggests that sellers may not readily adjust prices in response to demand shifts. First, there are administrative costs involved in continuously adjusting prices. Second, the demand response of habitual customers for the firm's product may be asymmetric with regard to a price rise and a price fall. While if the firm lowers its price it may not expect a large number of new customers because of search costs, if it raises its price it may alienate a number of its present customers. Thus, the demand curve for a firm's product may be 'kinked' at the current price, as originally set out in oligopoly theory. Third, given this uncertain response of demand to price changes, firms may prefer to adjust inventories or order books in response to demand shocks, to avoid uncertainty and to maintain customer goodwill. Finally, prices may respond more readily to cost changes than demand shifts, especially if all firms in an industry face similar cost structures.

Given the lack of responsiveness of prices to short-term variations in demand, 'customer' markets may provide the rationale for rational expectations models of the type described in subsection 4.1.2, which reject the strong invariance proposition. Nevertheless, as Okun recognises, the costs to buyers and sellers of severing a 'customer' market relationship, in terms of search and information collection costs, are typically less than those facing firms and workers breaking an 'implicit contract'. Thus, we would expect wages to be a greater source of inflexibility in the economy than prices in response to demand shocks. This to some extent justifies the greater attention paid to labour markets in the recent literature.

4.3. 'Bottlenecks' and the Rehabilitation of the Phillips Curve

4.3.1. The Phillips Curve Revisited

In the previous section, we have seen that implicit contract models suggest reasons why wages may be sticky, and employment flexible, in the face of demand shocks. However, they are essentially microeconomic in character, and as a result, do not in themselves provide a full picture of how the wage and employment determination process is likely to work in the economy on aggregate.

To overcome this difficulty, formal models of aggregate supply which take into account some of the specific features of labour markets outlined in section 2 have been developed. These models have their roots in Tobin's (1972) insightful re-evaluation of the Phillips curve which, unlike some of the original interpretations (including those of Phelps 1970a and Friedman 1968), introduced the notion that the economy is composed of different sectors, each of which may, at any given time, experience rather different demand conditions. Tobin (1972) also argued that labour markets are to some extent segmented between sectors, due to firm- or industry-specific skills, so that labour mobility across sectors may be limited.

Furthermore, individual sectoral labour markets may respond asymmetrically to changes in demand conditions. During a slump when there is an excess supply of labour, nominal wages may not fall readily, due to trade union power, or some (explicit or implicit) contractual arrangement between workers and firms. In contrast, during a boom, wages will rise in sectors where demand is buoyant and which therefore experience excess demand in labour markets. Such positions of excess demand have become commonly known as 'bottlenecks', and in this case are due to labour immobility between sectors, thus preventing an 'arbitrage effect' between those sectors experiencing booms and those experiencing slumps.

Models incorporating 'bottlenecks' may provide an interesting rationalisation of the original inflation–unemployment 'trade-off' estimated by Phillips (1958). Unlike subsequent studies of the relation between wage inflation and unemployment which concentrate on the *econometric* estimation of the trade-off, Phillips' original approach can only be described as somewhat *ad hoc*. There are contrasting views as to whether the techniques he employed in deriving the Phillips curve were interesting and sophisticated, or merely misplaced.

Phillips (1958) examined (annual) data on the percentage change in money wages and unemployment over the period 1861–1913. He found that over this period there were six cycles over which wage inflation and unemployment were negatively correlated, and took averages over the cycles, thus obtaining six data points, each an average of the particular cycle. He then fitted a non-linear relationship to these points, the celebrated Phillips curve. In addition, he noted that by superimposing the data for the period 1914–57 on this curve most of the latter observations did not diverge substantially from the fitted curve. This cannot be taken as econometric evidence that a Phillips curve existed, and neither can it be interpreted as an *exact* relationship between inflation and unemployment. It is therefore surprising that many Keynesians interpreted this relationship as a simple tool to be used for policy purposes as if the economy could be placed on some exact point on the curve (see, for example, Samuelson and Solow 1960). Phillips' original study (to its author's credit) does not make unrealistic policy claims, and indeed Desai (1975, 1981) argues that policy-makers' subsequent difficulties in exploiting the trade-off are a direct consequence of a mistaken interpretation of Phillips' study.

Phillips' *ad hoc* method may be re-evaluated positively in the light of the analysis provided by Tobin (1972). Unfortunately, Tobin's account is somewhat allusive in character, and only recently have there been attempts to crystallise his ideas into a formal economic model. Such models are essentially *disaggregated* accounts of wage determination, where aggregate supply is derived from the aggregation of events in individual labour markets (see for example, Iwai 1981, Evans 1985). As we have already noted in the case of implicit contracts, the aggregation of the wage and employment decisions of individual firms or industries is essential for a greater understanding of what government stabilisation policies can or cannot do. We now turn to an example of such aggregate 'bottleneck' models in the next subsection.

4.3.2. *A Model of 'Bottlenecks'*

In this subsection we concentrate on the model by Evans (1985), which may be interpreted as an accurate representation of Tobin's original ideas.

Evans assumes that there are T sectors in the economy, each producing a particular good. The output of each sector is denoted by q_{it}, and the price of its particular good is denoted by p_{it} (for $i = 1, \ldots, T$), where all the variables are in logarithms. The aggregate price and output level indices p_t and q_t are defined as the geometric means of the prices and outputs in each sector:

$$p_t = \left(\frac{1}{T}\right) \Sigma_{i=1}^{T} p_{it}$$

$$q_t = \left(\frac{1}{T}\right) \Sigma_{i=1}^{T} q_{it}$$

where for simplicity it is assumed that all sectors carry equal weight in the calculation of these indices. The aggregate demand part of the model has both money and goods markets. Money market equilibrium is defined, again for simplicity, by a quantity theory equation:

$$m_t + v_t = p_t + q_t \tag{4.30}$$

where the money supply m_t is exogenously determined. The demand for each good is given by the following demand function:

$$q_{it}^d = q_t - (p_{it} - p_t) + d_{it} \tag{4.31}$$

That is, the demand for an individual good q_{it}^d depends on aggregate output (income), and on the relative price of the good with respect to the aggregate price index. For simplicity, the income and price elasticities of demand are set equal to one. The d_{it} term represents a stochastic demand variable which follows a random walk:

$$d_{it} = d_{it-1} + u_{it} \tag{4.32}$$

where u_{it} is a white noise disturbance. This implies that demand in each sector has an exogenous element which changes each period by an amount governed by the random variable u_{it}. If we aggregate across sectors, the following adding-up restriction must hold:

$$\Sigma_i d_{it} = 0 \tag{4.33}$$

that is, the random effects across sectors must sum to zero, as they represent *relative* demand shifts between sectors, rather than changes in *aggregate* demand.

On the supply side, firms in each sector set their output q_{it}^s and price, p_{it} for their good according to the following equations:

$$q_{it}^s = n_{it} + k_i \tag{4.34}$$

$$p_{it} = w_{it} - k_i \tag{4.35}$$

where n_{it}, w_{it}, and k_i represent respectively the amount of labour employed, the wage paid to workers, and the average product of labour (which is assumed constant). This makes the simplifying assumption that labour is the only factor of production which firms use, and that there are constant returns to scale (k_i is constant) in (4.34) and (4.35). This implies that the marginal and average product in any given industry will coincide. We assume that there are no monopolistic or imperfectly competitive industries, so that price will be set equal to marginal cost (see (4.35)). Because of the assumption of constant returns to the variable factor, the marginal cost curve for each firm will be perfectly elastic with respect to output, and hence the firm's output will be demand-determined. However, the assumption of marginal cost pricing combined with the assumption of a perfectly elastic marginal cost curve means that the price for the firm's product will be primarily given by labour market conditions: from (4.35), given that k_i is constant, the price level, p_{it}, is directly proportional to the wage rate, w_{it}.

To complete the supply side of this model, therefore, we need to consider the way in which nominal wages w_{it} are determined. Assuming that each labour market contains N_{it} workers at any given time, and that labour is supplied at a constant wage $\bar{w}_{it}$ until all N_{it} workers are employed, the labour market can be described by Figure 4.3, at any given time t. The labour supply curve N^s is of a right-angle shape, and labour demand, N^d, is given by the marginal revenue product curve, which is downward sloping. Its downward slope does not depend on the shape of the marginal product curve which is perfectly elastic with respect to output (given that we have assumed constant returns to scale), but on the downward slope of the demand for the good produced by the firms (see (4.31)). The equilibrium in the labour market is point E, where not all labour is employed (there is an excess supply of labour of $(N_i - n_i)$). Note that even with this excess supply, wages cannot fall below the 'base' wage rate $\bar{w}_i$ because of labour market imperfections. When the labour demand curve shifts rightward to $N^{d'}$, equilibrium will be at E', where all labour is employed and actual wages rise above the 'base' wage to w_i. In this latter case a 'bottleneck' is said to exist.

Note the similarities between this view of the labour market and the implicit contract model of section 2 (see Figure 4.2). First, in both models, once labour demand falls below the point at which all the workers in the

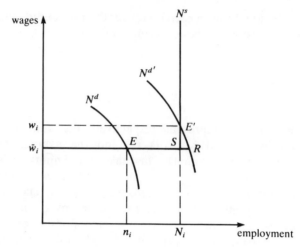

Figure 4.3 The Sectoral Labour Market in the 'Bottleneck' Model

industry are employed, the wage level stays constant at its 'wage floor' level. Second, the derived demand for labour depends on the stochastic demand variable d_{it} which creates either 'good times' (equilibrium E') or 'bad times' (equilibrium E) for the firm in the 'bottleneck' model. This may be seen as analogous to the state-dependent price level in the implicit contract model. The difference between these two models is that the 'base wage' in the 'bottleneck' approach is not determined by an explicit microeconomic contracting model, and as we shall see below, it is not exogenously fixed. It would be wrong to let $\bar{w}_{it}$ be fixed exogenously, and independently of market forces. As we pointed out in the case of implicit contract models, if the firm hits 'good' or 'bad' times permanently, we can expect contracts to be renegotiated, and the wage level (in this case the 'base' wage) to be readjusted. Therefore, Evans assumes that the 'base' wage adjusts in response to the excess demand (or supply) for labour, x_{it}, evaluated at the base wage.

In terms of Figure 4.3 x_{it} can be found as follows. When the demand curve is N^d, there is excess supply of ES in the labour market at the 'base' wage. According to our definition, therefore, $x_i = ES$. When labour demand is $N^{d'}$, however, excess demand x_i would be SR *if the wage were set at the 'base' wage*. In algebra, the definition of x_{it} can be found by the difference between the derived demand for labour evaluated at the base wage, and the supply of labour N_{it}:

$$x_{it} = p_t + q_t - \bar{w}_{it} - N_{it} + d_{it} \tag{4.36}$$

Across the economy as a whole, excess demand x_t is therefore defined as:

$$x_t = p_t + q_t - \bar{w}_t - N \tag{4.37}$$

where $\bar{w}_t$ is the average base wage in the economy as a whole, and N is the aggregate labour supply which is assumed to be fixed. 'Base' wages in each sector are assumed to adjust to excess demand x_{it} by the following mechanism:

$$\Delta \bar{w}_{it} = \alpha x_{it-1} + \pi_t + v_t + \Delta e_t \qquad (4.38)$$

where π_t is the 'inflationary momentum' in the economy, defined below, v_t is a white noise shock to the 'base' wage in sector i, and e_t is a white noise shock to the average 'base' wage in the economy. This may be interpreted as an expectations-augmented Phillips curve. Furthermore, it is assumed that $0 < \alpha < 1$, so that the 'base' wage does not totally adjust in response to excess demand in the sector. Inflationary momentum in the economy is merely defined by 'adaptive expectations' of *actual* wage growth:

$$\pi_t = \lambda \Delta w_{t-1} + (1 - \lambda)\pi_{t-1} \qquad 0 < \lambda < 1 \qquad (4.39)$$

It could be argued that such backward looking expectations accurately describe the wage-setting approach when there are non-clearing labour markets (see Okun 1981). Thus, (4.38) and (4.39) together describe the way in which 'base' wages will adjust in response to excess demand or supply in the labour market. The labour market is not a continuous auction market, but is segmented across different sectors, with wages set at a 'base' level, except where all workers in the sector are fully employed. Nevertheless, excess demand or supply for labour will tend to be eliminated in the long run as 'base' wages adjust over time. Furthermore, another factor tending to eliminate excess demand and supply for labour is labour mobility across sectors, so that N_{it} will change over time, as labour is reallocated between sectors:

$$\Delta N_{it} = \beta E_{t-1}(w_{it}^* - w_t^*) + z_t \qquad (4.40)$$

where w^* denotes the market-clearing wage, and β lies between 0 and 1 reflecting the costs of adjustment to labour in moving between sectors. For example, if β is zero, there is no mobility of labour across sectors. The term z_t represents a white noise disturbance. Equation (4.40) therefore states that the size of the workforce in each sector adjusts by some proportion of the expected difference between the market-clearing wage in the sector under consideration, and the prevailing average in the economy.

Using the above model, Evans derives some interesting propositions regarding the shape of the aggregate supply curve. First, one of the crucial factors determining the shape of the aggregate supply curve is the *distribution of bottlenecks* in the economy. This describes the extent of imbalance between different sectors. The distribution of 'bottlenecks' can be found as follows. First define the difference between excess labour demand in each sector x_i and total excess demand, x, as follows:

$$r_i = x_i - x$$

The set of r_i for all sectors $i = 1, \ldots, T$ will then represent the *distribution of 'bottlenecks'* in the economy. This distribution will have a certain dispersion which influences the shape and position of the aggregate supply curve. Consider two possible cases. First, in the *short-run*, over which 'base' wages are not allowed to adjust, labour supplies N_i in each sector are fixed, and demand shocks d_i across sectors are given. Increases in aggregate demand (due, say, to an increase in the money stock) will be reflected in price and output changes: from (4.30) we can see that if the government increases the money supply, this will require a rise in nominal income, $(p_t + q_t)$, to restore money market equilibrium. From (4.31) we can then see that this will raise the demand in all sectors of the economy by an equal amount (remembering that d_{it} is given and fixed in the short run). From (4.36) and (4.37) we can see that if this is the case, then a change in aggregate demand will not alter the distribution of bottlenecks in the short run, as the x_i and x rise in step leaving r_i unchanged. While more sectors will enter the 'bottleneck' state, the spread of such 'bottlenecks' in the economy will not alter, as demand has increased uniformly in all sectors. A rise in aggregate demand will therefore cause more sectors to enter the 'bottleneck' state, as it will shift the labour demand curve, N^d, of Figure 4.3 rightward in all sectors. The short-run aggregate supply curve then has the form given by schedule AS in Figure 4.4.

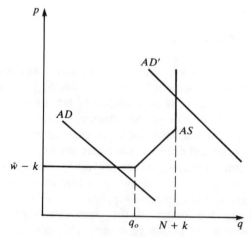

Figure 4.4 Short-Run Aggregate Supply in the 'Bottleneck' Model

The slope of the aggregate supply curve is given by $b/(1 - b)$, where b is the proportion of sectors experiencing 'bottlenecks'. Notice that when b becomes equal to unity, for very high levels of aggregate demand (curve AD'), the AS curve becomes vertical, and when it becomes zero, for low levels of aggregate demand (curve AD), the AS curve becomes horizontal, with all sectors paying their 'base wage'. It should be stressed that the 'distribution of bottlenecks' will not change as long as the 'base' wages differential $(w_i - \bar{w})$, the labour supply differential $(N_i - N)$, or exogenous demand disturbances d_i do not alter. Thus it is merely a measure of the *imbalance among sectors*, showing in which order sectors will hit the 'bottleneck state'. The larger the spread of the r_i, the greater the imbalance between sectors. If, for instance, the sectors are perfectly 'balanced' so that all sectors hit a 'bottleneck' at the same time, the aggregate supply curve will be of the right-angled shape shown in AS_1 of Figure 4.5, thus giving policy-makers the option of expanding the economy without inflationary consequences in the short run, until full employment is reached at output $(N + k)$, the sum of the (logarithms of) the total workforce in the economy and the aggregate average product. A wider spread of 'bottlenecks' would, however, imply that an aggregate demand expansion would cause wage and price inflation, even at low levels of output (see schedule AS_2 in Figure 4.5).

In the *long run*, we must allow for the evolution in exogenous demand factors, d_{it}, changes in 'base' wages, and the migration of labour between sectors. Given the dependence of the r_i on these factors, it follows that the 'distribution of bottlenecks' will vary, and will be endogenous to the model. One interesting question at this point is whether the economy

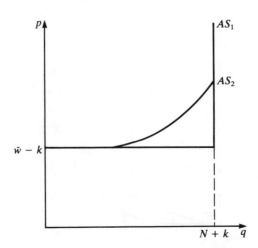

Figure 4.5 The Spread of 'Bottlenecks' and Aggregate Supply

will converge to a steady-state 'bottleneck' distribution. It can be shown that, if the authorities keep the money supply growth on a steady path (i.e. Δm_t is kept constant), then the distribution of 'bottlenecks' will reach a steady state, and furthermore output will settle at a long-run equilibrium level which is *independent of the rate of growth of the money stock*. This we may regard as the 'natural' level of output, and we may explain this result with reference to Figure 4.6, where price inflation is plotted against output.

Suppose the economy begins at point E in Figure 4.6 with a rate of monetary growth Δm_t^0, at the 'natural' output level q^*, and that the monetary authorities increase the rate of monetary expansion to Δm_t^1. At first, output will increase as well as inflation, as any sectors which have not yet reached a bottleneck state increase their output, and the economy will move along the short-run aggregate 'Phillips curve' SS. However, once excess demand is reflected in higher base wages in those sectors which experience 'bottlenecks', inflationary momentum will increase, causing output to fall back to q^*, as the short-run aggregate Phillips curve drifts upwards to $S'S'$. In the long run the economy settles down again at point E', at the natural level of output, with an inflation rate equal to the rate of growth of the money stock. Notice that q^*, the output at which the economy settles in the long run, is typically lower than the output at which all the economy's workforce is employed, $(N + k)$. The economic interpretation of this result is the following.

At q^* there will be some sectors in the 'bottleneck' state, with 'base' wages rising as a result. However, other sectors will have unemployed workers, with excess supply in the labour market, and 'base' wages will be falling as a result. Output level q^* is where these opposing forces exactly offset each other, thus creating a long-run equilibrium. Though labour is

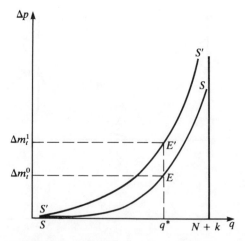

Figure 4.6   Long-Run Equilibrium in the 'Bottleneck' Model

free to move between sectors, there are costs involved, captured by the parameter β, and therefore such adjustments are not instantaneous. Also, because the d_i are constantly shifting over time, there will be a continuous imbalance in the economy, which is never eliminated. In the words of Tobin (1972), a situation arises where there is 'perpetual sectoral disequilibrium (and) stochastic macroequilibrium'. Thus, in the long run, some level of unemployment persists. Monetary growth cannot affect q^* because a permanent increase in aggregate demand affects all sectors to the same degree, and will not alter the distribution of 'bottlenecks' in the economy. The gap between 'full employment output', $(N + k)$, and the 'natural output level', q^*, can only be narrowed by reducing the variance of exogenous demand shocks, u_{it}, the variance of labour supply shocks z_t, or the cost of labour movement between sectors, β.

The long-run properties of this model may at first sight seem similar to Friedman's (1968) re-evaluation of the Phillips curve, as changes in aggregate demand can only affect output in the short run. In the long run, the economy settles at its 'natural' output level, which is independent of aggregate demand factors. However, despite this superficial similarity, there are marked differences between Friedman's account and this 'bottlenecks' model. First, the unemployment in this model given by the gap between $(N + k)$ and q^* is involuntary, as it is due to a structural imbalance between sectors. In those sectors which have not reached a 'bottleneck' state, an excess supply of labour persists in the long run. Thus, while the economy as a whole settles down to its long-run equilibrium, there are individual sectors which experience involuntary unemployment, due to non-market-clearing behaviour in their sectoral labour market. In contrast, any remaining unemployment in the long run in monetarist or new classical models is purely voluntary, as the neoclassical labour market is in equilibrium. This implication of 'bottleneck' models supports the contention of Solow (1980) and Modigliani (1977) that not all unemployment at the 'natural' rate (or in long-run equilibrium) may be regarded as voluntary.

Second, while the transition from the short run to the long run in monetarist and new classical models is likely to involve a short time period, as any short-run output response is due to temporary misperceptions of the aggregate price level on the part of firms and workers in aggregate, in 'bottlenecks' models a return to the 'natural' level of output following an aggregate demand shock may take a long time, given the nature of equilibrating forces in such models. The economy is driven back to its 'natural' output level by migration of labour between sectors, the gradual adjustment of base wages in the light of inflationary expectations, and the evolution of relative demand effects, all of which may be slow acting.

Thus, the policy implications of the 'bottlenecks' model are different from those of monetarist and new classical models. First, given that the 'short run' in 'bottleneck' models may persist for a long period of time, counter-cyclical stabilisation policies are justifiable. Second, the government may consider a selective expansionary policy more appropriate. If the government were skilful enough to recognise sectors which have not yet reached the 'bottleneck' state, and were to concentrate their policies in those sectors, they could reduce unemployment, even in the long run, by narrowing the gap between q^* and $(N + k)$. In Figure 4.6, q^* is independent of the rate of monetary growth only because spending is assumed to increase *pari passu* in all sectors. If aggregate demand policy becomes selective, q^* is no longer independent of aggregate demand. Third, bottleneck' models suggest a number of supply-side policies which may bring q^* closer to $(N + k)$ in the long run. The government may attempt to reduce the costs to workers of moving between sectors (i.e. increase β), thereby reducing structural imbalances. Alternatively, they may set up incomes policies to avoid rising wages in those sectors experiencing 'bottlenecks'. It should be recalled that neoclassical models primarily advocate supply-side policies to reduce any remaining long-run unemployment, yet one merit of Evans' model, in contrast, say, to Friedman's (1968) approach, is that it is more specific about the factors likely to affect the level of the 'natural' rate of unemployment.

Finally, as noted in subsection 4.3.1, this type of model provides an interesting reinterpretation of the Phillips curve in a number of respects. First, it provides a more solid theoretical underpinning for the Phillips curve than that offered by Lipsey (1960), as it is not dependent for any of its conclusions on long-run money illusion. Furthermore, some of the aspects incorporated within the model, such as 'base wages' and firm-specific workers, are readily derived from implicit contract models. Second, it suggests that the slope of the aggregate supply curve and the short-run Phillips curve may not be invariant over time, and may be endogenous to government policy. As we saw in Figure 4.5, the distribution of bottlenecks will affect the extent of the trade-off between output and inflation in the short run. This is to some extent consistent with Phillips (1958) original methods, which averaged data points over business cycles. Just as Phillips never claimed that a government could 'engineer' a precise shift of the economy along a Phillips curve, so 'bottleneck' models confirm that the exact nature of the trade-off will depend on the distribution of 'bottlenecks' and that we cannot speak of a 'unique' short-run Phillips curve.

4.4. Conclusion

We have seen in this chapter that the Keynesian belief that there is a role for stabilisation policies in an economy depends on four, not mutually exclusive, hypotheses. First, the rapid adjustment of wages and prices may be precluded by costs of adjustment in a modern economy. Second, governments may have an information advantage over economic agents and thus may have a comparative advantage in stabilising the economy at the 'natural' level of output. Third, the existence of implicit contracts may cause output and employment fluctuations around their 'natural' levels. In the presence of incomplete insurance contracts, this causes 'inefficiencies', in that some workers are involuntarily unemployed, and governments may then attempt to offset persistent cycles in output through stabilisation policies. Fourth, in an aggregate model where nominal wages are sticky in the presence of an excess supply of labour, but where 'bottlenecks' may occur, and labour migration between sectors is slow, there seems to be scope for stabilisation policies in the short run, and long-run unemployment may be involuntary. Demand and supply policies may be deployed to reduce the 'natural' rate of unemployment. However, one caveat in such models is that the government faces greater uncertainty in designing stabilisation policies, given the variable nature of the aggregate supply–Phillips curve trade-off.

One difficulty with Keynesian approaches to aggregate supply is that, despite presenting what may be regarded as 'intuitively plausible' accounts of the workings of the labour and goods market, they normally concentrate on individual aspects of the aggregate supply model. There is, as yet, no 'general theory' of Keynesian aggregate supply. In sharp contrast, monetarist and new classical models which are based on neoclassical accounts of the labour market, provide full, coherent accounts of macroeconomic behaviour, and as a result have an immediate aesthetic appeal. Furthermore, as we have seen in Chapter 3, casual empirical evidence cannot help us to discriminate between Keynesian and neoclassical accounts of the labour market. Despite arguments that large observed increases in unemployment in many Western countries during the 1970s and 1980s, coupled with high wage inflation, provide support for Keynesian accounts of the labour market (see *inter alia* Hall 1980, Okun 1981, Andrews and Nickell 1982), as we saw in Chapter 3 new classical models can also provide coherent accounts of the business cycle (see Lucas 1977, 1980). It is also difficult to draw conclusions from formal econometric evidence, as we saw from section 3 of Chapter 3, and the Keynesian models analysed in this chapter are not amenable to formal testing, given the partial nature of much of the analysis. As a result the debate on aggregate supply remains largely unresolved.

5
MONEY, FINANCIAL MARKETS, AND AGGREGATE DEMAND

In the preceding chapters of this book, we have been mainly concerned with the question of whether the macroeconomy is inherently self-stabilising, and therefore, by implication, of whether there is a role for government to play in managing aggregate demand in the interests of achieving some set of macroeconomic objectives. This discussion has been set against the background of the model of aggregate demand outlined in Chapter 1. In this chapter, and the succeeding one, we examine more closely the role of monetary and fiscal factors in the determination of aggregate demand.

This chapter is in four sections. In section 1, we briefly review the analysis of monetary policy set out in Chapter 1 as an introduction to the theoretical and empirical questions which are taken up in the remainder of the chapter. In section 2, we examine the determinants of the money supply, while in section 3, we analyse alternative theories of the transmission mechanism of monetary policy. Finally, in section 4, we review and evaluate recent developments in empirical studies of the demand for money.

5.1. Monetary Policy in the Simple IS–LM Model

In Chapter 1, we saw how monetary policy can be conveniently represented in the IS–LM model. For much of this chapter, we shall be concerned with demonstrating some of the shortcomings of that analysis. For the moment, however, let us review the main issues as presented in the IS–LM framework.

Let us define monetary policy as the control of the money stock by the authorities directed towards influencing aggregate demand. In IS–LM terms this may be represented as shifting the LM curve, as set out in Figure 5.1.

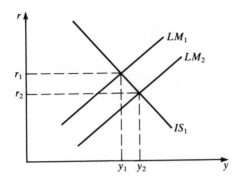

Figure 5.1 Monetary Expansion in the IS–LM Model

Starting from r_1 and y_1, an expansionary monetary policy increases the money stock, and therefore shifts the LM curve to the right, increasing aggregate demand and reducing the interest rate. Clearly, the effectiveness of monetary policy in affecting aggregate demand is determined by the slopes of the IS and LM curves, and extreme Keynesian and extreme monetarist positions are frequently described, as in Chapter 1, by correspondingly extreme assumptions about the slopes of the curves.

Monetarist optimism about the effectiveness of monetary policy is frequently represented by a steep LM curve and a flat IS curve, as illustrated in Figure 5.2. With an interest-inelastic demand for money and interest-sensitive expenditure, changes in the money stock exert a strong influence on aggregate demand. Shifting the LM curve from LM_1 to LM_2 increases aggregate demand from y_1 to y_2. However, as we shall see in subsection 5.3.3, wealth plays a key role in the monetarist transmission mechanism, and it could be argued that a more accurate representation of the monetarist mechanism would involve a simultaneous rightward shift of IS to IS_2 in Figure 5.2, reflecting direct wealth effects on expenditure. This has the effect of further increasing the effectiveness of monetary

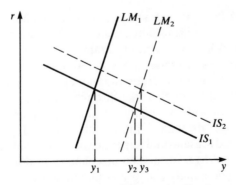

Figure 5.2 The 'Monetarist Case'

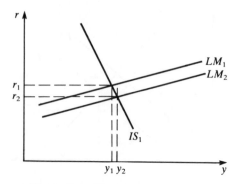

Figure 5.3   The 'Keynesian Case'

policy, increasing income to y_3, and reducing the role of the interest rate in the transmission mechanism, thus moving the debate about the efficacy of monetary policy away from the question of the relative slopes of IS and LM.

The textbook Keynesian doubts about the efficacy of monetary policy are represented by changing the relative slopes of the two curves, as in Figure 5.3. In this case, increasing the money stock has little effect, since the interest-elastic demand for money function underlying the flat LM curve ensures that changes in the money stock generate only small changes in the interest rate, while these changes, in turn, exert little impact on aggregate demand due to the interest-inelastic investment function underlying the steep IS curve.

For much of the 1950s and 1960s the debate between monetarists and Keynesians was conducted largely in terms of the relative slopes and stability of the IS and LM curves (see, for example, Gordon 1974). Focusing on monetary policy in particular, the remainder of this chapter is concerned with three general questions which the above analysis does not confront.

First, in simple IS–LM treatments of monetary policy, the money stock is exogenously given and is usually assumed to be under the control of the authorities. In section 2, we critically examine this assumption in the light of alternative theories of money stock determination.

Second, the mechanism whereby the money stock influences aggregate demand in the IS–LM model works through *the* interest rate. In a world characterised by a wide diversity of financial assets, a transmission mechanism working through a more fully specified portfolio than the simple money–bonds case would appear to be more realistic. An additional objection to the IS–LM transmission mechanism, as noted above, is that it is not capable of adequately encapsulating the monetarist view of the role of money in the macroeconomy, there being more to the monetarist 'black box' than a steep LM curve. In section 3, we examine alternative views of the transmission mechanism.

Finally, however the transmission mechanism of monetary policy may be described in theory, for practical policy debates the key issue is the stability of the demand for money function. This is an empirical issue, to which we turn in section 4, where recent developments in the econometric testing and interpretation of money demand functions are reviewed.

5.2. Money Supply Determination

Up to now, we have treated the money supply as exogenously determined by the authorities, who may seek to manipulate the money stock as an instrument of demand management. However, the process of money supply determination may be such that the assumption of an exogenous money stock under the control of the monetary authorities may be difficult to justify. In this section we examine this question by reviewing alternative theories of the determination of the money supply.

5.2.1. The Multiplier Theory of the Supply of Money

The standard textbook approach to money supply determination takes the form of the monetary base (or high powered money) multiplier, where the money stock is defined as notes and coins plus bank deposits, and the monetary base comprises bank reserves and assets eligible as bank reserves which are held by the non-bank private sector. In such a model the money stock is seen as the outcome of an interaction between the monetary authorities, as suppliers of monetary base, and the private sector (both bank and non-bank) as demanders of monetary base. This approach may be set out as follows.

The money stock is defined as cash (notes and coin) in circulation with the non-bank public (C_p) plus bank deposits (D). Thus,

$$M \equiv D + C_p \tag{5.1}$$

The stock of monetary base, H, is defined as bank reserves, R, comprising bankers' balances with the central bank (BB) and vault cash (C_b), plus cash held by the public, C_p, which is assumed to be eligible as bank reserves. Thus, we have:

$$R \equiv BB + C_b \tag{5.2}$$

$$H \equiv R + C_p \tag{5.3}$$

If we specify the non-bank holdings of cash as a proportion, c, of bank deposits, and the banks' reserve ratio as a proportion, r, of bank deposits, so that:

$$r = \frac{R}{D} \tag{5.4}$$

$$c = \frac{C_p}{D} \tag{5.5}$$

we may then find the ratio of the money stock to the monetary base by dividing (5.1) by (5.3):

$$\frac{M}{H} = \frac{(C_p + D)}{(R + C_p)} \tag{5.6}$$

Using (5.4) and (5.5) we may then write (5.6) as:

$$\frac{M}{H} = \frac{(1 + c)}{(r + c)} \tag{5.7}$$

That is, for given values of r and c, there is a fixed multiplier relation between the monetary base and the total money stock. As it stands, this relation is only meaningful if the ratios r and c remain constant throughout the monetary process. However, it may be regarded as a useful framework within which to analyse the key questions about money stock determination. First, is the supply of monetary base exogenous and under the control of the monetary authorities? Second, are the ratios c and r likely to be stable and predictable? Let us now examine these questions in turn.

We have already defined the monetary base as the supply of bank reserves and assets eligible as bank reserves. If we assume a fractional reserve system based on a cash reserve ratio, then we may alternatively regard the monetary base as the monetary liabilities of the central bank. A simplified central bank balance-sheet is set out in Table 5.1.

The liabilities of the central bank may be listed as notes and coins, bankers' deposits (that is, commercial banks' reserves deposited at the central bank), and government deposits. These liabilities reflect the central bank's function as issuer of currency, bankers' bank and the government's bank. Central bank assets comprise loans to the commercial banking system (reflecting its role as 'lender of last resort'), loans to the government (either in the form of government bonds or advances) and foreign exchange reserves (reflecting the central bank's interventions in the foreign exchange market as part of exchange rate policy). We assume that

Table 5.1   A Simplified Central Bank Balance-Sheet

Liabilities	Assets
Notes and coins (C)	Loans to the banking system (CLB)
Bankers' deposits (BB)	Loans to the government (CLG)
Government deposits (G)	Foreign exchange reserves (F)

government deposits at the central bank remain constant, since these represent the working transactions balances of the government, and as such are likely to be fairly constant except in the very short run, and do not play any role in money supply policy. Consequently, they are suppressed in the discussion which follows.

Substituting for R from (5.2) into (5.3) we see that we can define monetary base as total cash plus bankers' deposits:

$$H \equiv C + BB$$

where total cash, C, is given by $(C_p + C_b)$. Given this, it can be easily demonstrated that the supply of monetary base is the outcome of the balance of payments, fiscal budget finance and monetary policy. We begin by noting that:

$$PSD \equiv \Delta CLG + \Delta PrLG \tag{5.8}$$

where PSD is the public sector deficit, ΔCLG is the increase in loans to the government by the central bank, whether in the form of advances or bond purchases, and $\Delta PrLG$ is private sector lending to the government, which we may regard as largely comprising bond sales to the private sector, including banks. In specifying that the government borrows only from the private sector or from the central bank, we are making the simplifying assumption that the government does not borrow from overseas. From the balance-sheet of the central bank (suppressing government deposits), we may note that:

$$\Delta CLG \equiv \Delta C + \Delta BB - \Delta CLB - \Delta F \tag{5.9}$$

where ΔCLB is the change in central bank lending to the banking system. By simple substitution, and noting that $\Delta H = \Delta C + \Delta BB$, we obtain

$$\Delta H \equiv PSD - \Delta PrLG + \Delta F + \Delta CLB \tag{5.10}$$

Thus, changes in the stock of monetary base are brought about by fiscal policy, monetary policy and the balance of payments. Other things remaining equal, the stock of monetary base is increased by a fiscal deficit, a balance of payments surplus, and central bank lending to the banking system, and it is reduced by open-market bond sales to the private sector. Thus, although the supply of monetary base is under the control of the authorities in the sense that it comprises the liabilities of the central bank, in reality the actions of the monetary authorities to control the monetary base may affect, say, interest rates, prices or incomes in a manner which feeds back on one or more of the elements in the budget identity. For example, the monetary approach to the balance of payments is based on a feedback effect whereby monetary expansion may induce a fall in interest rates and a rise in prices and incomes such that the balance of payments goes into deficit, reducing foreign exchange reserves, and therefore the monetary base, to offset the original monetary expansion (see Chapter 7). A similar feedback mechanism could also operate through the endogeneity of the fiscal deficit via income-related tax receipts (see Chapter 6). Such interrelationships make the point that (5.10) is merely an identity where causal relationships cannot be established *a priori*.

Having outlined the factors which determine the stock of monetary base, can we be sure of a stable, predictable relationship between the monetary base and the total money stock? In a purely tautological sense, this must depend on the behaviour of r and c. In the simplest possible model, these two ratios would be regarded as constants. This might be justified on the basis of legally enforced minimum reserve requirements for commercial banks on the one hand, and some assertions about institutional and technological factors affecting the public's demand for cash (rather analogous to the argument for a constant velocity of circulation of money in the old quantity theory) on the other.

In fact, neither of these arguments is convincing. First, in those countries where meaningful legal reserve requirements are enforced (and this is far from universal practice), these stipulate a *minimum* ratio. Banks still have to determine their actual reserve ratio above this minimum. In both this case and, *a fortiori* in the case where reserve requirements are determined as a completely free portfolio decision by the banks, interest rates will be a determining factor. Since bank reserves are customarily non-interest-bearing, an increase in interest rates imposes increased opportunity costs on holding reserves, and therefore it is reasonable to specify r to be a negative function of interest rates in general. An additional consideration might be the composition of bank liabilities as between sight deposits and time deposits. Since the former may be more variable in terms of day to day withdrawals, banks may choose to maintain a higher reserve ratio against these deposits than against time deposits. Changes in the composition of deposits may then induce changes in the banks' overall reserve ratio. Finally, reserve ratios may also be variable in response to changes in the perceived riskiness of credit markets, which may reflect both economic and political factors.

To put the matter more generally, the multiplier approach places the portfolio decision of banks within a straitjacket. Bank reserves automatically back private sector lending, for which there is an assumed ready demand, interest rates playing no role. A more fully specified model would, at the very least, take account of interest differentials as between government bonds, foreign bonds and advances. (See Goodhart 1975, 1984 for examples of a more fully developed portfolio approach.)

A similar set of arguments may be advanced concerning the public's demand for cash. In particular, the demand for cash may also be negatively related to interest rates as, in the face of rising interest rates, individuals attempt to economise on their cash holdings. This could be analysed in a manner analogous to the inventory-theoretic approach to the demand for transactions balances in the demand for money literature (see Baumol 1952). To put the matter rather differently, even if the authorities were able to control the stock of monetary base, they might not be able to control its distribution as between the non-bank public and the banks. Thus, if the banks' reserve base is squeezed, they may increase their interest rates and attract reserve assets (cash) from the public. In addition, the demand for cash balances may change in the short run in response to institutional developments (such as changes in banking hours, the increased withdrawal facilities offered by cash dispensers, and the like) and in the longer run reflecting factors such as the growth of the so-called 'black economy'.

Where, then, does this leave the monetary base multiplier model? It is clearly an oversimplification to see the money supply process as a constant causal relation from monetary base to money stock. Not only is the value of the multiplier likely to change (both exogenously and endogenously), but the process of monetary expansion is likely to feed back on the supply of the monetary base itself. (This is merely another way of saying that there are more 'leakages' from the multiplier process than bank reserves and public cash holdings.) For example, consider an increase in the monetary base through the finance of the public sector deficit. Not only will this reduce interest rates, bidding up c and r and reducing the value of the multiplier, but it may also generate balance of payments outflows and increased tax revenues (through an increase in money income), thus dampening the initial increase in the stock of high powered money. A model where the multiplier process affects the value of both the multiplier itself and the multiplicand is clearly deficient.

The resilience of the multiplier approach, as reflected both in its continued presence in textbooks and aggregate macromodels, is largely due to the virtual absence of a tractable alternative which does not exhibit similar shortcomings. The principal alternative approach to emerge has been the so-called 'asset side' or 'flow of funds' approach, to which we now briefly turn.

5.2.2. The 'Flow of Funds' Approach

The flow of funds approach has similar methodological foundations to those of the multiplier model, in that it is derived directly from a series of identities. In this case, we extend the accounting relationships set out in the previous section.

We begin, as before, by defining the money stock as currency plus bank deposits:

$$M \equiv C_p + D \tag{5.1}$$

Since total bank liabilities must equal total bank assets, we may note that:

$$D \equiv C_b + BB - CLB + BLG + BLP \tag{5.11}$$

where BLG is bank lending to the government, BLP is bank lending to the private sector, and C_b is vault cash. Also included in (5.11) are bankers' deposits (BB) net of central bank lending to the banking sector (CLB). Substituting (5.11) into (5.1), and taking first differences, we have

$$\Delta M \equiv \Delta C + \Delta BB - \Delta CLB + \Delta BLG + \Delta BLP \tag{5.12}$$

Noting that private sector lending to the government, $PrLG$, comprises lending by the non-bank public, $NBLG$, and by the banks, BLG, we may rewrite (5.8) as:

$$\Delta BLG \equiv PSD - \Delta CLG - \Delta NBLG \tag{5.8'}$$

and recalling (5.9):

$$\Delta CLG \equiv \Delta C + \Delta BB - \Delta CLB - \Delta F \tag{5.9}$$

by substituting (5.8') and (5.9) into (5.12), we obtain:

$$\Delta M \equiv PSD - \Delta NBLG + \Delta F + \Delta BLP \tag{5.13}$$

This final identity bears a superficial similarity to the monetary base identity of (5.10), but there are two important differences. First, (5.13) does not include any transactions between the banking system and the monetary authorities. This is because, *of themselves*, neither bank borrowing at last resort from the central bank nor bank lending to the government affect bank deposits and therefore the money stock. Second, the money stock identity (5.13) includes bank lending to the private sector, whereas (5.10) does not. These two differences are connected if we assume a stable multiplier relation, since bank borrowing at last resort (or, alternatively, the sale of bonds to the government by the banks, BLG) by increasing the monetary base, will increase bank lending to the private sector BLP in (5.13), and therefore the money stock.

Does the flow of funds approach have any advantages over the multiplier approach? The first point to note is that, like the multiplier, it is best regarded as a framework rather than a theory. As in the case of all accounting identities, we cannot impose causal relations between the various elements in (5.13), and changes in one element may be associated with equal and offsetting changes in another. The principal advantage in setting out these accounting relations, however, is in focusing explicitly on the four main sectors which together determine the money stock, providing a framework within which policy-makers might seek to analyse how a given policy action may affect the money stock by examining each component of the identity. (It was, for example, largely the convenience of such an accounting system which induced the monetary authorities in the UK to adopt £M3, in preference to other definitions of the money stock, as a target.)

However, neither approach provides a convincing explanation of the behavioural relationships involved in the money supply process. In the same way as the multiplier provides no adequate account of what might determine the behaviour of the ratios, c and r, the flow of funds approach says nothing about the determinants of bank lending to the private sector and how this might respond to changes in other elements in (5.13). In short, to construct a *theory* of money supply, we need to model the behaviour of the principal agents involved. Such an approach involves the construction of a fully specified general equilibrium portfolio model, where the flows of funds described in the accounting identities are given 'life' by making them functions of portfolio preferences, wealth and relative financial yields (see Goodhart 1975).

Such an exercise is beyond both the scope and the needs of this chapter, but, in the light of the framework provided by the two approaches outlined above, it is clear that within such a model, a large number of parameter values would be important in determining the final effects of particular policy actions on the money stock. For example, in a model where the portfolio of the non-bank private sector includes cash, bank deposits, government bonds and foreign bonds, the own- and cross-interest elasticities of demand for these assets will be central to the monetary supply mechanism, as c adjusts endogenously in the multiplier model, and $NBLG$ and F adjust in the flow of funds identity. Similarly, the behaviour of the banks must be modelled, taking account of the interest elasticity of the demand for bank credit which is central to the endogenous adjustment of r in the multiplier and BLP in the flow of funds, together with the rate-setting behaviour of the banks. For example, the impact of contractionary monetary policy which raises central bank interest rates will be dependent on the banks' response to this. In particular, to the extent that the banks engage in liability management and raise their deposit rates in line, monetary policy will be weakened. The banks' ability to do this will depend not only on the interest elasticity of the demand for bank credit, but also on the extent to which the banks are able to practise price discrimination among depositors. This will be dependent, among other things, on the competitive structure of the banking system.

In the light of this discussion, it is clear that the assumption that the money stock is exogenously given by the authorities is seriously open to question, for two reasons. The first concerns the behaviour of the monetary authorities. The money stock will be determined endogenously if the monetary authorities seek to target another policy variable in preference to the money stock. The most familiar example is the pursuit of an interest rate target. This is simply illustrated in IS–LM terms in Figure 5.4. If the authorities seek to stabilise the interest rate at a level such as r^*, for reasons that we shall discuss in Chapter 9, then any exogenous change in private expenditure, say an increase from IS_1 to IS_2, must be accompanied by a change in the money stock so as to keep the interest rate constant at r^*. Thus, the monetary authorities increase the money stock so as to shift the LM curve to LM_2, and a change in private sector spending has induced a change in the money stock, rather than vice versa. Similarly, if the authorities target the exchange rate in preference to the money stock, the money stock becomes endogenous through the balance of payments (or ΔF in (5.13)). This is discussed at length in Chapter 7.

In the above examples, the money stock is endogenous through the adjustment of monetary base by the authorities. However, the money stock may also be endogenous through the behaviour of the banking system and the private sector. Once it is recognised that c and r in the multiplier are not constant, but are the outcome of portfolio adjustments on the part of banks and the non-bank public, which respond to, *inter alia*, interest rate changes, then one can argue that an exogenous increase in the demand for bank credit, reflecting a consumer boom for example, will generate an increase in bank loan rates and consequently bank deposit rates. This will reduce both c and r, allowing bank lending to increase, for a given stock of monetary base. It may also reduce demand for public sector assets, and induce capital inflows, reinforcing the rise in bank lending with an increase in monetary base. While the final outcome clearly depends on a whole range of factors, not least the authorities' reactions, it is clearly an

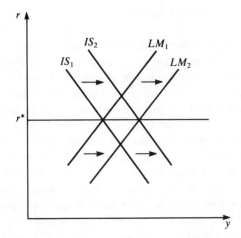

Figure 5.4　Interest Rate Stabilisation in the IS–LM Model

oversimplification to regard the money supply process as being a unidirectional one from central bank determined monetary base to bank lending and therefore the money supply.

These considerations have two general sets of implications. First, to the extent that the money supply is endogenously determined by private sector behaviour, doubt is cast on the efficacy of monetary policy as an instrument of stabilisation policy. Second, as we shall see in section 4, the question of whether the money supply is wholly or partly endogenous is central to the interpretation of the empirical evidence on the demand for money.

5.3.　Portfolio Analysis and the Monetary Transmission Mechanism

In this section we consider the question of the mechanism whereby changes in the money stock, however determined, affect the level of aggregate demand. In section 1 we examined the transmission mechanism of the IS–LM model where monetary changes work through a simple two-asset portfolio adjustment to affect the interest rate and therefore the level of investment. In this section we move away from that framework to consider the implications of a wider selection of financial assets for the monetary transmission mechanism. A necessary first step is to examine the microfoundations of the theory of portfolio diversification. We now turn to examine the way in which the demand functions for financial assets (including the demand for money) may be derived using a choice-theoretic framework.

5.3.1. Risk and Portfolio Selection

The microfoundations of the demand for financial assets were developed in the post-war period in the light of Keynes' theory of liquidity preference put forward in the *General Theory* (Keynes 1936). One unsatisfactory aspect of Keynes' account of the speculative demand for money was its prediction that individual economic agents at any given time will hold only money or bonds, but not both. In Keynes' original theory of liquidity preference, great emphasis was laid on the concept of a 'normal' level to which individuals expect the interest rate on bonds to return. This idea, however, carries with it a number of difficulties. First, if all investors in the market agreed on the 'normal' interest rate to which the market would return, it is apparent that the demand for money schedule would be horizontal in (M^d, r) space, as no individual would be prepared to hold bonds at an interest rate lower than the 'normal' level (a liquidity trap would exist). Thus, a downward sloping demand for money schedule like the one used to derive the LM curve in Chapter 1 has to rely on individuals differing in their views of the 'normal' rate, which presumably can be accounted for by Keynes' argument that uncertainty hangs over the behaviour of the interest rate: each individual investor has to form his opinion about the future interest rate knowing that there is a chance that the actual outcome may prove him wrong.

Second, at any given time, individuals are characterised as holding a portfolio consisting entirely of either money or bonds, but not both. Thus, individual investors will switch all their money holdings to bonds as soon as they believe that the interest rate has risen above its 'normal' level, and vice versa. In other words, Keynes' typical holder of speculative balances is a 'plunger', switching all his funds from one asset to the other as he sees fit. In contrast, casual empiricism suggests that investors, at any given time, hold a diversified portfolio, containing a range of assets and that they will attempt to reallocate their total holdings of wealth between assets in the face of changes in the assets' relative yields.

A theory of why investors should hold diversified portfolios was developed by Tobin (1958), Markowitz (1959), and Sharpe (1964). The framework used was that of choice under risk developed by von Neumann and Morgenstern (1947). In most portfolio models investors face a standard problem: how to allocate their given wealth between different assets, given that the yields on them are not known with certainty. Here we examine, for simplicity, the case where the investor is faced with the choice between two assets, but the results obtained may be readily generalised to the *n*-asset case. In practice, money is often described as an asset on which the return is known with certainty, and the simple model presented here may also be easily adapted to the case where one asset is riskless.

Suppose that we have two assets, denoted by i and j, and that a representative portfolio holder invests Z_i and Z_j (in real terms) respectively in these assets, such that his wealth budget constraint is satisfied:

$$Z_i + Z_j \equiv W/P \qquad (5.14)$$

where W/P is the investor's real wealth. Suppose that μ_i and μ_j are the returns on these two assets, and that they are random variables, so that the investor does not know with certainty what return will prevail in the period over which he allocates his portfolio. From simple probability we know that the expected value, $E(R)$, of the return from his total portfolio, R, is equal to:

$$E(R) = E(\mu_i)Z_i + E(\mu_j)Z_j \qquad (5.15)$$

where $E(.)$ denotes the expected value of a random variable. We also know that the variance of this total portfolio return, $\text{var}(R)$, is given by:

$$\text{var}(R) = Z_i^2 \text{var}(\mu_i) + Z_j^2 \text{var}(\mu_j) + 2Z_iZ_j\text{cov}(\mu_i\mu_j) \qquad (5.16)$$

where $\text{var}(.)$ denotes the variance of a random variable and $\text{cov}(.)$ denotes the covariance between two random variables. We assume that the investor has a utility function defined over the random return, R, on his portfolio. Though several types of utility function are plausible on *a priori* grounds, theorists have often preferred the so-called exponential utility function because of the readily interpretable results which may be derived from it, and because it is appropriate for the description of the behaviour of a *risk averse* investor. A risk averse individual may be *broadly* defined as an individual who experiences diminishing marginal utility from higher uncertain returns. In other words, the investor is risk averse if he prefers a certain return of £1 on his portfolio to an uncertain return with an *expected value* of £1 (see Arrow 1965, for a more detailed analysis of the concept and measures of risk aversion). Thus, we assume that:

$$U(R) = \alpha_0 - \alpha_1 \exp(-\alpha_2 R) \qquad (5.17)$$

where the α_i are positive coefficients. One advantage of this utility function is that, if we assume that the random returns on the two assets μ_i and μ_j are normally distributed:

$$\mu_s \sim N(r_s, \sigma_s^2) \qquad s = i, j \qquad (5.18)$$

then the variance of the total portfolio return, $\text{var}(R)$, may be seen as a measure of the riskiness of the portfolio. If the μ_s are normally distributed then the total return, R, is also normally distributed:

$$R \sim N(E(R), \text{var}(R)) \tag{5.19}$$

Furthermore, we assume that the investor maximises the expected utility of the return on his portfolio, $E(U(R))$:

$$E(U(R)) = \alpha_0 - \alpha_1 E(\exp(-\alpha_2 R)) \tag{5.20}$$

Given that R follows the normal distribution given in (5.19) above, we know that (5.20) may be written as:

$$E(U(R)) = \alpha_0 - \alpha_1 \exp(-\alpha_2[E(R) - \left(\frac{\alpha_2}{2}\right)\text{var}(R)]) \tag{5.20'}$$

It will be apparent from this expression that $E(U(R))$ will be maximised when

$$[E(R) - \left(\frac{\alpha_2}{2}\right)\text{var}(R)]$$

is maximised. From the definitions of $E(R)$ and $\text{var}(R)$ in (5.15) and (5.16) and the distributions of the μ_s in (5.19), we know that:

$$[E(R) - \left(\frac{\alpha_2}{2}\right)\text{var}(R)] = r_i Z_i + r_j Z_j$$

$$- \left(\frac{\alpha_2}{2}\right) [Z_i^2 \sigma_i^2 + Z_j^2 \sigma_j^2 + 2Z_i Z_j \sigma_{ij}] \tag{5.21}$$

where σ_{ij} is the covariance of the two random returns. The investor therefore has to maximise (5.21) with respect to the portfolio shares Z_i and Z_j subject to the wealth constraint in (5.14) above. This may be done by conventional Lagrangean maximisation. Defining the Lagrangean function, L, as:

$$L = r_i Z_i + r_j Z_j - \left(\frac{\alpha_2}{2}\right) [Z_i^2 \sigma_i^2 + Z_j^2 \sigma_j^2 + 2Z_i Z_j \sigma_{ij}]$$

$$+ \lambda \left(Z_i + Z_j - \left(\frac{W}{P}\right) \right) \tag{5.22}$$

where λ is the Lagrangean multiplier. We may apply the three first order conditions $\partial L/\partial Z_i = 0$, $\partial L/\partial Z_j = 0$, and $\partial L/\partial \lambda = 0$, to obtain the following expressions for the optimal portfolio shares which maximise the investor's expected utility, subject to his budget constraint:

$$Z_i = \frac{(r_i - r_j)}{\alpha_2(\sigma_i^2 + \sigma_j^2 - 2\sigma_{ij})} + \frac{(\sigma_j^2 - \sigma_{ij})}{(\sigma_i^2 + \sigma_j^2 - 2\sigma_{ij})} \cdot \left(\frac{W}{P}\right) \tag{5.23}$$

$$Z_j = \frac{(r_j - r_i)}{\alpha_2(\sigma_i^2 + \sigma_j^2 - 2\sigma_{ij})} + \frac{(\sigma_i^2 - \sigma_{ij})}{(\sigma_i^2 + \sigma_j^2 - 2\sigma_{ij})} \cdot \left(\frac{W}{P}\right) \tag{5.24}$$

These are the representative investor's asset demands for the two assets. The investor allocates a portion of his wealth to both assets given that, in the face of random yields, he may reduce the overall riskiness of his portfolio by diversifying his investments. The investor is trading off a lower risk against higher returns by maximising $[E(R) - (\alpha_2/2)\text{var}(R)]$ in (5.21).

We may simplify (5.23) and (5.24) by noting that, provided that the variances and covariances of the random returns (σ_i^2, σ_j^2, and σ_{ij}) may be regarded as constant in the period being considered, they may be consolidated into fixed coefficients, and thus these asset demands may be written in the form:

$$Z_i = \beta_0(r_i) - \beta_0(r_j) + \beta_1\left(\frac{W}{P}\right) \tag{5.25}$$

$$Z_j = -\gamma_0(r_i) + \gamma_0(r_j) + \gamma_1\left(\frac{W}{P}\right) \tag{5.26}$$

where the variances and covariance of the yields are now captured by the β and γ terms in (5.25) and (5.26). Thus, we have the intuitively plausible result that the demand for each asset is a positive function of its own rate of return, a negative function of the rate of return on alternative assets, and a positive function of wealth. Clearly, the two assets are to be regarded as imperfect, or gross, substitutes.

Furthermore, since the wealth constraint $Z_i + Z_j = W/P$ must hold, (5.25) and (5.26) must sum to W/P. It therefore follows that the own-rate and cross-rate effects on asset demands must satisfy an adding-up constraint:

$$\beta_0 - \gamma_0 = 0 \tag{5.27}$$

What this means is that when the rate of return on an asset increases, the increase in demand for that asset must necessarily equal the fall in demand for the alternative asset(s) in the portfolio. Furthermore, the coefficients on wealth must similarly satisfy the condition:

$$\beta_1 + \gamma_1 = 1 \tag{5.28}$$

Although the above analysis has been conducted with respect to two risky assets, it can be extended to cover any number of assets, including money. In the latter case, money is usually specified as an alternative asset of fixed yield (usually zero) which is therefore riskless. (In terms of (5.25) and (5.26), its yield has zero variance and covariance.) The outcome is to make the demand for money a positive function of wealth and a negative function of rates of return on alternative (risky) assets.

The following points should be noted about the above analysis. First, these results are totally dependent upon our choice of utility function. Alternative utility functions may be shown to lead to asset demands which are not linear functions of asset returns (see, for instance, Bhattacharyya 1979). Furthermore, there is no guarantee that asset demands will be homogeneous in wealth (i.e. that the wealth elasticity of asset demands equals one), although this property is assumed in Tobin (1969), since it ensures that as wealth grows in the economy, individuals will not hold ever-decreasing or ever-increasing shares of their portfolio in some assets. Furthermore, it has been argued (see Samuelson 1967a, 1967b, 1983) that the assumption of a normal distribution for asset returns is unrealistic, as it allows for the possibility of negative rates of return, which is clearly problematical. This difficulty has been largely ignored mainly because of the tractability of assuming normally distributed returns.

While we should certainly bear in mind that these and other criticisms raise a number of questions about the robustness of the results which are customarily derived from the mean-variance approach, it is convenient to adopt (5.25) and (5.26) as the basis of a portfolio model where the range of alternative assets available to wealth holders is wider than is envisaged in the simple money/bonds choice underlying the IS–LM model.

5.3.2. Portfolio Theory and Aggregate Demand

In this subsection, we now build on the microeconomic foundations of 5.3.1 to present a simple macroeconomic model which encapsulates the theory of the transmission mechanism usually identified with James Tobin (see Tobin 1961, 1969 and 1982).

The starting point for Tobin's macroeconomic portfolio analysis is the acknowledgement of an observation first made by Metzler (1951) that the IS–LM model is essentially a three-asset model comprising money, bonds and real capital, which is, in effect, collapsed into a two-asset model by the implicit assumption that bonds and real capital are perfect substitutes. This arises from the fact that in equilibrium in the IS–LM model, the rate of interest on bonds is equal to the marginal efficiency of capital. Much of the discussion in Tobin (1961) is concerned with the comparison of this case with an alternative two-asset model, where bonds and money are perfect substitutes, and are both in turn imperfect substitutes for real capital. In Tobin (1969), the more general case where all three assets are imperfect substitutes is analysed, and it is a version of this model which we present here. Throughout what follows, we assume that the price level, P, is fixed.

Building on the asset demand system (5.25) and (5.26) and extending it to the three-asset case where one asset, money, is riskless, we may write:

$$\frac{M^d}{P} = (\alpha_0 - \alpha_1 r_b - \alpha_2 r_k + \alpha_3 y)\frac{W}{P} \tag{5.29}$$

$$\frac{B^d}{P} = (\beta_0 + \beta_1 r_b - \beta_2 r_k - \alpha_3 y)\frac{W}{P} \tag{5.30}$$

$$\frac{V^d}{P} = (\gamma_0 - \gamma_1 r_b + \gamma_2 r_k)\frac{W}{P} \tag{5.31}$$

where total real wealth is given by:

$$\frac{W}{P} \equiv \frac{(M + B + V)}{P} \tag{5.32}$$

where r_b and r_k are the rates of return on bonds (B), and equity (V) (that is, claims on real capital). The nominal values of the outstanding stocks of money, bonds, and equity are denoted by M, B, and V respectively. In (5.29)–(5.32), in contrast to (5.25)–(5.26), we assume that asset demands are homogeneous in wealth, and, following IS–LM analysis, we allow for a transactions demand for money which depends on real income, y, in (5.29). Following Tobin (1969), changes in transactions balances are assumed to come exclusively out of bond holdings, and therefore the income term does not appear in (5.31). We should note that, in line with the results obtained from the microeconomic portfolio analysis, the demand for each asset is a positive function of its own rate of return, and a negative function of the rate of return on alternative assets, where money is non-interest-bearing. This confirms that all three assets are regarded as gross substitutes. Given that the wealth constraint (5.32) must hold, we again have adding-up constraints for the parameters of this model as follows:

$$\beta_1 - \alpha_1 - \gamma_1 = 0 \tag{5.33}$$

$$\gamma_2 - \beta_2 - \alpha_2 = 0 \tag{5.34}$$

$$\frac{M}{W} + \frac{B}{W} + \frac{V}{W} \equiv 1 \tag{5.35}$$

The model is completed by forging a link between the financial sector, set out in (5.29) to (5.32), and real expenditure. In the case of Tobin's model, this link is in the form of the so-called 'q' theory of investment, which relates the market value of equity (V), and therefore r_k, to the level of investment; it is to this theory that we now turn.

As a starting point, let us assume that firms finance their investment through retained earnings and the issue of equity. We may note that the market value of equity will be given by the total discounted value of the future returns accruing to equity holders over time. Thus, at time t, we have:

$$V_t = C_t + \frac{C_{t+1}}{(1 + r_k)} + \frac{C_{t+2}}{(1 + r_k)^2} + \dots \tag{5.36}$$

where C_{t+i} *is the expected return on capital at time* $t + i$, and r_k is the rate of return required by asset holders to induce them to hold the outstanding stock of equity. These returns, C, comprise dividend payments and expected capital gains. Equation (5.36) should be interpreted in the same way as the inverse relation between the market value and yield of fixed-coupon bonds. For simplicity, let us assume that all the C's are of the same value, C_0, so that we may rewrite (5.36) as:

$$V_t = \frac{C_0}{r_k} \tag{5.37}$$

In this case the relationship between V and r_k will be akin to that between the price and yield of a fixed-coupon irredeemable bond. (The relaxation of this assumption complicates the analysis without qualitatively affecting the results.)

The key relationship in Tobin's theory is that between the market value of equity, and the replacement cost of the outstanding capital stock. The latter is given by $P_k K$, where P_k is the price per unit of physical capital, and K is the total number of existing units of physical capital. The firm's investment decision will be based on a comparison between the marginal efficiency of capital relative to replacement cost, ρ_k, and the cost of capital to firms, which is represented by the rate of return required by equity holders, r_k. Given the replacement cost of capital and the prospective returns, C, we may identify the marginal efficiency of capital, ρ_k, from the following expression:

$$P_k K = C_t + \frac{C_{t+1}}{(1 + \rho_k)} + \frac{C_{t+2}}{(1 + \rho_k)^2} + \ldots \quad (5.36')$$

In an analogous manner to the derivation of (5.37), we may rewrite this as:

$$P_k K = \frac{C_0}{\rho_k} \quad (5.37')$$

The investment decision depends positively on the ratio of ρ_k to r_k. From (5.37) and (5.37'), this may be seen as equivalent to the ratio (q) of the market value of equity to the replacement cost, that is:

$$q = \frac{V}{P_k K} = \frac{\rho_k}{r_k} \quad (5.38)$$

Providing that newly acquired capital is assumed to generate the same returns at the margin for the firms as the existing capital stock, we may write the (net) investment function as:

$$I = f(q) \qquad f_q > 0, f(1) = 0 \quad (5.39)$$

In long-run full stock equilibrium, when the rate of return on investment to firms equals the rate of return to equity holders, q will equal one, and in a static model no new net investment will take place. (Within a growth context, when q equals one, investment will be at its long-run equilibrium level, associated with the equilibrium growth path of the economy; see Tobin 1982.) More significantly, in the short run, the larger is the value of q, the greater is the incentive for firms to invest, since when $q > 1$ the rate of return on investment projects exceeds the rate of return required by portfolio holders, and therefore the cost of borrowing to the firm.

There are three main factors which may cause q to change. First, a change in the price of capital goods, P_k, relative to the cost of labour and the price of the goods which the firm sells will alter the marginal efficiency of capital, thus affecting investment. Second, a change in expected future returns, C_{t+i}, will affect the firm's current stock market valuation relative to replacement cost, thus influencing the firm's cost of capital, and its incentive to invest. Finally, changes in the required rate of return on capital by asset holders, r_k, due to portfolio adjustments, will affect investment, and it is this last factor which is central to the transmission mechanism of monetary policy. Before examining this in further detail, however, there are a number of points to note about the 'q' theory of investment.

First, the investment function in (5.39) does not constitute a significant departure from the Keynesian investment function used in the IS–LM model. Keynes postulated that investment would take place if the cost of capital (the interest rate) was below the marginal efficiency of capital. A similar comparison is made here, except that the relevant cost variable is 'q'. However, given that 'q' is inversely related to the cost of capital, r_k, Tobin and Keynes' accounts are broadly equivalent. The only difference is that, while in IS–LM the relevant interest rate for firms' investment decision is the interest rate on bonds, given that bonds and equity are perfect substitutes, here Tobin differentiates between the two returns r_b and r_k.

Second, given that r_k and 'q' are inversely related, for a given marginal efficiency of capital, one may equivalently formulate Tobin's investment function in terms of the cost of capital:

$$I = g(r_k) \qquad g'(.) < 0 \tag{5.40}$$

This assumes, in line with the investment equation underlying IS–LM, that investment is mainly determined by asset markets, through changes in r_k, rather than through changes in the marginal efficiency of capital. In more familiar IS–LM terms, we consider movements along the investment function to be more important than shifts in it.

Third, as has been pointed out above, the market values of both fixed-coupon bonds and equities will vary inversely with their rates of return. Indeed, this is precisely the mechanism which drives investment in the IS–LM and Tobin 'q' models. However, these changes in nominal asset values will affect the total wealth of asset holders, and may in turn be expected to have repercussions in the allocation of portfolios. To allow for such factors, one would have to rewrite the wealth constraint in (5.32) as follows (where all bonds are perpetuities):

$$\frac{W}{P} \equiv \frac{M + \dfrac{B}{r_b} + qK}{P} \tag{5.32'}$$

However such 'revaluation effects' complicate the analysis of simple macromodels, and in the model outlined below we shall ignore these effects and continue to use (5.32), since including such effects would complicate our analysis without fundamentally altering the results.

Fourth, the simple IS–LM model ignores the effects of new net investment on the existing capital stock. This is even more important in portfolio models, as Tobin (1982) recognises, since this causes an increase in wealth, and hence potential portfolio effects. However, such capital accumulation effects will also be ignored in what follows.

Lastly, Tobin's 'q' theory of investment can allow a degree of volatility in the level of aggregate investment similar to Keynes' 'animal spirits'. If equity holders and firms have volatile expectations of future profits, this will cause 'q' (and hence investment) to display large fluctuations.

Returning now to our general model, in line with the above analysis we may relate aggregate investment to the rate of return on equity, r_k, and may set out goods market equilibrium as:

$$y = \lambda_0 + \lambda_1 y - \lambda_2 r_k \tag{5.41}$$

Essentially, (5.41) may be regarded as a modified IS curve, where investment is now a function of the rate of return on capital, and λ_1 is the marginal propensity to consume.

The integration of the real sector, as in (5.41), with the portfolio analysis of (5.29) to (5.32) completes the model, and we may now examine in some detail the transmission mechanism of monetary policy. To facilitate the discussion, let us first focus on the process of portfolio adjustment following a monetary disturbance, which we assume to take place in the very short run during which real income is unchanged.

The nature of portfolio equilibrium in this three-asset model can be conveniently illustrated by means of a diagram set out in Figure 5.5. In Figure 5.5, there are three asset equilibrium curves, each of which is drawn for given asset stocks. The *MM* curve describes the combinations of r_k and r_b at which the demand for money equals the exogenously given supply. The curve is downward sloping because an increase in r_k, for example, reduces the demand for money and to maintain monetary equilibrium r_b must fall. It will also be noted that the locus is stable in the sense that if we are at a point above *MM*, then r_k and r_b are 'too high', and consequently there is an excess supply of money. As individuals attempt to adjust their portfolios by buying bonds and equity, r_b and r_k are bid down and we move on to the *MM* curve.

Similarly, we may construct a *BB* curve for equilibrium in the bond market. In this case, the curve is upward sloping since an increase in r_k which reduces the demand for bonds is now required to be offset by a rise in the own rate of return on bonds, r_b. As in the case of the *MM* curve, the *BB* curve is stable in the sense that portfolio adjustments must always drive us on to the curve. The *KK* curve, which describes equilibrium in the market for equity, is also upward sloping, for analogous reasons, but it is flatter than the *BB* curve. This is explained by the 'adding-up' constraints within the portfolio. It will be recalled from (5.33) and (5.34) that the partial derivative of the demand for any asset with respect to its own rate of

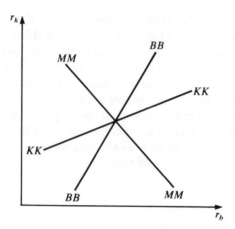

Figure 5.5 Portfolio Equilibrium

return must necessarily equal the sum of the cross-partial derivatives of the demand for the other assets with respect to that rate of return. Thus, a change in the rate of return of a given asset will affect the demand for that asset more strongly than the demand for other assets in the portfolio, so that a given change in r_b requires a relatively large change in r_k to maintain equilibrium in the bond market, and a relatively small change in r_k to maintain equilibrium in the market for real capital. Thus, *BB* must be steeper than *KK*.

Finally, it will be noted that since money, bonds and equity constitute the entire portfolio, when any two of these markets are in equilibrium, so too must be the third. Thus, all three curves in Figure 5.5 must intersect at the same point, and this equilibrium is globally stable.

It will be recalled that the *MM*, *BB* and *KK* curves are all drawn for given asset stocks. We may now analyse the consequences of changing these stocks exogenously, and in particular, the effect on r_k, which is the key link in the transmission mechanism. Let us begin with an increase in the money stock (unaccompanied by any other asset stock change) as set out in Figure 5.6. The *MM* curve must shift to the left, since the increased money supply requires increased money demand to maintain equilibrium, and this in turn requires lower rates of return on both bonds and equity. At the same time, the *BB* curve shifts to the left and the *KK* curve to the right. This is because the increased wealth deriving from the increased money stock exerts positive wealth effects, increasing the demand for both bonds and equity. As can be seen in Figure 5.6, the net outcome of the increase in the money stock is a fall in both r_b and r_k, the latter generating an increase in aggregate demand in the longer run.

This result is unexceptionable, but does reflect the assumption that the own rate of return on money is fixed (in this case, at zero). Thus, excess

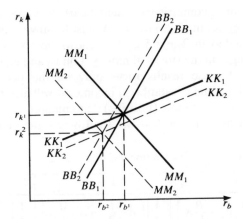

Figure 5.6 Monetary Expansion in Portfolio Analysis

supply in the money market must bid down the rate of return on alternative assets. However, when we change the supply of one of the other assets in the portfolio, the consequences for the rates on the alternative assets are less clear. In particular, if we increase the stock of bonds, will r_k rise or fall? In standard IS–LM analysis, an increase in the bonds stock is regarded as contractionary, since it reduces the money–bond ratio, increases the interest rate and depresses investment. In our portfolio model, the effect on r_k is less easily identified, as illustrated in Figure 5.7. As the bond stock is increased, this shifts the *BB* curve to the right as its own rate of return must be bid up to preserve portfolio equilibrium. The wealth effects on the demand for money and equity shift *MM* and *KK* to the right. The net outcome is clearly an increase in r_b, but the consequences for r_k depend on the relative shifts of the curves and their slopes, which in turn reflect the wealth and substitution effects referred to above. (As drawn, r_k falls, but this is not an inevitable outcome.)

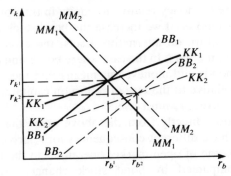

Figure 5.7 Bond Expansion in Portfolio Analysis

At this point, our geometric treatment clearly becomes less satisfactory, and the model set out in (5.29) to (5.32) must be solved formally. The key results are tabulated in Table 5.2. This shows how r_b and r_k change in response to changes in the stocks of money, bonds, and equity. It should be remembered that these results focus only on the period of portfolio adjustment, and assume constant real income. It will also be noted that all the coefficients share the same (positive) denominator, and therefore when comparing coefficients in the text, we shall ignore the denominator, Δ.

Table 5.2 Matrix of Portfolio Multipliers

	dM	dB	dK
dr_b	$-\dfrac{1}{\Delta}\left[\left(1-\dfrac{M}{W}\right)\beta_2+\dfrac{B}{W}\alpha_2\right]$	$\dfrac{1}{\Delta}\left[\left(1-\dfrac{B}{W}\right)\alpha_2+\dfrac{M}{W}\beta_2\right]$	$\dfrac{1}{\Delta}\left[\dfrac{M}{W}\beta_2-\dfrac{B}{W}\alpha_2\right]$
dr_k	$-\dfrac{1}{\Delta}\left[\dfrac{B}{W}\gamma_1+\dfrac{V}{W}\beta_1\right]$	$\dfrac{1}{\Delta}\left[\gamma_1\dfrac{M}{W}-\alpha_1\dfrac{V}{W}\right]$	$\dfrac{1}{\Delta}\left[\dfrac{B}{W}\alpha_1+\dfrac{M}{W}\beta_1\right]$

Note: Where $\Delta = W(\alpha_2\beta_1 + \beta_2\alpha_1)$

A number of points can be noted from these results. First, in two cases the multiplier coefficients are ambiguous in sign, i.e. dr_k/dB and dr_b/dK. Let us examine the effect of an increase in the bond stock on r_k. The value of dr_k/dB is calculated as

$$(\gamma_1 \frac{M}{W} - \alpha_1 \frac{V}{W})$$

This is more likely to be positive (that is, a bond expansion is more likely to be contractionary), the greater are γ_1 and (M/W) relative to α_1 and (V/W). That is, an increase in the bond stock is likely to bid up r_k if bonds and equity are closer substitutes than are bonds and money, and the greater is the share of money relative to equity in the portfolio. This may be rationalised as follows: if we increase the bond stock this tends to bid down the rate of return on alternative assets, those on near substitutes adjusting by less than others. In the case where bonds and equity are closer substitutes than bonds and money, this means that the rate of return on money must fall relative to the rate of return on capital. Since the former is, by assumption, fixed, r_k must rise.

Second, it follows directly from the above point that changes in the money stock will have different consequences for r_k according to whether these are the outcome of open-market operations in the bond market, or they are unaccompanied by bond stock changes. An open-market operations increase in the money stock is illustrated in Figure 5.8. In this case, as the money stock is increased, shifting *MM* to the left, the bond stock is reduced shifting the *BB* curve to the left. However, since the total wealth stock is unaltered by the money–bonds swap, and there is therefore no wealth effect on the demand for real capital, the *KK* curve does not shift. Portfolio equilibrium moves from point R to point S, with both r_b and r_k unambiguously reduced. What we cannot tell from this diagrammatic approach is whether r_k is reduced more by open-market operations or by the unaccompanied increase in the money stock. To answer this, we must return to Table 5.2.

The open-market operations multiplier for r_k is simply derived as $(dr_k/dM - dr_k/dB)$, which, again ignoring the common denominator and making use of the adding-up constraints, reduces to $-\gamma_1$. Clearly whether this is greater or smaller in absolute terms than (dr_k/dM) (which equals $-\gamma_1(B/W) + \beta_1(V/W)$ depends on whether dr_k/dB is positive or negative. Thus, the factors which determine whether bond expansion bids r_k up or down are the same factors which determine whether open-market operations are more or less powerful than unaccompanied changes in the money stock. In contrast, in the simple IS–LM model, open-market operations are generally to be regarded as unambiguously more powerful in their impact on the interest rate, and therefore on aggregate demand, since by definition in that model money and bonds are more distant substitutes than bonds and real capital which are assumed to be perfect substitutes. In the three-asset portfolio model, the result is dependent on the whole structure of asset demands and supplies.

Third, the results obtained in the above model reflect the assumption that the rate of return on money is fixed. If we relax this assumption and allow money to bear a market-determined rate of interest, then the impact of a change in the money stock on r_k will be reduced, as part of it is absorbed by changes in the own rate of interest on money, a point of some importance as financial markets are deregulated.

Fourth, it is also clear that an important factor determining the strength

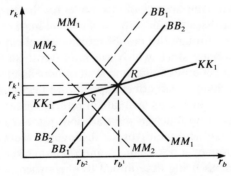

Figure 5.8 Open-Market Operations in Portfolio Analysis

of the impact of money stock changes on aggregate demand is the availability of close substitutes. Thus, if money and bonds are close substitutes (i.e. if α_1 is large), then the value of dr_k/dM is reduced in absolute terms. The intuition of this point is simply that the existence of a close substitute absorbs much of the disturbance imparted to the portfolio by a monetary disturbance.

Up to now we have been concerned with the short-run portfolio consequences of asset stock changes. In the longer run, any changes in r_k will affect real investment expenditure, as explained above. Once we incorporate the real consequences of portfolio adjustment by allowing real income to respond to changes in r_k and allowing for the increased transactions demand for money which results, we obtain the following monetary multiplier, by substituting (5.41) into our model:

$$\frac{dy}{dM} = \left(\frac{\lambda_2}{W\theta}\right)\left[\left(1 - \frac{M}{W}\right)\beta_1 - \alpha_1 \frac{B}{W}\right] \tag{5.42}$$

where $\theta = \lambda_2\alpha_3(\beta_1 - \alpha_1) + (1 - \lambda_1)(\beta_2\alpha_1 + \alpha_2\beta_1)$

Again, we may note that the existence of close money substitutes (a high value of α_1) reduces the impact of money stock changes on real income. In addition, as we would expect, the value of the multiplier is reduced by high value of α_3 (within θ) as the transactions demand for money dampens the effectiveness of monetary policy. We may also examine the consequences of bond expansion for real income:

$$\frac{dy}{dB} = \left(\frac{\lambda_2}{W\theta}\right)\left[\left(1 - \frac{B}{W}\right)\alpha_1 - \beta_1 \frac{M}{W}\right] \tag{5.43}$$

As expected, dy/dB may be positive or negative, depending on the values of α_1 and (M/W), with all the implications for the relative effectiveness of unaccompanied money stock changes and open-market operations discussed above, and this merely confirms the earlier portfolio analysis.

What, then, is the importance of this model for the analysis of monetary policy? First, it stresses that in so far as financial market conditions affect real expenditures (through the rate of return on real capital) it is not only changes in the money stock which are important. Since r_k is only one relative price in a general equilibrium system, *any* asset stock change (or, indeed, demand change) can affect expenditure decisions. Money is only unique in this system in that its own rate of return is assumed institutionally fixed, a conclusion very much in the tradition of the Yale school.

Second, the analysis enables us to distinguish more clearly between unaccompanied money stock changes and open-market operations, their relative effectiveness being determined by the structure of asset supplies and their relative substitutabilities within the portfolio.

Third, since the existence of close money substitutes reduces the impact of money stock changes on aggregate demand, the most effective monetary policy may not be that directed towards the money stock. Rather, in a developed and diversified financial system, a more appropriate strategy may be to control a bundle of assets which are close substitutes among themselves, but which are distant substitutes for the remainder of the assets in the portfolio; to do this, the monetary authorities should identify the clearest substitutability 'break' in the spectrum of assets, and select the financial aggregate to be controlled accordingly.

Fourth, while Tobin's portfolio model may be analysed in purely market-clearing terms, volatile expectations of future profits will lead to wild fluctuations in 'q' and investment expenditure. As Tobin (1978) points out, the stability of the monetary transmission mechanism in portfolio models depends critically on our view of the way in which asset markets operate. Portfolio theory merely offers a *framework* for analysis: the conclusions for monetary policy which may be derived from it depend on the structure of cross-elasticities and whether asset markets adjust smoothly to monetary shocks.

In conclusion, we may note that in this analysis all asset stocks are exogenously determined. However, a more complete model of the financial sector would include supply as well as demand functions for all assets, and indeed many of the debates about the design and conduct of monetary policy in a diversified financial system revolve around the endogenous behaviour of asset stocks in response to monetary policy. We have already touched on some of these issues in section 2, and we return to them at the end of this section. Before that, however, we examine the monetarist view of the transmission mechanism, in the light of the portfolio framework set out here.

5.3.3. *Monetarist Views of the Transmission Mechanism*

The portfolio model of the previous section can be seen as more realistic than the simple IS–LM approach; but it still preserves the two-stage view of the transmission mechanism whereby, in the first instance, changes in the money stock (or, indeed, any other asset) generate relative price (or rate of return) changes in financial markets which ensure that the new structure of asset stocks will be willingly held in individuals' portfolios. This process of portfolio adjustment does not, of itself, involve any real expenditure decisions. The second stage of the process occurs when a key relative price change affects private sector expenditure, usually invest-ment. In the IS–LM model, the key relative asset price is the only one available, the interest rate, while in Tobin's model it is 'q' (the reciprocal of r_k in the previous section). In both cases, the strength of the transmission mechanism is affected by the structure of portfolio preferences. In the IS–LM model, the interest elasticity of the demand for money is critical. In the portfolio model it is the general structure of portfolio demands and supplies which is important. In both cases, there is ample scope for 'elasticity pessimism' to play down the role of monetary policy.

It is interesting to note that the development of the monetarist counter-position, where the transmission mechanism is more direct and powerful, has also involved the extension of the portfolio decision behind the simple money–bonds world of the IS–LM model. In at least one case, this has led to the development of a model with a similar portfolio structure to that set out in the previous section (see Brunner and Meltzer 1972, 1976, and B. M. Friedman 1978a). However, in this section we review briefly the approach of Milton Friedman, as the principal monetarist spokesman, and argue that although the monetarist transmission mechanism may be regarded as in some sense an extension of the portfolio adjustment process, this superficial similarity is much less significant than the underlying differences of assumption and focus which combine to render Friedman's theory fundamentally distinct from its Keynesian counterparts.

The starting point for Friedman's analysis of the transmission mechanism is the 'restatement' of the quantity theory (Friedman 1956), which sets out his view of the theory of the demand for money. It is tempting to draw a number of general parallels between this approach and the portfolio analysis of the previous section. In particular, the restatement firmly sets the demand for money within the theory of wealth. Money is an asset which yields a flow of services to the holder. The demand for money is, therefore, to be regarded as a function of its own rate of return, the rate of return on other assets, and the total wealth stock. An increase in the money stock generates excess demand for all alternative assets in the portfolio, bidding up their prices (bidding down their rates of return) until all asset stocks are willingly held is equal and the portfolio is brought back into equilibrium. In this very general sense, the theory is in line with the portfolio approach. However, the differences are more important than the similarities.

First, and most fundamentally, the definition of wealth appropriate to the portfolio decision in Friedman's theory is much wider than that in conventional Keynesian analysis. All forms of wealth are to be included, even as far as human capital, the individual's lifetime earning capacity. However, Friedman recognises that the scope for substitution into and out of human capital is severely limited in the short term, at least in the absence of slavery, and therefore the ratio of human to non-human wealth is regarded as a constraint on portfolio adjustment. However, even in respect of non-human wealth, the monetarist portfolio includes a wider range of assets. Not only are bonds and equity recognised as alternatives to money, but so too are physical capital itself and durable consumption goods, since they too generate a flow of returns to the asset holder, although the rates of return on these assets are not readily observable in financial markets (in contrast to the assets included in Tobin's portfolio). Thus, an increase in the money stock will increase the demand for all other assets, including consumer durables, until their rates of return are bid down so as to re-establish portfolio equilibrium. This differs from the earlier portfolio analysis in that it specifies a direct transmission mechanism from the money stock to expenditure on physical assets.

Second, the microfoundations of Friedman's portfolio analysis differ fundamentally from those of Tobin in that the motives for holding money do not derive from considerations of risk and return which are central to the mean-variance approach. Rather, money is regarded as an asset which yields to the holder a flow of services which derive from its uniqueness as a 'temporary abode of purchasing power'.

Third, although rates of return on bonds and equity are included in the demand for money function these play only a transitory role in the transmission mechanism. The reason for this is that, although interest rates may influence the demand for money, they are not determined in the money market. Rather, rates of return on bonds and equity, which are assumed to move together, are fundamentally determined in real markets by real factors. Thus, productivity and thrift provide the long-run anchors for interest rates in the Friedman model, and monetary disturbances serve to affect interest rates only transitorily.

Fourth, in contrast to many Keynesian theories, increases in the money stock influence expenditure not only through the portfolio mechanism outlined here, but also directly through the consumption function. We have already noted in Chapter 1 how consumption expenditure may be related to wealth, and Friedman's permanent income theory may be seen as a variant of this approach. (For a comprehensive discussion of the permanent income hypothesis, see Friedman 1957, Sargent 1979.) Increases in the money stock, to the extent that these are perceived as permanent increases in net wealth (and therefore permanent income) will therefore generate increases in aggregate expenditure on both durable and non-durable consumption. The key point here is that this mechanism will only operate if the increased money stock comprises outside money, and therefore net wealth. (Note however that this caveat does not apply to the portfolio adjustment mechanism outlined above.)

Finally, the monetarist transmission mechanism is normally set within the context of a fully employed economy (or at the natural level of output) so that any increase in expenditure generates increased prices and not increased output.

In the light of these considerations, what is the transmission mechanism implied by Friedman's theory? An increase in the nominal money stock produces excess supply in the money market and excess demand for all alternative assets. Initially, interest rates are bid down, but this is only temporary as real factors dominate in the longer run and the permanent impact falls on the market for real assets, as expenditure on physical capital and consumer durables is increased. This, in addition to the increased level of consumption brought about by the increase in wealth which the monetary expansion represents, increases the price level, until the real money stock is reduced to its original level. This result is in the spirit of the quantity theory of money, whereby money is held to be neutral with respect to real variables. Real output and interest rates are unchanged at their natural levels. However it should be noted that although, as the price level increases in line with the nominal money stock and the real money stock is unchanged, the real stock of other nominally denominated assets is reduced. Portfolio theory suggests that this should result in falling interest rates on these assets, which, as we saw in Chapter 2, raises questions about the neutrality of money. (For a full discussion of these issues, see Harris 1981, Sargent 1979.)

It is clear from this discussion that, although a portfolio mechanism lies at the heart of the monetarist view of the transmission of monetary policy, the view taken about the strength and stability of this mechanism is different from many Keynesian models. The direct nature of the monetarist mechanism stems from the view about the determination of interest rates, the assumed absence of near-money substitutes, the inclusion of real assets, including consumer durables, within the portfolio, and the role of money, as one component of wealth, in the consumption function. In contrast, Keynesian models see the transmission mechanism as being less direct and therefore potentially more unstable and weaker. Ultimately, these issues have to be debated on empirical grounds, in terms of the stability of the demand for money function and the values of the key parameters, and the final section of this chapter surveys recent developments in this debate. Before we embark on that discussion, however, we turn to the question of how endogenous changes in private sector asset stocks can affect the effectiveness of monetary policy, and in particular the role of non-bank financial intermediaries.

5.3.4. The Role of Non-Bank Financial Intermediaries and Endogenous Asset Stocks

Up to now in our discussion of the transmission mechanism, we have made the important *ceteris paribus* assumption that, after an exogenous change in the money stock, other asset stocks in the model remain unchanged. As we have seen in section 2, however, it is difficult to justify monetary models which regard the private financial sector as a passive mechanical partner to official monetary policy. In this section, we remove this assumption by means of the didactic device of introducing an uncontrolled financial sector in the form of non-bank financial intermediaries (NFIs), whose behaviour is such as to change relative asset stocks in response to official monetary policy.

Let us begin with a simple model, where individuals hold a portfolio comprising money (cash plus bank deposits), NFI deposits, bonds and equity. Let us assume that money and NFI deposits are very close substitutes and both are, in turn, highly imperfect substitutes for equity. On the asset side of their balance-sheet, NFIs hold equity. (Alternatively they could be assumed to extend loans to the private sector at rates equal to equity rates.) In line with the Tobin model, it is the rate of return on equity (and associated loan rates) which is the relative price within the portfolio which affects real expenditure decisions.

Suppose, now, that the authorities wish to implement contractionary monetary policy, by means of effectively reducing the money stock. According to portfolio analysis, this will bid up the rates of return on alternative assets, including that on equity, reducing aggregate demand. As we have seen in our earlier analysis, the very *existence* of near-money substitutes (in the form of NFIs' deposits) weakens this portfolio adjustment effect on expenditure. However, how would we expect NFIs to *respond* to this situation? In fact, contractionary monetary policy has provided an incentive for NFIs to expand their deposits. In line with portfolio theory, while the rate of return on all assets in the portfolio has been bid up, the rate on NFIs' deposits, as near-money substitutes, has been bid up by less than that on equity, a distant money substitute. The rates on NFI assets have therefore risen relative to the rates on their liabilities, increasing their profit margins and encouraging an expansion. The NFIs therefore seek to increase their deposits, and if they are able to do so, then the stock of a near-money substitute will have *increased*, serving further to offset the initial policy of monetary contraction.

The question of whether NFIs do in fact tend to offset official monetary policy was first raised by Gurley and Shaw (1960) and the *Radcliffe Report* (1959), with further notable contributions by Tobin and Brainard (1963) and Brunner and Meltzer (1963). We do not survey this literature here, but we may examine the central issues by reference to an extended version of the simple multiplier model of the money supply, designed to take account of 'financial layering'. This describes a financial structure where a so-called 'pyramid of credit' involving both banks and NFIs is built on the reserve base of the system.

Following Chick (1977) and our analysis in section 2, we assume for simplicity that the banks operate on a reserve base system, with a given reserve ratio, r_b, as in (5.4):

$$R = r_b D \qquad\qquad (5.4')$$

where reserves, as previously, comprise bankers' balances (BB) and vault cash (C_b):

$$R \equiv BB + C_b \tag{5.2}$$

Bank deposits (D) are held by both the public (D_p) and NFIs (D_n), the latter holding them as reserves against their deposits, at a given ratio, r_n. That is:

$$D \equiv D_p + D_n \tag{5.44}$$

$$r_n = \frac{D_n}{N} \tag{5.45}$$

Again for simplicity, we assume that NFIs do not hold cash, so that total cash is given by:

$$C \equiv C_b + C_p \tag{5.46}$$

We also assume that the public holds NFI deposits (N) but the banks do not. Finally, we assume the public holds a given ratio of cash to bank deposits, c, (as in section 2), and a given ratio of NFI deposits to cash, n:

$$c = \frac{C_p}{D_p} \tag{5.47}$$

$$n = \frac{N}{C_p} \tag{5.48}$$

For given values of all the key ratios, this describes a system where bank deposits are founded on the cash reserve base, and NFI deposits are founded on a base of bank deposits. At both levels of this pyramid, however, there is a leakage to the public, in the form of the public's cash holdings at the first level, and public's holdings of bank deposits at the second. The so-called pyramid is illustrated in Figure 5.9. Thus, an increase in the cash base increases the supply of bank deposits, which, allowing for the public's demand for bank deposits, increases in turn the potential reserve base of the NFIs, and therefore NFI deposits. Retaining the definition introduced in section 2 of the money stock as public holdings of cash plus bank deposits:

$$M \equiv C_p + D \tag{5.1}$$

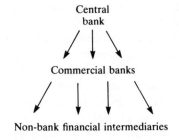

Figure 5.9 The 'Credit Pyramid'

We may derive the monetary base money multiplier by dividing (5.1) by (5.3), and using (5.2), (5.4′), and (5.44)–(5.48):

$$\frac{M}{H} = \frac{(1 + c + r_n nc)}{(c + r_b + r_n r_b nc)} \tag{5.49}$$

Comparing (5.49) to (5.7), it will be noted that this multiplier is increased by the presence of NFIs, tending to strengthen monetary policy, though this result is dependent on including bank deposits held by NFIs within the definition of the money stock. Rather more interesting is the total liquidity multiplier which we may measure as the increase in total liquid assets held by the public ($L = C_p + D_p + N$) brought about by an increase in high powered money. This multiplier is given by:

$$\frac{L}{H} = \frac{(1 + c + nc)}{(c + r_b + r_n r_b nc)} \tag{5.50}$$

If the key ratios remain constant, then the existence of NFIs tends to reinforce the transmission mechanism of monetary policy. For example, a fall in the monetary base reduces the stock of both bank and NFI deposits, which bids up the rate of return on equity further than in the absence of NFIs. However, as in the case of the simple multiplier of section 2, such results depend critically on the constancy of the ratios r_n, r_b, n and c. We have already noted that the banks' reserve ratio is likely to move in an offsetting manner due to the interest effects of monetary policy, and the same point may be made with reference to NFI reserves. However, equally important is the behaviour of n and c. The higher is nc, then the greater is the value of the multiplier, and nc describes the public's desired ratio of NFI deposits to bank deposits. Returning to our original example, a contractionary monetary policy, by its effects on the structure of returns in the portfolio, will tend to provide an incentive to NFIs expand their deposits, by bidding deposits away from the banks. This is another way of describing an increase in *nc*.

The ability of the NFIs to bid deposits away from banks will depend on a number of factors. First, if the deposits of the two sets of institutions are very close substitutes for each other, then a relatively small interest rate rise by the NFIs is necessary to bid the deposits away. However, this pre-supposes a passive attitude by the banks, which is usually justified in one of two ways. The first is the possibility that the banks are under such monetary control that they are unable to compete with the NFIs. Recent developments in monetary policy in many countries make this less than convincing. The second argument is that there is no incentive for the banks to compete, because the basic arithmetic of the credit pyramid is such that the switching of deposits by the public from banks to NFIs merely changes the identity of the deposit holder since it returns to the banking system in the form of NFI reserves. This argument is questionable on at least two grounds. First, in reality the reserves of NFIs (for example building societies in the UK) are not held entirely in the form of bank deposits, but also include other liquid assets, which implies a net drain of deposits from the banking system. Second, the banks may not regard the relative growth of NFIs with complete indifference. In particular, if credit markets are not significantly segmented, and NFIs are able to compete successfully on the asset side of the balance-sheet, then it may be possible for NFIs to bid away both loans and deposits from the banking system. Under these circumstances, banks contract relative to NFIs, and become less profitable. For these reasons, therefore, the banks can be expected to defend their liabilities position against the non-banks, rendering the final outcome uncertain.

In conclusion, we have, in this subsection, concentrated on a particularly stylised example of the way in which asset stocks may change in response to exogenous shocks to a portfolio model. More generally, we may note that a key contribution of the portfolio approach is that it formally focuses on the contention that the nature of the transmission mechanism necessarily reflects the general financial structure, and therefore that structural change (or financial innovation) is of central importance to the analysis of monetary policy. Such a view was fundamental to the belief of the Radcliffe Committee in reaching its general conclusion that monetary policy was likely to be less effective and reliable than fiscal policy, as the financial structure 'adapted' in the face of monetary controls. In addition, structural change may be actively encouraged by the authorities on microeconomic grounds, by policies of deregulation. While the dynamic *process* of structural change may generate uncertainty in the operation of monetary policy, in the long run, it may also have the consequence of increasing the diversity of financial assets available to wealth holders. In so doing, the pattern of substitutabilities within the portfolio may be smoothed so that monetary policy is pushed towards the control of more widely defined financial aggregates.

Finally, we may note that throughout this section, we have been concerned with *theories* of the transmission mechanism. Once we turn to issues of practical policy-making, the central question concerns the identification of a monetary, or financial, aggregate for which there is a stable demand function. The search for a stable demand for money function has dominated empirical monetary research for the past twenty years, and it is to recent developments in this area that we finally turn in this chapter.

5.4. The Demand for Money: Empirical Evidence

In this section, we extend the discussion of the theoretical issues of section 3 by examining the empirical evidence on the demand for money. The main problem in comparing the multitude of empirical studies on the demand for money is that the data series used vary between studies. First, a wide range of definitions of the money stock may be adopted, and the principal definitions are given in Table 5.3. Second, a further difficulty lies in the different scale variables used to explain money demand, and in particular, different definitions of real income are often used. Finally, while interest rates clearly play a role in the demand for money, it is not clear whether a single or a number of interest rates on alternative assets should be used, and which rates should be chosen.

Bearing in mind these differences between empirical studies, in this section we shall concentrate on their common themes, and in particular the problems which have been encountered in finding a stable demand for money relationship in the 1970s. As we have seen so far, the stability of the monetary transmission mechanism, and hence the useful deployment of monetary policy, requires the existence of a stable demand for money function. As a result, our main interest in this section will be in those studies which model the aggregates which have been targeted in the UK and US, £M3 and M1 respectively. Furthermore, we shall show how the apparent empirical breakdown of the demand for money function in the 1970s has led to the development of alternative theories of money demand.

5.4.1. The Demand for Money in the 1960s

Most empirical studies are based on traditional demand for money theories which build on the transactions motive for holding money (Baumol 1952, Tobin 1956) or the portfolio motive (Tobin 1958, Friedman 1956). Many

Table 5.3 Money Stock Definitions

Definition	UK	USA
M1	Notes and coin in circulation with public + UK private sector sterling sight deposits (interest and non-interest bearing)	Currency + Demand deposits at commercial banks + 'Now' accounts
M2	M1 + Other UK private sector retail deposits with banks + UK private sector retail shares and deposits with building societies + National Savings Bank ordinary accounts	M1 + Time deposits at commercial banks + Shares in money market mutual funds + Money market certificates issued by commercial banks
£M3	M1 + UK private sector sterling time deposits + UK public sector sterling deposits	—
M3	£M3 + UK residents' deposits in currencies other than sterling	—

$$m = \alpha_0 + \alpha_1 y + \alpha_2 p + \alpha_3 r \qquad (5.51)$$

where m is the nominal money stock, y is real income, p is the price level, and r is the rate of return on an appropriate alternative asset to money. All the variables (except r) are in logarithms. Such models of money demand are usually described as 'static', because they assume that the holdings of money always instantaneously adjust to the changes in the determinants of the demand function, and thus no lags of these latter variables appear in the estimated equation.

Generally most US and UK studies (see for example Meltzer 1963, Brunner and Meltzer 1964, Laidler 1966, for the US and Barratt and Walters 1966, Laidler 1971, for the UK) found 'well determined' and stable demand for money functions, for various definitions of money, income, interest rate, and data period. Furthermore, though most studies used conventional ordinary least squares (OLS) estimators, it was also shown that the adoption of simultaneous equations estimators did not significantly alter OLS results (see, for example, Teigen 1964). Thus the apparent lack of simultaneity problems meant that the demand for money could be legitimately modelled without reference to the supply of money. As we shall see below, though, this conclusion seems to have been turned on its head by the use of active monetary policy in the 1970s.

Before turning to the 1970s, it should be noted that although equations of the form of (5.51) were common for annual data, the use of quarterly data required the use of lags in the regressors or, more typically, in the dependent variable, m. (See, for instance, Feige 1967, for the US, and Laidler and Parkin 1970, for the UK.) Usually these studies incorporated the assumption of partial adjustment in money holdings. Assuming that (5.51) now represents *desired* money holdings:

$$m_t^* = \alpha_0 + \alpha_1 y_t + \alpha_2 p_t + \alpha_3 r_t \tag{5.52}$$

and assuming that agents do not instantaneously adjust actual money holdings, m, to desired levels, m^*, but rather, by a partial adjustment mechanism:

$$m_t - m_{t-1} = \lambda(m_t^* - m_{t-1}) \qquad 0 < \lambda < 1 \tag{5.53}$$

then, substituting (5.52) into (5.53), the equation to be estimated becomes:

$$m_t = \alpha_0\lambda + \alpha_1\lambda y_t + \alpha_2\lambda p_t + \alpha_3\lambda r_t + (1 - \lambda)m_{t-1} \tag{5.54}$$

In addition to the use of partial adjustment, dynamics were also introduced by means of replacing current income by expected income, with expectations usually modelled with the adaptive mechanism outlined in Chapter 3. These *dynamic* models generally performed well on quarterly data, and most of the arguments centred on the magnitude of the interest elasticity of demand which was supposed to shed light on the debate regarding the relative slopes of the IS and LM curves.

5.4.2. The 1970s and the Apparent 'Breakdown' of the Demand for Money

Unfortunately, the 1970s have proved to be troubled times for the demand for money function, as models previously estimated using the methods described above apparently became unstable. This instability could not be attributed to national institutional factors, as the breakdown of the function occurred in many OECD countries (see OECD 1979). Although these events were not simultaneous across national boundaries, and different countries' experiences were not entirely similar, the failure on such a global scale of an econometric relationship was probably indicative of the volatile economic environment of the 1970s. For example, in the UK, Artis and Lewis (1976) showed, for different specifications of the demand for money, that the parameters of these functions did not remain stable over the period 1971–73. Similarly, in the US, Goldfeld (1976) estimated a stable demand function for M1 on quarterly data over the period 1952–73, but this equation failed to predict the demand for money accurately over the 1970s.

In general, the problems encountered with parameter stability and with poor forecasting equations have not been solved by extending the list of explanatory variables used in the estimated functions. Variables which account for the introduction of financial innovation (see for example the US study by Judd and Scadding 1982), or which allow for the payment of interest on money balances (an 'own rate' variable), (see Goodhart 1984) at best make only marginal contributions to the acute problems encountered in modelling the demand for money.

However, the late 1970s and 1980s have seen the development of both theoretical and empirical techniques which attempt to overcome these problems. These two parts of the literature are intimately related. The first response to the breakdown of conventional demand for money functions was in the development of improved econometric techniques, which have contributed to the partial 'rebuilding' of the demand for money function.

5.4.3. The Econometric Response to the Breakdown in the Demand for Money

As we saw in subsection 5.4.1, many studies of the UK demand for money (Laidler and Parkin 1970, Goodhart and Crockett 1970, Price 1972) based on quarterly data used the assumption of partial adjustment and/or adaptive expectations in obtaining an equation with a particular lag structure, e.g. (5.54). Equations of this type, however, did not provide an adequate explanation of M3 after 1970. Hacche (1974) further developed equation (5.54), to obtain an improved estimating equation for M3, first imposing the constraint on the estimating equation that $\alpha_2 = 1$ so that the elasticity of the demand for money with respect to price is set arbitrarily equal to one, and then estimating the model with the variables entered not in terms of levels, but in first differences.

This is equivalent to considering an equation with lagged explanatory and dependent variables of the type:

$$(m_t - p_t) = \alpha_0 + \alpha_1 y_t + \beta_1 y_{t-1} + \alpha_2 r_t$$
$$+ \beta_2 r_{t-1} + \beta_3 (m_{t-1} - p_{t-1}) + u_t \qquad (5.55)$$

and setting $\alpha_i = -\beta_i$ for $i = 1, 2$ and $\beta_3 = -1$, where u_t represents a stochastic disturbance term. Furthermore, Hacche corrects his model for first-order serial correlation, thus assuming that the disturbance term u_t follows the autoregressive pattern:

$$u_t = \rho u_{t-1} + \varepsilon_t$$

where ε_t is a white noise disturbance term.

Thus, Hacche imposes *a priori* restrictions on the dynamics of the demand for money. Note that the simple models of the 1960s also imposed a particular lag structure on the estimating equations, by assuming that the adjustment of the actual demand for money towards the desired level followed a simple first-order partial adjustment. Hacche's model imposes two *additional* restrictions by assuming a very particular lag structure so as to allow the estimation of the model in first differences, and by correcting for first-order serial correlation in the residuals.

This approach to modelling has been criticised at length, notably by Hendry and Mizon (1978), Courakis (1978), and Hendry (1979). These authors argue that the prior imposition of restrictions on the lag structure of the regressors or the disturbance term dynamics as in (5.54) and (5.55) is incorrect, given that there are no *a priori* theoretical reasons for imposing a particular type of adjustment of the actual demand for money towards its desired level. They argue that these restrictions should be verified empirically through appropriate statistical tests.

Hendry and Mizon (1978) begin their search for a suitable demand for money function by specifying a general lag formulation of the type:

$$m_t = \alpha_0 + \Sigma_{i=0}^{n} (\beta_i y_{t-i} + \gamma_i p_{t-i} + \delta_i r_{t-i})$$
$$+ \Sigma_{i=1}^{n} (\varepsilon_i m_{t-i}) + u_t \tag{5.56}$$

where n is chosen to be equal to 4, to avoid the loss of too many degrees of freedom. However, this specification is too general, leading to a model with suboptimal statistical properties. Not all of these regressors are likely to be significant, and they adopt a modelling strategy which imposes constraints on (5.56), so as to simplify its structure. However, all the restrictions imposed are tested statistically, and thus the model obtained is seen to be 'data acceptable'. The final model must satisfy a number of desirable statistical properties, among which are an adequate explanation of the data within the sample period, a reasonable out of sample forecasting performance, and parameter stability. The model preferred by Hendry and Mizon is:

$$\Delta(m - p)_t = \underset{(0.65)}{1.60} + \underset{(0.09)}{0.21\Delta y_t} + \underset{(0.31)}{0.81\Delta r_t} + \underset{(0.12)}{0.26\Delta(m - p)_{t-1}}$$

$$- \underset{(0.15)}{0.40\Delta p_t} - \underset{(0.05)}{0.23(m - p - y)_{t-1}} - \underset{(0.21)}{0.61 r_{t-4}} + \underset{(0.04)}{0.14 y_{t-4}} \tag{5.57}$$

$$SE = 0.0091 \quad R^2 = 0.69 \quad \text{chi}^2(12) = 6.4$$

where the values in parentheses represent standard errors for the estimated coefficients.

This model has a reasonable fit, and shows no signs of residual autocorrelation from the Box–Pierce portmanteau statistic, $\text{chi}^2(12)$ for 12 lags. This equation is very different from that estimated by Hacche, and Hendry and Mizon (1978) show that the restrictions imposed by Hacche are not consistent with the data. It is argued, therefore, that the adoption of an untested, and unduly restrictive, dynamic model is not likely to lead to demand for money equations which remain stable over long periods of time.

One further interesting feature of dynamic models of the type shown in (5.57) is that they have a form which is readily interpretable in economic terms. The term $(m - p - y)_{t-1}$ in (5.57) represents an *error correction mechanism*, with the negative coefficient showing that, while the growth in real balances depends on the growth of prices and income, there is a correction for any divergence from an equilibrium static demand for money function, such as (5.51). Thus, this type of specification explicitly shows the short-run dynamics around a long-run 'equilibrium' demand for money function. Furthermore, equations of this type can be solved to obtain the long-run elasticities with respect to the independent variables.

This model selection procedure advocated by Hendry and Mizon (1978), and Hendry (1979), known as 'general to specific' (GTS), has been widely adopted in many spheres of applied economics where single equation estimation is seen as appropriate. The resulting models often embody an error correction mechanism of the type described above, and may be described as ECM models. In the case of the demand for money, this method has been remarkably successful in obtaining a stable demand function for M1 in the UK which also forecasts well (see Hendry 1979, 1985). In contrast, attempts to model the demand for the targeted aggregate £M3 have been notably less successful, and have required the addition of other variables to explain the large expansion in the money stock following the Competition and Credit Control episode, and the large post-1980 expansion. Grice and Bennett (1984) attempt to formulate a general dynamic model by incorporating a financial wealth variable, and expected capital gains. However, problems still remain in accurately forecasting these broad monetary aggregates in the UK.

In contrast, in the US, the greatest problems appear to lie in estimating a stable M1 equation, and M2 has proved more stable (see Laidler 1980). In particular, early attempts to develop successful ECM models for M1 failed (see Gordon 1984). More recent evidence (see, for example, Hendry 1985) suggests that the introduction of additional explanatory variables as well as the use of a general dynamic model may help in the estimation of a stable M1 function for the US.

It is interesting to note that the main difficulties have arisen in the estimation of *targeted* aggregates, in both the US and the UK. There are two possible (and related) reasons for this. First, the demand for targeted monetary aggregates proved stable during the 1960s when the determinants of the demand for money were less volatile. It seems likely that conventional demand for money theories are unable to explain the behaviour of the money stock during periods of greater economic upheaval such as that experienced in the 1970s and the 1980s. Second, estimated demand for money functions typically take the observed money stock as being equivalent to the demand for money, even though the short-run actual demand for money diverges from the long-run desired demand in dynamic models of the type described in equations (5.54), (5.55), (5.56), and (5.57). During periods of substantial monetary disturbance, it is argued that it is unreasonable to assume that the determinants of the demand for money will adjust immediately to equal the new level of the money stock. We now examine the way in which the theory of the demand for money has been modified to account for the recent experience in empirical modelling.

5.4.4. Disequilibrium in the Money Market and the 'Buffer Stock' Approach to the Demand for Money

As we have seen so far, traditional empirical models of the demand for money have ignored any independent role for the supply of money, with models such as (5.54) adopting the nominal money stock as the dependent variable, thus making the implicit assumption that the money supply adjusts endogenously to changes in income, the price level, or the interest rate. In such a model the money supply is demand determined, and money demand always equals money supply.

Laidler (1982, 1984) argues that this view of the money market runs counter to traditional monetarist analysis, which postulates that money supply changes are exogenous to the determinants of money demand, and that there are 'long and variable lags' in the transmission mechanism of monetary policy to nominal income. However, as Laidler points out, it is difficult to reconcile the concept of 'long and variable lags' with a model of the money market in which 'equilibrium' prevails at all times. This is clearly seen in the following argument: suppose the money stock is increased exogenously, but prices are sticky in the short run. If we impose the condition that money supply and demand be equal at all times, the slow adjustment in prices implies that the other determinants of the demand for money must adjust by more to compensate (notably the interest rate, as asset prices are usually assumed to be flexible). As a result, one would expect the interest rate to 'overshoot' its long-run value to compensate for price stickiness (as we shall see in Chapter 8, a similar argument applies in some exchange rate models). Since such interest rate overshooting is not apparent, Laidler concludes that the monetary transmission mechanism is more usefully described in terms of short-run disequilibrium: after a monetary shock, individuals find that their actual and desired money balances will diverge due to lags in the adjustment of money demand determinants.

However, this critique does not represent a total indictment of the models presented in the previous sections. First, partial adjustment models are in fact in line with Laidler's 'disequilibrium' approach in suggesting that short-run money holdings adjust gradually to their long-run desired values. However, partial adjustment models such as (5.54) are still open to the criticism that the lefthand side variable is the exogenous variable, though this criticism does not apply to models such as (5.55) and (5.57), where the lefthand side variable is the real money stock, which is clearly endogenous. Furthermore, the natural conclusion from Laidler's critique is that one should 'invert' the money demand equation, and model instead the way in which the determinants of money demand adjust to the exogenous money supply. However, this raises the problem of which variable should be chosen to be the dependent variable. Does one model a price equation, as Laidler's analysis seems to suggest, or an income, or even an interest rate equation (following Artis and Lewis 1976)? The alternative is to build a full simultaneous equation model which captures several channels of the transmission mechanism (see, for instance, Davidson 1985).

Thus, while recognising that Laidler's 'disequilibrium' approach provides an interesting rationalisation for the existence of lags in demand for money functions, it appears that equations such as (5.57) with real balances as the dependent variable, still represent a valid approach.

However, in addition to attacking the 'equilibrium' approach to the money market, Laidler (1984) also provides an interesting description of why the monetary transmission mechanism may be subject to 'long and variable lags'. This in turn has led to the development of the 'buffer stock approach' (BSA) to the demand for money. The BSA essentially argues that money fulfils a special role in the economic system (see Goodhart 1984). Due to the liquid nature of money assets, the costs of adjusting money holdings are typically less than the costs involved in changing one's holdings in real or illiquid financial assets. In an uncertain environment, economic agents are likely to adjust their portfolios only when they perceive changes in the economic environment to be permanent rather than transitory.

For example, consider an exogenous rise in the money supply. If this increase is perceived as permanent, then it will pay agents to adjust their portfolios. However, if agents expect the increase in the money stock to be reversed in the next time period, it would be costly for them to adjust their expenditures on real and financial assets and to reverse these decisions in the next period. As we shall see below, this results in a lag in the transmission mechanism, as an unexpected monetary shock leads to a gradual portfolio adjustment. Furthermore, the BSA is not limited to the case where the money stock is exogenous. Consider the case where economic agents find that their income has suddenly risen. Unless this change is perceived as permanent, they are unlikely to adjust their portfolio to augment their transactions balances.

The interesting aspect of the BSA is that it introduces the concept of forward looking expectations in the demand for money. Holdings of money are not only dependent upon a 'small number of economic variables', but also on expectations regarding both the likely evolution of the money supply and the determinants of the demand for money. Agents attempt to find their optimal holdings of money given that there are costs of adjustment involved in reallocating their portfolios.

Early studies on the BSA centred mainly on simple empirical models. For instance, Carr and Darby (1981) propose a model where 'unanticipated' changes in the supply of money lead to temporary changes in holdings of money, while anticipated changes in the money supply are entirely reflected in changes in the price level, and hence in an immediate adjustment of money holdings. Note that this type of model is very much in the tradition of the 'rational expectations' approach to monetary economics (see Chapter 3), and that the money supply is treated as entirely exogenous. In fact, a measure of 'anticipated money' in the Carr–Darby model is obtained by specifying a forecasting equation for the money stock in a similar way to that proposed by Barro (1977b) in the study discussed in Chapter 3. There are three main difficulties with the Carr–Darby model of the 'buffer stock'. First, there are econometric difficulties with their estimated model. MacKinnon and Milbourne (1984) propose an alternative estimation procedure for the Carr–Darby model, and suggest that the evidence does not confirm Carr and Darby's simple 'shock absorber' approach. Second, the Carr–Darby model is one which relies on a very simple 'shock absorbing' mechanism: anticipated changes in the money stock are *immediately* reflected in price changes, while unanticipated changes are not. There is no role for costs of adjustment, and no explicit microfoundations of the BSA are presented. Third, it concentrates on money supply shocks, thus ignoring expected changes in the money demand determinants.

Alternative 'buffer stock' models have been developed, which are of interest because they may explain the reason for the parameter instability in demand for money functions by means of the incorporation of forward looking behaviour. We now present a model of intertemporal optimisation, based on the work of Hall *et al.* (1984), Nickell (1985), and Cuthbertson (1985a, 1985b). Suppose that the *desired* demand for money M^* depends, conventionally, on price, real income, and the interest rate:

$$M_t^* = \alpha_0 + \alpha_1 y_t + \alpha_2 P_t + \alpha_3 r_t \tag{5.58}$$

Assume that the individual chooses his actual money holdings, M, so as to minimise the following intertemporal quadratic cost function:

$$C = \Sigma_{t=1}^{\infty} a(M_t - M_t^*)^2 + b(M_t - M_{t-1})^2 \tag{5.59}$$

This cost function measures both the costs of being away from equilibrium (the first bracketed term in (5.59)), and the costs of changing money holdings (the second bracketed term in (5.59)). The parameters a and b are the weights which the individual places on the costs of being away from equilibrium and the costs of adjusting money holdings. It may seem strange, at first sight, to assume that the individual finds it costly to adjust his money balances, given that it is money which is the financial 'buffer'. However, one can note that in a model with only money and one alternative asset, bonds, changes in money holdings must correspond to changes in bond holdings. To minimise this cost function, we have to assume that economic agents form expectations with regard to the future values of y, P, and r so that C becomes an expected cost function, and agents minimise expected costs subject to expectations at time $t - 1$. Effectively, the individual is assumed to use (5.59) so as to form an optimal plan for his money holdings over an infinite time horizon. (This problem is similar to that analysed in the new classical theories of the business cycle in Chapter 3, where firms and workers make an intertemporal labour supply and demand plan.)

The solution to the cost minimisation problem may be shown to lead to a second-order difference equation which describes the behaviour of money holdings over time (see Sargent 1979, Cuthbertson 1985a, 1985b). The optimal choice of money holdings is then found to be:

$$M_t = \mu M_{t-1} + \left(\frac{\mu}{1-\mu}\right)\left(\frac{a}{b}\right)\alpha_0 + \left(\frac{a}{b}\right)\mu\alpha_1 \Sigma_{i=0}^{\infty} (\mu)^i y_{t+i}^e$$

$$+ \left(\frac{a}{b}\right)\mu\alpha_2 \Sigma_{i=0}^{\infty} (\mu)^i P_{t+i}^e + \left(\frac{a}{b}\right)\mu\alpha_3 \Sigma_{i=0}^{\infty} (\mu)^i r_{t+i}^e \tag{5.60}$$

where μ is a coefficient which depends on a and b (it is the stable characteristic root of the difference equation mentioned above) and the superscript e denotes expectations. To develop this model further, it is necessary to make some assumption with regard to the way in which expectations are formed. Given that this is a forward looking model, it is natural to employ the rational expectations hypothesis. Thus (5.60) shows how economic agents will vary their current holdings of money in response to 'news' about the future evolution of nominal income. This model has been empirically tested for the demand for M1 in the UK by Cuthbertson (1985a) and Cuthbertson and Taylor (1987), using different forecasting methods to obtain estimates for expected variables. Equation (5.60) has some plausible theoretical features. Most important of all, it stresses the shock absorbing nature of money balances. Consider for example an *expected* future rise in P, y, or an expected future fall in r. This will have an immediate effect on present holdings of money, discounted by μ. (The reader will note the similarity between this model and the rational expectations models of fiscal policy and of exchange rates, outlined in Chapters 6 and 8 respectively.)

In contrast, an *unexpected* rise in y, P or fall in r will initially be reflected in a rise in money balances, except to the extent that they represent 'news' about a change in the process generating P, y and r, in which case the effect on holdings of money will again depend on the future expected values of these variables. Though this emphasises the endogenous nature of money holdings, the above approach may be easily modified to include the main feature of the Carr–Darby model where exogenous money shocks may occur. This may be done by defining the M in (5.60) above as an individual's planned holdings of money, M^p:

$$M_t^p = \mu M_{t-1} + \left(\frac{\mu}{1-\mu}\right)\left(\frac{a}{b}\right)\alpha_0 + \left(\frac{a}{b}\right)\mu\alpha_1 \Sigma_{i=0}^{\infty} (\mu)^i y_{t+i}^e$$

$$+ \left(\frac{a}{b}\right)\mu\alpha_2 \Sigma_{i=0}^{\infty} (\mu)^i P_{t+i}^e + \left(\frac{a}{b}\right)\mu\alpha_3 \Sigma_{i=0}^{\infty} (\mu)^i r_{t+i}^e \qquad (5.60')$$

and then adding a term, M^u to this equation to represent individuals' unplanned holdings of money:

$$M_t = M_t^p + M_t^u \qquad (5.61)$$

If there is an exogenous shock to the money supply, this may be interpreted as a rise in M^u, which is then slowly dissipated through the money demand function to price, income and interest rates, given that the rise in M leads to a revision of desired long-run money holdings from (5.58), and given the lag structure in (5.60) and (5.60'). Thus, this buffer stock approach has the advantage, compared to the simpler Carr–Darby model, of explicitly incorporating intertemporal costs into the individual's decision, which is shown to lead to a particular dynamic structure for the demand for money, while encompassing (in the theoretical sense) Carr and Darby's own shock absorbing mechanism, following a money supply shock.

These BSA equations tend to perform as well as the more conventional ECM dynamic equations. However, the fact that both 'forward looking' buffer stock models of the type described in (5.60) and 'backward looking' ECM models of the type described in (5.57) have been successful in explaining the behaviour of the demand for money is not surprising. The reason for this may be illustrated with a simple example, following Cuthbertson (1985a). Suppose, for simplicity, that α_0, α_2, and α_3 are set equal to zero in (5.58) and (5.60), and that expectations of y are generated using the following autoregressive forecasting equation:

$$y_t = \alpha_0 y_{t-1} + \alpha_1 y_{t-2} + u_t \tag{5.62}$$

By repeated substitution of (5.62) into (5.60) we obtain (see Cuthbertson 1985b):

$$\Delta M_t = (\mu - 1)M_{t-1} - \delta_1 \Delta y_t + (\delta_0 + \delta_1)y_t \tag{5.63}$$

which has a similar structure to the ECM models. It can also be formally shown that if agents are assumed to engage in an intertemporal optimisation exercise, and the explanatory variables of the behavioural relationship (in the case of money demand P, y and r) are assumed to follow a random walk, a simple ECM model is always obtained (see Nickell 1985, Hendry, Pagan and Sargan 1984). This problem in distinguishing between 'backward' and 'forward looking' models, known as *observational equivalence*, is common to the rational expectations literature, and has parallels in the Keynesian–new classical debate on the aggregate supply function (see Chapter 3).

Thus we have shown that our ECM models have some underlying theoretical justifications, and that they may not simply represent the sluggish adjustment of money demand through some backward looking, myopic adjustment, but may actually be the result of rational forward looking behaviour. Furthermore, the above argument may explain why the parameters in 'backward looking' demand for money equations such as (5.57) and (5.63) may be unstable. The δ_i in (5.63) are combinations of the parameters a and b in (5.60), and α_i in(5.62). Thus, if any of the costs of adjustment (a and b) change, or if a change in government policy causes a change in the behaviour of y (a change in α_i), then the parameters of the demand for money equations will vary. This is the well known Lucas (1976) critique, which argues that if agents form forward looking expectations, one may not expect structural equations to remain invariant across different policy periods. This indictment is not unique to ECM models, but applies to most econometric models particularly when employed for policy evaluation purposes, a point highlighted by Lucas. This point may be of supreme importance in the case of the demand for money, given the emphasis placed on monetary targeting in the 1970s and early 1980s.

However, there are two main criticisms of the simple BSA model presented here (i.e. equation (5.60)). First, it is not inconceivable that agents will conduct their intertemporal optimisation by taking into account their expectations of the government's future policies with regard to the money supply. Second, the assumption that individuals have only two assets to choose from, and that adjustments in money holdings correspond exactly to adjustments in bond holdings is a heroic one, and more complex models may be derived if it is relaxed (see Muscatelli 1986).

To summarise, the contribution of the BSA to the demand for money has been twofold: first, it has provided the theoretical underpinning for much empirical work on the demand for money since the late 1970s which could not easily be reconciled with traditional static demand for money theories. Second, it has led to some initial successes in the search for a stable demand for money function, particularly in suggesting different types of expectations generating mechanisms (see Cuthbertson and Taylor 1986) which to some extent circumvent the Lucas critique by explicitly modelling expectations. However, most applications so far have been on UK data for M1, and work still remains to be done on the demand for broad aggregates in the UK.

5.4.5. Conclusion

The results from empirical demand for money studies generally suggest that there is some long-run demand for money relationship. However, the short-run lags of adjustment appear to be variable, thus leading to problems in estimating a stable short-run demand for money function for targeted aggregates. This evidence has profound implications for the use of active monetary policy. First, even if the underlying long-run demand for money is stable, governments are unlikely to know the lags between changes in the money stock and prices and incomes, especially given the Lucas critique. Second, in the case where the authorities use the interest rate as their instrument of policy, and adopt a money supply target as an intermediate objective (see Chapter 9), the uncertain structural lags between money stock changes and variations in the final objectives may render the money stock less useful as an intermediate objective. This broadly reflects the experience of practical policy-making in the UK and the US in the 1970s, where increasingly greater attention has been directed to final targets of economic policy.

6
FISCAL POLICY AND AGGREGATE DEMAND

In this chapter, we examine how fiscal policy can influence aggregate demand, and we discuss some of the problems in assessing its likely impact in both the short and long run. In the first section, we review some familiar issues concerning the mechanism and measurement of fiscal policy within the framework of the IS–LM system. In section 2, we introduce the government's budget constraint and concentrate on the case of money-financed fiscal policy. In section 3, we examine the more contentious case of bond-financed fiscal policy, focusing on problems of portfolio equilibrium, long-run stability and the key question of whether government bonds may be regarded as net wealth. Finally, in section 4, we examine the implications of rational expectations for the analysis of fiscal policy.

6.1. Fiscal Policy in the Simple IS–LM Model

6.1.1. Fiscal Multipliers and Fiscal Stance

Fiscal policy may be defined as the manipulation of government expenditure and taxes for the purpose of influencing aggregate demand. As we have already seen in Chapter 1, in the simple IS–LM model, this is represented by shifts in the IS curve. To recapitulate that analysis, we present a simple closed economy linear IS–LM model (following Artis 1979):

$$c = c_0 + c_1(y - t) \tag{6.1}$$

$$t = t_0 + t_1 y \tag{6.2}$$

$$g = g_0 \tag{6.3}$$

$$i = i_0 - i_1 r \tag{6.4}$$

$$y = c + i + g \tag{6.5}$$

$$m = m_1 y - m_2 r \tag{6.6}$$

In the above model, all variables are expressed in real terms. Consumption (c) is a function of disposable income ($y - t$), with the marginal tax rate given as t_1. Government expenditure (g_0) is exogenous, while investment (i) is a negative function of the interest rate (r). Goods market equilibrium is given by (6.5) while money market equilibrium is given in conventional fashion in (6.6).

Full equilibrium, where both the goods and money markets clear, is given by:

$$y = \frac{e}{z + (i_1 m_1/m_2)} + \frac{m}{m_1 + (z m_2/i_1)} \tag{6.7}$$

where $e = c_0 - c_1 t_0 + i_0 + g_0$ and $z = 1 - c_1(1 - t_1)$.

Equation (6.7) is the algebraic form of the intersection of the IS and LM curves in Figure 6.1. Fiscal policy is to be regarded as shifting the IS curve. Thus, fiscal expansion, whether in the form of increases in the flow of government expenditure or reduced taxation, will shift the IS curve to the right, increasing aggregate demand. Clearly, the extent of the increase in aggregate demand for a given IS shift is dependent on the slopes of IS and LM, and we may note from Figure 6.1 that fiscal policy will be the more effective, the steeper is the IS curve and the flatter is the LM curve.

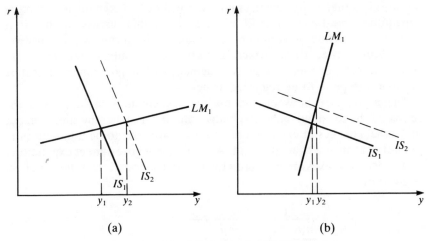

(a)   (b)

Figure 6.1 Fiscal Policy in the IS–LM Model

In Figure 6.1(a), we show what is sometimes referred to as the extreme Keynesian case, where the LM curve is flat and the IS curve is steep. A given rightward shift of IS representing expansionary fiscal policy is much more effective here than in the extreme monetarist case in Figure 6.1(b), where the LM curve is relatively steep and the IS curve is relatively flat. We may confirm this from (6.7) by noting that:

$$\frac{dy}{de}\left(=\frac{dy}{dg_0}\right) = \frac{1}{\dfrac{m_1 i_1}{m_2} + z} \tag{6.8}$$

and that dy/de is greater, the smaller is $m_1 i_1/m_2$. Thus, in this simple analysis, fiscal policy will be more effective the greater is the interest sensitivity of the demand for money, and the smaller is the interest sensitivity of investment and the income sensitivity of the demand for money.

However, it will be noted that government expenditure changes and tax changes are not equivalent in their effects on shifting the IS curve and therefore in affecting aggregate demand. While the government expenditure multiplier is given by $dy/dg = dy/de$, the taxation multiplier, for a given change in t_0 is given by $dy/dt_0 = -c_1/([m_1 i_1/m_2] + z)$. Thus, a given cut in exogenous taxes, while increasing aggregate demand, increases it by less than does an equal increase in government expenditure. The reason for this is simply that, whereas government expenditure is, in itself, a component of aggregate demand, changes in taxes only affect expenditure in so far as the changes in disposable income which they bring about affect aggregate consumption. Thus, tax changes affect aggregate demand through the 'filter' of the marginal propensity to consume. So long as this is less than unity, the tax multiplier will be less than the government expenditure multiplier. It will be clear from this discussion that it is essential to define government expenditure in terms of 'exhaustive' expenditures (i.e. those which absorb real resources and therefore constitute components of aggregate demand) while government transfers are more properly to be regarded as negative taxes.

The asymmetry between the tax and expenditure multipliers is the source of the so-called 'balanced budget multiplier', whereby simultaneous and equal changes in expenditure and taxes are seen to be non-neutral in their effects on aggregate demand. Assuming that government expenditure and exogenous taxes are increased by the same amount, then the net effect is given by:

$$\frac{dy}{dg_0} + \frac{dy}{dt_0} = \frac{1}{\dfrac{m_1 i_1}{m_2} + z} - \frac{c_1}{\dfrac{m_1 i_1}{m_2} + z}$$

Thus, a balanced increase in both government expenditure and taxes is net expansionary in its impact on aggregate demand.

6.1.2. The Endogeneity of the Budget and Problems of Measuring Fiscal Stance

The standard assumption in models such as that outlined in the previous section is that tax revenues are endogenous to income while government expenditure is not, and this means that the budget deficit $(g - t)$ is a negative function of income, which in turn raises the problem of how to interpret changes in the budget deficit as an indicator of fiscal policy. The problem is illustrated in Figure 6.2.

In Figure 6.2, we set out a simple exogenous government expenditure function together with a tax function whose slope reflects the marginal tax rate, t_1. Assume we start from an equilibrium level of income, y_1, which is associated with a balanced budget, and then government expenditure is increased from g_1 to g_2, which, via the multiplier relation set out in (6.8) increases the equilibrium level of income to, say, y_2. While the budget has gone into deficit, the size of the deficit is much smaller than the initial increase in government expenditure because of the endogenous increase in tax revenue resultant upon the increase in real income. The misleading character of the budget position as an indicator of fiscal stance is increased if the increase in government expenditure is reinforced by an increase in private sector expenditure which further increases income to, say, y_3. At this higher income level, tax receipts now exceed the increased level of government expenditure, and the budget has gone into surplus even though in terms of discrete policy actions, fiscal policy has been unambiguously expansionary. The problems of interpretation raised by the endogeneity of the budget position were recognised by Brown (1956), who

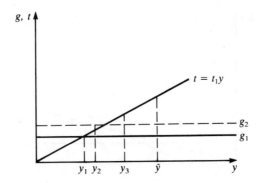

Figure 6.2 Fiscal Stance with Endogenous Taxes

proposed that fiscal stance be judged in terms of the budget position, not at the current level of national income, but rather at a predetermined income level. Conventionally, the level of income selected is the full employment level.

The 'full employment budget surplus' would be represented by the budget positon at $\bar{y}$ in Figure 6.2, and the increase in government expenditure leads to an unambiguous fall in the budget surplus measured in this manner, so providing a more accurate reflection of fiscal stance. In a simple model such as that set out here, this procedure seems to resolve the problems of measurement caused by endogenous tax revenues. However, in a more realistic analytical setting, the full employment budget surplus is not without its problems. (For a full discussion of the points raised below, see Shaw 1979.)

Even in the simple IS–LM model, the full employment budget surplus is deficient in so far as it does not distinguish between changes in the budget position arising out of tax changes and those arising out of expenditure changes. It will be clear from the discussion in the earlier subsection that an increase in the (full employment) budget surplus arising out of tax increases will be less contractionary than an equal increase in the surplus due to expenditure cuts. Therefore, it has been suggested that the full employment budget surplus be 'weighted' to take account of this. Another problem arises when the tax or expenditure change is associated with a change in the slope of the relevant function. For example, how are we to interpret an increase in the full employment budget surplus stemming from an increase in the progressivity of the tax function which, nevertheless) leaves the budget deficit at the current income level unaltered? Such a case is illustrated in Figure 6.3. An alternative example would be a cut in unemployment benefit, since this would increase the budget deficit to a greater extent at lower levels of national income (and employment) than at full employment.

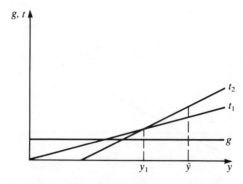

Figure 6.3 Fiscal Stance with Changing Tax Rates

Once we relax the fix-price assumption of the IS–LM model, further difficulties appear, in the form of fiscal drag (increases in the real tax yield due to a progressive tax structure denominated in nominal terms), and the selection of the appropriate price index to apply to full employment (as compared with current) income. In addition, once the macromodel is more fully specified, a whole range of adjustments may be suggested, including those designed to take account of the differential effects of various taxes on the price level (and therefore interest rates) and the distribution of income (and therefore consumption), together with the impact of different categories of government expenditure on aggregate demand and the balance of payments. Clearly, beyond a certain level of disaggregation, general measures of fiscal stance give way to measures which may be more rigorous but which are also highly model-specific. Thus, the development of large econometric models has replaced single measures of fiscal stance in assessing the impact of fiscal policy on aggregate demand.

Associated with the increasing tendency to set the measurement of fiscal policy within a wider framework has been the recognition of the ongoing financial consequences of fiscal deficits/surpluses. Indeed, many economists, especially monetarists, see these implications as being central to the analysis of the effects of fiscal actions on aggregate demand. It is to these crucial interrelationships between fiscal policy and monetary policy that we now turn in the next section.

6.2. Money-Financed Fiscal Policy

We have already encountered the macroeconomic budget constraint in Chapter 1 and Chapter 5. At its most general level, it expresses the accounting identity that transactions between the private sector on the one hand, and the government and overseas sectors on the other, must be reflected in changes in private sector holdings of financial assets. The integration of this fundamental identity in its various forms into macro-economic models has generated interesting results, particularly in drawing attention to the distinction between short-run flow equilibrium (a characteristic focus of many Keynesian models) and long-run stock equilibrium. This distinction is of vital significance to open economy macroeconomics, as we shall see in the chapters which follow; but in this chapter, we examine the implications of the budget identity for the analysis of fiscal policy.

It will be recalled from Chapter 5 that the budget identity may be given the following general form:

$$\Delta H \equiv PSD - \Delta PrLG + \Delta F \tag{6.9}$$

To facilitate the discussion in this chapter, we make the following amendments to (6.9). First, we assume there is no banking system since this makes no substantive difference to the analysis and it enables us to equate monetary base (H) with the total money stock (M). Second, we equate the public sector deficit (PSD) with the budget deficit $(G - T)$, recognising that this skims over a number of accounting problems of measurement, but again at little cost to the present analysis. Third, we assume that private sector lending to the government $(PrLG)$ consists entirely of the purchase of government bonds by the private sector (ΔB). Finally, and much more significantly, we assume a closed economy, which enables us to remove the balance of payments, in the form of the change in foreign exchange reserves (ΔF) from the identity, and we postpone discussion of the open economy aspects of fiscal policy to Chapter 7.

Thus, we may rewrite (6.9) as:

$$\Delta M \equiv G - T - \Delta B$$

which may be re-arranged as

$$G - T \equiv \Delta M + \Delta B \tag{6.9'}$$

Thus, the government's budget deficit may be financed in a closed economy either by increasing the money stock, or by increasing the private sector's holdings of government bonds. It is this necessary accounting relationship which ensures that monetary and fiscal policies cannot be regarded as entirely independent policy instruments. In this section, we restrict our attention to the case of money-financed fiscal policy. (For early examples of the type of analysis set out here, see Ott and Ott 1965, Christ 1967, 1968, and Silber 1970.)

Starting from a balanced budget, we may illustrate the consequences of a money-financed increase in government expenditure with reference to an extended version (following Artis 1979) of the familiar IS–LM diagram, as in Figure 6.4. While the top quadrant contains the familiar IS–LM apparatus, we set out the government's budget schedules in the lower quadrant, with taxes as a positive function of real income. An increase in government expenditure shifts the IS curve from IS_1 to IS_2, increasing income and the interest rate to y_2 and r_2 respectively. At this income level, however, there is now a budget deficit equal to RS, which, given our assumption that the deficit is money-financed, must have the consequence of shifting the LM curve to the right, further increasing the level of income.

At this point, we encounter the stock–flow interaction which is crucial in analysing the financial asset consequences of fiscal policy. The fiscal deficit (incorporated in the position of the IS curve) is a *flow* magnitude which has to be financed over time, while the financial assets which are issued to

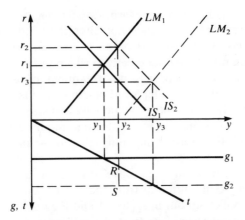

Figure 6.4 Money-Financed Fiscal Expansion

finance it are *stocks* which, as they are increased, shift the position of the LM curve. Therefore, although the increase in government expenditure generates a *once-for-all* shift in the IS curve, the increases in the money stock which finance it continue to shift the LM curve so long as the deficit finance continues. Thus, while the IS curve stays at its new position, IS_2, the LM curve continues to shift to the right so long as the deficit persists.

In the light of this, y_2 cannot be regarded as the long-run equilibrium level of income. Rather the money stock will continue to increase until the income level has risen by enough to generate the additional tax revenue to bring the budget back into balance. As may be seen from the lower quadrant, this is achieved at y_3.

Four final points may be noted about this analysis. First, wealth effects may be incorporated into the story without seriously amending the outcome. It will be recalled from Chapter 1 that wealth effects may operate on the LM curve as increases in the wealth stock increase the demand for money, and on the IS curve through wealth effects on consumption. In the case of money-financed fiscal expansion in Figure 6.4, the rightward shift of the LM curve would be dampened, but not reversed, by wealth effects on the demand for money, but the adjustment to long-run equilibrium at y_3 would be reinforced by rightward shifts in the IS curve, reflecting wealth effects on consumption. The final equilibrium would only be affected in that the long-run equilibrium interest rate might be higher than r_3.

Second, in the open economy case, not analysed here, the budget need not be balanced in full equilibrium, if the authorities are prepared to run a balance of payments deficit, the selling of foreign exchange reserves contributing to the financing of the budget. It is possible to include the balance of payments in the model, so that in full equilibrium, a fiscal deficit is financed by an external deficit; these are matters to which we turn in the next chapter.

Third, the inclusion of an upward sloping aggregate supply curve complicates the analysis, but does not alter the nature of the results. Clearly, the effects of fiscal expansion on real income are dampened, via Keynes and Pigou effects, by the extent to which the price level rises; but a more untidy problem concerns the treatment of endogenous fiscal revenues under conditions of inflation. For example, the existence of fiscal drag will have the effect of making the tax function steeper (with respect to real income), reducing the rise in real income required to attain budgetary balance, and therefore dampening the long-run impact of fiscal policy.

Finally, it is clear from the above discussion that long-run fiscal multipliers are markedly different from their short-run counterparts. The analysis of fiscal policy set out in section 1 and Figure 6.1 can be regarded at best as focusing on the impact effects of fiscal expansion. Short-run flow equilibrium does not equate with long-run stock equilibrium which, in a closed economy, now clear, can only obtain when the budget is balanced. Consequently, long-run equilibrium is obtained once income levels have changed so as to generate changes in tax revenues sufficient to restore budgetary balance. In fact, this makes the calculation of the long-run government expenditure multiplier a remarkably straightforward matter. Since in long-run equilibrium, the budget must be balanced, we may write: $dg = dt$ and $dt = t_1 dy$ then

$$\frac{dy}{dg} = \frac{1}{t_1}$$

In other words, the long-run fiscal multiplier necessarily equals the reciprocal of the marginal rate of tax. A given increase in government expenditure must generate enough tax revenue to balance the budget in the long run, and it is the expansionary monetary implications of the initial deficit which ensures that this is achieved. However, it is clear from the budget identity that money finance is not the only option open to the authorities, and we examine the implications of the alternative regime, of bond finance, in the next section.

6.3.   Bond-Financed Fiscal Policy

6.3.1.   'Pure' Fiscal Policy and the Question of Crowding-Out

The central importance of the government's budget constraint lies in the recognition of the financial consequences of fiscal actions. Again assuming a closed economy, we may note from (6.9′) that unless fiscal expansion, in the form of an increase in the budget deficit, is financed by selling bonds, then fiscal policy will be reinforced by monetary policy in the form of increases in the money stock. Monetary policy and fiscal policy may then be seen as operating hand in hand. This would appear to be the appropriate financing regime for a government wishing to exert the strongest expansionary impact on aggregate demand. Yet the attention of the economics profession has been focused much more sharply on the alternative financing regime — that of bond finance. There are several explanations for this preoccupation. First, the economics of bond-financed expenditures still need to be analysed since the consequences of a given level of government expenditure will be dependent on the money–bonds mix; in reality deficits are rarely entirely money-financed. Second, it is in any case not at all clear, as we shall see, that money-financed expenditures are, in fact, unambiguously more expansionary, especially in the long run. Finally, in the context of the discussion between monetarists and Keynesians on the relative efficacy of monetary policy compared to fiscal policy, starting with Friedman and Meiselman (1963), and then continuing through the debate about the contribution of the St Louis school (see, for example, Andersen and Jordan 1968, Andersen and Carlson 1970, Ando and Modigliani 1976), the most meaningful comparison is that between monetary policy and 'pure' fiscal policy, defined as fiscal actions unaccompanied by any changes in the money stock. Setting aside the question of tax-financed expenditure, which relies on the balanced budget multiplier for its impact, we therefore focus on bond-financed fiscal actions.

The hard line monetarist contention about bond-financed increases in government expenditure is that they must be ineffective, since they leave the money stock unaltered. For this to be the case, the increase in government expenditure must be accompanied by an equal reduction in private sector expenditure to leave aggregate demand unchanged. In other words, the increase in government expenditure 'crowds out' private expenditure. The mechanism whereby this crowding-out might occur has become the central question in the analysis of bond-financed fiscal policy. (For a full taxonomy of crowding-out theories, see Buiter 1977.)

To define our area of interest in this debate, we may at the outset dispose of two suggested mechanisms for crowding-out, one of which relies on extreme assumptions of rationality, while the other is unexceptionable. The first is the so-called ultra-rationality hypothesis (see David and Scadding 1974), whereby public expenditures are seen as direct substitutes for private sector expenditure. Thus, if public sector expenditure is perceived by the private sector to be meeting needs on behalf of the private sector, then increased public investment, say, may be automatically matched by increased private sector saving. Crowding-out which is brought about in this manner is essentially voluntary, and requires no relative price or wealth effects to generate it. While this argument can certainly be put forward in the case of certain categories of government expenditure (e.g. public utilities), it is difficult to render it credible for government expenditure in the aggregate. In addition, it might be argued that in some cases, public and private expenditures may be regarded as complements (for example, public provision of infrastructure may induce private sector investment), and this could cause 'crowding-in'.

The second crowding-out mechanism works through the general price level, and the Keynes and Pigou effects outlined in Chapter 1. Quite simply, if the increase in government expenditure generates a rise in prices, then the real money stock is reduced, increasing interest rates and reducing wealth, both of which tend to reduce private expenditure. For complete crowding-out to take place through this mechanism, however, the aggregate supply curve must be vertical, that is, the economy must be at full employment. It is clearly not in dispute that an increase in real government expenditure at full employment must be associated with a fall in real private expenditure. In short, the debate about crowding-out can only take place meaningfully at less than full employment. In what follows, therefore, we set out the debate on crowding-out in fix-price terms, employing the IS–LM model.

The third general set of crowding-out mechanisms focuses on the wealth and interest rate consequences of bond-financed expenditure, and on how these consequences might affect private sector demand. (We may also include exchange rate effects within this category, but we postpone discussion of this important mechanism until Chapter 8.) Let us first examine the simplest specification of the question.

In Figure 6.5, we start from IS_1 and LM_1, with income determined at y_1. Suppose we now increase the flow of government expenditure, such that the IS curve shifts to IS_2. It is clear that income will increase to y_2 but is this a position of long-run equilibrium? It could be argued that it is, since under a regime of bond-financing the money stock is not changing, and therefore

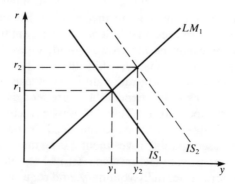

Figure 6.5   'Hicksian' Crowding-Out

the LM curve is stationary. If this is accepted, then it is clear that the extent of crowding-out will be determined by the familiar empirical issue of the relative slopes of IS and LM. This rather limited analysis has been labelled, perhaps somewhat unfairly, 'Hicksian crowding-out'. In this case, the monetarist result of 100 per cent crowding-out obtains only when the extreme assumption of a vertical LM curve is applied.

However, this analysis, apart from recognising that the money stock is unaltered by bond-financed fiscal policy, makes no reference to the government's budget constraint. In fact, private sector holdings of government bonds are increasing as long as the deficit persists, and it is certainly wrong to identify the slope of the LM curve as describing the interest rate consequences of this bond finance. In the simple analysis of Figure 6.5, the increase in the interest rate from r_1 to r_2 has nothing directly to do with the requirement of the government to induce the private sector to buy bonds. Rather, it only reflects the interest cost of increasing the stock of transactions money balances out of asset money balances. In order to incorporate the long-run implications of the increasing bond stock into the analysis, the simple IS–LM model must be extended to take into account wealth effects.

6.3.2. *Crowding-Out and the Role of Wealth and Portfolio Effects*

As we have already noted, wealth may play a role in both the goods and money markets in the IS–LM model. An increase in the bond stock, therefore, has two sets of effects. On the one hand, as the bond stock is increased, with a given money stock the interest rate must rise to preserve portfolio equilibrium, and this may be expressed as a leftward shift in the LM curve. On the other hand, the increasing bond stock increases aggregate demand through a wealth effect on consumption, shifting the IS curve to the right. In the light of these two effects, how is the IS–LM analysis of bond-financed government expenditure to be amended? This question was tackled in a seminal paper by Blinder and Solow (1973), and we set out the main lines of their analysis in Figure 6.6. The flow impact of the increased government expenditure is retained, shifting the IS curve to IS_2. This once-for-all shift is, however, ultimately swamped in the longer run by the two sets of wealth effects which stem from the increasing bond stock as the deficit persists. The LM curve drifts to the left and the IS curve to the right, with the interest rate increasing continuously, but with ambiguous consequences for real income. If the wealth effect on expenditure outweighs that on the demand for money, then the long-run consequences of bond-financed fiscal expansion are indeed expansionary. On the other hand, if the wealth effect on the demand for money prevails, then although the immediate impact of the policy will be expansionary, the

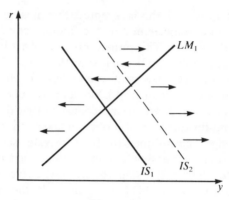

Figure 6.6

longer-run consequences will be negative. (A similar general result is obtained by Stein 1976.)

This is not the end of the story, however, since we still have to take into account the behaviour of the fiscal deficit in the face of these effects. As we noted in the previous section, as long as the fiscal deficit is non-zero, asset stocks continue to change, but as incomes rise, the fiscal deficit will be removed by the endogenous growth in tax revenues. Thus, with reference to Figure 6.6, in the case where the wealth effect on expenditure prevails, and income levels rise in the longer run, the fiscal deficit will be removed at a higher income level which is the long-run equilibrium of the model. This is a parallel result to that obtained in the money-financed case, even to the extent that in both cases the long-run fiscal multiplier is given by the reciprocal of the marginal tax rate, a result to which we return below. In the case where the wealth effect on the demand for money prevails, however, the model is unstable, since as the deficit induces a fall in the level of income, tax revenues fall as incomes fall, increasing the deficit and therefore the flow of bonds into private sector portfolios, and therefore driving the economy further into contraction. The peculiarity of this result tends to encourage the belief that the relative strength of the wealth effects is in favour of expansion.

A number of additional points may be noted from this analysis. First, it is extremely difficult to obtain the classic monetarist result of 100 per cent crowding-out from this model. This requires not only that the initial increase in government expenditure has no net impact on real income, but also that the ensuing structure of wealth effects is neutral (that is, the IS and LM shifts are exactly offsetting). This serves to demonstrate that the IS–LM model provides an uncomfortable vehicle for monetarist analysis.

Second, thus far we have ignored the fact that the outstanding stock of government bonds carries with it service costs in the form of coupon payments. Since coupon payments contribute to the fiscal deficit, the increasing stock of bonds must itself add to the deficit. On the assumption that other components of government expenditure are not reduced to offset the burden of these coupon payments, then this has two implications for our earlier analysis. First, on the assumption that the model is stable (i.e. that the wealth effects on IS outweigh those on LM), then coupon payments serve to make bond-financed expenditure *more* expansionary than money-financed expenditure. The reason for this somewhat bizarre result is that as the bond stock increases with the ongoing deficit, the deficit itself is reinforced by interest payments by the government. Such a reinforcing effect is, of course, absent in the case of money-financed expenditure. The second implication of the 'coupon effect' is that it introduces the possibility of instability in an expansionary direction, since it is conceivable that the relative strength of the two wealth effects may be such that bond-financed expenditure is expansionary, but only weakly so, such that as income rises, tax revenues rise less fast than debt service costs so that the deficit is never closed and income rises without limit.

Third, the Blinder–Solow analysis is based on the assumption that the government bonds which are issued to finance the expenditure constitute net wealth to the private sector. This is a matter which has aroused some debate and revived discussion of what has become known as the 'Ricardian debt equivalence theorem' (see Buchanan 1976). Put most simply, the Ricardian equivalence theorem states that the burden of government expenditure on the private sector is the same whether it is financed by taxation or by selling interest-bearing debt to the private sector. Borrowing is equivalent to levying taxes. This is because the sale of the bond today carries with it the obligation to pay interest (and ultimately the capital, if the bond is not a perpetuity), which in turn implies a future tax liability. If individuals take into account this future tax liability, then they will not regard the bond as net wealth. (An elegant exposition of this argument has been presented by Barro 1974.) In that case, the wealth effects on expenditure which make bond-financed expenditure potentially expansionary in the long run in the Blinder–Solow model are no longer operative.

Three main arguments have been levelled against the Ricardian equivalence theorem. First, the future tax liability implied by the current issue of the bond may fall on a future generation, leaving the present generation wealthier. However, Barro argues that in a model where the present generation bequeaths wealth to the succeeding generation, the future tax liability will still be relevant to the present generation. The argument is that the very existence of bequests implies that the present generation takes into account the utility of its children, and therefore an expected tax liability on the children will induce the present generation to increase its bequest accordingly, thus saving more and consuming less. The wealth effect of the bond issue is therefore nullified. A number of objections have been raised against this argument (see, for example, Tobin 1980). Not all parents will be so far-sighted (or even so selfless) as to take into account their children's expected tax liabilities. Indeed, not everyone is a parent. In addition, it may be that the utility of bequests to the parent stems simply from the act of bequeathing rather than in carefully taking into account the utility of the receivers. (For a detailed discussion of the implications of adopting different time horizons in the analysis of fiscal policy, see Blanchard 1985.)

A second argument in favour of regarding government bonds as net wealth is that the rate of interest paid on the bond, which determines the size of the future tax liability, may be less than the rate of discount relevant to the private sector when calculating the present value of the tax liability. This might reflect the fact that the government's access to capital markets is more favourable than that of the individual. Under these circumstances, bond-financed expenditures (or tax cuts) effectively increase private sector wealth.

Finally, the Ricardian debt equivalence theorem assumes that the relevant future taxes are lump-sum taxes. The relaxation of this assumption opens the door for tax avoiding behaviour by the private sector. For example, anticipated future taxes on wealth will clearly discourage current saving, and therefore, bond-financed fiscal expansion will tend to increase current consumption.

For all these reasons, then, the debt equivalence theorem is regarded by many economists as a 'theoretical curiosum' (Buiter 1985), and, to the extent that wealth effects on expenditure are indeed significant, increases in the stock of government debt are an important element in the longer-run transmission mechanism of fiscal policy.

Before concluding this section, we may introduce a final argument for supposing that bond-financed fiscal policy is likely to be expansionary. The portfolio effects on the LM curve, which are potentially contractionary, operate through the simple money-bonds portfolio of the IS–LM model. However, as we saw in Chapter 5, this is equivalent to regarding bonds and real capital (or equity) as perfect substitutes (see Metzler 1951 and Tobin 1961). If we now relax this assumption and allow money, bonds and real capital to be gross substitutes, and assign to the rate of return on equity (or, alternatively, Tobin's 'q') the key role of determining private sector investment, then the portfolio consequences of increasing the stock of government bonds may be either expansionary or contractionary. More particularly, if government bonds are closer substitutes for money than for equity, and the share of equity in the portfolio is large relative to that of money, then increasing the bond stock will bid down the rate of return on equity (bid up q), and therefore encourage private sector investment (see Chapter 5 for a detailed discussion of this point). Under these circumstances, bond-financed expenditure is expansionary irrespective of the wealth effect on expenditure. Instead of crowding-out, we may have 'crowding-in' (see B. M. Friedman 1978b).

6.4. Fiscal Policy and Expectations

So far in this chapter the analysis of fiscal policy has been conducted in terms of the simple IS–LM model, which does not contain expectational variables. In practice, however, there are a number of ways in which households' and firms' expectations of *future* fiscal policy may have effects on *current* aggregate demand. As we shall see in this section, allowing for such expectations effects has implications for the accurate measurement of fiscal stance, and for the predictability of fiscal policy's influence on aggregate demand. As a corollary, familiar from Chapter 3, this also implies that fiscal actions will have different effects depending on whether they are anticipated or unanticipated. We shall concentrate our attention on two examples of the role of fiscal expectations in the determination of output, the first focusing on current consumption behaviour and wealth effects, and the second on portfolio effects and investment expenditure. In order to make the analysis tractable, we treat these two examples separately, and for similar reasons we do not incorporate the more rigorous implications of the budget identity treated in the previous section.

6.4.1. Fiscal Policy, Expectations and Consumption Expenditure

The link between expectations and consumption expenditure has been stressed on numerous occasions by both Keynesian and neoclassical economists. The permanent income and life-cycle hypotheses of consumption behaviour of Friedman (1957) and Modigliani and Brumberg (1954) were based on the link between consumer expenditure and wealth. In these models consumers form a view of their current wealth on the basis of their expectations of their income over their lifetime (or a shorter time horizon). While initial attempts at modelling expectations of future income levels were based mainly on the adaptive expectations hypothesis (see, for example Friedman 1957), recently there have been attempts to allow for forward looking expectations through the application of the rational expectations hypothesis to the theory of consumption (see, for example Hall 1978, Flavin 1981, Begg 1982). In this section we show that, if consumers base their consumption decisions on wealth and have forward looking expectations (even with very short time horizons), then current consumer expenditure and income will be affected by expected future fiscal policies.

We begin by defining consumers' current wealth, W_t, as the present value of future disposable income flows (Y_{t+i}^d) over the time horizon N. The length of the time horizon may reflect individuals' expected lifespan, or alternatively, may be assumed to be infinite, as in the case of Friedman's (1957) permanent income hypothesis. For simplicity, this definition ignores consumers' past accumulated wealth:

$$W_t = \Sigma_{i=0}^{N} Y_{t+i}^d (1 + r)^{-i} \qquad (6.10)$$

where r is the rate of interest, and disposable income is found by subtracting taxation from current income:

$$Y_t^d = Y_t - T_t \qquad (6.11)$$

Note that we have assumed that all taxation is of a lump-sum variety, avoiding the complication of income-related taxes. This does not affect our results. We assume, for simplicity, that current consumption, C_t, depends only on current wealth, W_t:

$$C_t = \alpha W_t \qquad (6.12)$$

Equation (6.12), though simple, captures the essence of the modern theories of consumption referred to above. To complete the model, we specify a conventional IS relation:

$$Y_t = C_t + I_t + G_t \qquad (6.13)$$

and we assume that the interest rate and price level are fixed exogenously, thus restricting our attention to the goods market.

Note that, though current consumption and hence current income depend on current wealth, the latter depends on consumers' expectations of their future disposable incomes. To render our analysis more tractable, we make the extreme assumption that consumers' time horizon N in (6.10) is equal to 1. While this apparently reduces the forward looking nature of the model, as we shall see below this short horizon is still sufficient for our simple expenditure model to yield some significant results. Setting $N = 1$ in (6.10), and substituting for W_t into (6.12), we obtain:

$$C_t = \alpha(Y_t - T_t) + \frac{\alpha}{1 + r}(Y_{t+1}^e - T_{t+1}^e) \qquad (6.14)$$

where the superscript e denotes the expected value of the variable concerned. Thus current consumption depends on disposable income in the current and subsequent time periods. Subsituting (6.14) into (6.13), we obtain:

$$Y_t = \alpha(Y_t - T_t) + \frac{\alpha}{1 + r}(Y_{t+1}^e - T_{t+1}^e) + I_t + G_t$$

and, solving for Y_t:

$$Y_t = \frac{(I_t + G_t)}{(1 - \alpha)} - \frac{\alpha T_t}{(1 - \alpha)} + \frac{\alpha}{(1 - \alpha)(1 + r)}(Y_{t+1}^e - T_{t+1}^e) \qquad (6.15)$$

This type of 'forward looking' difference equation may be solved by repeated substitution of the lead income variables, Y_{t+i}^e. For instance, by leading all variables in (6.15) by one period we obtain:

$$Y_{t+1}^e = \frac{(I_{t+1}^e + G_{t+1}^e)}{(1 - \alpha)} - \frac{\alpha T_{t+1}^e}{(1 - \alpha)} + \frac{\alpha}{(1 - \alpha)(1 + r)}(Y_{t+2}^e - T_{t+2}^e)$$

$$(6.15')$$

and a similar operation may be performed on (6.15') to obtain an expression for Y_{t+2}^e, and so on. By repeated substitution of Y_{t+1}^e, $Y_{t+2}^e, \ldots$ into (6.15), we eliminate all future values of income and obtain the following expression for current income:

$$Y_t = \frac{1}{(1 - \alpha)}\Sigma_{i=0}^{\infty} \left(\frac{\alpha}{(1 + r)(1 - \alpha)}\right)^i I_{t+i}^e \qquad (6.16)$$

$$+ \frac{1}{(1 - \alpha)}\Sigma_{i=0}^{\infty} \left(\frac{\alpha}{(1 + r)(1 - \alpha)}\right)^i G_{t+i}^e$$

$$- \left(\frac{\alpha}{(1 - \alpha)}\right) T_t - \left(\left(\frac{\alpha}{(1 - \alpha)}\right) + 1\right) \Sigma_{i=1}^{\infty} \left(\frac{\alpha}{(1 + r)(1 - \alpha)}\right)^i T_{t+i}^e$$

The essence of this rather daunting result is that current income depends not only on current investment, government expenditure and taxation, as in the standard IS–LM model, but also on all future values of these variables. This implies that individuals' expectations of these variables will affect their perceptions of future income, and hence *current* wealth. It is unimportant for the purposes of this model that current wealth depends at most on next period's income, Y_{t+1}, since Y_{t+1} depends on W_{t+1}, which depends on Y_{t+2}, and so on, *ad infinitum*. Even a short intertemporal link may have important implications for the determination of current income. This is one of the main conclusions resulting from the adoption of forward looking expectations, as we saw in Chapter 3.

As a result, current consumption and income will react to 'news' about future government fiscal policy, through the terms G^e_{t+i} and T^e_{t+i} in (6.16). We may analyse these effects with the aid of Figure 6.7. In Figure 6.7(a) we examine the effect on current income of an unanticipated permanent increase in government spending (or cut in taxation) at time t_0. Assuming that the system was in equilibrium at Y_0 before the shock, the income level will immediately rise to its new equilibrium level, Y_1 in response to the unanticipated shock. The instant the shock has taken place, consumers perceive it to be permanent, and incorporate the effect into their expectations of future incomes and current wealth. Given that there are no *structural* lags in the system, the adjustment is immediate. This result is analogous to the consequences of an unanticipated permanent rise in aggregate demand in the new classical model of Chapter 3 (see Figure 3.8), where the price level immediately 'jumps' to its new equilibrium level.

Let us now turn to the case where changes in fiscal policy have not yet been implemented, but consumers perceive such changes in advance. In Figure 6.7(b) we assume that consumers perceive at time t_0 that at some future time t_1 the government will increase government spending or decrease taxation, so as to carry the economy to a higher level of income y_1, as in the case of Figure 6.7(a). In reality such announcements of future fiscal plans are not uncommon. From (6.16) it will be apparent that if consumers predict such a fiscal shock at some future date, there will be an impact (or 'announcement') effect, as individuals evaluate the consequences of the shock for future incomes and current wealth. However, such impact effects will not immediately carry the economy to its new equilibrium, since between t_0 and t_1 government fiscal policy will remain unaltered, and households will discount the future fiscal change at

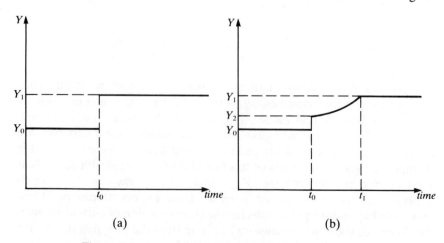

Figure 6.7   Unanticipated and Anticipated Fiscal Shocks

the current interest rate. Thus in terms of Figure 6.7(b), income at t_0 suddenly rises to some intermediate value y_2, which depends on the value of α and the discount rate, r. Income will then gradually rise until at the time when the fiscal policy is implemented, t_1, the system will reach its new equilibrium, y_1. The idea here is that if individuals are forward looking, and anticipate future policy changes, they will act so as to carry the economy to its new equilibrium at the time when the new policy comes into force: they will not be caught unawares at time t_1.

The above analysis might be regarded as being incomplete in that it focuses on only the expenditure wealth effects of fiscal policy. As we have seen earlier in this chapter, fiscal actions also have implications for financial markets, and in the above model, the interest rate is treated as exogenous with respect to fiscal actions. We now take account of this by considering how forward looking fiscal expectations affect investment, through a portfolio mechanism, following Blanchard (1981).

6.4.2. *Fiscal Policy, Expectations and Investment Expenditure*

Blanchard (1981) constructs a model which extends IS–LM analysis in two important ways. First, output is assumed to adjust to expenditure with a lag, so that the model adjusts sluggishly to IS equilibrium. Second, investment is assumed to depend positively on 'q', the ratio of the stock market value of capital to its replacement cost, following Tobin (1969) (see Chapter 5 for a detailed exposition of Tobin's 'q' theory of investment). As a result, expectations of future stock market prices will affect current investment, and this provides the crucial link between future fiscal policy and current investment.

We begin by setting out a conventional definition of real aggregate expenditure, d:

$$d = \alpha q + \beta y + g \tag{6.17}$$

where y is real income, and g represents an index of government expenditure. All the variables in this model are written in logarithms. The αq term represents the effect on investment of 'q', and βy the influence of income on consumption. For simplicity, we assume that all changes in fiscal policy in this model are due to changes in the balanced budget, enabling us to avoid the complications of bond finance outlined in the previous section. Furthermore, the price level is assumed fixed. Thus, an increase in g represents an equal increase in both total government expenditure and total taxation. Since we assume that real output adjusts to a change in expenditure with a lag, then in the short run firms will alter their inventories to cope with changes in demand:

$$\dot{y} = \sigma(d - y) \tag{6.18}$$

Simplifying Blanchard's treatment of asset markets, we assume that portfolio holders allocate their wealth between money, bonds, and equity. Furthermore, we assume that bonds and equity are perfect substitutes. Thus, we only need the demand for money equation to characterise the portfolio decision, and we may write down a conventional LM relationship:

$$m = \delta y - \lambda r_b \tag{6.19}$$

where r_b and m are the interest rate on bonds and the real money stock respectively. To complete the model, we need to specify a relationship between q and r_b. Given that bonds and equities are perfect substitutes, the rates of return on these two assets must be equal. Recall from Chapter 5 that the yield on capital, r_k is given by the ratio of the return on capital to the market value of equity (see (5.37) in Chapter 5). We follow Blanchard in assuming that firms' profits, c, and hence returns on capital, depend on current output:

$$c = \gamma_0 + \gamma_1 y \tag{6.20}$$

As a result, the rate of return on holding equity is given by the ratio of current profits to q (reflecting the return on capital), plus any expected capital gains due to a change in q, i.e. $(c - q + \dot{q}^e)$, where again all the variables are in logarithms. The capital gains term is necessary in this model since, while in Chapter 5 we made the simplifying assumption that future profits and returns were fixed for all time, profits are now a function of output, and hence expectations of future output changes will cause investors to re-evaluate the present value of their equity, given the implied future rise in dividends.

We therefore complete the model by specifying the equality of the rates of return on bonds and capital, due to the assumption of perfect substitutability:

$$r_b = (c - q + \dot{q}^e) \tag{6.21}$$

The model has two dynamic variables, of which one, $\dot{q}^e$, is an expectational variable. We assume that individuals have perfect foresight (rational expectations), so that $\dot{q}^e = \dot{q}$. Substituting for d from (6.17) into (6.18), and for r_b and c from (6.19) and (6.20) into (6.21), the model reduces to the following two dynamic equations:

$$\dot{y} = \sigma(\alpha q + (\beta-1)y + g) \qquad (6.22)$$

$$\dot{q}^e = q + \left(\frac{\delta}{\lambda} - \gamma_1 \right) y - \gamma_0 - \frac{m}{\lambda} \qquad (6.23)$$

These equations may be plotted in (y, q) space to give a graphical representation of the model, as shown in Figure 6.8. The $\dot{y} = 0$ locus shows the combinations of q and y which ensure goods market equilibrium, and is analogous to the IS locus in the IS–LM model: a higher value of q (a lower interest rate on bonds) generates more investment, which requires a larger savings flow, and hence a higher level of income, to offset it. By setting $\dot{y} = 0$ in (6.22), we see that the equation of this IS curve is given by:

$$q = -\left(\frac{g}{\alpha} \right) + \frac{(1 - \beta)y}{\alpha} \qquad (6.24)$$

and thus it is upward sloping. The $\dot{q} = 0$ locus shows the combinations of q and y which ensure asset market equilibrium, and setting $\dot{q} = 0$ in (6.23), its equation is given by:

$$q = \left(\gamma_1 - \frac{\delta}{\lambda} \right) y + \gamma_0 + \frac{m}{\lambda} \qquad (6.25)$$

Its slope coefficient is ambiguous in sign, and depends on the relative size of (δ/λ) and γ_1. The economic rationale for this is as follows. A higher value of output will cause q to rise through its effect on profits, but it will also increase the demand for money (and decrease the demand for bonds and equity), which cause q to fall. Which of these two effects dominates depends to a large extent on whether output changes are reflected in large increases in profits, for a given interest and income elasticity of the demand for money. In Figure 6.8, we have assumed that the γ_1 parameter is small, so that an increase in output will require a fall in q (a rise in the interest rate) to bring asset markets back into equilibrium. This may be interpreted as corresponding to the conventional upward sloping LM curve in IS–LM analysis. Blanchard refers to this as the 'bad news' case because it implies a relatively small effect of output on profits (γ_1). We will not analyse the alternative case, where $\dot{q} = 0$ is upward sloping, but the interested reader is referred to Blanchard (1981).

The system is saddlepoint stable (see the appendix to Chapter 3), so that the forward looking price, q, 'jumps' in response to exogenous shocks to carry the economy on to its saddlepath. In Figure 6.8, the initial equilibrium is E. Assume that the system is subjected to an unanticipated fiscal expansion. From (6.24) and (6.25) we see that if g increases, this shifts the $\dot{y} = 0$ schedule downward and to the right, to $\dot{y}' = 0$, but leaves $\dot{q} = 0$ unchanged. (In IS–LM terms, a fiscal expansion only shifts the IS curve to IS', leaving LM unchanged.) The new long-run equilibrium is at E', where both goods and asset markets are in equilibrium. The dynamics of this result are more complex, however. Since income adjusts sluggishly in this model, the immediate impact of the fiscal shock is to generate expectations of a future rise in income and thus a future fall in q (assuming the bad news case). This, therefore, increases the demand for money today, generating disequilibrium in asset markets. This is resolved by an immediate fall in q, from q_0 to q_1, represented by the movement on to the new saddlepath $A'A'$ at point R in Figure 6.8. In the longer run, as income responds to the fiscal shock, the economy moves along the saddlepath to full equilibrium at point E'.

However, the short-run impact of an *anticipated future* fiscal shock is somewhat different, and this is illustrated in Figure 6.9. Suppose that economic agents suddenly perceive a balanced budget expansion sometime in the future. Then, as in the case of Figure 6.7(b), they can be expected to react immediately, as asset markets perceive future profits (through an increase in future output), and consequently interest rates rise now in response to the expected increase in the demand for transactions balances, and q falls. In fact, q will not jump as far as in the case of an anticipated expansion, since in this case, the expansion has not yet taken place, and

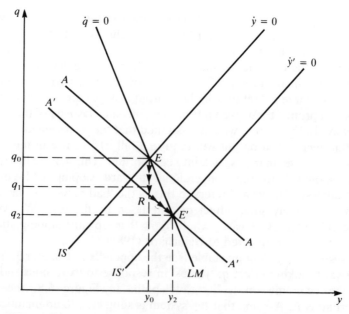

Figure 6.8 An Unanticipated Fiscal Shock in the Blanchard Model

therefore the new saddlepath is not yet relevant. Thus, q will typically jump to an intermediate position such as R (see Wilson 1979), and move along a path such as RR', so that it reaches the saddlepath $A'A'$ at the time when the fiscal expansion takes place. In other words, asset markets react immediately to the 'news' of future output growth, and stock market prices will fall, to q_1. The expectations effect brings forward the future expected interest rate rise to the present and causes present output to *fall*, until it reaches y_1. Thus, the impact effect of announced fiscal expansion is negative and aggregate demand rises to y_2 only once the fiscal expansion is actually implemented (moving from R' to E').

6.4.3. *Fiscal Policy and Expectations: Conclusions*

The net impact effect on output of announced fiscal changes is, therefore, likely to be ambiguous. The effects on consumption, as analysed in 6.4.1, are likely to be positive as households respond to the perceived improvement in their net wealth position. On the other hand, the impact effect on investment may be negative, as the expected rise in interest rates feeds back on current equity prices, driving them down and discouraging new investment. However, this latter effect is not inevitable, since it depends on the 'bad news' case, where expected income growth pushes up

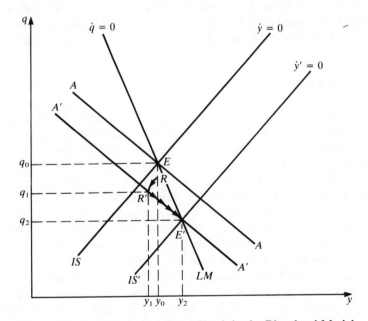

Figure 6.9 An Anticipated Fiscal Shock in the Blanchard Model

interest rates. If, in contrast, expected income growth is perceived as leading to higher profits, then current equity prices (q) may be bid up by the fiscal announcement ('the good news' case), increasing investment and reinforcing the consumption effect. However, it should be pointed out that the likelihood of the 'good news' case prevailing is reduced once the budget identity is taken into account. Thus, anticipated 'pure' (bond-financed) fiscal expansion *must* be associated with increasing interest rates, and therefore, falling equity prices, if the Blinder–Solow analysis of the previous section is accepted (though even this seemingly unambiguous conclusion may have to be amended, if the assumption of perfect substitutability between bonds and equity is relaxed).

What both these models show is that the effects of fiscal policy on aggregate demand may be more difficult to predict than the simple IS–LM model suggests. If the private sector has volatile expectations of future fiscal policies, then these models suggest that current income would respond accordingly. This in turn suggests the need for caution in drawing up fiscal policy for the stabilisation of the domestic economy. One frequently cited advantage of a regime of preannounced policy *rules*, in preference to pure discretion, is that it reduces uncertainty concerning the future conduct of stabilisation policy, providing the government has a sufficiently good reputation of sticking to its announced policies. Furthermore, it also suggests that it is difficult to devise a measure of fiscal stance for any given time period, because any proper measure would have to include not only *actual* fiscal policies, but also *perceived future* changes in these policies. A given size of fiscal deficit may have quite different effects on current income depending on the private sector's future perceptions.

6.5. Conclusion

In this chapter we have demonstrated that the simple IS–LM analysis of fiscal policy, where the efficacy of government expenditure and tax changes is determined by the relative slopes of the IS and LM curves, is seriously deficient in three key respects. First, the government's budget constraint draws attention to the fact that the impact of fiscal actions will be determined to some extent by the means of their finance. Second, it is important to distinguish between the short- and long-run consequences of fiscal policy, the key point being that, once wealth and portfolio effects are incorporated into the analysis, long-run equilibrium must be associated with a balanced budget, at least in a closed economy. Finally, the introduction of forward looking expectations in the analysis demonstrates the need to distinguish between anticipated and unanticipated fiscal policy, a conclusion which has notable counterparts in our discussion of monetary policy in Chapters 3 and 5, and exchange rates in Chapter 8.

7

MACROECONOMIC POLICY AND THE BALANCE OF PAYMENTS

In this chapter we introduce the problems of operating macroeconomic policy in an open economy. In so doing, we are again confronted with alternative schools of economic thought, and in the case of open economy macroeconomics, the problems of arriving at a meaningful consensus are compounded by the sheer number of alternative scenarios which can be analysed. Policy conclusions vary according to whether the domestic economy is large or small relative to the rest of the world, and according to the degree of competitiveness of world markets and the international mobility of capital. In addition, of course, the exchange rate regime is of fundamental importance to any open economy model. In this chapter, we consider only the case of fixed exchange rates. While the abandonment of the Bretton Woods system and the movement to flexible exchange rates in 1971 may seem to relegate such a discussion to being of historical interest only, it should be stressed that, since 1971, exchange rates have not been freely flexible, in so far as governments have frequently intervened in foreign exchange markets. This so-called 'dirty floating' means that the balance of payments does not sum to zero, as under freely floating rates. In addition, the problems of exchange rate instability in the 1980s have prompted some economists and government officials to consider the case for returning to some form of fixed exchange rate regime in the future. For these reasons, the issues raised in this chapter remain relevant.

The chapter is in three sections, treating the Fleming–Mundell model, the monetary approach and the portfolio approach in turn. Throughout the chapter, however, we are concerned with the basic issue of the extent to which world economic conditions impose a constraint on domestic monetary and fiscal policy.

7.1. Balance of Payments Policy in a Keynesian Framework

In this section, we examine how Keynesian analysis has typically tackled the question of how internal objectives, in the form of real income and employment, can be reconciled with external objectives, in the form of the balance of payments. The mainstream Keynesian model on which we focus is that developed by Fleming and Mundell in the early 1960s (see Fleming 1962, and Mundell 1962, 1963), which has become one of the more resilient models in the rapidly developing field of open economy macroeconomics, partly because it is a formal extension of the equally resilient IS–LM system outlined in Chapter 1.

7.1.1. The Fleming–Mundell Model

Our starting point is the determination of the current account in the standard fix-price Keynesian model. To simplify the analysis, we assume that the world real income and price level are given and that the domestic country is small in the sense that its macroeconomic policies will not affect world macroeconomic aggregates. We also ignore net property income from abroad and unilateral transfers such as emigrants' remittances, so that the current account is identical to the trade balance (or net exports). For simplicity, we assume net exports to be a function of domestic real income (reflecting the familiar Keynesian assumption that imports are a positive function of income) and competitiveness (defined as eP^*/P, where P^* and P are the world and domestic price levels respectively, and e is the domestic currency price of foreign exchange). Thus, the current account equation may be written as:

$$CA = c(y, eP^*/P) \qquad c_y < 0, \; c_{(eP^*/P)} > 0$$

Assuming that P and P* are fixed, this can be rewritten as:

$$CA = c(y,e) \qquad c_y < 0, c_e > 0 \tag{7.1}$$

The fact that c_y is negative is due to the marginal propensity to import, while the positive value of c_e assumes that a rise in the real exchange rate generates an increase in net exports. The mechanism whereby this latter effect comes about depends on the assumptions made about pricing behaviour and the domestic country's position in international markets, and we turn our attention briefly to this question.

For the moment, we assume that the country produces and exports a relatively specialised good such that, although it may be deemed to be a small country in the sense that it cannot influence such global aggregates as the world money supply or world income, the country is nevertheless a sufficiently important producer and exporter in its somewhat specialised markets for it to be a price-maker rather than a price-taker. Additionally, however, it is assumed that the country imports goods which compete in consumption but not production, and that the country is sufficiently small in these markets for it to be a price-taker. Thus, the current account is taken to be a function of the relative price of exports *vis-à-vis* imports, given by eP^*/P. For the current account to be a positive function of eP^*/P it is required that the Marshall–Lerner conditions be fulfilled.

The Marshall–Lerner conditions require that, starting from a balanced current account, and assuming perfectly price-elastic supply curves for exports and imports, the sum of the price elasticities of demand for exports and imports must exceed unity for a rise in the real exchange rate to generate a current account surplus. More generally, the more elastic are the import and export demand functions, the more responsive will the current account be to exchange rate changes. A similar line of reasoning can be applied to changes in the real exchange rate brought about by changes in the domestic price level (of production). In both cases, it is a crucial assumption that foreign currency export prices precisely reflect exchange rate or domestic price level changes. It should also be noted that relaxing the assumption of perfectly price-elastic supplies of exports and imports requires a modification of the simple Marshall–Lerner conditions. However, in general terms, we may note that a devaluation will tend to be effective if the demand for imports and exports is price-elastic, and the supply of exports is price-elastic.

This model is the one most frequently favoured by Keynesian economists, and in employing it, two points should be borne in mind. First, an important assumption of this model is that the domestic price level can vary with respect to the world price level, and that therefore the 'law of one price', which is a central part of the monetary approach set out in section 2, does not apply. Second, whether or not the Marshall–Lerner conditions obtain is entirely an empirical matter which first received attention in the 1940s, and then later in the post-war years in the context of the debate about the efficacy of devaluation as a policy for balance of payments adjustment under the Bretton Woods system of international monetary arrangements. Early estimates of the elasticities yielded low values such that the current account balance would be a negative function of the real exchange rate, and gave rise to what became known as 'elasticity pessimism', since the implication was that devaluation would not 'work'. However, subsequent research, carried out in the context of considerably freer trade, has produced somewhat higher estimates of the trade elasticities (see Stern, Francis and Schumaker 1976).

A similar but distinct source of pessimism surrounds the lags in the response of the current account to relative price changes, the argument being that trade volumes respond sluggishly to price changes because of the inertia in importers changing their supplier from one country to another, and the existence of contracts. Thus, if the domestic country devalues, then in the short run trade volumes are unchanged but, assuming the normal practice of invoicing in the exporter's currency, then in domestic currency terms export receipts are unchanged while the import bill is increased. Similarly, if the domestic price level falls, with a given exchange rate, then until trade volumes respond, export receipts fall while the import bill remains unchanged. This short-run perverse response of the current account to a change in relative prices is known as the J-curve, so-called since a graph of the current account over time (along the horizontal axis) in response to a change in eP^*/P would, in the short run, trace out the letter J.

There are several criticisms of the elasticities approach. First, it ignores any direct effects which a devaluation may have on the domestic price level, or indeed on the domestic rate of inflation. We have so far assumed that a devaluation only affects the domestic economy through its effects on net exports and hence *aggregate demand*. In practice, however, imports may be used in the production of domestic goods, and increasing prices of imports in terms of the domestic currency will directly affect the prices of domestic goods. In a model where the *aggregate supply* curve takes account of such factors, this shortcoming would be crucial. Second, domestic nominal wages will probably be set with reference to the *consumption price index*. Such an index will normally be made up of a basket of commodities, including imports, and therefore increasing import prices may lead to real wage resistance (that is, nominal wages are adjusted in the face of the rise in import prices brought about by the devaluation). This represents another direct channel from a devaluation to domestic prices. These problems are taken up later in this section, but for the moment, we retain our fix-price framework, treating the real exchange rate as a parametric constant which can be directly determined by policy-makers.

The Fleming–Mundell model is completed by integrating the capital account into the analysis. This is done by making the capital account a function of the differential between the domestic interest rate and the world interest rate. The argument here is simply that the higher the domestic interest rate is relative to the world rate, the more attractive are domestic assets and therefore the greater is the inflow of capital, K. Thus, we can write

$$K = k(r-r^*) \qquad k_r > 0 \tag{7.2}$$

where k_r is the partial derivative of $k(.)$ with respect to $(r-r^*)$.

This specification of the capital account has been questioned, principally on the grounds that it relates interest differentials to capital *flows*. It can be argued that a given international structure of interest rates will be associated with a given distribution of asset stocks among countries, and that only *changes* in interest rates will generate capital flows, as stocks are adjusted. This is an application of portfolio theory, as pioneered by Tobin and Markovitz (see Tobin 1958, and Markowitz 1959), and outlined in Chapter 5, whereby investors seek to diversify their portfolios in the interests of producing an overall combination of risk and return to accord with the individual investor's preferences and thus maximise utility. In such a model, the demand for a particular asset is a function of its own rate of return, the rate of return on alternative assets, the perceived riskiness of the assets and the overall size of the portfolio or wealth stock. This approach can be applied to international capital markets, illustrated as follows.

Assume for simplicity that there are only two traded assets, domestic bonds (B) and foreign bonds (F), and the demand functions for these two assets are given as follows:

$$\frac{B}{W} = b(r, r^*) \qquad b_r > 0, b_{r^*} < 0 \tag{7.3}$$

$$\frac{F}{W} = f(r, r^*) \qquad f_r < 0, f_{r^*} > 0 \tag{7.4}$$

A rise in the domestic interest rate (perhaps reflecting open-market operations on the part of the domestic authorities) increases the stock demand for domestic bonds and reduces the stock demand for foreign bonds. The increased preference for domestic bonds will result in a capital inflow. However, this will not be an ongoing inflow as implied in the Fleming–Mundell formulation of the capital account as expressed in (7.2). Rather, in the portfolio specification of (7.3) and (7.4), the capital inflow reflects the process of portfolio adjustment and generates only a temporary surplus on capital account. This approach suggests that an ongoing capital inflow would require a continuous rise in domestic rates relative to world rates over time, with obvious implications for the Fleming–Mundell model, as we shall see.

However, there are two grounds on which the flow theory may be defended. The first of these concerns the so-called portfolio growth effect, that in a growing world economy individuals' wealth portfolios will be growing continuously over time. Let us assume that the domestic country is a net debtor which holds no foreign assets and where, therefore, capital inflows consist entirely of sales of domestic bonds to non-residents. A given interest differential will be associated with a given foreign stock demand for domestic assets, as a proportion of the total portfolio. If the portfolio is growing, then this will be associated with net bond sales (a capital inflow) whose size is determined by the initial stock demand for domestic bonds (related to the interest differential) and the rate of growth of the portfolio. Thus, if domestic interest rates rise, the stock demand for domestic bonds rises, generating an increased capital inflow (as long as the total portfolio continues to grow).

The second defence of the flow theory is the familiar one that, although the portfolio approach is correct in specifying the capital account in stock adjustment terms, the process of stock adjustment may be sufficiently slow to permit analysis in flow terms in the short run. Thus, a change in the interest rate will change the stock demand for domestic assets. However, in a partial adjustment model, the new interest rate will be associated with a capital inflow/outflow as long as the process of adjustment is incomplete. Thus, with lagged adjustment in the short run, the capital account is determined by the level of interest rates rather than their rate of change, and the flow theory of the capital account is, at least partially, salvaged.

Thus, for the moment, we may retain the flow theory of capital movements, and combine (7.1) and (7.2) to produce the overall balance of payments equation:

$$BP = CA + K = c(y, e) + k(r - r^*) \qquad\qquad (7.5)$$

The Fleming–Mundell model essentially consists of a formal integration of (7.5) into a standard fix-price IS–LM model, where goods market and money market equilibrium are described in (7.6) and (7.7) respectively:

$$y = g(y, r, e, a) \qquad g_y, g_e, g_a > 0, g_r < 0 \qquad\qquad (7.6)$$

where a is autonomous expenditure:

$$m = m(y, r) \qquad m_y > 0, m_r < 0 \qquad\qquad (7.7)$$

Assuming linear forms for (7.5), (7.6) and (7.7), the Fleming–Mundell model can be set out in the context of the familiar IS–LM diagram as in Figure 7.1. At every point on the BP line the balance of payments is in equilibrium. The locus is upward sloping with the increasing current account deficit generated by higher income levels being offset by an increasing capital account surplus brought about by higher domestic interest rates. The slope of the BP line is positively related to the marginal propensity to import, c_y, and negatively to the interest sensitivity of international capital movements, k_r. With respect to the latter, the two limiting cases of perfect capital mobility (horizontal BP) and zero capital mobility (vertical BP) should be noted. It will also be noted that points above (to the left of) the BP line represent combinations of y and r which generate balance of payments surpluses, while points below (to the right of) BP are associated with deficits.

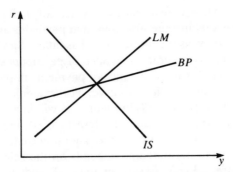

Figure 7.1 The Fleming–Mundell Model

7.1.2. *Internal and External Balance and the Fiscal–Monetary Mix*

The principal purpose of the Fleming–Mundell model is to demonstrate how domestic monetary and fiscal policies, though both are instruments of demand management, can be regarded as two separate instruments which can be combined to secure internal (domestic real income–employment) and external (balance of payments) objectives simultaneously (see, for example, Mundell 1962, and Swoboda 1973). As a preface to this discussion, however, let us examine the consequences for the balance of payments of domestic monetary and fiscal policies, starting with monetary expansion.

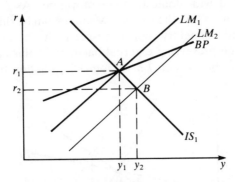

Figure 7.2 Monetary Expansion in the Fleming–Mundell Model

Starting from a position such as point A in Figure 7.2, where the goods and money markets clear with the balance of payments in equilibrium, an increase in the money stock shifts LM_1 to LM_2, reducing the rate of interest to r_2 and increasing the level of real income to y_2 at B. The balance of payments is now in deficit, partly because of a deterioration in the current account as real income has risen, and partly because of a tendency towards capital outflow as the interest rate has fallen. Similarly, a fall in the money supply tends to generate a balance of payments surplus.

Slightly more complex is the balance of payments impact of fiscal policy as represented by shifts in the IS curve. For example, an expansionary fiscal policy which shifts IS to IS_2 in Figure 7.3 will increase both the level of real income (to y_2) and the rate of interest (to r_2), tending to move the current account towards deficit and the capital account towards surplus. Diagrammatically, the net outcome depends on the relative slopes of BP and LM. In Figure 7.3, LM is steeper than BP and the fiscal expansion results in a balance of payments surplus. Equally, with a flatter LM and/or a steeper BP the net outcome could have been a deficit. Either case is possible, depending on the values of c_y, k_r, m_y and m_r. Formally, fiscal expansion will generate a balance of payments surplus if $c_y/k_r < m_y/m_r$. Thus, a surplus is more likely the greater is the interest sensitivity of international capital movements and the income sensitivity of the demand for money, and the smaller is the marginal propensity to import and the interest sensitivity of the demand for money.

As we noted above, the key result from the Fleming–Mundell model is that it provides a solution to the problem of securing simultaneously internal and external balance (if we define external balance as a zero balance on current plus capital account), solely by means of the appropriate mix of monetary and fiscal policies, and without recourse to changes in exchange rates, tariffs or any other balance of payments policies. To illustrate this, in Figure 7.4 we start from a position of external balance associated with domestic unemployment. As long as there is a degree of capital mobility, the IS and LM curves can be shifted by means of fiscal policy and monetary policy respectively so as to secure full employment while preserving external balance. In this case, the relevant new curves would be IS_2 and LM_2. Domestic reflation by means of both

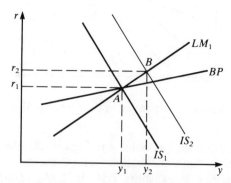

Figure 7.3   Fiscal Expansion in the Fleming–Mundell Model

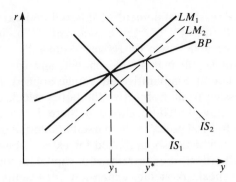

Figure 7.4   Internal and External Balance

monetary and fiscal policy has generated full employment, while the negative current account consequences of this increase in real income have been offset by a capital account surplus generated by the higher interest rate induced by fiscal expansion.

One might at this point question whether a situation where the current account is in continual deficit matched by a capital account surplus constitutes 'external equilibrium'. This is open to serious question for three main reasons. First, so long as the current account is not in balance, whatever the capital account position, domestic wealth holdings will be changing. For example, with a current account deficit, domestic wealth will be falling, and this may be associated with falling or rising interest rates and/or falling domestic expenditure, both of which would further affect the balance of payments. In short, if wealth is introduced into the model, full stock equilibrium requires current balance. This is a point developed at length in the final section of this chapter. Second, we may note that a country running a continual current account deficit may be regarded in international capital markets as being diminishingly credit-worthy and that, as a consequence, the capital account surplus required for overall external balance may only be able to be secured at progressively higher domestic interest rates. Finally, we may recall that the Fleming–Mundell model is based on a flow theory of capital movements. If this is replaced by the stock theory, then this provides another argument suggesting that the required capital account surplus (assuming a current account deficit) will in turn require rising domestic interest rates over time.

7.1.3.   The Assignment Problem

It may also be noted that the policy implementation as outlined above is characterised by complete coordination of monetary and fiscal policy instruments. In a world where such perfect coordination is not to be expected, the successful attainment of internal and external equilibrium depends critically on the correct assignment of monetary and fiscal instruments between the twin objectives. Mundell's solution to the so-called assignment problem is simple enough and can be viewed as an example of the law of comparative advantage applied to the problem of policy design: assign to that objective the policy which is relatively more efficient at pursuing it. Thus, although there is no reason to prefer monetary policy to fiscal policy in the pursuit of internal balance, monetary policy is to be unambiguously preferred for external balance, since while fiscal policy will affect the current and capital accounts in opposite directions, so to speak, monetary expansion, for example, will push both accounts towards deficit via real income and interest rate effects. Thus, Mundell's (1962) solution to the assignment problem is to use monetary policy for balance of payments adjustment and fiscal policy for domestic employment/real income objectives. (The reader may illustrate this result for himself/herself in Figure 7.4. First, shift the IS curve to reach y^*, then shift the LM curve to intersect with IS on the BP line. Then shift IS to re-attain y^*, and so on. Compare the outcome with that when the LM curve is shifted to reach y^* and the IS curve is used to return to the BP line.)

7.1.4. The Monetary Consequences of the Balance of Payments

The model outlined so far could be criticised on the grounds that it is incomplete in that no account is taken of the monetary consequences of the balance of payments, or alternatively, that it implicitly assumes that the monetary effects of the balance of payments are sterilised. Let us now examine the consequences of relaxing this assumption.

It will be recalled from Chapters 1 and 5 that changes in the money stock may be conveniently decomposed into four main components as in (7.8) below:

$$\Delta M \equiv PSD - \Delta B + BP + \Delta BLP \tag{7.8}$$

Thus, it is clear that, *other things remaining equal*, a balance of payments surplus will increase the domestic money stock. The important point to bear in mind is that other things may not remain equal and, in particular, the authorities may seek to change the fiscal deficit, domestic bond sales or bank lending in order to offset the balance of payments effects on the money stock. Such systematic policies are usually referred to as 'sterilisation', and the motives for sterilisation and the factors which determine its effectiveness are discussed later in this chapter. For the moment, let us assume that the authorities do not choose to, or are unable to, carry out effective sterilisation policies, so that a balance of payments surplus increases the domestic money stock, and vice versa.

The implications of this for our analysis can be illustrated by referring back to Figure 7.2. Let us allow the authorities to increase the money stock by, say, open market purchases of government debt from the private sector. The immediate result is as we analysed earlier. The LM curve shifts to LM_2, the interest rate falls to r_2, the income level rises to y_2 and the balance of payments moves unambiguously into deficit. However, this is now no longer the end of the story. According to (7.8), the balance of payments deficit will reduce the money stock by the amount of the deficit every time period. Thus, over time the money stock will be reduced as long as the deficit persists, and the LM curve will move back to the left until it re-attains its original position.

There are a number of points to note about this. First, it provides a self-correcting mechanism for the balance of payments whereby deficits or surpluses generate changes in the money stock which in turn restore external equilibrium via interest rate and real income changes. Second, at the end of the day, monetary policy has had no permanent effect other than to alter the composition of the money stock. Domestic credit (money supply minus foreign exchange reserves) has increased and foreign currency holdings (or foreign exchange reserves) have fallen to offset this. The domestic interest rate and real income are unchanged.

Third, the assignment problem, as analysed by Mundell, is rendered trivial since monetary policy can no longer control the money stock, but only its domestic component. Thus, as long as the authorities continue to employ fiscal policy to attain internal balance, then endogenous changes in the money stock will automatically adjust the balance of payments to attain external balance.

Finally, it can be simply demonstrated that in the Fleming–Mundell model without sterilisation, while the impact of monetary policy on real income is ultimately zero, the impact of fiscal policy is enhanced, except in the case where capital is relatively immobile. These results are illustrated in Figure 7.5. In Figure 7.5, we start with IS_1 and LM_1, with income at y_1 and the interest rate at r_1. We have already noted that monetary policy designed to, say, increase real income to y_2 will serve only to bring about a balance of payments deficit which, in the absence of sterilisation, will reduce the money stock and ultimately shift LM back to its original position. Contrast this result with that for fiscal policy. If IS is shifted to IS_2, the position required to attain y_2 in a closed economy, then, given that BP is flatter than LM (as drawn), this fiscal expansion will generate a balance of payments surplus, which in turn will increase the money stock and shift the LM curve to LM_2 where it cuts IS_2 and BP at y_3. The proposed fiscal expansion has been underwritten, and hence reinforced, by the monetary consequences of the balance of payments surplus.

Clearly the extent of this effect will depend on the slope of the BP line,

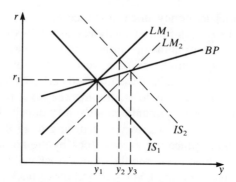

Figure 7.5   Fiscal Policy without Sterilisation

being more significant the greater is the interest sensitivity of the capital account. In the case not illustrated in Figure 7.5 where the BP line is steeper than the LM curve, fiscal policy will be ultimately less effective than in a closed economy; but it will always be more effective than monetary policy in an open economy except in the limiting case of zero capital mobility, when both policies are completely ineffective.

With the exception of the last point, these conclusions are of a distinctly monetarist character. The balance of payments is seen to be automatically self-correcting via a monetary mechanism, and monetary policy is rendered impotent by its balance of payments consequences. These are the main conclusions of the monetary approach to the balance of payments, to be discussed in the next section, although the adjustment mechanism in the Fleming–Mundell model works through interest rate and real income changes, which is in contrast to the monetary approach, as we shall see.

However, zero sterilisation is customarily regarded as an extreme case by Keynesian economists, and in the next section we discuss the rationale for pursuing sterilisation policies in a Keynesian framework, and then examine the factors which determine the likely effectiveness of such a strategy.

7.1.5.   Sterilisation Policies

Sterilisation policies may be defined as actions designed to change domestic credit in order to offset the monetary consequences of the balance of payments. Such policies may be viewed either as attempts by the authorities to thwart the automatic adjustment of the balance of payments via the monetary mechanism, or alternatively, as attempts to pursue policies independent of world monetary conditions. In either case, the problems facing the authorities are the same. Before examining these problems, however, let us consider the possible rationale for pursuing sterilisation policies in the first place.

Assuming that macroeconomic policy is directed towards securing internal and external balance, as analysed above, it is not immediately clear why the authorities should wish to sterilise. Indeed, as we noted in the previous section, a strategy of zero sterilisation considerably simplifies the assignment problem. Suppose, however, that policy is conducted under conditions of uncertainty, where structural equations are subject to stochastic disturbances. Under these circumstances, it is possible that sterilisation may be the preferred strategy.

Let us assume a stochastic version of the Fleming–Mundell model where the IS, LM and BP functions are liable to additive stochastic disturbances with zero mean. In addition, let us assume that, although the monetary consequences of external imbalance occur immediately, discretionary fiscal policy to stabilise real income is not carried out in this short time period, given the problems of recognition and implementation lags. Finally, we assume that the internal macroeconomic objective takes the form of the stabilisation of real income at $\bar{y}$, and that this objective is afforded priority over external balance. We now examine the implications of three alternative stochastic disturbances to the model.

In Figure 7.6, we analyse a balance of payments disturbance, which shifts the BP line from BP_1 to BP_2. (For simplicity, we assume a capital account disturbance so that the IS curve is unaffected.) The balance of payments is now unambiguously in deficit, irrespective of the relative slopes of BP and LM. The important question is what happens to real income. Under zero sterilisation, the LM curve moves to the left as the money stock is reduced, until at LM_2 the balance of payments is back in equilibrium. Real income has fallen to y_2. However, if the monetary consequences of the deficit are effectively sterilised, the LM curve does not shift, and income remains at $\bar{y}$. If the key objective is to stabilise real income, a strategy of sterilisation is therefore preferable when the shocks are of external origin.

The case for sterilisation is less clear cut when the shocks are of domestic

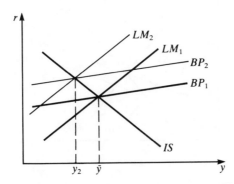

Figure 7.6 Fleming–Mundell and External Shocks

origin and affect the IS curve. In Figure 7.7, there is a stochastic disturbance which shifts the IS curve from IS_1 to IS_2. In the case of Figure 7.7(a), the BP function is flatter than the LM curve, and therefore the IS shift generates not only a fall in real income to y_1, but also a balance of payments deficit. Under zero sterilisation, this will shift the LM curve to the left reducing real income still further, to y_2. A policy of sterilisation, though not preventing the initial fall in income, is, therefore, nevertheless preferable. However, this result is reversed when the LM curve is flatter than the BP line, as in Figure 7.7(b). In this case, the shift in IS reduces income and generates a surplus, which increases the domestic money stock. With zero sterilisation, the initial fall in income is partially offset and we move to y_1 to y_2 (offsetting it entirely in the case of complete capital immobility).

Finally, where the stochastic disturbance affects the LM curve, there is no case for sterilisation, as we can see from Figure 7.8, where the leftward shift of the LM curve, possibly reflecting an exogenous increase in the demand for money, unambiguously generates a balance of payments

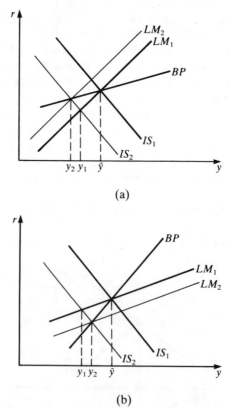

(a)

(b)

Figure 7.7   Fleming–Mundell and IS Shocks

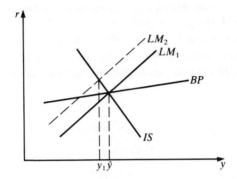

Figure 7.8 Fleming–Mundell and LM Shocks

surplus at y_1. Under zero sterilisation, the consequent increase in the domestic money stock leads to a rise in real income back towards $\bar{y}$. In other words, changes in the demand for money are underwritten by changes in the supply of money through the balance of payments, and the level of income is undisturbed.

In the very short run, then, when fiscal policy cannot be expected to operate in the ultra-discretionary manner implied in the earlier deterministic analysis, there is a case for sterilisation. Even under these circumstances, however, the case for sterilisation is not clear cut, but it is stronger the greater the incidence of external shocks, the greater the degree of international capital mobility and the smaller the interest elasticity of the demand for money. The size of the stochastic disturbances will determine the optimal stock of foreign exchange reserves to be held. Thus, should the extent of these disturbances be increased, then the authorities' external objective will be to run a balance of payments surplus until the stock of reserves has increased in line with this. Under these circumstances also, then, the authorities will wish to pursue sterilisation strategies.

Let us now examine whether such policies will be effective in the context of a simplified linear version of the Fleming–Mundell model as set out in equations (7.9)–(7.13) below.

$$y = a - \beta r \tag{7.9}$$

$$m^d = -\alpha_1 r + \alpha_2 y \tag{7.10}$$

$$\Delta m^s = K + CA + DCE \tag{7.11}$$

$$K = \gamma r \tag{7.12}$$

$$CA = -\delta y \tag{7.13}$$

DCE is changes in domestic credit, and the world interest rate are assumed constant and therefore suppressed.

Assuming that the goods and money markets clear instantaneously (we are always at the intersection of the IS and LM curves), then by substitution and re-arrangement, we can obtain the following dynamic equation:

$$\Delta m = DCE + \frac{[(\gamma\alpha_2 - \delta\alpha_1)a - (\gamma + \beta\delta)m]}{(\alpha_1 + \beta\alpha_2)} \tag{7.14}$$

That is, the change in the money stock is composed of changes in domestic credit, DCE, and balance of payments effects (the second term in (7.14)), the latter being entirely a function of exogenous expenditure and the money stock itself. It will be noted that the coefficient on m is negative, reflecting the fact that increases in the domestic money stock tend to generate deficits on both current and capital accounts, while autonomous expenditure, a, has an ambiguous effect on the balance of payments, and therefore changes in the money stock, depending on the relative slopes of the LM and BP curves.

In this model, for the authorities to control the money stock, in the sense of maintaining it at a given level, external effects on the money stock from the current and capital accounts of the balance of payments must be offset by changes in domestic credit. That is, independent monetary policy requires effective sterilisation. This is shown by setting Δm equal to zero in (7.14) and by solving for m:

$$\bar{m} = \frac{(\alpha_1 + \beta\alpha_2)DCE + (\gamma\alpha_2 - \delta\alpha_1)a}{(\gamma + \beta\delta)} \tag{7.15}$$

The key point about this result is that, since DCE represents changes in domestic credit, in order to maintain a given money stock, $\bar{m}$, the authorities must continuously increase domestic credit, unless the balance of payments happens to be zero, and the greater is the money stock desired by the authorities, the faster domestic credit needs to be expanded. Such a policy will be associated with ongoing changes in the country's stock of foreign exchange reserves which, in the case of a deficit, is untenable in the long run. It will be noted that the extent of domestic credit expansion required to maintain a given money stock is dependent on the coefficient on DCE in (7.15). The smaller this coefficient, the greater is the required DCE for the maintenance of a given money stock (and the greater is the consequent balance of payments deficit and therefore reserve loss). Two key elements in the coefficient on DCE are γ and δ. Clearly, sterilisation policies become more expensive in terms of foreign exchange losses the greater are γ and δ. In the case of perfect capital mobility, where the BP line becomes horizontal, γ assumes a value of infinity, and sterilisation clearly beomes impractical.

The above result, an uncomfortable one for advocates of sterilisation policies, stems directly from the fact that domestic money stock changes have offsetting *flow* consequences for the balance of payments. However, in recent work on the efficacy of sterilisation policies, the Fleming–Mundell model has been amended in a manner which breaks this stock–flow relation, and casts sterilisation policies in a somewhat different light.

Following Argy (1981), we may set out a model similar in structure to that outlined in (7.9)–(7.13) above, with two important differences. First, our amended model is concerned with the very short run so that real income and the current account are assumed to be exogenous. Second, the flow theory of capital movements is replaced by the equivalent stock version. Thus, we can write:

$$y = \bar{y} \tag{7.9'}$$

$$K = \gamma(\Delta r) \tag{7.12'}$$

$$CA = \overline{CA} \tag{7.13'}$$

From these relations, together with (7.10) and (7.11), it is possible to derive the following reduced form:

$$K = \mu_1 \Delta \bar{y} - \mu_2 DCE - \mu_3 \overline{CA} \tag{7.16}$$

where $\mu_1 = \gamma \alpha_2/(\alpha_1 + \gamma)$ and $\mu_2 = \mu_3 = \gamma/(\alpha_1 + \gamma)$. In this simplified model, we can see that a capital inflow is generated by rising domestic income (increasing interest rates via the transactions demand for money), falling domestic credit and/or a current account deficit (increasing interest rates via a reduction in the money stock). The *offset coefficient*, measured by μ_2, shows the extent to which a once-for-all increase in domestic credit 'leaks abroad' in the form of a once-for-all capital outflow. It is less than unity as long as γ is less than infinity, that is as long as capital is less than perfectly mobile. Where capital is perfectly mobile, sterilisation is impossible, as in the previous model. However, in contrast to the previous model, (7.16) implies that, since a *flow* increase in domestic credit generates a *flow* deficit on capital account, a *stock* increase in domestic credit will generate only a *once-for-all* capital outflow. Thus, with an exogenous current account and an offset coefficient of less than unity, a given increase in the money stock can be effected by a given (larger) increase in domestic credit. Suppressing the current account income, and the constant μ, and noting therefore that $\Delta m = K + DCE$, we can write:

$$\Delta m = (1-\mu_2)DCE$$

Thus, a once-for-all increase in the money stock no longer requires an ongoing increase in domestic credit, because the potential offset to monetary policy is in stock, not flow, terms, a result which makes independent monetary policy a more feasible proposition (at least in the short run).

Kouri and Porter (1974) estimated offset coefficients significantly less than unity for West Germany, Italy, Australia and the Netherlands (77, 43, 47, and 59 per cent respectively), while Argy and Kouri (1974) found offset coefficients of 53, 51 and 91 per cent for Italy, the Netherlands and West Germany respectively. These reduced form studies have met with some criticisms on econometric grounds, however (see, for example, Obstfeld 1982.) Consequently, structural models which specify the asset markets which lie behind the reduced form have also been tested. For example, Herring and Marston (1977) indicated considerable interest sensitivity of capital movements in the West German case, which implies a reduced ability to sterilise (although the study did imply that direct controls were effective in constraining capital movements). Finally, we may note that further empirical light has been thrown on the interest sensitivity of capital movements, the key parameter in deriving offset coefficients, by work in the 1980s estimating risk premia in the context of flexible exchange rates, since the existence of risk premia implies less than perfect substitutability between domestic and foreign assets, and therefore less than perfect capital mobility.

Finally, it should be noted that the empirical model outlined above deals with the question of sterilisation within a highly specific context. In particular, it focuses on the very short run, in so far as real income and the current account are assumed exogenous with respect to monetary policy. In the longer run, the offset coefficient will not only be increased as the current account adjusts, but the offset will be an ongoing flow, rather than a once-for-all stock adjustment.

In addition, the analysis sheds little light on the problems which the monetary authorities might encounter in attempting to sterilise the monetary consequences of a current account imbalance. Equation (7.16) implies that this should present no problem, since both domestic credit and the current account appear with the same coefficient, and therefore a current account surplus, say, can be offset by a fall in domestic credit with no net effect on the capital account. This example draws attention to a key weakness in the model, namely that the budget identity in (7.8) is not fully incorporated into the analysis, and therefore that there is no indication of how changes in domestic credit are brought about. This is a point which we take up in section 3 of this chapter in our discussion of portfolio models of the balance of payments.

7.1.6. *Macroeconomic Policy under Capital Immobility*

It will be clear from the analysis so far that the central Fleming–Mundell result, that internal and external objectives can be achieved by the appropriate fiscal/monetary mix, relies upon at least a degree of interest-sensitive capital mobility. If capital is immobile, then the BP line becomes vertical, and the reconciliation of internal and external objectives requires the introduction of a new policy instrument. This is the context in which Keynesian open economy macroeconomic analysis was conducted prior to the development of the Fleming–Mundell model, and we briefly examine some of the issues here.

In Figure 7.9, the BP line is vertical, reflecting the assumption of complete capital immobility. External balance is equated with current balance and, with fixed prices and a given exchange rate, there is only one level of domestic income at which the current account is in equilibrium, and this is given as y_1. At higher income levels, the current account is in deficit, and vice versa. If internal balance is given by $\bar{y}$, then in the absence of other policy instruments, internal and external objectives are incompatible. In the spirit of Tinbergen's (1952) famous theorem, whereby policy-makers require as many independent policy instruments as there are independent policy objectives to be pursued, it was Meade who first pointed out that if monetary and fiscal policies were employed to achieve internal balance, then some other policy instrument was required to attain

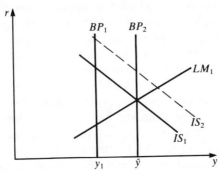

Figure 7.9 Fleming–Mundell under Zero Capital Mobility

external balance (see Meade 1951). In terms of Figure 7.9, once monetary/fiscal policies have attained $\bar{y}$, additional policies are required to shift the BP line. Such policies might include exchange rate changes, tariffs, subsidies, quotas or any other device the effect of which is to change the current account position at a given level of income. Such policies are normally designated as 'expenditure-switching' policies.

An important point to note, however, is that such policies, to the extent that they succeed in improving the trade balance, also shift the IS curve to the right since net exports are a component of aggregate demand. Consequently, in the present example, if domestic demand management has secured full employment and expenditure-switching policies are then directed towards shifting the BP line to BP_2, then the IS curve will shift to the right, generating inflation as there is now excess demand at full employment. As eP^*/P falls, the current account will deteriorate and the BP line will shift back to the left. This represents the familiar conclusion that for economies operating at full employment, a current account deficit cannot be corrected by expenditure-switching policies alone. They must be accompanied by appropriate 'expenditure-reducing' policies. A more general conclusion is that whenever expenditure-switching policies are implemented, demand management policies must take account of the aggregate demand consequences of the change in the current account.

The synthesis of internal and external objectives under capital immobility can also be illustrated using a diagram first introduced by Salter (1959) and Swan (1960), and set out in Figure 7.10. Measuring 'competitiveness', to include all factors affecting the current account, other than real income changes, up the vertical axis, and domestic expenditure on domestic goods, or absorption along the horizontal, we can draw loci of internal and external balance. *AA* is the internal balance function, at every point on which the economy is at full employment. It is downward sloping because the rise in aggregate demand associated with a rise in absorption must be offset by a fall in net exports via falling competitiveness to keep aggregate demand at the full employment level. Alternatively, at any point on *BB* the current account is in equilibrium. Since a rise in absorption tends to lead to a deterioration in the current account and must be offset by increased competitiveness for external balance to be maintained, *BB* must be upward sloping.

At point X, both internal and external balance are attained. In our earlier example, where the economy has achieved internal balance (full employment) but is running a current account deficit, the economy is at a point such as T, which is on the *AA* line but is below, or to the right of, *BB*. A policy of undiluted deflation to correct the current account deficit would move the economy to point S, achieving external balance at the expense of full employment. On the other hand, an expenditure-switching policy, such as a devaluation, with no change in demand management policy, would

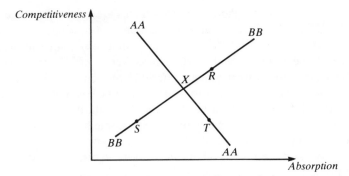

Figure 7.10   The Swan–Salter Analysis

push the economy to point R on the BB curve, again removing the current account deficit but now generating excess demand and inflation since R is above the AA line. The lesson is clearly that both sets of policies are required to work in a complementary manner to secure the twin objectives and arrive safely at point X.

How is this analysis affected when we allow for the monetary consequences of the external deficit? Let us return for a moment to the case outlined in Figure 7.9. Once monetary and fiscal policies have secured $\bar{y}$, the current account (and therefore the balance of payments) is in deficit. If the balance of payments effects on the money supply are allowed for and not sterilised, then the current account deficit in Figure 7.9 will adjust to a zero balance over time, as the LM curve drifts to the left until income falls to y_1. In terms of Figure 7.10, this adjustment would be described by a movement from point T to point S. In short, the monetary mechanism automatically ensures external equilibrium, but at the expense of internal balance. In the capital mobility case, the fiscal–monetary mix can be adjusted to secure both internal and external objectives, but with zero capital mobility, this escape route is not available, and a change in eP^*/P is required.

7.1.7.   The Fleming–Mundell Model under Flexible Prices

Finally in this section, we note that the Fleming–Mundell model shares the restrictive fix-price assumptions of the IS–LM system within which it is located. In a closed economy model, it is a relatively simple matter to extend the IS–LM model by integrating an aggregate supply side into the analysis, as demonstrated in Chapter 2. Such an extension is a rather more complicated exercise in the case of the Fleming–Mundell model. In a closed economy, the main amendment is to recognise that a change in the domestic price level reduces the real domestic money stock, with consequent Keynes and Pigou effects which determine the slope of the aggregate demand curve. In the open economy case, domestic price level changes have an additional set of consequences stemming from the presence of the international relative price term, eP^*/P, in both the IS curve and the balance of payments equilibrium locus. An increase in the domestic price level, for example, reduces competitiveness and therefore net exports, shifting the IS curve to the left. Similarly, an increase in the domestic price level means that a given real income level is associated with a larger current account deficit (or smaller surplus) requiring a greater capital inflow and therefore higher interest rate to offset it, shifting the BP line to the left.

These effects tend to complicate the diagrammatic treatment of the Fleming–Mundell model, but do not change the basic analysis, since, assuming an upward sloping aggregate supply curve, the price and real income effects operate in the same direction. We examine the case of domestic monetary expansion, to illustrate the general point. In Figure 7.11(a), we start with LM_1, IS_1 and BP_1. Domestic income is therefore at y_1 and the balance of payments is in equilibrium. It is assumed that capital is imperfectly mobile and thus BP slopes upwards from left to right. In Figure 7.11(b), we show the aggregate demand and supply curves also intersecting at y_1, and we assume that the aggregate supply curve is upward sloping.

Now let the monetary authorities increase the domestic money stock (from M_1 to M_2). This will shift the aggregate demand curve to the right, increasing the income level to y_2 and the price level to P_2. In IS–LM terms, this summarises three separate effects. First, the nominal money stock is increased, shifting the LM curve to the right. Second, the increase in the price level reduces the real money stock, dampening the rightward shift in LM. These two effects taken together shift the LM curve to LM_2. Third, the rise in the price level reduces eP^*/P and therefore competitiveness, reducing net exports and shifting the IS curve to the left, to IS_2. All three effects are reflected in the slope of the aggregate demand curve in Figure 7.11(b), and the final outcome for income and the price level is y_2 and P_2. In addition, however, the fall in eP^*/P has also shifted the BP line to the left, to BP_2, since decreased competitiveness dictates that, for a given interest rate, external balance now requires lower domestic income.

Qualitatively, the net outcome of the expansionary monetary policy is the same as under fixed prices, namely an increase in domestic real income accompanied by a balance of payments deficit. However, while the increase in income is unambiguously smaller relative to the fixed price case, the relative size of the external deficit is unclear and depends on the relative price and income effects on net exports. In the extreme case of a vertical aggregate supply curve with real income 'pegged' at its 'natural' level, all of the adjustment takes place through the price level; but this is a

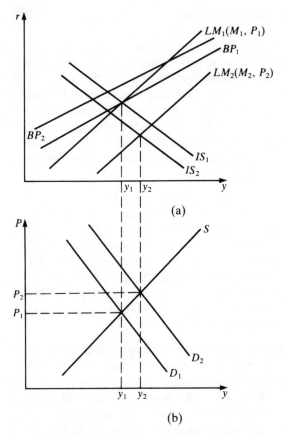

Figure 7.11   Fleming–Mundell and Flexible Prices

case more closely associated with the monetary approach discussed in the next section.

The relaxation of the fixed price assumption, then, complicates the analysis, but does not materially alter the end results, and the familiar Fleming–Mundell conclusions about the relative efficacy of monetary and fiscal policy (under zero sterilisation) and the assignment problem remain valid. The more central criticisms surrounding the Fleming–Mundell approach concern the treatment of the capital account, the absence of wealth effects, and the issue of whether the authorities can effectively sterilise the monetary consequences of the balance of payments, and indeed whether they should wish to do so. Before we confront these issues further, however, we turn to what might be regarded as the polar counterpart to the Fleming–Mundell model, the monetary approach to the balance of payments.

7.2. The Monetary Approach

The monetary approach to the balance of payments is the modern version
of the theory of international adjustment first introduced by David Hume
in the eighteenth century (see Hume 1752). In the course of the late 1960s
and the 1970s, a whole literature was spawned comprising models of
differing specifications but all of which shared the common view that the
balance of payments was a monetary phenomenon and the appropriate
focus for analysis of international adjustment was the money market, the
balance of payments being the mechanism whereby the domestic goods
and money markets are cleared.

> The main characteristic of the monetary approach to the balance of
> payments can be summarised in the proposition that the balance of
> payments is essentially a monetary phenomenon . . . In general, the
> approach emphasises the budget constraint imposed on the country's
> international spending and views the various accounts of the balance of
> payments as the 'windows' to the outside world, through which the
> excesses of domestic flow demands over domestic flow supplies, and of
> excess domestic flow supplies over domestic flow demands, are cleared
> (Frenkel and Johnson 1976, p.21).

Our discussion of the monetary approach is in three parts. In the first
subsection, we outline a simple two-country model of current account
adjustment, which shows how the law of one price affects the transmission
mechanism of both domestic monetary policy and exchange rate changes
with respect to the current account. In subsection 7.2.2, we extend the
model to take account of capital movements, and analyse the balance of
payments consequences of excessive growth rates of domestic credit.
Finally, we contrast the results of the monetary approach with those of the
Fleming–Mundell model, highlighting the policy issues raised. (For a
comprehensive collection of the main contributions to the monetary
approach, see Frenkel and Johnson 1976. For a critical view, see Whitman
1975.)

7.2.1. The Monetary Approach to the Current Account

The simple monetary approach to the current account can be summarised
in the following equations, following Dornsbusch (1973):

$$M^d = f(P, y) \qquad f_P > 0, f_y > 0 \tag{7.17}$$

$$M^s = D + R \tag{7.18}$$

$$A = Py - H \tag{7.19}$$

$$H = h(M^d - M^s) \qquad h_m > 0 \tag{7.20}$$

$$CA = Py - A = H \tag{7.21}$$

$$P = eP^* \tag{7.22}$$

$$y = \bar{y} \tag{7.23}$$

where h_m is $\partial H/\partial(M^d - M^s)$. Equation (7.17) sets out the demand for money as in a simple version of the quantity theory, while (7.18) is the stock equivalent of (7.9), where domestic credit (D) reflects fiscal finance and bank lending, and foreign exchange reserves (R) are the accumulated monetary stock consequences of the balance of payments. Equation (7.19) states that nominal absorption (A) equals nominal income less hoarding (H), that is, the excess of income over domestic expenditure must be reflected in increasing holdings of money balances. H can be regarded as the *flow* adjustment of money holdings. Equation (7.20) relates this to the difference between desired and actual *stock* holdings of money balances.

The monetary approach is completed by assuming the law of one price, (7.22) and setting the level of income at its full employment or natural level, (7.23). While the latter is a familiar feature of monetarist models, the law of one price requires a word of explanation. In the Fleming–Mundell model, we assumed that exporters faced downward sloping demand curves i.e. although the country itself might be small relative to the rest of the world, its exports were sufficiently specialised so that, in terms of the markets in which they traded, exporters had some discretion over pricing behaviour and could be regarded as operating under conditions of imperfect competition. In contrast, the assumption underlying (7.22) is that exporters operate under conditions of perfect competition. That is, traded goods are assumed to be homogeneous and exporters are price-takers in international markets. (For a full discussion of the law of one price together with a considerable volume of empirical evidence, see *Journal of International Economics*, Vol. 8, 1978.) This assumption has important implications for the external consequences of aggregate demand policy and for the analysis of how a change in the exchange rate might be expected to affect the current account. In addition, it is an important point of divergence between the modern monetary approach and the original theory put forward by Hume.

The essence of the monetary model can be illustrated by examining the consequences of a once-for-all increase in the domestic money stock. Were we dealing with a closed economy, the standard quantity theory result would obtain, the domestic price level rising until the demand for nominal money is equal to the increased supply. In the open economy case, however, the demand for money will not adjust to the increased supply because both the arguments in the demand for money function are exogenously given. Real income is fixed at full employment and the domestic price level is tied to the world price level (assuming a fixed exchange rate). Under these circumstances, the demand for money is fixed and the excess supply of money generates dishoarding, (7.20), and therefore increased absorption, (7.19), and a current account deficit, (7.21). Assuming that the authorities do not attempt to sterilise the consequent currency outflow (i.e. that the fall in R is not offset by a rise in D in (7.18)), the current account deficit results in a fall in the domestic money stock, and this process continues until the entire increase in the money stock has leaked abroad. That is, the system returns to equilibrium by an adjustment of money supply rather than money demand.

The above process can be illustrated in a two-country context by Figure 7.12. This diagram, employed in Dornbusch (1973), sets out domestic hoarding (H) and foreign dishoarding ($-eH^*$) schedules, in domestic currency, as positive and negative functions respectively of the domestic price level. The domestic hoarding function is upward sloping since an increase in the price level increases the demand for money and therefore, by (7.20) and for a given money stock, increases hoarding. Similarly, an increase in the domestic price level is equally an increase in the foreign price level, by (7.22) for a given exchange rate. This increases foreign hoarding or, alternatively, reduces foreign dishoarding.

Now, goods market equilibrium will obtain when the world goods market clears, that is, when total output equals total absorption. From (7.19), it is clear that this will occur when, across the two countries, net hoarding equals zero, that is, the world goods market clears when domestic

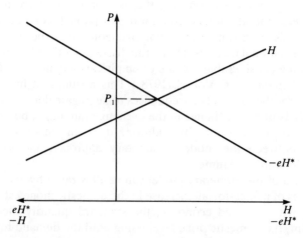

Figure 7.12 The Monetary Approach to the Current Account

hoarding equals foreign dishoarding, or vice versa. In Figure 7.12, the price level clears the world goods market at P_1. At prices higher than P_1, for example, domestic hoarding exceeds foreign dishoarding, and this is necessarily associated with excess supply in the goods market, pushing prices down towards P_1.

However, this does not describe monetary equilibrium, since hoarding in the domestic country (matched by dishoarding in the foreign country) is associated with a current account surplus in the domestic country (from (7.21)), which will in turn increase the domestic money stock and reduce the foreign money stock. In terms of Figure 7.12, this will shift both the H schedule and the $-eH^*$ schedule to the left until hoarding in both countries equals zero, and current balance is restored.

Similarly, starting from full equilibrium, we can analyse the consequences of an increase in domestic credit in one of the countries, say the domestic country. This will initially shift H to H' as hoarding is reduced, as shown in Figure 7.13. The resulting current account deficit then reduces the domestic money stock and increases the foreign country's money stock, shifting both schedules to the right (to H'' and $eH^{*'}$), until current balance is again restored. In this case, the domestic monetary expansion has increased the domestic price level, to P_2, but only to the extent that it has increased the world price level. In the case where the domestic country is infinitely small relative to the foreign country (which in this case might be regarded as the rest of the world), the increase in the domestic country's money stock will have a negligible effect on the world money stock and therefore on the world price level. This could be represented by a horizontal $-eH^*$ schedule, so that domestic monetary policy cannot affect the world price level, and consequently the domestic price level. In this

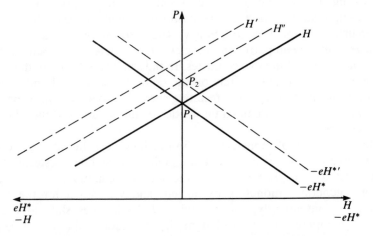

Figure 7.13 Monetary Policy in the Monetary Model

'small country' case, then, the only lasting consequence of the monetary expansion is the equivalent loss of foreign exchange reserves.

It should also be noted that changes in the exchange rate affect the current account by a different mechanism in the monetary model. In our discussion of the Fleming–Mundell model, we assumed that exporters operated in imperfectly competitive markets and that a devaluation enabled them to alter the relative price of their exports in foreign currency terms, with the consequences of exchange rate changes for the current account depending on demand elasticities, as summarised in the Marshall–Lerner conditions. Under the law of one price, however, such relative price changes are by definition impossible to secure. How, then, can a devaluation generate an increase in net exports? We examine this question with reference to Figure 7.14.

Starting from equilibrium at P_1, the immediate effect of a devaluation is to shift the foreign dishoarding function upwards to $-e'H^*$. This is because, for monetary equilibrium to be maintained, the nominal demand for money in the foreign country must be unaltered. This requires an unaltered foreign price level, which in turn requires a higher domestic price level, given the devalued exchange rate. In terms of (7.22), the rise in e must be offset by an equiproportionate rise in P, for P^*, and therefore the foreign demand for money, to remain unaltered. At P_1, there is now excess demand in the world goods market, since foreign dishoarding exceeds domestic (zero) hoarding. The price level will rise until domestic hoarding rises and foreign dishoarding falls, to reduce total absorption and bring the world goods market back into equilibrium at P_2. At this point, the domestic country is running a current account surplus. The mechanism bringing this about has worked through the effects of the exchange rate change on the price levels in the respective countries. The devaluing country's price is now higher, increasing the demand for money relative to the supply, and therefore increasing hoarding and reducing absorption, while precisely the opposite is occurring in the foreign country. The distribution of the price level changes will depend partly on the relevant parameter values and partly on the relative size of the two countries. In the small country case, the burden of adjustment will fall entirely on the domestic price level and domestic absorption. In any event, the resulting current account surplus is obtained without reference to demand elasticities or the securing of the Marshall–Lerner conditions.

As in the case of monetary expansion, however, the non-zero current balance cannot be regarded as full equilibrium, as long as sterilisation is not effected. Thus, in Figure 7.14, the domestic country's current account surplus generates monetary expansion, and vice versa for the foreign country. Consequently, the H and $-eH^*$ schedules shift to the left, generating increased absorption in the domestic country and reduced absorption in the foreign country, and bringing the current account back

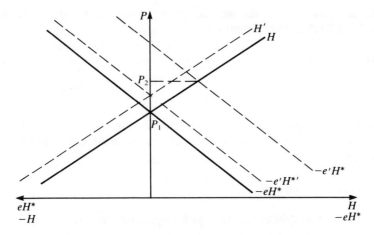

Figure 7.14 Devaluation in the Monetary Model

into balance at H' and $-e'H^{*\prime}$. The often quoted result of the monetary approach that devaluation cannot secure a current account surplus is based not on the actual mechanism whereby exchange rate changes affect the current account, but rather on the separate issue of the impossibility of effective sterilisation policies. It will be noted that a similar point follows from the Fleming–Mundell model outlined in the previous section.

Thus far, we have been concerned with the monetary approach to the current account, concentrating on the consequences of one-off changes in the money stock. In the next section, we extend the analysis to include capital movements, and analyse the implications of the monetary approach when policy is conducted in terms of monetary growth rates, rather than once-for-all changes.

7.2.2. The Monetary Approach to the Balance of Payments

In this section, we modify slightly the model set out in sub section 7.2.1, following Johnson (1972). First, we include the domestic interest rate in the demand for money function, so that we can write:

$$M^d = m(y, r, P) \qquad m_y > 0, m_r < 0, m_P > 0 \qquad (7.17')$$

Second, we assume that the law of one price applies not only to the goods market, but also to the asset market. That is, all assets are traded at the world interest rate, so that we can write:

$$r = r^* \qquad (7.24)$$

To complete the model, we may simply remind ourselves of the money supply and price level equations:

$$M^s = D + R \qquad\qquad (7.18)$$

$$P = eP^* \qquad\qquad (7.22)$$

As in the simple model in the previous section, it is the market-clearing process in the money market which drives the model. In equilibrium we can write:

$$m(y, r, P) = D + R$$

Re-arranging and differentiating with respect to time, we obtain:

$$\frac{dR}{dt} = \left(\frac{\partial m}{\partial y}\right)\left(\frac{dy}{dt}\right) + \left(\frac{\partial m}{\partial r}\right)\left(\frac{dr}{dt}\right) + \left(\frac{\partial m}{\partial P}\right)\left(\frac{dP}{dt}\right) - \frac{dD}{dt}$$

Dividing throughout by M, and by further re-arranging, we can write this as:

$$\left(\frac{1}{M}\right)\left(\frac{dR}{dt}\right) = \left(\frac{y}{M}\right)\left(\frac{\delta m}{\delta y}\right)\left(\frac{1}{y}\right)\left(\frac{dy}{dt}\right) + \left(\frac{r}{M}\right)\left(\frac{\delta m}{\delta r}\right)\left(\frac{1}{r}\right)\left(\frac{dr}{dt}\right)$$

$$+ \left(\frac{P}{M}\right)\left(\frac{\delta m}{\delta P}\right)\left(\frac{1}{P}\right)\left(\frac{dP}{dt}\right) - \left(\frac{1}{M}\right)\left(\frac{dD}{dt}\right)$$

This can be rewritten as:

$$\frac{BP}{M} = e(y).g(y) + e(r).g(r) + e(P).g(P) - \left(\frac{1}{M}\right)\left(\frac{dD}{dt}\right)$$

where BP is the balance of payments over time period t, $e(.)$ is the corresponding elasticity of demand for money, and $g(.)$ is the proportionate rate of growth of the variable in question over time period t. Therefore, we obtain:

$$BP = M(e(y).g(y) + e(r).g(r) + e(P).g(P)) - \left(\frac{dD}{dt}\right) \qquad (7.25)$$

Given the operation of the law of one price and a neoclassical aggregate supply function, together with the assumption that the demand for money has a unit price elasticity (i.e. $e(P) = 1$), (7.25) may be rewritten as:

$$BP = M(e(y).g(y^*) + e(r).g(r^*) + g(P^*)) - \frac{\mathrm{d}D}{\mathrm{d}t} \qquad (7.25')$$

This is the fundamental equation on which the monetary approach to the balance of payments is based. The balance of payments is the outcome of a flow divergence between the growth of the demand for money and the growth of domestic credit, with the money stock consequences of the balance of payments bringing the money market into equilibrium. It will be noted, therefore, that $(7.25')$ describes an equilibrium condition where BP may be positive or negative.

The economic process underlying this simple result is exactly equivalent to that outlined in our monetary model of the current account, but extended to include capital transactions as well as real expenditure. Starting from equilibrium, suppose the monetary authorities increase the money supply. Given that real income is fixed at its natural level, y^*, and the interest rate and the price level are tied to international levels by the law of one price, individuals will run down their excess money balances by buying goods and services and financial assets from abroad, and the necessary result of the increase in the domestic money supply is a balance of payments deficit equal in magnitude to that increase. The money stock remains at its original level, the increase in domestic credit being offset by a fall in foreign currency holdings.

The model presented here extends the result of the previous subsection in two ways. First, the offsetting deficit will occur on capital account as well as on current acount. It is very much in the style of the monetary approach that the decomposition of the external deficit into current and capital transactions is not confronted, in contrast to the Fleming–Mundell approach. However, although the law of one price is applied to both goods and asset markets, it may be assumed that the burden of adjustment will be borne by capital movements, given the greater ease with which capital transactions can be effected internationally. This dynamic assumption will become familiar to the reader in the discussion of asset market theories of exchange rate determination in the next chapter.

The second important difference is that it would appear from $(7.25')$ that the balance of payments need not be zero over time, and that money market equilibrium may be associated with external deficits or surpluses. The difference here is that the analysis is conducted in dynamic terms, whereas previously we were concerned with once-for-all changes. Thus, $(7.25')$ may be interpreted as describing a situation where the excessive growth in domestic credit (in the deficit case) may be regarded as a policy of continual sterilisation over successive time periods which prevents external adjustment from taking place. The policy implications of this analysis are clear. If the authorities wish to pursue a particular balance of payments objective, then the expected growth in the demand for money should be estimated and an appropriate target growth rate for domestic credit adopted. However, it should be noted that excessive growth of domestic credit, generating an ongoing external deficit, can be maintained only so long as the country in question has the foreign exchange reserves to finance the deficit.

However, whereas it is possible to conceive of a rationale for sterilisation policies within a Keynesian framework, it is much more difficult to rationalise such a strategy under the monetary approach, particularly in its hard line form. Given the law of one price in goods and asset markets, together with the natural rate hypothesis, domestic prices and interest rates, and income and employment levels are all exogenously given, and therefore there is nothing for independent monetary policy to determine other than the stock of foreign exchange reserves; and given that the monetary mechanism is perceived to correct external imbalance with minimal friction, there is no strong case for an individual country to build up its holdings of foreign exchange reserves.

7.2.3.   Policy Implications and Contrasts with the Fleming–Mundell Model

It is possible to see the monetary approach and the Fleming–Mundell model as extreme variants of one common model. (For an attempted synthesis, see Frenkel, Gylfason and Helliwell 1980.) However, it is clear that adherents to the two approaches draw different policy conclusions and interpretations. We now examine three examples of such differences.

(a) The Role of Monetary Policy   Under the monetary approach, domestic monetary policy is impotent. Two points should be noted about this conclusion. First, exactly the same result can be obtained from the Fleming–Mundell model, assuming zero sterilisation. The main differences are in the mechanisms involved. In the monetary approach, the law of one price ensures that, during the operation of the monetary mechanism, the price level, interest rate and real income are unaffected. In the Fleming–Mundell case, an increase in the money stock will increase real income and reduce the domestic interest rate while the balance of payments is in deficit, and, in an extended version of the model, the domestic price level may increase. In the longer term, as the balance of payments deficit reduces the money stock, these variables will return to their original values, in line with the monetary approach, but while the system is adjusting, monetary policy is not neutral.

Second, although monetary policy is impotent in its effects on domestic variables, it becomes all-powerful in its effects on the balance of payments. If the authorities have a balance of payments objective, say a surplus to build up depleted reserves, then a target growth rate of domestic credit which is lower than the projected growth in the demand for money should be adopted. This is generally the strategy adopted by the International Monetary Fund when granting credit arrangements for debtor countries. Thus, for example, when the UK negotiated special credit facilities with the IMF, first in the wake of the 1967 devaluation and then again during the sterling crisis of 1976, DCE ceilings were the conditions attached to the credit facilities by the IMF and agreed to in the Letters of Intent to the IMF by the UK authorities.

(b) The Monetary Mechanism as Automatic Adjustment   As a corollary to the above, the monetary approach also provides an automatic adjustment mechanism for the balance of payments. That is, an exogenous shock to the balance of payments, from whatever source, will have no permanent effect on the balance of payments as long as it is not underwritten by a change in domestic credit. For example, a devaluation can only generate a temporary external surplus by increasing the domestic price level (via the law of one price) and therefore the demand for money. With a given stock of domestic credit, this excess demand for money will indeed generate a balance of payments surplus M but only as long as the excess demand persists. In the absence of sterilisation, the balance of payments surplus will remove the excess demand by increasing the supply of foreign currency, thereby in turn removing the source of the surplus itself. This argument applies with equal force to any shock or 'expenditure-switching' policy designed to push the balance of payments into surplus (or deficit). Again, this argument can be made with equal force, though through a different mechanism, with respect to the Fleming–Mundell model, as long as the proviso of zero sterilisation is retained.

(c) Export-Led Growth   An interesting contrast in prediction between the two models reviewed here concerns the expected impact of real income growth on the balance of payments, and in particular, the explanation of the 1960s phenomenon whereby those countries experiencing rapid real income growth, such as West Germany and Japan, also exhibited persistent balance of payments surpluses. Monetarists have customarily cited these countries' experience as supportive evidence for the monetary approach, the argument being that rapid real income growth, which, it is implicitly assumed, is a supply-side phenomenon, increases the demand for money relative to the domestic supply, thus generating a balance of payments surplus. It is, of course, necessary to assume that the monetary authorities do not increase the supply of domestic credit in line with this real income growth.

The simple Fleming–Mundell model is somewhat wrong-footed by this issue, since real income growth is likely to generate balance of payments weakness through increased absorption. The escape route for Keynesians is provided by the dynamic theories of export-led growth, first introduced by Beckerman, Lamfalussy and Kaldor in the early 1960s. In these theories, exports and real income growth feed off each other in a 'virtuous circle', whereby export growth generates increased productivity, whether by Verdoorn's Law (Kaldor 1966) or by induced investment (Beckerman 1962, and Lamfalussy 1963), which not only increases real income but also increases competitiveness and therefore exports, so completing the circle. However, two fundamental questions are raised, and perhaps not entirely answered, by these models. First, what determines which countries enjoy the virtuous circle of export-led growth rather than the vicious circle of consumption-led growth? Second, under what circumstances will the link from productivity to competitiveness be broken by excessive real wage growth? It was this latter question which prompted some economists (e.g. Kindleberger 1967, Balassa 1963) to see export-led growth theories as models of long-run convergence as different economies 'matured' or reached full employment.

7.2.4. Conclusion

There are essentially two points of contrast between the monetary approach and the Fleming–Mundell model. The first relates to the pricing environment within which the two models operate. The Fleming–Mundell model is customarily set in fix-price terms domestically, with real income and employment being demand-determined, but allowing international relative prices to vary. The monetary model, in contrast, assumes clearing markets and supply-determined income and employment, and the law of one price in international markets. These differences render different variables exogenous as between the two models and therefore alter the transmission mechanism from macroeconomic policy and exchange rates to the balance of payments.

The second difference concerns the view taken of sterilisation policies. In the monetary approach, sterilisation is assumed to be impracticable and irrational. In the Fleming–Mundell model, zero sterilisation is seen as a special case. Clearly, the question of the efficacy of sterilisation policies and the desirability of pursuing them is central to the discussion of macroeconomic policy under fixed exchange rates.

Finally, both the models reviewed so far can be criticised for focusing exclusively on the money stock in their respective analyses of asset markets; it is this focus which leads both models to define external balance in terms of the overall balance of payments. Assuming a degree of capital mobility, the current account can be in surplus or deficit in long-run equilibrium in both cases, even in the absence of sterilisation. This is an uncomfortable result, and the incorporation of wealth effects into the analysis renders this view of external balance invalid. It is to wealth-based current account models that we now turn in section 3.

7.3. Wealth Effects and Portfolio Models of the Balance of Payments

In this section we introduce and examine a portfolio model of the balance of payments. (Early examples of fixed exchange rate portfolio models are to be found in Oates 1966, McKinnon 1969, and Branson 1974.) The main contribution of such a model is twofold. First, it formally integrates the stock theory of the capital account which we mentioned in section 1. Second, it enables us to examine the role of wealth effects in an open economy under fixed exchange rates, which in turn affords a central role for the current account, casting doubt on the long-run validity of the Fleming–Mundell contention that external and internal balance can be attained by the fiscal–monetary mix without recourse to additional (expenditure-switching) policies. In so doing, it also has implications for the design and implementation of effective sterilisation strategies.

The model which we present is an extension of the Fleming–Mundell model and is fix-price in character. This is appropriate for three reasons. First, macroeconomic portfolio models have been developed generally within a Keynesian framework (e.g. Tobin, 1982). Second, the monetary approach does not comfortably incorporate the main elements of portfolio models. The assumption of perfect substitutability of domestic and foreign assets removes one of the principal features of the portfolio approach, while the monetary tradition of not treating current and capital accounts individually is clearly at odds with the model to be presented here. Finally, though the fix-price assumption of the Fleming–Mundell model is both restrictive and unrealistic, it is our view that it is preferable for didactic purposes to the alternative natural rate assumptions of the monetary approach.

7.3.1. *A Simple Portfolio Model of the Open Economy*

We begin with an analysis of short-run equilibrium in asset markets, which draws heavily on the closed economy analysis of Tobin presented in Chapter 5. We assume that domestic residents may hold three assets— non-interest-bearing domestic money (M), domestic bonds (B), which bear interest r, but which are non-tradable (following Branson 1974, 1975), and foreign assets (F), which bear interest r^*. (The domestic currency value of foreign assets is, in fact, given by eF, but we suppress the fixed exchange rate in the current discussion.) We adopt the 'small country' assumption, such that r^* is exogenously given at $\bar{r}^*$. Taking the stocks of the three assets as exogenously given, we may set out the equilibrium conditions in asset markets as follows:

$$M = m(r, r^*)W \qquad m_r, m_{r^*} < 0 \tag{7.26}$$

$$B = b(r, r^*)W \qquad b_r > 0, b_{r^*} < 0 \tag{7.27}$$

$$F = f(r, r^*)W \qquad f_r < 0, f_{r^*} > 0 \tag{7.28}$$

In a manner entirely analogous to our treatment of the Tobin model in a closed economy, we can describe asset market equilibrium in diagrammatic form, as in Figure 7.15. The *MM*, *BB* and *FF* functions describe the combinations of r and r^* which generate equilibrium in the money, bond and foreign asset markets respectively. (The analysis is identical to that contained in Chapter 5, except for the fact that the portfolio contains foreign assets in place of equity, and for simplicity we ignore transactions balances.)

The model is completed by integrating the goods market and the current account into the analysis, as in (7.29) to (7.31):

$$y = y(W, r) \qquad y_W > 0, y_r < 0 \tag{7.29}$$

$$CA = c(y) \qquad c_y < 0 \tag{7.30}$$

$$CA = \Delta M + \Delta F \tag{7.31}$$

In the goods market, domestic expenditure is a function of wealth, rather than income, and the rate of interest, while the current account is solely a function of income, suppressing the fixed exchange rate. Equation (7.31) expresses the budget identity whereby a current account surplus is associated with increasing asset holdings by domestic residents. These increased holdings may be in the form of domestic currency, or foreign

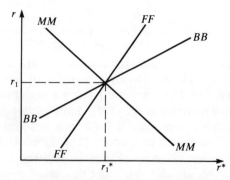

Figure 7.15 Portfolio Equilibrium in an Open Economy

assets which may be purchased at the exogenously given world interest rate, but not of domestic bonds which are non-traded and exogenously fixed in supply. Let us now examine the working of this model by analysing the short- and long-run consequences of an increase in the domestic money stock. We define the short run as the time period within which asset markets clear.

We begin in full equilibrium in Figure 7.16, with asset stocks and interest rates such as to give schedules *MM*, *BB* and *FF* intersecting at point *X*, where $\bar{r}^*$ equals the prevailing world interest rate. Let us also assume that we start from a position of current account balance.

Let us now allow an increase in the domestic money stock. The *MM* schedule shifts to MM_1, since with a larger money stock the rate of return on alternative assets must be reduced to maintain asset market equilibrium. In addition, the *BB* schedule shifts to BB_1 as the increase in wealth represented by the increased money stock increases the demand for bonds, pushing down the interest rate, *r*. Similarly, the *FF* schedule shifts to FF_1 for analogous reasons. The new asset market equilibrium is at point *Y*. (It will be recalled from the discussion in Chapter 5 that all three functions must necessarily intersect at the one point.) In the absence of capital movements, point *Y* would represent full asset market equilibrium. However, it will be noted that in domestic portfolios, the market-clearing interest rate on foreign assets has fallen to r_1^*. Thus, domestic residents are prepared to hold foreign assets at an interest rate lower than the prevailing world interest rate, and a capital outflow will result as domestic residents accumulate foreign assets and decumulate money. Diagrammatically, this is represented by a rightward shift of both *MM* and *FF* to MM_2 and FF_2 intersecting at *Z*. (*BB* does not shift during this phase, since total

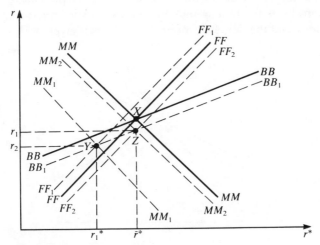

Figure 7.16 Monetary Expansion in the Portfolio Model

wealth is not changing, and there is merely a substitution effect along BB and no net wealth effect to shift BB). Thus, the final asset market equilibrium is attained at Z with a lower domestic interest rate, but at the same world rate $\bar{r}^*$.

A similar exercise may be carried out to illustrate the consequences of an exogenous increase in foreign assets, as in Figure 7.17. Again starting from point X, the increase in foreign assets shifts FF to FF_1, BB to BB_1 and MM to MM_1. The difference in this case is that the initial change in the domestic interest rate is ambiguous, being dependent, in a manner familiar from Chapter 5, on the pattern of substitutabilities and relative assets shares within the portfolio. In the case illustrated in Figure 7.17 (i.e. point Y), the domestic interest rate rises, reflecting close substitutability between domestic and foreign bonds.

Again, however, this is not asset market equilibrium, since r^* is now above its world level. The resultant capital inflow shifts FF_1 and MM_1 to FF_2 and MM_2 respectively, and again the final effect (point Z) is a fall in the domestic interest rate. Such a result would obtain whatever the cross-elasticities within the portfolio and the intuition behind this result is quite simple. An increase in the stock of foreign assets and/or money is an increase in the assets alternative to domestic bonds, and can be expected to bid down the rate of interest on domestic bonds *relative* to other assets. Since the rates on the alternative assets are fixed (at zero and $\bar{r}^*$), this necessarily means a fall in the rate on bonds *in absolute terms*. The asset market consequence of a current account surplus, increasing M and F, is necessarily to bid down the domestic interest rate. This result is also illustrated in Figure 7.18.

Since domestic money and foreign assets can be freely exchanged for each other at the given world interest rate, it is possible to draw an equilibrium locus for money plus foreign assets with respect to the total wealth stock and the domestic interest rate. This is given in Figure 7.18 by

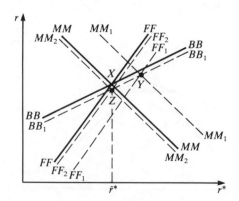

Figure 7.17   Foreign Asset Accumulation in the Portfolio Model

the *MF* curve, which is upward sloping, reflecting the fact that the demand for both foreign assets and money is a positive function of wealth and a negative function of the domestic interest rate. The *BB* function, describing equilibrium in the bond market, is downward sloping since the demand for bonds is a positive function of both the wealth stock and the domestic interest rate. Clearly, full asset market equilibrium is obtained at the point of intersection *A*. An increase in the money stock (or the foreign asset stock) will shift the *MF* curve to the right, increasing domestic wealth and reducing the domestic interest rate, confirming the outcomes in Figures 7.16 and 7.17. By contrast, an open-market operations increase in the money stock (i.e. accompanied by a fall in the bond stock) will shift both the *MF* and *BB* curves downward by the same amount (to MF_1 and BB_1), so that the wealth stock is unaltered but the fall in the domestic interest rate is greater than in the case of an increase in the money stock alone.

To return to our original example of an increase in the domestic money stock, with the bond stock held constant, it is clear that while the immediate consequence is a rise in domestic wealth and a fall in the domestic interest rate, this is only a position of short-run equilibrium, since from (7.29) and (7.30) the current account will now be in deficit. This can be illustrated in Figure 7.19.

In Figure 7.19, we superimpose on the two asset equilibrium functions an equilibrium locus for the current account, denoted as the *CA* curve. This is an upward sloping function, as income (and therefore the current account) is a negative (positive) function of the interest rate and a positive (negative) function of wealth. In the absence of policies which shift the *CA* line, we may also note that current account balance is associated with a given income level, and therefore at all points on *CA*, income is constant at this level. At points below *CA*, income is greater than this level, and the current account is in deficit, and vice versa for points above *CA*. Obviously

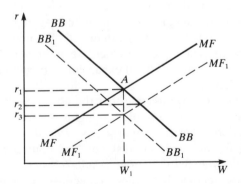

Figure 7.18 Portfolio Equilibrium in an Open Economy

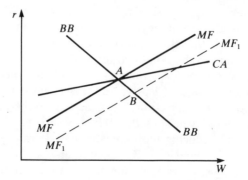

Figure 7.19   Portfolio Equilibrium and the Current Account

it is not clear *a priori* whether CA is steeper or flatter than MF.

Starting from an initial equilibrium at point A, where asset markets clear and the current account is in balance, an increase in the money stock shifts MF to MF_1 and asset market equilibrium is now represented by point B. Point B is unambiguously below the CA line and therefore, while income has risen in response to the monetary expansion, the current account is now in deficit. From (7.31), this deficit must be reducing domestic holdings of money and foreign assets, which in turn shifts the MF function back towards the left, and this process will continue until it has reattained its original position, with income back at its initial level and the current account back in balance.

While this analysis is reminiscent of the Fleming–Mundell model under zero sterilisation, where monetary policy is rendered impotent by its balance of payments consequences, the key difference is that this model is driven by wealth and portfolio effects, and that full stock equilibrium requires a zero current account rather than balance in the overall balance of payments.

It is also possible to analyse a particular form of fiscal policy in this model. Since the expenditure function in (7.29) is wealth-based, the only channel through which fiscal policy can affect aggregate demand, and therefore real income, is through wealth effects. We may therefore regard pure fiscal expansion as an exogenous increase in the domestic bond stock. The consequences of a one-off fiscal expansion expressed in this form are shown in Figure 7.20.

In this particular case, we assume that the CA curve is flatter than the MF curve (reflecting, for example, a highly interest-elastic domestic expenditure function). Expansionary fiscal policy shifts the BB curve to the right, increasing the domestic interest rate and domestic wealth, which, because of the relatively flat CA curve, results in a current account surplus at point B. (Thus, income has fallen, reflecting the assumed degree of interest sensitivity of domestic expenditure in this case.) The current

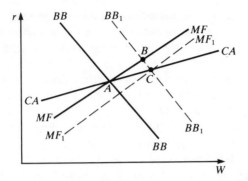

Figure 7.20 Fiscal Expansion and the Current Account

account surplus shifts the *MF* curve to the right until the current account returns to equilibrium at point *C*, and income rises to its initial level. In the case where *CA* is steeper than *MF*, the short-run consequence of fiscal expansion is a current account deficit, but the final equilibrium remains associated with current balance.

It is clear from the above discussion that any current account disturbance will give rise to wealth and substitution effects such as to generate current balance. Thus, since the current account is a function of the level of income, long-run equilibrium in this model is uniquely associated with the income level at which the current account clears. Neither monetary nor fiscal policy is able to affect domestic income in the long run, unless some expenditure-switching policy is employed, which would have the effect of shifting the *CA* curve in Figures 7.19 and 7.20. This is in line with the conclusion reached in the Swan–Salter analysis in section 1, but is now not restricted to the case of capital immobility. Even with mobile capital, the Fleming–Mundell conclusion that internal and external balance can be attained by means of the appropriate fiscal–monetary mix is untenable once the wealth effects of the current account are incorporated. If these wealth effects are not offset, or sterilised, then the long-run equilibrium income level is given by the current account, and can only be changed by means of an exchange rate change or some other expenditure-switching policy.

Within this analysis, it is clearly a key issue as to whether the ongoing wealth effects of the non-zero current balance can be effectively sterilised, and it is to this question that we now turn.

7.3.2. Sterilisation Policies and the Current Account

From the outset, it is obvious that effective sterilisation policies will not be defined in terms of keeping the domestic money stock constant, as was the case in sections 1 and 2. In this wealth-based model, what is required is for the domestic wealth to be maintained at a constant level in the face of current imbalance. What are the implications of entrusting this task to monetary policy?

It is clear that for monetary policy to offset the domestic wealth effects of, say, a current account surplus, not only will it be required to reduce domestic credit by the amount of the current account surplus every time period, it will also need to do this by changes in the domestic credit which do not involve offsetting changes in the domestic bond stock. In Figure 7.21, we start from point *A*, where domestic asset markets are in equilibrium, but the current account is in surplus. In the absence of sterilisation policies, the *MF* function would drift to the right as domestic residents accumulate wealth. This, together with the resulting fall in the interest rate, increases domestic real income and expenditure until the current account is back in balance, and the *MF* curve intersects with *BB* and *CA* at *B*. Effective sterilisation policies will stop the *MF* curve from shifting in this manner, and preserve real income at the lower level implied by *A*. Effective sterilisation requires that domestic credit be reduced at the rate of the current account surplus, since this will have the effect of stabilising the position of the *MF* curve in the face of the current account surplus. Under these circumstances, the domestic interest rate and wealth stock are constant, and the current account surplus remains intact.

Similarly, the above analysis could be carried out for the case of a current account deficit (resulting from attempts to keep income levels higher than those associated with current balance) which would be sterilised by increasing domestic credit at a rate equal to the deficit. The problem here is that such a policy, though effective in the short run, would ultimately run up against a foreign exchange reserves constraint, as the current account deficit (without an offsetting capital account surplus) persists.

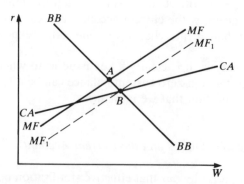

Figure 7.21 Sterilisation by Fiat Money Changes

Suppose, alternatively, that the authorities pursue sterilisation by means of open-market operations, and that these are aimed at offsetting the current account surplus rather than maintaining a given money stock. The outcome of such a policy is less clear cut than in the previous example, and in particular depends on the relative slopes of the *MF* and *CA* curves. As we noted earlier, the slopes of these curves are determined by completely unrelated parameter values. In Figure 7.22, we take the case where *CA* is steeper than *MF*. Again starting from a position of surplus, sterilisation by means of open-market operations has the effect of shifting the *BB* curve to the right, leaving *MF* stationary. This is because the fall in domestic credit engineered by the open-market operations offsets the increase in *M* and *F* arising from the current account surplus, but it increases the stock of domestic bonds outstanding. It is clear that this policy will have the effect of pushing the economy to point *B*, where the current account is in equilibrium. Thus, sterilisation policy via open-market operations in this case is doomed to failure, and the economics of this result is quite straightforward. The current account surplus increases domestic wealth, while open-market operations merely redistribute it as between money and domestic bonds. Thus, the net accumulation of wealth is not offset, and as wealth increases there are two opposing effects on the current account. The wealth effect on expenditure reduces the current surplus, while the increase in the domestic interest rate tends to increase it. In Figure 7.22 the former effect prevails, and the adjustment of the current account to equilibrium is not averted. Precisely the same argument may be implemented in reverse in the case of a current account deficit.

However, it should be noted that the above result does not apply in the case where the *CA* line is flatter than the *MF* curve. This case is illustrated in Figure 7.23. Starting once more from point *A* where the current account is in surplus, it is clear that open-market bond sales which push *BB* to the right will now have the effect of generating a larger current account

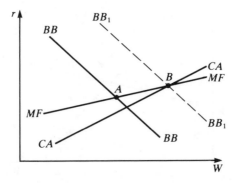

Figure 7.22 Sterilisation by Open-Market Operations — I

surplus. This is because the wealth effect on expenditure is now outweighed by the interest rate effect, and the model is unstable. Thus, attempts to sterilise the current account surplus actually serve to increase it. Again, these arguments apply symmetrically to the deficit case.

It will be recalled that the principal motive for a sterilisation strategy in this model is to enable the authorities to employ demand management policies to affect real income without recourse to expenditure-switching policies. The general conclusion of the foregoing analysis must be that, once a more fully diversified portfolio approach is adopted, together with the incorporation of wealth effects, sterilisation policies appear much more complex than is implied by the Fleming–Mundell approach of the first section. In addition, it is clear that open-market operations based policies are likely to be less effective than policies based on pure changes in domestic credit. Indeed, the latter point can be extended to include changes in any single component of domestic wealth if interest rate effects on domestic expenditure are suppressed or, alternatively, if domestic and foreign bonds are assumed to be perfect substitutes. Once such a streamlined model is adopted, where domestic aggregate demand, and therefore the current account and real income, is a function of total domestic wealth holdings, irrespective of their composition as between different assets, it is a simple matter to integrate into the analysis a government budget constraint, where the public sector deficit is endogenous to real income — with powerful results for the efficacy of macroeconomic policy. It is to a model of this type that we now finally turn. (The analysis which follows may be regarded as a highly simplified version of that contained in Currie 1976. Note also the contributions of Turnovsky 1976, and Branson 1976.)

Given our simplifying assumptions on the asset market side of the model, we are centrally concerned with the relations between the public sector surplus (*PSS*) and the current account surplus, wealth stocks and

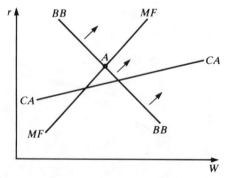

Figure 7.23   Sterilisation by Open-Market Operations — II

the level of income. Thus, we can set out the model as follows, retaining (7.30) from the earlier version.

$$y = y(W) \qquad y_W > 0 \qquad\qquad (7.29')$$

$$CA = c(y) \qquad c_y < 0 \qquad\qquad (7.30)$$

$$PSS = p(y) \qquad p_y > 0 \qquad\qquad (7.32)$$

$$\Delta W = CA - PSS \qquad\qquad (7.33)$$

Equation (7.32) expresses the public sector surplus as a positive function of the income level, on the familiar assumption that tax receipts rise with real income, while (7.33) is a simplified budget identity whereby increased wealth holdings by domestic residents must come either from the government via fiscal finance or from abroad via a current account surplus. The model can be set out as in Figure 7.24. From (7.29'), it is clear that equilibrium is obtained only when $\Delta W = 0$, and from (7.33), this can be located where CA cuts PSS. At income levels greater than y_1, the public sector surplus exceeds the current account surplus, generating a fall in domestic wealth and pushing income down, and vice versa for income levels lower than y_1. To put the matter another way, in the absence of sterilisation, the current account surplus at y_1 would increase wealth, and therefore aggregate demand, until income rose to y_1 and the current account equalled zero. This does not happen in this model because fiscal policy acts as a steriliser.

Furthermore, it is now clear that fiscal policy can affect real income without the aid of expenditure-switching policies in this model. For example, expansionary fiscal policy shifts the PSS function to the right to PSS_1 (reducing the fiscal surplus at every level of income). At income

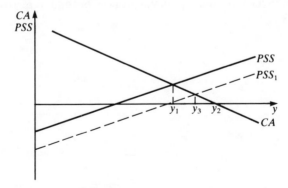

Figure 7.24 Sterilisation with an Endogenous Fiscal Sector

level y_1, wealth is now increasing since the current account surplus exceeds the fiscal surplus, increasing wealth and therefore driving income towards y_3. Similarly, the familiar tenet of the monetary approach that devaluation, tariffs or the like cannot permanently affect the external balance does not hold here. Such policies shift the *CA* line upwards, increasing both income and the current account surplus. In short, the policy conclusions which the monetary approach sought to invalidate by assuming zero sterilisation have been rehabilitated by the introduction of sterilisation not by pure monetary policy, but by fiscal policy.

7.4. Conclusion

The fundamental question which runs through this entire chapter is whether a country whose monetary authorities pursue a fixed exchange rate target can enjoy a degree of sovereignty in its domestic macroeconomic policy. The answer supplied by the monetary approach is not so much negative, but rather that the question does not really arise, since the degree of domestic wage flexibility normally assumed in these models makes income levels supply-determined, while price and interest rate levels are tied to competitive world markets. In any case, the latter assumptions render impracticable sterilisation and, therefore, independent macro-economic policy.

The Fleming–Mundell model retains a role for domestic policy, partly by means of allowing for effective sterilisation. However, even in the case of zero sterilisation, fiscal policy can affect domestic real income; but this result relies upon a flow theory of the capital account. The portfolio approach not only replaces this flow theory with a more acceptable stock adjustment approach, but also integrates wealth effects into the analysis. The net outcome is that the current account now becomes central to the analysis and that appropriately specified sterilisation policies, and therefore independent macroeconomic policy, can now become effective.

8

MACROECONOMIC POLICY AND THE EXCHANGE RATE

In this chapter we extend the discussion of open economy monetary and fiscal policy to consider the case of flexible exchange rates. Throughout the chapter we shall assume that the domestic currency is freely floating against other currencies, i.e. that the authorities do not intervene in the foreign exchange market to influence the exchange rate, and that consequently the current and capital accounts of the balance of payments sum to zero at all times. However, it must be recognised that in the period after the breakdown of the Bretton Woods system in 1971, the authorities have in fact consistently intervened in the foreign exchange market and that the exchange rate regime since then has been one of managed or 'dirty' floating. In Chapter 9, we consider some of the criteria whereby official intervention might be part of an optimal monetary policy rule. For the moment, however, we are concerned with the behaviour of the exchange rate in the absence of official intervention.

Exchange rates are important for macroeconomic policy for a number of reasons. First, the exchange rate can play an important role in the transmission mechanism of monetary and fiscal policy, affecting real income (as in the Fleming–Mundell model), and/or the domestic price level (as in the monetary approach). Thus, alternative theories of exchange rate behaviour present different conclusions about the relative efficacy of monetary and fiscal policy as instruments of demand management. Second, the exchange rate may be viewed as a kind of filter through which developments in the world economy affect the domestic economy. The expected impact of such external shocks varies depending on the exchange rate model in question. Finally, the short-run dynamics of exchange rate adjustment may be an important consideration in formulating and implementing aggregate demand policies. In particular, the exchange rate may 'jump', and possibly oscillate, in response to actual or expected domestic policy developments. Again, the possibility and implications of such exchange rate behaviour are of importance to macroeconomic policy.

Exchange rate economics has been one of the most rapidly developing areas of research in recent years, where the bewildering variety of models has made it difficult to reach consensus answers to the issues introduced above. (For a survey of this literature see Jones and Kenen 1985.) In this chapter, we set out the main alternative approaches, assessing the implications of these models for the analysis of macroeconomic policy. In sections 1 and 2, we review the flexible exchange rate versions of the Fleming–Mundell and monetary models whose fixed rate versions are familiar from Chapter 7. In section 3, within the framework of the monetary model, we introduce imperfect price flexibility and the Dornbusch model of 'overshooting', while in section 4 we focus on the role of the current account in exchange rate determination by integrating wealth effects in a portfolio framework. Finally, in section 5, we examine some of the empirical evidence and policy issues raised by these alternative approaches to exchange rate economics.

8.1. The Fleming–Mundell Model

The general lines of the Fleming–Mundell model are already familiar to us from the previous chapter, and can be summarised in the following three equations, set out in linear form. Throughout the analysis, we adopt the small country assumption, so that world income and the world interest rate are exogenously given.

$$y = \alpha_0 + \alpha_1 y - \alpha_2 r + \alpha_3 e - \alpha_4 y + \alpha_5 y^* \tag{8.1}$$

$$M = \beta_1 y - \beta_2 r \tag{8.2}$$

$$BP = CA + K = \alpha_3 e - \alpha_4 y + \alpha_5 y^* + \Omega(r - r^*) = 0 \tag{8.3}$$

Equation (8.1) is the open economy IS curve where α_0 is autonomous expenditure, which may be regarded as encompassing fiscal policy, and the last three terms set net exports (CA) as a positive function of the exchange rate (where the Marshall–Lerner conditions are assumed to obtain and the exchange rate is defined as the domestic currency price of a unit of foreign currency), a positive function of world real income and a negative function of domestic income, reflecting a positive marginal propensity to import. Equation (8.2) is the LM curve with the price level fixed and therefore suppressed as a determinant of the demand for nominal money. In (8.3), the balance of payments comprises net exports and the capital account (K), the latter set as a positive function of the differential between the domestic interest rate and the world interest rate, with the value of Ω reflecting the degree of international capital mobility. Under flexible exchange rates, the balance of payments is set equal to zero with the exchange rate determined endogenously.

The model can be solved for real income, with the money stock, autonomous expenditure and the world interest rate as exogenous variables. Thus, we can write:

$$y = \frac{[\alpha_0 + (\alpha_2 + \Omega)(M/\beta_2) + \Omega r^*]}{\Delta} \tag{8.4}$$

where $\Delta = 1 - \alpha_1 + \left(\frac{\beta_1}{\beta_2}\right)(\alpha_2 + \Omega)$

The diagrammatic treatment of the model may be set out as in Figure 8.1, which is drawn on the assumption of imperfect capital mobility (i.e. $\Omega < \infty$). We may illustrate the comparative statics of the model by analysing the impact on real income of fiscal and monetary policy. We begin by increasing the money stock so as to shift the LM curve from LM_1 to LM_2. Under fixed exchange rates, this would generate a balance of payments deficit, which, in the absence of sterilisation, would neutralise the domestic monetary policy, shifting the LM curve back to LM_1. Under flexible exchange rates, however, it is the IS and BP curves which shift to restore equilibrium. The incipient balance of payments deficit, implied by point S in Figure 8.1, generates excess supply of the domestic currency on foreign exchange markets, and the exchange rate depreciates. This has two sets of consequences. On the one hand, the depreciation renders the domestic country more competitive, shifting the BP line to the right. On the other hand, the improved trading position of the domestic country also generates an increase in aggregate demand, as net exports increase, and this shifts the IS curve to the right. The rise in the exchange rate will

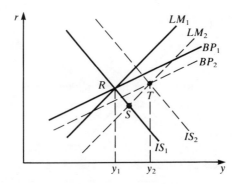

Figure 8.1 Expansionary Monetary Policy in the Fleming–Mundell Model

continue until a new equilibrium is attained at point T, where LM_2, IS_2 and BP_2 all intersect. Thus, the exchange rate adjustment serves to reinforce domestic monetary policy, to an extent which is dependent on the slopes of all the three schedules, but most significantly on that of the BP curve, which in turn reflects the degree of capital mobility. This may be seen explicitly by examining the monetary multiplier, which may be obtained from (8.4):

$$\frac{dy}{dM} = \frac{\alpha_2 + \Omega}{\beta_2 \Delta} \tag{8.5}$$

It is clear from (8.5) that the greater is the value of Ω, the greater is the monetary multiplier. In the case of zero capital mobility, for example, the initial monetary expansion will generate a smaller incipient balance of payments deficit, and therefore a smaller depreciation, than in the case illustrated in Figure 8.1, since there can be no capital outflow to reinforce the current account deficit. Conversely, in the case of perfect capital mobility, the value of Ω is infinity, and dy/dM is given by $1/\beta_1$, exactly the same result as when the IS curve is horizontal in a closed economy. This result is obtained because under perfect capital mobility the BP line is horizontal, and the exchange rate must adjust to shift the IS curve enough to clear the goods market at the given world interest rate. This extreme case is illustrated in Figure 8.2. Again, if we start from equilibrium at point R and consider a shift of LM to LM_2, then the domestic interest rate will tend to fall towards r_2, below the world interest rate r^*. The resulting capital outflow will push the exchange rate up and the improving trade balance shifts IS to the right, until equilibrium S is reached. Monetary policy is now at its most effective.

The model can also be employed to analyse the effectiveness of fiscal policy under flexible rates. To simplify the analysis, we restrict the discussion to two cases of capital mobility. In Figure 8.3 we illustrate the case where capital is imperfectly mobile and where the BP line is steeper

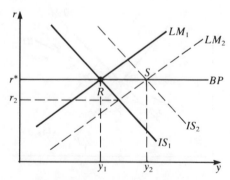

Figure 8.2   Monetary Expansion under Perfect Capital Mobility

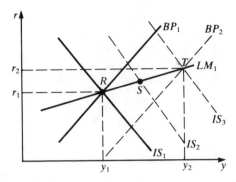

Figure 8.3 Fiscal Policy under Imperfect Capital Mobility

than the LM curve. Again, starting from equilibrium at point R, a fiscal expansion shifts the IS curve to IS_2. In a closed economy this would result in an increase in real income and the interest rate, as summarised by point S. However, in the open economy case when BP is steeper than LM, this is a position of incipient balance of payments deficit and the exchange rate will depreciate, shifting both IS and BP curves rightwards, until a new equilibrium is attained at r_2 and y_2, at point T. In this case, fiscal policy is rendered more powerful by its exchange rate consequences, but its effectiveness relative to monetary policy depends on the slopes of all three curves. This is easily seen by comparing the monetary multiplier with the fiscal multiplier given in (8.6):

$$\frac{dy}{d\alpha_o} = \frac{1}{\Delta} \tag{8.6}$$

Fiscal policy is more powerful than monetary policy under flexible rates only if $\alpha_2 + \Omega < \beta_2$. Thus, the more mobile is capital, the more interest-elastic is the expenditure function and the less interest-elastic is the demand for money, the more powerful is monetary policy relative to fiscal policy. In other words, it is only in the particular case where BP and IS are steep, and LM is flat that fiscal policy outperforms monetary policy. Taking the extreme case where capital is perfectly mobile, we see that in this case not only is monetary policy more effective, but also that fiscal policy is completely unable to affect real income. This situation is depicted in Figure 8.4. With the domestic interest rate tied to the world rate, r^*, the attempted fiscal expansion must generate an incipient capital inflow which causes the exchange rate to fall, thus reducing the country's net exports, and shifting the IS curve back towards its original position. In the case of perfect capital mobility, full equilibrium obtains only when there is no further tendency for the domestic interest rate to rise above the world rate. This can only occur when the exchange rate has appreciated sufficiently for

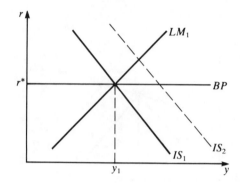

Figure 8.4   Fiscal Policy under Perfect Capital Mobility

net exports to have fallen so as to offset exactly the initial fiscal expansion. In terms of (8.5), as Ω approaches infinity, $dy/d\alpha_0$ approaches zero, and, to borrow some terminology from Chapter 6, fiscal expansion has crowded out net exports, and there is no change in real income as a consequence.

Thus, the Fleming–Mundell model throws up an interesting asymmetry in the relative effectiveness of fiscal and monetary policy under fixed and flexible exchange rates. As we saw in Chapter 7, under fixed exchange rates fiscal policy is underwritten by the monetary consequences of the balance of payments, while monetary policy is correspondingly offset. As we have seen in the analysis above, the situation is broadly reversed under flexible rates.

In addition, this asymmetry in the Fleming–Mundell model is extended to the response of real income to exogenous shocks from abroad. We can characterise a foreign monetary shock as a change in the world interest rate. The consequences for domestic real income are given by:

$$\frac{dy}{dr^*} = \frac{\Omega}{\Delta} \tag{8.7}$$

Thus, the impact of an increase in the world interest rate on domestic income is positive as long as capital is not entirely immobile, and increases with the degree of capital mobility. In the case of perfect mobility, $dy/dr^* = \beta_2/\beta_1$. The mechanism at work here is that an increase in the world interest rate generates an incipient capital outflow from the domestic country, pushing the exchange rate up. The consequent increase in net exports then increases real income until the increased transactions demand for money has brought the domestic interest rate up into line with the world rate.

In contrast, a foreign real shock, such as an increase in world real income, would impact in the first instance on net exports. For example, a rise in world income would tend to raise domestic net exports, and thus shift both the BP and IS curves to the right. However, since the BP curve is shifted further to the right than is the IS curve (so long as the marginal propensity to save is positive), the net outcome for the balance of payments is an incipient surplus, whatever the degree of capital mobility. The consequent appreciation in the exchange rate must then reduce net exports until the balance of payments is back in equilibrium, which is necessarily at the original level of income. The domestic economy is therefore perfectly insulated from foreign real shocks, a conclusion which is confirmed algebraically by the absence of y^* in the reduced form equation (8.4).

The principal shortcoming of the Fleming–Mundell model is, of course, the fix-price assumption. It will be recalled from the discussion in the previous chapter that the Fleming–Mundell approach is more properly to be regarded as an analysis of aggregate demand in an open economy, and that allowing for price flexibility has the effect of dampening the real income consequences of exogenous shocks, policy induced or otherwise. The same caveat applies here, but with an additional element. Exchange rate changes may also affect the domestic price level through the aggregate supply side in two ways. First, the depreciating exchange rate tends to increase import costs, which, if imports are used as factors of production, will tend to shift the aggregate supply curve upwards. Second, this effect may be magnified if workers base their wage claims on a consumer price index which includes imports. Thus, changes in the exchange rate will not only affect aggregate demand, by shifting the BP and IS curves, but also shift aggregate supply.

Let us consider an increase in the domestic money stock, under perfect capital mobility, as is illustrated in Figure 8.5. In Figure 8.5(a), we shift the LM curve from LM_1 to LM_2. In the simple fix-price model, this would increase real income to y_2. Suppose, however, the economy faces an upward sloping aggregate supply curve such as SS_1 in Figure 8.5(b). Then the increased money stock would shift the aggregate demand curve to DD_2, but the price level would rise to P_2, dampening the increase in income to y_3, as the rising price level shifts LM back to LM_3 in Figure 8.5(a), and IS shifts to IS_3 as the exchange rate adjusts. Clearly, the steeper is aggregate supply, the less real income will rise and the more inflationary will the increase in the money stock be.

However, it is also likely that the exchange rate depreciation implied in Figure 8.5(a) will displace the aggregate supply curve upwards, say to SS_2, raising the price level, and further dampening the rise in real income by shifting the IS and LM curves to IS_4 and LM_4. The importance of this secondary effect depends on the openness of the economy and the extent of real wage resistance of the labour force to changes in the consumer price index shocks (or, alternatively, the extent of wage indexation in the economy).

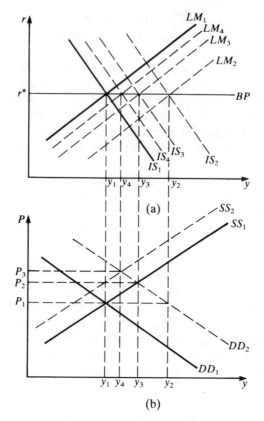

Figure 8.5   Fleming–Mundell with Flexible Prices

Therefore, to the extent that this effect is significant, it must be incorporated into the analysis of the various policies/shocks set out above. Thus, not only is the effectiveness of monetary policy called into question, but also expansionary fiscal policy may be helped by a rightward shift in the aggregate supply curve as the exchange rate appreciates. (For further details on the incorporation of such aggregate supply effects in exchange rate models, see Neary and Purvis 1983, Bruce and Purvis 1985.)

Other criticisms of the model are familiar from the previous chapter. The treatment of capital movements remains unsatisfactory, being cast in flow rather than in stock terms, and, although the current account plays a leading role in the adjustment mechanism, no account is taken of the wealth effects, either on portfolio allocation or on real expenditures. This criticism is given all the greater force when it is noted that equilibrium in the Fleming–Mundell model requires only overall payments balance, and that a current account deficit/surplus, with corresponding wealth stock changes, is allowed to persist in the long run. Recognition of this point lies at the centre of the portfolio theories outlined later in this chapter.

Finally, there is no role for exchange rate expectations in the model. Capital movements are solely a function of the interest differential between the domestic economy and the rest of the world, taken to measure the differential yield on the respective assets. However, another component in the prospective asset yields is the expected capital gain/loss through expected exchange rate variations. Expectations play a crucial role in many theories of the exchange rate, and their neglect in the simple Fleming–Mundell model is a fundamental criticism of that approach.

8.2. The Monetary Model of Exchange Rates

8.2.1. *The Simple Monetary Model with Static Expectations*

The monetary approach to the analysis of exchange rate determination is a direct application of the monetary approach to the balance of payments to the case of floating exchange rates. (For a collection of the seminal papers in this area, see Frenkel and Johnson 1978.) The key characteristics and assumptions of the monetary approach are retained as follows: first, asset market equilibrium lies at the centre of the model, where the asset in question is money and where the demand for money function is stable and the supply of money is determined by the authorities. Thus, adopting a log-linear form, we can write:

$$m = \lambda y + p - \rho r \tag{8.8}$$

Second, international goods markets are sufficiently competitive for the domestic and world price level to be equal when expressed in a common currency. Thus, we can write:

$$p = e + p^* \tag{8.9}$$

which may be rewritten as:

$$e = p - p^* \tag{8.9'}$$

That is to say, the exchange rate matches the difference in own currency price levels between the domestic country and the rest of the world, and thus equates the two price levels in terms of either currency. This is in accordance with purchasing power parity (PPP).

The law of one price in asset markets is reflected in (8.10), where the domestic interest rate is tied to the world interest rate. Thus, we have:

$$r = r^* \tag{8.10}$$

This equation is the exact equivalent of the perfect capital mobility case in Fleming–Mundell, and is open to the criticism, which applies equally to the Fleming–Mundell model, that it neglects exchange rate expectations in comparing the relative yield of assets denominated in different currencies. The neglect of expectations is remedied later in this section. By substituting (8.8) into (8.9), we obtain:

$$e = m - p^* - \lambda y + \rho r \qquad (8.11)$$

In addition, assuming a demand for money function in the rest of the world which is analogous to the domestic demand for money function, we can write:

$$p^* = m^* - \lambda^* y^* + \rho^* r^* \qquad (8.12)$$

where world variables are denoted by *. Substituting (8.12) into (8.11) we obtain:

$$e = m - m^* - \lambda y + \lambda^* y^* - \rho^* r^* + \rho r \qquad (8.13)$$

The central feature of the above model is that the exchange rate is determined in the money market in the two economies, and in particular by the relative money supplies, the exchange rate being the relative price of the two monies. The PPP condition plays a central role in this. Any incipient divergence between national price levels, which must stem from changes in money market conditions as summarised in (8.8) and (8.12), will give rise to an exactly offsetting change in the exchange rate. Furthermore, it is frequently assumed that the domestic (and the world) economy is operating at the 'natural' or full employment level of output, such that changes in y (or y^*) are seen to originate from the supply side rather than from an increase in, say, the money stock. Finally, in what follows, since m^*, y^* and r^* can be taken as exogenously given in analysing domestic policy, we suppress these variables in the interests of stream-lining the analysis.

What, then, is the mechanism whereby a change in the money stock affects the exchange rate in this model? An increase in the domestic money stock generates excess supply in the money market. Since real income is exogenously given at its natural level, and the interest rate is tied to the world rate, then the excess supply in the money market can only be removed by an increase in the domestic price level, which in turn must come about through a change in the exchange rate, if the country is too small to affect world prices, p^*. The excess supply of money generates increased demand for foreign goods and assets, with the resulting excess supply of domestic currency on foreign exchange markets causing the exchange rate to rise. By the PPP theorem, this will drive up the domestic price level (in the same proportion as the devaluation) and therefore the demand for money, to bring the money market back into equilibrium. Note that it is the fall in the exchange rate which drives up the domestic price level rather than vice versa.

Is there a role for fiscal policy in the monetary approach? The absence of an expenditure function means that the analysis of fiscal policy is excluded in such models. As we shall see later, this shortcoming, in conjunction with the PPP theorem, makes the monetary model particularly unsuited for explaining changes in the real exchange rate.

Alternatively, what are the insulating properties of the monetary model? With real income in the domestic economy tied to its supply-determined level, these questions are clearly less critical than in the Fleming–Mundell model, and the relevant question is whether foreign shocks will affect the domestic price level. A foreign monetary shock (say, a rise in m^*), will lead to a rise in p^*, but this will be offset by a fall in the exchange rate, thus insulating the domestic economy from world inflation. This is the converse case to the fixed exchange rate monetary model where money flows between countries tend to equalise inflation rates internationally, and has led some monetarists to advocate flexible exchange rates to prevent the international transmission of inflation due to monetary shocks (for an early example see Friedman 1953).

The monetary model falls firmly within what has come to be called the 'asset market approach', with the exchange rate being the 'relative price of two monies' which brings about asset market equilibrium. However, the central role assigned to PPP is seen by many as the crucial weakness of the model, the principal objection to it being simply that it does not appear to hold empirical validity, at least in the short run. PPP in its strongest form states that the real exchange rate should be constant. As we shall see in the final section of this chapter, this does not stand up to empirical scrutiny. A second general criticism of the monetary approach, counter to the fix-price charge conventionally levelled against the Fleming–Mundell model, is that the monetary model assumes perfect domestic price flexibility. One model which relaxes this assumption, with important consequences for the short-run dynamics of exchange rate behaviour, is that of Dornbusch (1976), (see section 3 below).

The simple monetary model is also open to other criticisms shared with the Fleming–Mundell model — namely, the concentration on the money market to the exclusion of all other asset markets, the absence of an explicit role for wealth, and the indeterminacy of the current account. These shortcomings are the starting point for portfolio models of the exchange rate, which we examine in section 4. However, as with Fleming–Mundell, the simple monetary approach is also open to the fundamental criticism that there is no role for expectations in the explanation of exchange rate behaviour; it is this aspect of monetary models to which we now turn.

8.2.2. Exchange Rate Expectations in the Monetary Model

It is easy to conceive of a role for exchange rate expectations in the asset market approach, since asset market equilibrium in an open economy must take account of the relative yields on domestic and foreign assets, and one component of the relative yield on assets denominated in different currencies is derived from expected changes in the exchange rate. However, it will be useful to preface the analysis at this stage with a brief discussion of the role of risk in international asset markets.

We have already noted in the previous section that an integral element in the monetary approach is the assumption that international markets are sufficiently competitive for arbitrage operations to validate the law of one price. For this to operate, it is required that domestic and foreign assets are perfect substitutes. Let us now examine this notion a little more closely.

Let us first assume that both domestic and foreign assets are identical as far as default risk and interest rate risk are concerned. (We can assume that both are riskless or alternatively that they have identical risks and changes in their yields are perfectly correlated. The consequences of relaxing this assumption are analysed at length in section 4.) However, foreign assets might be regarded as carrying exchange risk, i.e. the risk of exchange rate variations which inflict capital gains/losses on domestic holders of foreign assets. The attitude of portfolio holders to such risk is the key to how exchange rate expectations can enter the model. Let us assume, for purely didactic purposes, that there is a group of agents in the market who are risk averse. In any contract across currencies, these agents will wish to avoid exchange risk. They are able to achieve this by 'covering' their contract in the forward exchange market. Suppose, for example, that exporters wish to guard against the risk of the domestic currency value of their export proceeds being reduced by a fall in the exchange rate (an appreciation) during the period of the export contract. They would then buy domestic currency in the forward market (i.e. contract to buy domestic currency next period at an exchange rate, the forward rate, determined this period). Similarly, risk averse importers will contract to buy foreign currency (and sell domestic currency) in the forward market. The net outcome of these forward transactions for the forward rate will depend on the relative importance of risk averse importers and exporters.

Suppose market conditions drive the forward rate up such that the domestic currency is at a forward discount — that is the forward rate is above the spot rate — at a time when the domestic interest rate r equals the world rate r^*. There is now scope for arbitrage in international asset markets, since agents can now risklessly sell domestic currency in the spot market, invest the foreign currency in foreign assets, and sell foreign currency on the forward market at the higher forward exchange rate. Such arbitrage operations will continue, bidding up the domestic interest rate and bidding down the foreign interest rate, until the interest differential exactly matches the spot–forward differential. That is, until:

$$r_t - r_t^* = F_t \qquad (8.14)$$

where F is defined as the forward/spot differential expressed as a proportion of the spot rate, all set at time period t. This condition is referred to as *covered interest parity* (CIP) and it is assumed that arbitrage secures this equality, an assumption widely supported by empirical evidence. (See, for example, Frenkel and Levich 1975, 1977.)

Thus far, however, we have introduced no role for exchange rate expectations. Suppose that international asset markets also contain agents who are risk neutral and who are prepared to be exposed to exchange risk by engaging in uncovered transactions based on exchange rate expectations. Then, if it is expected that the spot rate will rise, these speculators will buy foreign assets to seek out the expected capital gain. In the extreme case, where the market is dominated by risk neutral speculators, the forward–spot differential will be bid up until it corresponds exactly to the expected depreciation. Thus, under these assumptions, (8.14) can be rewritten as:

$$r_t - r_t^* = E_t e_{t+1} - e_t \qquad (8.15)$$

where $E_t e_{t+1}$ is the expectation formed in time period t of the exchange rate in period $t+1$. This condition is known as *uncovered interest parity* (UIP) and implies that the expected depreciation of the domestic currency equals the forward discount (F) i.e. that exchange rate expectations are fully incorporated in the forward exchange rate and that the forward rate is an unbiased estimator of the future spot rate. The key difference between CIP and UIP is the role played by exchange rate expectations in UIP. So long as risk neutral speculators dominate the market, and domestic and foreign assets are identical in all respects except for exchange risk, then, in equilibrium the returns on domestic and foreign assets should be equalised. Thus, any expected capital gain/loss as represented by expected exchange rate changes in (8.15) must be exactly offset by the interest differential between the two assets. If risk neutral speculators do not dominate the market, and/or the assets are not identical, then a risk premium must be incorporated into (8.15). That is to say, interest rate differentials between countries will reflect not only exchange rate expectations, but also the fact that assets may be qualitatively different between countries and/or that international portfolio holders need to be rewarded for accepting the exchange risk inherent in uncovered transactions. If such considerations are relevant, then (8.15) must be rewritten as:

$$r_t - r_t^* = E_t e_{t+1} - e_t - x \qquad (8.16)$$

where x is the risk premium. (In this particular case, foreign assets are assumed to be riskier than domestic assets.) The existence of risk premia means a departure from UIP, and we return to this possibility in section 4. In the meantime, we adopt UIP as a characteristic assumption of the monetary approach. (For a comprehensive discussion of the different implications of CIP and UIP in exchange rate models, see Eaton and Turnovsky 1983.)

Returning to the monetary model of the previous subsection, we can now integrate exchange rate expectations into the model via the UIP equation. Substituting (8.15) into (8.13), we can write:

$$e_t = \frac{(m_t - m_t^* - \lambda y_t + \lambda^* y_t^* - (\rho^* - \rho) r_t^*)}{(1 + \rho)} + \frac{\rho(E_t e_{t+1})}{(1 + \rho)} \qquad (8.17)$$

This rather complicated expression simply states that the exchange rate, as well as being determined by all the exogenous factors which affect the demand and supply of money, is also determined by the expected exchange rate in the next period. Indeed, we may simplify our notation by defining:

$$Z_t = m_t - m_t^* - \lambda y_t + \lambda^* y_t^* - (\rho^* - \rho) r_t^*$$

and substituting in (8.17) to obtain:

$$e_t = \frac{Z_t}{1 + \rho} + \frac{\rho(E_t e_{t+1})}{1 + \rho} \qquad (8.17')$$

The point to note is that the effect which expectations have on the current exchange rate is determined by the value of ρ, the interest elasticity of the demand for money. Thus, expectations are no different from any other influence on the exchange rate in the monetary model in that they only affect the exchange rate in so far as they affect the money market, in this case through the demand for money. The transmission mechanism is as follows. An expected depreciation makes foreign assets more attractive relative to domestic assets, causing individuals to adjust their portfolios, and bidding up the domestic interest rate (the foreign interest rate is unaffected, in line with the small country assumption), which in turn tends to reduce the demand for money. At the same time, however, the exchange rate is bid up, which preserves money market equilibrium by increasing the price level via PPP, and therefore the demand for money. Note that, implicitly, this is a three-asset portfolio model, comprising money, domestic bonds and foreign bonds, but where the two latter assets are perfect substitutes, so that we only have to consider the money market to characterise asset market equilibrium. Note also that there would be no channel through which expectations could affect the exchange rate in the monetary model if $\rho = 0$, that is if the LM curve was vertical, as in the simple characterisations of the 'extreme monetarist' models of the 1960s and 1970s.

Thus far, our treatment has assumed expectations to be given exogenously. Let us now assume that expectations are formed 'rationally' in accordance with the rational expectations hypothesis discussed in Chapter 3.

From (8.17), we know that the current exchange rate is a function of the current values of the exogenous variables affecting the money market, together with the expected value of the exchange rate in the next time period $(t+1)$. The latter, in turn, is given by the expected values of the exogenous variables in $(t+1)$ together with the expected exchange rate in $(t+2)$, and so on. By repeated substitution of the expected exchange rate in (8.17) we can write:

$$e_t = \left(\frac{1}{1 + \rho} \right) \Sigma_{j=0}^{\infty} \left(\frac{\rho}{1 + \rho} \right)^j E_t(Z_{t+j}) \qquad (8.18)$$

Thus, all information about the future course of the relevant exogenous variables is discounted back into the current exchange rate, the rate of discount being determined by the interest elasticity of the demand for money. What does this model tell us about the impact of domestic monetary policy on the exchange rate? From (8.17), it is clear that a given change in the domestic money stock has a direct (supply-side) and an indirect (demand-side) effect on the exchange rate. An increase in the money stock tends to bid up the exchange rate in the manner analysed in the simple monetary model in the previous section. However, if the change in the money stock also gives rise to expectations about the future course of monetary policy, then it will also affect exchange rate expectations. This will affect the domestic interest rate (via UIP), the demand for money, and therefore (via PPP) the current exchange rate. Whether this indirect expectations effect tends to reinforce or offset the direct money supply effect depends on the effect of monetary policy on exchange rate expectations. This, in turn, is determined by economic agents' perception of the future conduct of monetary policy.

For example, the exchange rate consequences of an increase in the money stock will depend on whether this is interpreted by economic agents as a permanent or a transitory increase. In the former case, the exchange rate will adjust upwards (depreciate) once-for-all in accordance with the simple model of the previous subsection. In the latter case, however, agents will expect a fall in the money stock, and therefore a fall in the exchange rate, in the near future. As a consequence, and in line with UIP, this expectation will drive down domestic interest rates, increasing the demand for money, and therefore offsetting, to an extent dependent on the interest elasticity of the demand for money, the current rise in the spot rate. That is to say, where monetary policy gives rise to regressive expectations, fluctuations in the exchange rate will be damped relative to fluctuations in the money stock.

On the other hand, a third possibility is that the change in the money supply is interpreted as the onset of a period of sustained monetary expansion, and not simply as a one-off disturbance. In this case, the exchange rate will increase by proportionately more than the increase in the money stock in the current period. The rise in the exchange rate directly attributable to the increase in the money stock will be reinforced by a fall in money demand due to the rise in domestic interest rates as exchange rate expectations are revised upwards in line with the perceived new monetary rule. These propositions have been further developed, and placed in a formal dynamic context by Mussa (1976). In general, the conclusion from models which incorporate exchange rate expectations is that uncertainty with regard to future monetary policy may result in volatile exchange rates in the current time period. This may be one argument in favour of the adoption of understandable policy rules in place of discretionary monetary policy, which may lead to volatile exchange markets.

Finally, it should be noted that the general proposition that expectations about the future affect the current spot rate has a necessary corollary. In any given period, anticipated future events have less impact on the exchange rate than current unanticipated events, since the impact of the former is spread over the time period during which the anticipation was formed. In the monetary model, the rate at which the impact of anticipated disturbances is discounted into the spot rate in advance is determined by the interest elasticity of money demand, and the period over which the disturbance has been discounted. This proposition can be demonstrated in a simple two-period version of the monetary model set out in (8.18). Thus, we can write:

$$e_t = \frac{Z_t}{1 + \rho} + \frac{\rho \, (E_t Z_{t+1})}{1 + \rho} \tag{8.19}$$

and

$$Z_{t+1} = E_t(Z_{t+1}) + u_{t+1}$$

where u_{t+1} is an unanticipated component in Z_{t+1}. If we assume, for simplicity, that the exchange rate is not expected to change after $t+1$, then we can write:

$$e_{t+1} = \frac{Z_{t+1}}{1 + \rho}$$

and by substitution, we can obtain:

$$e_{t+1} - e_t = \left(\frac{1 - \rho}{1 + \rho}\right) E_t(Z_{t+1}) + \frac{u_{t+1}}{1 + \rho} - \frac{Z_t}{1 + \rho} \qquad (8.20)$$

It is clear that the coefficient on the anticipated value of Z_{t+1}, $(1 - \rho)/(1 + \rho)$, is less than that on its unanticipated component u_{t+1}, $1/(1 + \rho)$, so long as ρ is greater than zero.

It is clear from this section that expectations can exert a strong influence which could disturb the equiproportionate relationship between the money stock and the exchange rate which lies at the centre of the simple monetary model. While this is an important result, it should not be confused with the notion of the exchange rate deviating from its PPP value. The monetary model outlined here, complete with rational expectations and the role of 'news' about future monetary policy, cannot generate other than PPP results for the exchange rate, for the simple reason that the PPP equation remains part of the underlying structural model, and is the point of entry whereby the exchange rate can affect the demand for money and clear the money market. Thus, changes in exchange rate expectations, say an expected appreciation, will indeed cause the spot rate to change in the same direction, but only because the domestic interest rate has fallen, generating excess demand in the money market which can only be resolved by a fall in the price level via a fall in the exchange rate (PPP).

In conclusion, the expectations-augmented model outlined here remains wedded to PPP and serves only to explain fluctuations in the exchange rate which may not be in line with concurrent changes in the money stock. Departures from PPP require asset markets to be cleared by the exchange rate in a manner which does not depend on PPP. One possibility is to make the demand for money a function of domestic wealth rather than nominal income. The exchange rate then clears asset markets via wealth effects rather than price level effects. This (together with the introduction of gross substitutability between domestic and foreign assets) is the main contribution of the portfolio approach outlined in section 4.

Another alternative is to preserve the notion of PPP as a long-run equilibrium phenomenon, at least with reference to monetary shocks, but to explain short-run deviations from it by reference to imperfect price flexibility. This was the approach adopted by Dornbusch (1976) with interesting results for the short-run dynamics of exchange rate adjustment, as we shall see in the next section.

8.3.   The Monetary Model, Rational Expectations, and Imperfect Price Flexibility

Both the Fleming–Mundell and the monetary approach may be seen as relying on extreme or unrealistic assumptions. While the former model is fix-price in character, the monetary approach relies on perfect price flexibility such that real income is exogenously given at its natural level. While the Fleming–Mundell treatment of capital flows is at best appropriate to only very short-run situations, the monetary assumption of perfect capital mobility is a special case. In both models, the equilibrium exchange rate clears the overall balance of payments, with no requirement that the current account be balanced in the long run — an uncomfortable result. The models to which we now turn attempt to secure the middle ground by removing some of these extreme assumptions. The first example is afforded by the model of Dornbusch (1976). Its long-run properties are generally in accord with the monetary model outlined in the previous section. In the short run, however, prices are sticky and the impact of a change in the domestic money supply is to change the real exchange rate, with at least the possibility of real consequences for the domestic economy, in the spirit of the Fleming–Mundell model. In this sense, the Dornbusch model is an example of a halfway house which is somewhat familiar in modern macroeconomics, where monetary policy has real (Keynesian) effects in the short run and is neutral (in a neoclassical manner) in the long run.

As we shall see, the consequences for the short-run behaviour of the exchange rate, given imperfect price flexibility, are to generate 'overshooting'. That is, given an initial disturbance, the exchange rate first moves beyond its long-run equilibrium level, and then in the longer run moves back. This provides an explanation for an empirical phenomenon which attracted much attention in the late 1970s and early 1980s (*after* the publication of the Dornbusch model in 1976). In particular, it was the common experience of Switzerland, West Germany and the UK that the adoption of heavily publicised strict monetary targets was followed by a substantial appreciation in the real exchange rates of the respective currencies.

Let us note first of all that the long-run equilibrium properties of the model are identical to those of the monetary approach outlined in the previous section. The demand for money function is retained in its original form from the simple monetary model in section 8.2. Thus, we have (where all the variables are in logarithms):

$$m = \lambda\bar{y} + p - \rho r \tag{8.8}$$

where real income is at its natural level, $\bar{y}$.

We retain the assumption of uncovered interest parity, in its continuous time form:

$$r - r^* = \dot{e}^e \tag{8.15'}$$

where $\dot{e}^e$ denotes the expected exchange rate depreciation. When asset markets are in long-run equilibrium, $\dot{e}^e = 0$, and by substituting for r from (8.8) into (8.15'), we may write:

$$p = \rho r^* + m - \lambda\bar{y} \tag{8.21}$$

Bearing in mind that r^*, m and $\bar{y}$ are exogenously given, this locus may be represented as a horizontal line in (p, e) space, as in Figure 8.6.

Goods market equilibrium is obtained where aggregate demand equals aggregate supply. While aggregate supply is given by $\bar{y}$, the natural level of output, the aggregate demand function is given by:

$$d = \omega + \delta(e - p) + \gamma\bar{y} - \sigma r \tag{8.22}$$

where ω is autonomous expenditure which may be regarded as including fiscal policy. The second term in (8.22) determines net exports via a competitiveness effect ($\delta > 0$ reflecting the assumption that the Marshall–Lerner conditions are satisfied), while γ captures income effects on consumption, and σ interest effects on investment. Due to the small country assumption, we shall assume that foreign income effects on net exports are exogenous, and this term is therefore suppressed.

The rate of inflation is a positive function of excess aggregate demand over aggregate supply:

$$\dot{p} = \Phi(d - \bar{y}) \tag{8.23}$$

Thus, goods market equilibrium ($\dot{p} = 0$) is obtained where $\bar{y} = d$. Substituting for d from (8.22) into (8.23), and setting $\dot{p} = 0$, we may write:

$$p = \left(\frac{\delta}{\beta}\right)e + \frac{\omega}{\beta} - \left(\frac{(1 - \gamma)\rho + \sigma\lambda}{\rho\beta}\right)\bar{y} + \left(\frac{\sigma}{\rho\beta}\right)m \tag{8.24}$$

where $\beta = \delta + \dfrac{\sigma}{\rho}$

This may be represented in Figure 8.6 by an upward sloping *GG* function, at every point on which aggregate demand equals the natural level of output. The economic interpretation of this schedule is quite straightforward. As the exchange rate rises, aggregate demand rises as net exports respond to increased competitiveness. This is offset by a rising price level which reduces aggregate demand via two mechanisms. First, the increased price level reduces competitiveness and therefore net exports. If this were the only price level effect, then the GG function would be a 45° line, the price level and the nominal exchange rate changing in equal proportions to keep the real exchange rate, and therefore competitiveness, constant. However, the increasing price level also has the effect of reducing the real money stock, therefore increasing the domestic interest rate (the 'Keynes effect') which also reduces aggregate demand. The presence of this second effect renders the GG schedule flatter than 45°. This is confirmed from (8.24) by the fact that the coefficient on the exchange rate (δ/β) is less than unity. The position of the GG schedule is given by the exogenous variables in the model, an increase in the money stock, for example, shifting GG to the right.

Full equilibrium is obtained where the goods and asset markets both clear, at point X, with $\bar{e}$ and $\bar{p}$. We can solve for $\bar{e}$ and $\bar{p}$ from (8.21) and (8.24):

$$\bar{e} = \bar{p} + \frac{1}{\delta}(\sigma r^* + (1 - \gamma)\bar{y} - \omega) \tag{8.25}$$

It is clear from (8.25) that the long-run equilibrium real exchange rate $(\bar{e} - \bar{p})$ is a function of the world interest rate, domestic autonomous expenditure (including fiscal variables) and real income. Thus, in the long run domestic monetary policy can only affect the nominal exchange rate, and not the real exchange rate, and it is in this sense that long-run equilibrium in the Dornbusch model is tied to PPP. However, it should be stressed that departures from long-run PPP can be effected by fiscal policy, or changes in the world interest rate or world income.

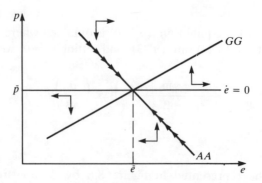

Figure 8.6 Long-Run Equilibrium in the Dornbusch Model

The stability properties of long-run equilibrium require a further word of explanation. While the GG function is a stable locus in that at points below GG there is excess demand and therefore rising prices, and vice versa, the $\dot{e} = 0$ schedule is unstable in that at price levels above $\bar{p}$ the exchange rate tends to rise, and vice versa. These stability properties are summarised by the 'arrows' in Figure 8.6, the net outcome being that full equilibrium at $\bar{p}$ and $\bar{e}$ can only be approached along the unique saddlepath, AA, a familiar, and indeed necessary, characteristic of rational expectations models. (See the appendix to Chapter 3.)

In order to analyse more fully the process of adjustment along the saddlepath we can analyse how the asset market clears in the short run when e and p are not equal to their long-run equilibrium values. In so doing, we follow Dornbusch (1976) in specifying that exchange rate expectations are formed according to (8.26):

$$\dot{e}^e = \mu(\bar{e} - e) \tag{8.26}$$

Thus, exchange rate expectations are a function of the divergence between the current exchange rate and its long-run equilibrium level, where the value of μ is specified so as to be consistent with the rational expectations structure of the model. Incorporating (8.26) into UIP and substituting into (8.8), we obtain:

$$p = \rho r^* + \rho\mu(\bar{e} - e) + m - \lambda\bar{y} \tag{8.27}$$

and subtracting (8.21) from this, we obtain:

$$p = \bar{p} + \rho\mu(\bar{e} - e) \tag{8.28}$$

This expression describes short-run asset market equilibrium, but this does not correspond to goods market equilibrium so long as e does not equal $\bar{e}$, since under these circumstances p does not equal $\bar{p}$. The reason why this may still be consistent with asset market equilibrium is that exchange rate expectations, formed regressively with respect to e, play a role in the asset demand function via UIP. In effect, (8.28) describes the saddlepath AA in Figure 8.7. At every point on AA the money market clears, and its negative slope may be explained in the following fashion. With a given money stock, a rise in p (relative to $\bar{p}$) generates excess demand in the money market, which is resolved by an increase in the domestic interest rate. This is now above the world rate and, by UIP, this newly emerged differential must be matched by the expectation of an exchange rate depreciation. Thus, from (8.26), the exchange rate must fall below the (unchanged) long-run equilibrium exchange rate, $\bar{e}$. This is brought about by increased demand for domestic financial assets, and therefore domestic currency, in world portfolios following the rise in the domestic interest rate. In the short run, then, the exchange rate clears the money market, not through changes in the price level as in the flexible-price PPP model, but through its effect on exchange rate expectations and therefore the domestic interest rate via UIP.

The Dornbusch model is interesting for its properties of dynamic adjustment, once the crucial (but empirically reasonable) assumption is made that asset markets adjust more quickly than do goods markets and that in the short run the price level is sticky. To throw the implications of this assumption into clearer relief, we take the extreme case where interest rates and exchange rates adjust instantaneously (that is, agents 'jump' immediately on to the saddlepath following a disturbance), while goods prices are fixed in the short run and only adjust gradually in the long run.

Starting from full long-run equilibrium, let us analyse the short- and long-run impact of an unanticipated increase in the domestic money stock. The immediate effect is to shift both the $\dot{e} = 0$ and GG schedules (and hence the AA schedule), as shown in Figure 8.7. From (8.25), we know that in the long run the real exchange rate will be unaffected by domestic monetary policy. More precisely, we know that positions of long-run equilibrium must lie along a 45° line with horizontal intercept given by $(1/\delta)(\sigma r^* + (1 - \gamma)\bar{y} - \omega)$. Following Dornbusch, we have scaled the axes such that this intercept is zero. Thus, the shift in AA and GG must be such as to generate equal changes in the exchange rate and the price level, so that the new intersection between AA_1 and GG_1, X_1, must lie on the 45° line, at $\bar{e}_1$ and $\bar{p}_1$.

In the short run, however, we have assumed that prices are fixed, and that asset markets clear instantaneously. Thus, at all times we must be operating on the relevant AA curve. From Figure 8.7 it is clear that, following a money supply increase, the exchange rate temporarily overshoots its long-run equilibrium level of $\bar{e}_1$ to reach e_2.

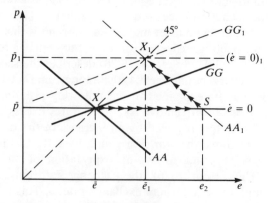

Figure 8.7

What is the economic process underlying this result? In this fixed price case, the real money supply has been increased, and equilibrium in the money market requires a fall in the interest rate. To preserve equilibrium in the international bond market, this new interest differential must be matched by the emergence of the expectation of a fall in the exchange rate. Since the market is aware (given rational expectations) that the long-run equilibrium exchange rate is $\bar{e}_1$, the expectation of an appreciation can only be generated by a rise in the exchange rate relative to $\bar{e}_1$, in this case to e_2. The market produces such an outcome since, at an exchange rate below e_2, the expected appreciation will not be adequate compensation for the unfavourable interest differential caused by the increase in the money supply, and the exchange rate will be bid up by an incipient capital outflow, until e_2 is reached.

Point e_2 is a position of short-run equilibrium, where asset markets are clearing. However, at e_2 and $\bar{p}$ the goods market is no longer in equilibrium. Since S is below and to the right of GG_1, there is now excess demand in the goods market. In the longer run, prices will start to rise and tend to reduce the real money stock, pushing up the domestic interest rate. At e_2, the expected rate of appreciation (to $\bar{e}_1$) is greater than the now shrinking interest differential. Thus, foreign demand for domestic assets, and therefore domestic currency, will rise, pushing down the spot rate. This is represented by a movement up the AA_1 curve, and full equilibrium is eventually established at $\bar{e}_1$ and $\bar{p}_1$.

An obvious extension of the above analysis is to allow for real income effects during the short run when prices are sticky. As things stand in our account so far, the short-run equilibrium point S is a position of goods market disequilibrium (rationing in the goods market) due to price stickiness. It is a simple matter to allow output to adjust to this excess demand and thus allow a temporary increase in real income until prices eventually adjust, and income falls back to $\bar{y}$. Thus, an increase in the money stock increases real income in the short run, both because of the fall in the interest rate and because of the (overshooting) rise in the real exchange rate. In this guise, it is tempting to see the Dornbusch model as a reconciliation between Fleming–Mundell as a short-run exercise, and the monetary approach as the long-run equilibrium to which it tends.

The long-run constancy of the real exchange rate, in line with PPP, which is a feature of the above analysis is, however, only relevant when we are considering monetary shocks. We now turn briefly to the question of how the model responds to fiscal shocks. A fiscal expansion will not shift the $\dot{e} = 0$ schedule since fiscal influences do not appear in (8.21). However, from (8.24) it will shift the GG schedule leftwards to GG_1, since an increase in autonomous expenditure, ω, must be offset by a fall in the exchange rate (for a given domestic price level), to preserve goods market equilibrium. Consequently, the new equilibrium position is at point Z, to which there corresponds a new saddlepath AA_1. This is set out in Figure 8.8. The economics of this result are similar to the Fleming–Mundell case. With the domestic price level anchored by the money stock, fiscal expansion must necessarily generate excess demand in the goods market which is removed by a fall in the real exchange rate and a deterioration in the trade balance.

Four points should be noted about the above analysis. First, unlike the response to a monetary shock, the exchange rate does not overshoot following a fiscal shock. This is simply because the source of overshooting in the model lies in the sticky price adjustment, and in this case, the equilibrium price level does not change. Second, fiscal policy (or a change in the world interest rate or the natural level of domestic real income) will generate a change in the real exchange rate, and therefore a departure from the initial PPP relation. Diagrammatically, fiscal expansion shifts the intercept of the 45° line horizontally, to the left of the origin. (This may be confirmed by inspection of the second righthand term in (8.25).) Third, we may note that the phenomenon of short-run overshooting is introduced in the Dornbusch model by means of sticky prices. Similarly, overshooting may be generated in models of quite different structure by assuming sticky adjustment in a relevant endogenous variable. For example, an analogous overshooting result may be obtained using an expectations-augmented Fleming–Mundell model, and introducing lagged real income (rather than price level) adjustment to bring the money market into equilibrium. Lagged real income adjustment in the face of exchange rate changes may be introduced by invoking lags in trade flows' response to exchange rate changes, as described in the J-curve (see Chapter 7.) This is the approach adopted in Vines and Moutos (1987).

Finally, it is clear from (8.22) that changes in the real exchange rate affect the current account, and therefore that long-run equilibrium in the Dornbusch model (as in the simple monetary model and the Fleming–

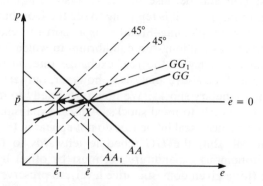

Figure 8.8 Fiscal Shocks in the Dornbusch Model

Mundell model) is consistent with a non-zero current account. If, in the analysis set out above, the current account were in balance before the fiscal shock, then the new equilibrium following the fiscal expansion must be associated with a current account deficit, and with floating rates this must be matched by a capital account surplus. Under UIP, this is explained in the following way. The current account deficit, by tending to reduce the domestic money stock, generates an incipient rise in domestic interest rates, which is immediately and continuously countered by a capital inflow. The consistency of a non-zero current account with long-run equilibrium has been regarded as a point of weakness in all these exchange rate models. In the next section, however, we examine some recent developments in exchange rate theory which place the current account at the centre of the stage, and which at the same time cast a rather different light on the impact of monetary and fiscal policy.

8.4. Wealth Effects, the Current Account, and Exchange Rates

8.4.1. Introduction: The Current Account and the Stock of Wealth

One criticism of the models discussed so far is their neglect of trade flows and the current account. However, the development of the asset market approach to incorporate wealth effects has restored the current account to a more central role, and we devote the major part of this section to a discussion of one model of this character.

The development of current account models involves the incorporation of two general elements into exchange rate theory. The first is the budget identity, whereby it is recognised that under floating rates, a non-zero current account must change domestic private sector wealth stocks, other things (particularly the public sector deficit/surplus) remaining equal. Since the current account plus the capital account must sum to zero under floating rates, a current account surplus must be matched by a capital account deficit and the net outcome is an unchanged money stock together with an increase in domestic holdings of assets acquired from abroad. In the analysis which follows, we shall assume for simplicity (following Branson 1979) that domestic assets are non-tradable and that therefore current account surpluses/deficits are associated with increased/reduced holdings of foreign assets, which are denominated in foreign currency.

The second element follows on directly from the above, namely the inclusion of wealth effects in asset markets and/or goods markets. Thus, a current account surplus, increasing domestic wealth, will increase the demand for money and other domestic assets and, in addition, may directly affect domestic expenditure through wealth effects on consumption. Through these mechanisms, the current account will influence the exchange rate and, possibly, domestic real income, which in turn will feed back on the current account, until the model is in full equilibrium once the current account is brought back into balance.

Over the past decade, a large number of such models have been developed. (See, for example, Kouri 1976, Dornbusch and Fischer 1980, Allen and Kenen 1980, Tobin and de Macedo 1981, Branson and Buiter 1983, Branson and Henderson 1985.) In this section, we restrict our discussion to the model developed by Branson in a number of papers (Branson 1977, 1979, 1981) which is important for its detailed analysis of the asset market, taking account of different degrees of international substitutability of assets and for its demonstration that, even when prices are flexible, monetary shocks, as well as real shocks, can effect long-run departures from PPP. This model does not, however, incorporate wealth effects in the goods market though, as we shall see subsequently, such an extension is possible.

8.4.2. The Branson Model

The Branson model parallels the closed economy approach of Tobin which we discussed in Chapter 5, where asset market equilibrium cannot be adequately analysed by reference to the money market only. A richer menu of assets is introduced, together with the assumption of gross substitutability.

As with Dornbusch, the Branson model sees exchange rate determination as a two-stage process, with the exchange rate clearing asset markets in the short run. There are three assets, which are all imperfect substitutes in the Branson model: money (M), which is non-interest-bearing, domestic bonds (B), which bear the domestic rate of interest (r), but which are non-tradable, and foreign bonds (F), which bear the world interest rate (r^*) and which are denominated in foreign currency. Under the small country assumption, r^* is exogenously given. The assumption of imperfect substitutability between domestic and foreign assets is a departure from UIP and implies the existence of risk premia (see Dornbusch 1983b). This imperfect substitutability can arise from exchange risk or country risk (the latter reflecting interest risk and/or default risk).

In line with the portfolio model outlined in Chapter 5, the demand for each asset is a function of its own rate of return and of the rates of return on alternative assets, together with the total wealth stock. Thus, we can set out the equilibrium conditions for all three assets as follows:

$$\frac{M}{P} = m(r, r^*)\left(\frac{W}{P}\right) \qquad m_r < 0, m_{r^*} < 0 \qquad (8.29)$$

$$\frac{B}{P} = b(r, r^*)\left(\frac{W}{P}\right) \qquad b_r > 0, b_{r^*} < 0 \tag{8.30}$$

$$\frac{eF}{P} = f(r, r^*)\left(\frac{W}{P}\right) \qquad f_r < 0, f_{r^*} > 0 \tag{8.31}$$

Given that the three asset demand functions are homogeneous in real wealth, we are able to eliminate the price level from the above equations. In addition, we should note the balance-sheet identity:

$$W \equiv M + B + eF \tag{8.32}$$

Arising out of this, we have the following 'adding-up' constraints whereby:

$$m_r + f_r + b_r = 0$$

and

$$m_{r^*} + b_{r^*} + f_{r^*} = 0$$

Finally, we also assume for the moment that the stocks of all three assets are exogenously given.

Full asset market equilibrium can be conveniently illustrated by means of a variant of the diagram we met in Chapter 7. In Figure 8.9 we set out three equilibrium functions. The money market equilibrium curve, *MM*, is upward sloping because the demand for money is a negative function of the domestic interest rate, r, and a positive function of the exchange rate, e. (The latter is the case because of wealth effects on the demand for money. As the exchange rate rises, the domestic currency value of foreign bonds, eF, and therefore total wealth, rises, increasing the demand for money.)

The *BB* curve, which represents equilibrium in the bond market, must, by similar reasoning, be negatively sloped, since the demand for bonds is a positive function of the interest rate and a positive function of the exchange rate. Finally, the foreign bonds equilibrium curve, *FF*, is negatively sloped. A rise in the interest rate reduces the demand for foreign assets and this must be offset by a fall in the domestic currency price of foreign assets, that is, a fall in the exchange rate. Given the adding-up constraints, *FF* must be flatter than *BB*.

Asset markets will be in full equilibrium where any two of the curves intersect, the third market necessarily clearing by residual. Thus, the equilibrium interest rate and exchange rate can be located at point R, with e_0 and r_0, and this is a globally stable equilibrium.

The short-run impact of monetary policy can be simply illustrated in Figure 8.9. An increase in the money stock will shift the *MM* curve to the

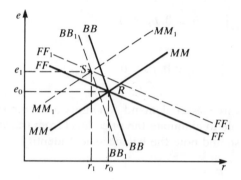

Figure 8.9   Portfolio Equilibrium in the Branson Model

left to M_1M_1 since at r_0 and e_0 there is now excess supply in the money market. However, the increase in the money stock also increases total wealth and therefore the demand for domestic and foreign bonds, shifting BB to B_1B_1 and FF to F_1F_1. The net outcome is a new intersection at S and a fall in the interest rate and a rise in the exchange rate to r_1 and e_1 respectively. The exchange rate brings about asset market equilibrium by affecting the domestic currency value of foreign wealth which in turn generates wealth and substitution effects across the portfolio. There is no mention of PPP, real income changes, or expectations effects.

Asset market equilibrium is not necessarily long-run equilibrium, however. To reach long-run equilibrium, we need to incorporate the current account into the analysis. As we noted earlier, a current account surplus, say, must be associated with the domestic accumulation of foreign assets, F. In terms of Figure 8.9, a current account surplus would increase the stock of foreign assets, shifting the FF curve downward with the associated wealth effects shifting BB to the left and the MM curve to the right. The net effect must be to generate a falling exchange rate. Thus, the model generates the reassuring result that current account surpluses/deficits are associated with appreciating/depreciating currencies. To close the model, however, we need to set out the determinants of the current account.

It is assumed that the current account equation is of the form:

$$CA = c(eP^*/P, \bar{y}) + r^*F \qquad c_{(eP^*/P)} > 0, c_y < 0 \qquad (8.33)$$

The first term relates net exports to the real exchange rate, and assumes that the Marshall–Lerner conditions are satisfied and that real income is fixed at $\bar{y}$. The second term refers to interest income accruing to holders of foreign assets.

The dynamics of exchange rate adjustment share the Dornbusch (1976) assumption that prices respond only gradually to monetary changes; but the key difference here lies in the emphasis on the portfolio effects of the current account response to exchange rate changes. The dynamics of the model are best explained by an example, using Figure 8.10.

Let us start in full equilibrium at point A in figure 8.10(a), where asset markets clear, and the real exchange rate is such that the current account is in balance. In Figure 8.10(b) the CA line traces out the combinations of exchange rate and domestic price level which clear the current account. It is a ray from the origin whose slope reflects the real exchange rate which clears the current account which is in turn determined by P^*, r^* and F. An exogenous increase in P^*, F, or r^* will rotate the CA line clockwise, as a lower exchange rate is needed, for every level of P, to keep the current account in equilibrium (see (8.33)). At full equilibrium, the exchange rate is e_1 (determined in figure 8.10(a)), and we are at point R, with a price level p_1.

Suppose the domestic money stock is now increased, say by open market domestic bond purchases. (See Chapter 5 for an explanation of why only MM and BB shift in this case.) In Figure 8.10(a), we move to a new asset equilibrium position B, with the exchange rate rising to e_2. This is only a short-run equilibrium, however, since, as is clear from Figure 8.10(b), exchange rate e_2 and price level p_1 combine to produce a current account surplus at point X, and therefore an appreciating exchange rate in the longer run (to restore current account equilibrium).

However, the adjustment to final equilibrium is complicated, and comprises three elements. First, as we noted earlier, the current account surplus means that domestic residents are accumulating foreign assets. In terms of Figure 8.10(a), this will bid down the exchange rate in the asset

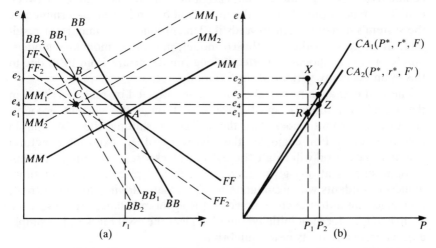

Figure 8.10 Short- and Long-Run Adjustment in the Branson Model

market by shifting the *FF* curve, and therefore the *MM* and *BB* curves, downward. If this were the only adjustment, then the exchange rate would fall back from e_2 to e_1, and we would move from point X to point R in Figure 8.10(b). However, two other elements are involved. First, in the longer run, the price level also responds to the increase in the money stock. In the model set out here, there is no explicit analysis of the determinants of the price level, and the simple assumption is that the price level is proportionate to the money stock in the long run, and we show the new equilibrium price level following the monetary disturbance as P_2. In the absence of any other adjustments, this would imply that asset markets would have to bid down the nominal exchange rate to e_3, and we would move to point Y in Figure 8.10(b), where we return to CA_1 and the real exchange rate attains its original value.

However, a third adjustment has to be taken into account. While the current account was in surplus, domestic residents have accumulated additional stocks of foreign assets. From (8.33), it will be recalled that income from foreign assets comprises one component in the current account. Thus, interest income from abroad will have increased, which means that at the original real exchange rate (and therefore the original level of net exports), the current account will be in overall surplus. Current account balance, and therefore long-run equilibrium, requires a fall in the real exchange rate, a key result. This is represented by a clockwise rotation of the *CA* line to CA_2. Thus, we can see that long-run equilibrium is attained at point Z in Figure 8.10(b), and asset markets will ultimately bid down the exchange rate to e_4, at the intersection of FF_2, MM_2 and BB_2 in Figure 8.10(a).

Thus, the eventual real exchange rate change is determined by the cumulative size of the current account surplus generated between equilibrium positions. That is, the final equilibrium is itself determined by the system's dynamic path towards it. This produces the important result that, in contrast to the Dornbusch model, and other monetary models, purely monetary shocks can effect a long-run departure from PPP, due to this open economy variant of the 'coupon effect'.

The real exchange rate is also, of course, affected by real shocks (as in the Dornbusch model), most obviously through the current account. A current account shock has the effect of shifting the *CA* line in Figure 8.10(b). For example, the discovery of an exportable natural resource such as oil will rotate the *CA* line clockwise, generating a current account surplus at any given exchange rate and price level. Over time, domestic residents will accumulate foreign assets, driving down the (real) exchange rate until the current account is again in balance. However, the exchange rate does not initially 'jump' to clear the asset market, but simply adjusts gradually to its new equilibrium.

While it is intuitively appealing that 'surplus shocks' should appreciate the exchange rate, it is less convincing that the appreciation should be gradual. Clearly, the exchange rate should be expected to 'jump' in response to 'news' about the current account or any other relevant exogenous variable, by affording a role to expectations. Thus is done by amending (8.29)–(8.31) to read:

$$\frac{M}{P} = m(r, r^* + \dot{e}^e) \left(\frac{W}{P}\right) \qquad m_r < 0, m_{r^* + \dot{e}^e} < 0 \qquad (8.29')$$

$$\frac{B}{P} = b(r, r^* + \dot{e}^e) \left(\frac{W}{P}\right) \qquad b_r > 0, b_{r^* + \dot{e}^e} < 0 \qquad (8.30')$$

$$\frac{eF}{P} = f(r, r^* + \dot{e}^e) \left(\frac{W}{P}\right) \qquad f_r < 0, f_{r^* + \dot{e}^e} > 0 \qquad (8.31')$$

where $\dot{e}^e$ is the expected depreciation in the exchange rate. Thus the rate of return on foreign assets now takes account of exchange rate expectations, though foreign and domestic assets remain imperfect substitutes. Assuming rational expectations and no stochastic disturbances, the model becomes in effect a perfect foresight model, with $\dot{e}^e$ measuring the actual rate of change of the exchange rate.

What are the implications of this amended formulation for the analysis of a current account shock, for example? Expressed simply, the *MM*, *BB* and *FF* curves are drawn for a given state of exchange rate expectations, so that an exogenous current account improvement (or its announcement) will generate expectations of a fall in the exchange rate, reducing the demand for foreign assets and increasing the demand for money and domestic bonds, thus shifting the *FF* and *BB* curves to the left and the *MM* curve to the right. The result is a downward 'jump' in the exchange rate.

To examine the dynamics of the expectations-augmented model in detail we solve the model for two dynamic variables, $\dot{e}$ and $\dot{F}$. In diagrammatic terms, we derive a $\dot{F} = 0$ locus and a $\dot{e} = 0$ locus. The former is easily obtained by rewriting (8.33) as:

$$\dot{F} = c(eP^*/P) + r^*F \qquad (8.33')$$

In (e, F) space, $\dot{F} = 0$ is a downward sloping line, where an increasing exchange rate generates a positive value for $\dot{F}$ through the trade balance, which is to be offset by falling interest income through falling F, given r^*. The $\dot{e} = 0$ locus is a rectangular hyperbola, reflecting the fact that, given M and B, asset market equilibrium requires a given value of eF.

The $\dot{e} = 0$ and $\dot{F} = 0$ schedules are drawn in Figure 8.11. The dynamic characteristics of the system are such that full equilibrium is represented by a saddlepoint which can be approached only along the unique

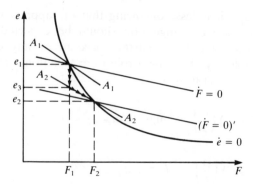

Figure 8.11   Rational Expectations in the Branson Model

saddlepath A_1A_1. The effect of a positive current account shock is to shift the $\dot{F} = 0$ curve downwards, from (8.33′). The new long-run equilibrium rate moves from e_1 to e_2, with a corresponding shift in the saddlepath to A_2A_2. Given that F is initially fixed at F_1, and we are assuming rational expectations, the exchange rate must jump on to its new saddlepath, at e_3, so as to maintain asset market equilibrium. The resulting current account surplus and accumulation of foreign assets from F_1 to F_2, moves the economy to its new long-run equilibrium. One unusual aspect of this analysis is that the long-run consequence of the positive shock to the current account is an eventual fall in net exports. This is because of the accumulation of foreign assets during the period of current account surplus and the resultant 'coupon effect' which, in current balance, must crowd out net exports.

8.4.3.   Conclusion

What conclusions can we draw from the Branson model? First, it represents a more radical break from PPP-based models than the Dornbusch model, by explicitly focusing on the current account as the long-run 'anchor' of the system on the one hand, and by introducing the 'coupon effect' to enable even purely monetary shocks to generate changes in the real exchange rate, on the other.

Second, in line with the Dornbusch model, the dynamics of exchange rate adjustment are derived from an assumption that the exchange rate 'jumps' to clear the asset market instantaneously, while goods markets and the current account adjust gradually to restore the economy to full equilibrium.

Third, in contrast to the Fleming–Mundell and Dornbusch models, where a temporary fiscal 'binge', say a one-off increase in government expenditure, has only temporary consequences for the exchange rate, the Branson model provides a key insight into the importance of the financing of fiscal policy for the exchange rate. A one-off, bond-financed, fiscal deficit permanently increases the stock of B, thus shifting the BB function to the right in Figure 8.12, and causing MM and FF to shift to the right with it. As will be familiar from Chapter 5, the net outcome for the exchange rate is ambiguous, and depends on the pattern of wealth and substitution effects. The case shown in Figure 8.12 is a rise in the exchange rate, implying that domestic and foreign bonds are relatively distant substitutes. Asset market equilibrium, then, requires the exchange rate to adjust to take account of the financial legacy of the fiscal 'binge'. Whether the exchange rate subsequently returns to its original level depends on the behaviour of the price level and the importance of the 'coupon effect'.

Finally, as we noted above, in this model, as in all current account models, the current account not only provides a mechanism for the long-run adjustment of the exchange rate, but also generates short-run changes in the exchange rate as 'news' about the future course of the current account affects expectations.

However, it should be noted that the model outlined in subsection 8.4.2 concentrates on wealth effects in asset markets. As we have seen in Chapter 6, so long as financial assets may be regarded as net wealth, then increases in the stock of financial wealth may also affect consumption behaviour. Thus, assuming that foreign assets are net wealth, a current account surplus may be expected to increase domestic expenditure, as well as bidding down the exchange rate in asset markets. If we additionally assume that the economy is at less than full employment, then the current account is adjusted through two sets of effects. A current account surplus, as well as generating an exchange rate appreciation, will also increase domestic expenditure, and both effects will serve to bring the current

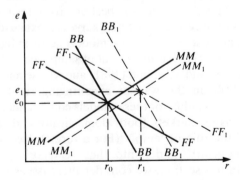

Figure 8.12 A Fiscal 'Binge' in the Branson Model

account into equilibrium. (See, for example, Dornbusch and Fischer 1980, Branson and Buiter 1983, Eaton and Turnovsky 1983.)

While all these models share the property of long-run current account equilibrium, the full incorporation of wealth effects in both asset and goods markets, together with price dynamics and expectations effects, can render the analysis somewhat intractable, and further development of these models often requires numerical simulation techniques to obtain insights into their economic properties.

Overall, the above analysis suggests that once the current account is placed once more at the centre of our analysis of exchange rates, even the longer-run properties of monetary models disappear. While the Dornbusch model attacked the short-run properties of monetary models by suggesting a reduction in the short-run insulating properties of flexible exchange rates, current account models represent a more dramatic departure from monetary models in that the introduction of wealth effects in asset markets, goods markets and the current account (see 'coupon effect') render both fiscal *and* monetary policy non-neutral with respect to real interest rates, real exchange rates and real wealth, even in the long run.

This discussion of the role of the current account completes our review of exchange rate theory. It is clear that a multiplicity of approaches to the analysis of open economy macroeconomics under floating rates has been developed over the past fifteen years. In the next section, we assess the empirical validity of these different models and their relevance to policy issues.

8.5. Some Empirical Issues

The exchange rate literature has produced a wide range of competing models, and although in recent years a number of 'middle ground' models have been developed (see, for example, Dornbusch 1980, and Eaton and Turnovsky 1983), no single 'representative' model has emerged. The question of which approach yields the best empirical results has generated an econometric literature too vast to be surveyed exhaustively here. The central point is that most exchange rate models perform badly in empirical tests, at least in terms of forecasting in out of sample periods. For example, the studies by Hacche and Townend (1981) and Meese and Rogoff (1983a, 1983b) provide little in the way of encouraging results for the main structural models. The failure of these models could reflect their treatment of goods prices, asset markets (both domestically and internationally), expectations and the role of 'news'. (For a formal decomposition of the failure of the monetary model into these categories, see Smith and Wickens 1986.) In this section, we consider these issues in turn.

8.5.1. Purchasing Power Parity

As we saw in section 2, the monetary model is wedded in both the short run and the long run to flexible domestic prices and PPP, and the empirical validity of these assumptions has been seriously questioned. Certainly at the most casual empirical level, the real exchange rates for certain currencies have shown marked fluctuations in recent years, a prominent example being the real appreciation of sterling's trade-weighted index between 1979 and 1982, and its subsequent reversal.

However, we should note that such empirical evidence should not be accepted entirely without comment. First, the choice of an appropriate price index is not a trivial one. At a general level, it is quite possible for perfect goods arbitrage to operate for individual goods (or categories of goods) and at the same time for different weightings within the indices involved to generate markedly divergent movements in the measured aggregate price levels.

Second, given that the arbitrage mechanism underpinning the law of one price, and therefore the PPP theorem, applies only to tradable goods, then there is no mechanism for the equalisation of the prices of non-tradables. To this extent, the simple monetary model in section 2 is clearly under-specified. One way of retaining a variant of the PPP theorem, however, is to relate the divergence of aggregate national price levels from the world price level to differential rates of productivity growth, along the lines suggested by the so-called Scandinavian model (see Edgren *et al*. 1969). In this case, the price of tradables is tied to world levels, so that the growth in wages is determined by productivity growth in the tradables sector. If the wage level in the non-tradables sector is set with at least some reference to the tradables sector, then rapid productivty growth in the tradables sector will generate rapid wage growth and therefore inflation in the non-tradables sector. The higher is the rate of productivity growth in the tradables relative to the non-tradables sector, the more pronounced will this effect be. Thus, even in the case where arbitrage validates the law of one price in international goods markets, there will still be scope for divergence of the pattern of exchange rates away from that consistent with PPP, to be explained by differential productivity growth and the different relative shares of non-tradables between countries.

Nevertheless, more formal tests of PPP and of PPP-based monetary models have also met with failure (for an early survey, see Officer 1976). In direct tests of PPP, encouraging results have been presented by Frenkel (1978) for data from the 1920s, but the experience of the 1970s is less encouraging (see Frenkel 1981a). While it might be argued that PPP is to be regarded as a long-run condition, it is clear that, in the discussion of macroeconomic policy, the exchange rate model selected must address the issue of short-run fluctuations in the real exchange rate. Given the apparent failure of PPP, it is not surprising that in a number of empirical studies PPP-based monetary models have been shown to perform badly (see for instance Frenkel 1979, Driskill 1981, Driskill and Sheffrin 1981, Meese and Rogoff 1983a, 1983b). However, one variant of the simple PPP model is to allow for short-term price stickiness, following Dornbusch (1976). This idea has been incorporated in an empirical model by Frenkel (1979), but with mixed success (see Driskill and Sheffrin 1981, Meese and Rogoff 1983b).

8.5.2. Asset Markets and Capital Mobility

As is pointed out by Smith and Wickens (1986), and suggested by Meese and Rogoff (1983a and 1983b), the misspecification of asset market models can also lie in their treatment of asset markets themselves, both domestically and in terms of the assumption of UIP. For example, both these studies attribute the failure of the simple monetary model to instability in the demand for money function. It is possible that a more fully specified portfolio approach is to be preferred to a simple demand for money function, and such a model is tested in Branson, Haltunnen and Masson (1977), with mixed results. The key problem in testing portfolio models of this character is the difficulty of obtaining reliable data on asset stocks denominated in different currencies.

   Another key issue in selecting the appropriate exchange rate model is the degree of capital mobility, in that the relative failure of the Frenkel–Dornbusch model in empirical studies might also stem from the assumption in these models of UIP. Empirical tests for the existence of UIP take as their starting point the well established contention that CIP holds. That is:

$$r_t - r_t^* = F_t \qquad\qquad\qquad (8.14)$$

To move from (8.14) to the condition of UIP it is necessary to establish that the forward exchange rate is an unbiased predictor of e_{t+1}, that is, that the forward rate accurately reflects exchange rate expectations. In the event, this contention has not been well supported by empirical evidence. However, one potential explanation for this can be sought in the role of 'news'. As we noted in section 2, developments in relevant exogenous variables can change expectations and this could cause the spot rate to diverge from the path predicted by the forward rate.

   In modelling 'news', two general approaches can be adopted. The first is to provide some independent measure of available information on relevant variables. A good example of this approach is that of Dornbusch (1980), where unexpected changes in real income and the current account are to be regarded as 'news', and are measured as deviations of these variables from

OECD forecasts. An alternative approach, similar to that adopted by Barro (1977b) in the context of domestic monetary policy, is to generate forecasting equations for the relevant exogenous variables so that actual changes in these variables may be decomposed into anticipated and unanticipated components, the latter being regarded as 'news', and measured by the residuals in the forecasting equation. The 'news' hypothesis would then be that these residuals explain the unexpected exchange rate changes as measured by the spot–lagged forward differential.

A large number of studies along these lines have been published in recent years, differentiated mainly by the choice of exogenous variables to carry the 'news'. For example, in Frenkel (1981b), 'news' is measured by the residuals in an interest rate forecasting equation, where, in line with the monetary model, unanticipated increases in the interest rate explain unanticipated depreciations. In another study, by Edwards (1983), a whole range of residuals, including both real and monetary variables, generated from forecasting equations, are employed to explain unanticipated fluctuations in the exchange rate between the dollar and a number of other currencies.

To some extent, the results from these and other studies are encouraging, in that a greater degree of exchange rate variability is explained; but they still do not rescue the theoretical models set out above, since the out of sample forecasting performance remains weak. There are several possible reasons for this. First, and most fundamentally, the structural models on which the 'news' tests are carried out may be deficient. Second, the econometric measures of expectations may be imperfect in that changes in expectations which affect the spot rate may not be picked up by the measure of 'news' adopted. Third, and closely related to the previous point, there is the so-called 'finance minister' problem whereby expectations and the spot rate are affected by policy announcements which are not subsequently put into effect.

Fourth, we must consider the possibility that the exchange rate does not in practice 'jump' on to the saddlepath, as is assumed to be the case in theoretical models. The imposition of this 'transversality condition' may be seen as somewhat restrictive if we believe that the exchange rate may exhibit 'speculative bubbles' (see the appendix to Chapter 3). The latter are self-fulfilling expectations paths which do not converge to equilibrium, and have been studied at the theoretical and empirical level by Blanchard (1979), Flood and Garber (1983) and Obstfeld (1984). Empirical investigations on the possibility of such divergent rational expectations paths in the exchange rate literature are limited, though Evans (1986) has developed a non-parametric test for the existence of such 'bubbles', and has used it to interpret the pound–dollar exchange rate over the floating exchange rate period. His tests seem to indicate that such a bubble may have been present in the early 1980s.

Finally, the failure of the incorporation of 'news' into exchange rate models to explain entirely the divergence of the spot rate from that predicted by the forward rate may imply the existence of variable risk premia. This is the conclusion suggested in Hansen and Hodrick (1980) and Cumby and Obstfeld (1981), and is clearly at odds with the assumption of UIP. Further research into the question of assessing country and exchange rate risk and explaining movements in risk premiums seems to be one way forward in this area, and in this sense the portfolio models may hold a comparative advantage.

8.5.3. North Sea Oil and the Current Account

An alternative explanation of the movements in the real sterling exchange rate assigns a key role to the discovery and subsequent exploitation of North Sea oil. In the course of the 1970s, it is argued, sterling became a 'petrocurrency', with the real exchange rate appreciating and contributing to the UK's worsening non-oil current account and generating increasing unemployment through the falling competitiveness of manufacturing industry, and with recent fluctuations in the exchange rate being explicable in terms of fluctuating world oil prices. How can such an argument be incorporated into the models outlined in this chapter?

A straightforward account can be provided by the Fleming–Mundell model, where the impact of an oil shock is exactly equivalent to the foreign real shock analysed in section 1. Thus, the exogenous increase in exports, assumed to be relatively price-inelastic, brings about a real appreciation which crowds out non-oil manufactured exports. On the plausible assumption that manufactured exports are more labour-intensive than oil exports, employment will fall. However, in a version of the Fleming–Mundell model which does not incorporate expectations, oil *discoveries* have no effect on the exchange rate until the oil is flowing and the current account is moving into actual surplus (an unrealistic interpretation of the experience of the 1970s).

The simple monetary model also predicts an appreciation in the face of an oil shock, but by a somewhat different mechanism. North Sea oil may be seen as an aggregate supply shock which raises real income, the demand for money and therefore appreciates the exchange rate through PPP. This result depends on the monetary authorities refraining from accommodating the increase in real income by increasing the nominal money stock. Incorporating exchange rate expectations, the announcement of oil discoveries could be sufficient to generate expectations of an appreciation and thus to push down the exchange rate in advance of the experienced rise in real income.

The above argument is, however, still tethered to PPP, but the adoption of imperfect price flexibility *à la* Dornbusch not only avoids this problem but also generates a real appreciation, and therefore a fall in non-oil exports, in response to the oil shock, in a manner entirely analogous to that described in the earlier discussion of fiscal policy in the Dornbusch model. (For a more fully specified analysis of the impact of oil shocks in a Dornbusch-style model, see Eastwood and Venables 1982.)

None of these monetary models assigns a specific role to the current account, however, and it is in this respect that the portfolio models appear more appropriate. In the Branson model, the oil shock generates a current account surplus, appreciating the exchange rate, and once expectations effects are incorporated, the exchange rate will 'jump' in response to oil 'news'. A somewhat surprising feature of the long-run response of the Branson model to an oil shock is not only that net non-oil exports are reduced by the real appreciation, but also that total net exports are reduced. This is explained by the requirement of current account balance in full equilibrium and the consequent 'crowding-out' of net exports through the 'coupon effect' as foreign assets are accumulated by domestic residents during the period of adjustment.

8.6. Conclusion

It is no easy task to draw together general conclusions for macroeconomic policy from a model-specific literature such as that on exchange rate determination. However, we offer the following observations.

First, the asset market view of exchange rate determination has provided fertile ground for the development of alternative dynamic paths of exchange rate adjustment. Different results are derived depending on whether the domestic shocks are monetary or fiscal, and whether they are anticipated or unanticipated. If, as is widely agreed, the exchange rate does indeed perform a key role in the transmission mechanisms of monetary and fiscal policy, then these dynamic considerations make the design of short-run stabilisation strategies much more complex than in a closed economy.

Second, the general proposition that flexible exchange rates insulate the domestic economy from foreign shocks does not necessary hold once all the short-run dynamics of prices and exchange rates are taken into account.

Third, as in the discussion of macroeconomic policy under fixed exchange rates, exchange rate theory in recent years has suggested that the appropriate definition of external balance is in terms of the current account rather than the overall balance of payments. Thus, under either exchange regime, the economy is in full equilibrium only when the current account is in balance.

Fourth, it should be remembered that the models outlined here assume no exchange rate intervention by the authorities. In fact, 'dirty floating' means that these models are only a framework within which discussion of actual exchange rate policy can be conducted, a point which should be borne in mind when interpreting and assessing the empirical evidence on the determinants of exchange rate behaviour cited in section 5.

Finally, it is clear that the exchange rate plays an intermediate role in the transmission mechanism of monetary and fiscal policy. Thus, when open economy policy is conducted within a stochastic framework, the authorities may wish to focus on an intermediate objective rather than directly on the final objective. Under these circumstances, the exchange rate may emerge as a possible intermediate objective, as an alternative to the money stock or the interest rate. To put the point somewhat differently, we may need to develop a theory of optimal exchange rate intervention. It is to these matters that we turn in the next chapter.

9
THE DESIGN OF MACROECONOMIC POLICY

Up to now, we have been concerned with the analysis of how macro-economic policy works, in terms of its transmission mechanism to aggregate demand and the complications of operating in an open economy, and of what it can be expected to achieve. In this chapter, we turn to a somewhat different set of questions, which are all essentially concerned with how macroeconomic policy should be designed and conducted. While it might seem that we have been concerned with this issue from the outset, in this chapter we introduce a new range of problems for policy-makers to confront.

In section 1, we analyse within a simple static IS–LM model the implications for policy design of moving the analysis into a stochastic framework. In this context, we examine the role to be performed by intermediate objectives and targets. In section 2, we focus on a longer-run perspective where policy is designed to cope with the dynamic problems introduced by structural lags and lags in policy implementation. In so doing, we outline the general principles of techniques of optimal control and assess, within that framework, the case for fixed policy rules relative to feedback rules. In addition, we consider the application of these techniques to the question of optimal exchange rate intervention in an open economy. Finally, in section 3 we consider whether techniques of optimal control can offer any guidance to policy-makers in the real world, extending the discussion to include consideration of problems of policy credibility and time consistency.

9.1. Instruments, Targets, and Intermediate Objectives

Up to now, when analysing macroeconomic policy within the IS–LM framework, we have generally assumed that the authorities conducted policy in full knowledge of the structure of the model and the positions of the schedules. In the simplest case, fiscal policy and monetary policy shift

297

the IS and LM schedules respectively, to attain the desired level of aggregate demand, and much of the earlier discussion has been about the relative effectiveness of these actions and how the resulting changes in aggregate demand could be expected to affect real income, employment and the price level.

In reality, however, policy is conducted under conditions of uncertainty. Over time, the structure of the model may change, and such structural uncertainty may be represented, at the very least, by changes in the slopes of the IS and LM schedules. Such *multiplicative* disturbances pose severe problems for policy-makers, and this issue is analysed at length in Courakis (1981). In this section, we shall restrict our discussion to *additive* disturbances i.e. those which shift the IS and LM curves without changing their slopes. Thus, the authorities are assumed to know the general form of the model, but the positions of the functions are subject to stochastic variation.

The existence of stochastic disturbances to the system has prompted the adoption of *intermediate objectives* as an aid to the formulation of macroeconomic policy. In fact, the literature on the role of intermediate objectives has concentrated on monetary rather than fiscal policy, and we follow that approach in this section.

The general role of intermediate objectives can be explained by means of the following analogy. Suppose we wish to make a journey by train from Glasgow to London. In a *deterministic* world (i.e. one with no stochastic disturbances), we could be sure that the train would run on time and that it would run to its prescribed destination. Under these circumstances, it would be of no consequence or interest to us, travelling on the train, at what time we pass through an intermediate station, say Carlisle. However, if the train (or its driver) were subject to stochastic shocks, then the situation is altered. If the train faces possible delays (or, potentially more calamitous, wrong turnings), then the time at which we pass through Carlisle will convey information to us about how well our journey is progressing.

Similarly, in the IS–LM model, when we have perfect information about the positions of the IS and LM curves, our policy instruments (such as tax rates or minimum bank reserve ratios) which are assumed to be under the direct control of the authorities, may be aimed directly at the *final objective* of real income (or aggregate demand). In contrast, when there are stochastic disturbances to the system, there may be advantages to be derived from focusing on some intermediate variable lying between the policy instruments and the final objective. In particular, this has prompted some economists and central bankers to characterise monetary policy as a two-stage process, whereby policy instruments are directed at the intermediate objective (which in turn is held to affect the final objective) as if it were itself the final objective.

Clearly, there are a number of properties which the intermediate objective must possess. In the first place, it must be controllable by the instruments at the disposal of the authorities. Second, it should have a stable relationship with the final objective. Third, information about the behaviour of the intermediate objective should be more quickly and regularly available than data on the final objective. In reality, an intermediate objective will not fulfil all these requirements perfectly, and indeed, one may have to be traded off against another. For example, in our discussion of the portfolio approach to monetary policy in Chapter 5, we suggested that a wider monetary aggregate may have a more stable relation to aggregate demand than, say, a narrow definition of the money stock. However, while such an aggregate may be 'close' to the final objective, it may also be remote from the policy instruments available.

What are the advantages to be derived from focusing policy instruments on an intermediate objective rather than directly on the final objective? In the first place, it affords early warning of a shock impacting between the instrument and the intermediate target. For example, suppose that the money stock is the intermediate objective and it is only imperfectly under the control of the authorities, so that a surge in bank lending increases the money stock without any change in instrument-settings by the authorities. In the absence of an intermediate objective, such a disturbance would affect the final objective before corrective action was taken. In contrast, focusing on the money stock as an intermediate objective enables the authorities to revise their instrument-setting so as to offset the shock, assuming that the disturbance was sustained and not purely random. The advantage afforded by the intermediate objective strategy in this case is clearly a function of the extent of the early warning provided, which in turn is determined by the differential data lag on the intermediate objective relative to the final objective, and the existence of a structural lag between the two objectives.

What of disturbances which occur between the intermediate objective and the final objective? Here the argument is a little more complicated, and again we need to distinguish carefully between shocks which are sustained (i.e. disturbances which are serially correlated) and shocks which are purely random. In the former case, the authorities may wish to revise their instrument-settings to offset the shocks, and again the function of intermediate objectives is to convey early information to the authorities. In this case, the intermediate objective is more appropriately to be regarded as an *indicator*. In contrast, if the disturbances are purely stochastic, then corrective action on the part of the monetary authorities is, by definition, impossible, and it was this case which was analysed in a highly influential paper by Poole (1970).

Poole's analysis focuses on shocks which impact between the intermediate objective and the final objective, and assumes that all shocks are purely random, and that discretionary corrective action by the authorities is therefore impractical. This has two consequences for the analysis. First, since there is no 'instrumental uncertainty' (i.e. instruments perfectly control the intermediate objective), monetary policy collapses into a single-stage process, instruments and intermediate objectives being consolidated. Second, since all shocks are random and discretionary policy is ruled out, the intermediate objective essentially becomes an intermediate *target*, which is adhered to in the face of the shocks. Poole's analysis then confronts the question of whether it is the money stock or the interest rate which 'rides out' these shocks the better, in terms of stabilising real income at a predetermined desired level. The analysis is set within the IS–LM framework, and is summarised below.

In Figure 9.1, *IS** and *LM** establish equilibrium income at its target level, y^*. In the absence of stochastic disturbances, the question of whether monetary policy should focus on the money stock or the interest rate does not arise. One is indifferent as to whether monetary policy is described as establishing the interest rate at r^*, or the money stock at M^* (reflected in the position LM^*). (This is analogous to our indifference as to the time at which we reach Carlisle in our earlier deterministic train journey.) However, suppose the IS curve is subject to stochastic variation between IS_1 and IS_2. It now makes a difference as to whether we use monetary policy to fix the interest rate or the money stock. If the money stock is the target, then income will vary between y_1 and y_2. However, if the interest rate is selected as the target, then income will vary between y_3 and y_4. The reason for this is simply that the monetary consequences of achieving the interest rate target serve to underwrite the fluctuations in real expenditure, thus exacerbating their effects on real income. If the stochastic shocks are predominantly on the IS side of the model, a money stock target is preferable to an interest rate target.

On the other hand, this result is reversed if the stochastic disturbances are concentrated on the monetary sector, as illustrated in Figure 9.2. In

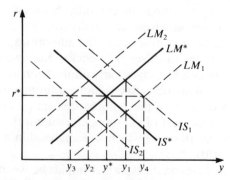

Figure 9.1 Monetary Policy under IS Instability

the case, it is the LM curve which is unstable, varying between LM_1 and LM_2. The pursuit of a money stock target means that real income varies between y_1 and y_2. In contrast, an interest rate strategy now has the effect of perfectly stabilising real income at y^*. Thus, if the stochastic disturbances lie predominantly on the LM side of the model (for example, in the form of an unstable demand for money function), then an interest rate target becomes preferable to a money stock strategy.

Poole's analysis, then, arrives at the conclusion that in the face of real sector instability (in the consumption or investment functions, for example), a money supply target is preferable, while instability in the demand for (or supply of) money implies an interest rate strategy. This result can be comfortably located within the familiar Keynesian–monetarist debates of the 1960s (starting from the Friedman–Meiselman (1963) contribution) about the relative stability of monetary and Keynesian multipliers. In addition, one could also justify the adoption of Tobin's 'q' as an intermediate target of monetary policy in the context of a portfolio model where asset demands and supplies are subject to instability.

However, a number of points should be noted about this analysis. First, its results may be regarded as being largely specific to the IS–LM framework. In particular, the relaxation of the fix-price assumption tends to strengthen the case for a money stock target for two main reasons. First, variations in aggregate demand which generate changes in the price level will tend to be stabilised by the Keynes and Pigou effects if the nominal money stock is constant, while they will tend to be underwritten by changes in the money stock under an interest rate strategy. Second, if we allow for inflation in the model, then the interest rate target must be set in real terms. It is a simple matter to demonstrate that a nominal interest rate target can be destabilising, if we assume that expenditure is a function of the real interest rate (defined as the nominal interest rate minus the expected inflation rate). Suppose, for example, the nominal (and real) interest rate is set 'too low', so that excess demand generates inflation, and

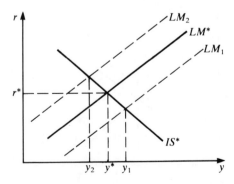

Figure 9.2 Monetary Policy under LM Instability

therefore the expectation of further inflation. Under a nominal interest rate target, the real interest rate will therefore fall, further increasing aggregate demand, and therefore inflation, and so on. Under flexible prices, the interest rate target must be the *real* interest rate, and this, in turn, requires policy-makers to estimate what they cannot directly observe, namely inflationary expectations. (For a further consideration of this point, see Goodhart 1984.)

A second point to note about Poole's analysis is that it does not represent a case for a targeting procedure (or fixed rules) *per se*. The reason why targets are adopted in the Poole case is because it is assumed that the authorities are confronting stochastic shocks which they are, by definition, unable to offset by discretionary policy. Subsequent analysis by B. M. Friedman (1975) has demonstrated that the Poole procedure is not optimal once we assume that the stochastic shocks are serially correlated, and that the authorities therefore have time to respond to them. A simple example demonstrates the point (see Courakis 1981) by reference to Figure 9.3.

Let us assume that the authorities have formed the view (correctly) that the system is subject to IS shocks, and have followed the Poole procedure to target the money stock. Suppose now that the IS curve shifts to IS_1. If this were a purely white noise disturbance as assumed in the earlier analysis, then IS can be expected to shift back to its long-run position IS^* next time period, and there is therefore nothing to be gained by discretionary policy, but money stock target ensures that the IS shock is at least partially damped by the increase in the interest rate to r_1.

However, suppose now that the IS shock is sustained over time (i.e. IS is subject to serially correlated disturbances), then a money stock target is suboptimal, unless the LM curve is vertical. This is because the authorities are not using all the information available in determining their monetary strategy. Although the authorities have no direct information on the behaviour of the final objective, y, in the short run, they can observe

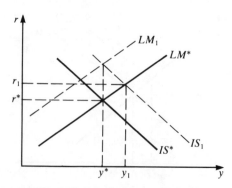

Figure 9.3 The Interest Rate as an Information Variable

the money stock and the interest rate. They are therefore aware that the interest rate has risen to r_1, and since they have already formed the view that the IS curve is the source of the instability of the system, they will now form the view that the interest rate has risen because the IS curve has shifted to the right (rather than because the LM curve has shifted to the left). Under these circumstances, then, they are aware that the money stock should be reduced, by shifting LM^* to LM_1, rather than held constant.

In this case, then, the interest rate is an *information variable* which, in the face of serially correlated disturbances, provides the authorities with guidance as to how to improve upon a simple fixed money supply rule. In fact, this represents a form of optimal policy procedure whereby feedback rules are demonstrated to be superior to fixed rules, a subject treated further in section 2, in the context of dynamic models. (For further analysis of how the authorities might make the best use of all information available to them in setting their monetary policy, see B. M. Friedman 1977.)

Finally, and departing from the Poole identification of instruments with intermediate targets, we may note that the two-stage analysis of monetary policy is not without its problems, even as a framework. In particular, there is some confusion as to what may be properly regarded as an instrument and what is an intermediate objective. For example, in deciding how to control the money stock, the authorities may wish to choose between the central bank's discount rate, and the availability of non-borrowed bank reserves (or monetary base) as alternative policy instruments. Indeed, an analogous exercise to that of Poole has been carried out by Pierce and Thomson (1972) in choosing between these two instruments. However, the interest rate appears again as an alternative to the money stock as an intermediate objective at the second stage of the procedure, suggesting that the two-stage division may not be entirely legitimate (see B. M. Friedman 1975).

In conclusion, it is clear that, under conditions of uncertainty, there is a role for intermediate objectives/targets to play, though the precise nature of this role depends on the nature and origin of the disturbances to which the economy is subjected, i.e. whether the stochastic shocks are purely random or serially correlated, and where they impinge on the model. However, throughout this section we have assumed a simple static model. The problems of policy design are compounded once we move to a dynamic setting, as we shall see in the next section.

9.2. Feasible and Optimal Policy in a Dynamic Setting

So far we have dealt with the pursuit of policy objectives in a static setting, illustrating the role of uncertainty in policy-making following Poole (1970), and B. M. Friedman (1975, 1977). However, when policy is pursued within a dynamic setting, that is, when the structure of the economy may more usefully be described by a set of difference or differential equations, an increased degree of complexity is added to the problem of devising optimal macroeconomic policies.

At the outset we have to distinguish between two strands of the literature. The first, which we outline in the next subsection, may be seen as representing the beginnings of the study of stabilisation policies in a dynamic economic setting with the work of Phillips (1954, 1957). Phillips' work is mainly concerned with the relative effectiveness of different *types of policy* which governments may employ in attempting to achieve their objectives. In examining this work we are therefore not concerned with the selection of a single optimal policy *within a given class of policies*, but rather whether a particular class of policies can achieve the policy-makers' objectives. Thus, in subsection 9.2.1 we deal mainly with what Turnovsky (1977) labels the 'descriptive theory of stabilisation policy'. In contrast, the second approach to policy in a dynamic setting assumes that policy-makers undertake an explicit optimisation exercise, and have some objective (or social welfare) function which they wish to maximise. We turn to this second approach in subsection 9.2.2.

9.2.1. *Feasible Stabilisation Policies in a Dynamic Economic Model*

In a model with a dynamic structure, Phillips analysed the relative performance of three types of stabilisation policies (or policy reaction functions) in achieving a particular policy objective in a model with a dynamic structure, and in achieving a rapid convergence to steady-state equilibrium. To simplify our analysis, we examine the relative effectiveness of Phillips' proposed policy rules in the context of a very simple linear dynamic IS–LM model of the economy:

$$C = \alpha Y, \quad \alpha > 0 \tag{9.1a}$$

$$I = -\beta r, \quad \beta > 0 \tag{9.1b}$$

$$E = C + I + G \tag{9.1c}$$

$$\dot{Y} = \mu(E - Y) \quad \mu > 0 \tag{9.1d}$$

$$M^d = \sigma Y - \lambda r \quad \sigma, \lambda > 0 \tag{9.1e}$$

$$M^s = \bar{M} \tag{9.1f}$$

$$M^d = M^s \tag{9.1g}$$

The problem faced by the authorities in this model is that income, Y, adjusts only slowly to expenditure, E, (see (9.1d)). Suppose that the authorities wish to use government expenditure, G, to achieve a particular income objective, Y^*, and also wish to ensure that their policies stabilise the economy, i.e. ensure a more rapid convergence to equilibrium. Phillips considers three types of policy rules which the authorities may wish to employ in meeting these objectives.

The first type of policy examined by Phillips is the so-called *proportional policy* rule, which is of the type:

$$G = \pi(Y^* - Y) \qquad \pi > 0 \tag{9.2}$$

The logic behind this policy is simply to increase government expenditure whenever income is below its target level, and to decrease it when it is above its target. The system of equations in (9.1a)–(9.1g) and (9.2) may be solved by substituting out all the non-dynamic endogenous variables (namely E, C, I, G, M^d, and r) into (9.1d) to yield a first order differential equation in Y which contains only exogenous variables:

$$\dot{Y} = \mu\left[\left(\alpha - \left(\frac{\beta\sigma}{\lambda}\right) - \pi - 1\right)Y + \pi Y^* + \left(\frac{\beta}{\lambda}\right)\bar{M}\right] \tag{9.3}$$

The stability of this economic system depends on the sign of the term $(\alpha - (\beta\sigma/\lambda) - \pi - 1)$. If this term is negative, the system will be stable, which suggests that the implementation of a proportional policy rule tends to stabilise the economy. The larger the value of π, the more likely it is that this term is negative, and hence the economy is rendered more stable. More significantly, however, (9.3) suggests that the authorities will never achieve their objective of Y^*. This may be demonstrated by noting that equilibrium income, $\tilde{Y}$, is found by setting $\dot{Y} = 0$:

$$\tilde{Y} = \frac{\pi Y^* + \left(\frac{\beta}{\lambda}\right)\bar{M}}{\left(1 + \pi + \left(\frac{\beta\sigma}{\lambda}\right) - \alpha\right)} \tag{9.4}$$

Note that $\tilde{Y}$ will only equal Y^* when $\pi = \infty$, and therefore the policy objective will never be achieved without a modification of this policy rule. To achieve its objective the authorities have to modify (9.2) by finding that level of government expenditure, G^*, which is consistent with a static equilibrium level of income of Y^*. This yields a policy rule of the type:

$$G - G^* = \pi(Y^* - Y), \qquad \pi > 0 \tag{9.2'}$$

Thus our policy rule in (9.2) has to be amended to (9.2′), to enable the authorities to meet their income objective. This is analogous to the problem faced by the government in assessing fiscal stance, where the latter may only be accurately gauged by reference to the full employment fiscal deficit. The above argument shows that it is not sufficient for a government to alter its policy instrument as output moves around their target. To achieve their final objective, the authorities must know the setting of its policy instrument in steady state (G^*). In other words, policy has to be executed with respect to some equilibrium frame of reference.

The second type of policy rule which Phillips considered is the so-called *integral control rule*:

$$\dot{G} = \pi(Y^* - Y) \qquad \pi > 0 \tag{9.5}$$

The name of this policy rule derives from the fact that (9.5) may also be written as:

$$G = \pi \int_{-\infty}^{t} (Y^* - Y(\tau)) d\tau \tag{9.5′}$$

Thus shows that, when implementing this policy rule, the authorities determine current expenditure not solely with regard to the current gap between actual income and its desired level, but also *vis-à-vis* all past deviations of income from target. Considering (9.5) in conjunction with our IS–LM model of (9.1) we obtain a pair of simultaneous differential equations by substituting out all non-dynamic endogenous variables $(E, r, M^d, C, \text{ and } I)$:

$$\begin{bmatrix} \dot{Y} \\ \dot{G} \end{bmatrix} = \begin{bmatrix} \mu(\alpha - (\beta\sigma/\lambda) - 1) & \mu \\ -\pi & 0 \end{bmatrix} \begin{bmatrix} Y \\ G \end{bmatrix} + \begin{bmatrix} (\mu\beta/\lambda)\bar{M} \\ \pi Y^* \end{bmatrix} \tag{9.6}$$

$$\qquad\qquad\qquad\qquad \text{A} \qquad\qquad\qquad\qquad \text{B}$$

It may be shown that this economic model is globally stable, and that, the larger the value of π, the more rapidly the system will converge to equilibrium. Thus, the integral policy rule is stabilising in its effect. We may also solve for the equilibrium of this macromodel as follows (see Gandolfo 1972):

$$[\bar{Y} \ \bar{G}] = -\mathbf{A}^{-1}\mathbf{B}$$

which yields:

$$\bar{Y} = Y^* \qquad\qquad \bar{G} = -(\beta/\lambda)\bar{M} + Y^*(1 + (\beta\sigma/\lambda) - \alpha)$$

Thus, income converges in equilibrium to the level desired by the policy-makers, in contrast to the unmodified proportional policy rule in (9.2).

The third type of policy introduced by Phillips is a *derivative policy rule*, which is of the type:

$$G = -\pi(\dot{Y}) \qquad \pi > 0 \tag{9.7}$$

This policy rule implies that government expenditure increases whenever the rate of change of income is negative, and vice versa. Note that once more we only have a single dynamic endogenous variable, Y. We can therefore substitute for G in the IS–LM model from (9.7) to obtain a single first-order differential equation:

$$\dot{Y} = \frac{\mu\left[(\alpha - \left(\frac{\beta\sigma}{\lambda}\right) - 1)Y + \left(\frac{\beta}{\lambda}\right)\bar{M}\right]}{(1 + \mu\pi)} \tag{9.8}$$

Once more, as in (9.3), stability requires $\alpha < 1 + (\beta\sigma/\lambda)$. Furthermore, in the case of the derivative policy, as for the proportional policy, unless (9.7) is modified to take account of the final target, there is no guarantee that income will reach Y^* in equilibrium. The above analysis shows that only under certain circumstances will systematic policy responses enable the authorities to achieve their final objectives. None the less, all three of these policy rules tend to stabilise the economic system.

However, Phillips' policy rules are *ad hoc*, and not derived from an explicit optimisation process. Furthermore, the criteria used to evaluate such policies are limited, being based purely on whether a single policy objective, Y^*, can be met, and on whether a more rapid convergence to equilibrium can be ensured. This analysis does not take into account possible costs involved in manipulating policy instruments, the possibility that the authorities may have multiple final objectives, and also whether, given such considerations, there is some *optimal* value of the policy rule parameter, π, which enables the authorities to achieve their policy objectives. To answer such questions, we have to turn away from Phillips' analysis, and analyse the problem as one of the government maximising some government objective function over time. This is the approach followed in the application of optimal control theory to economic policy, and we turn to this in the next subsection.

As Turnovsky (1977) shows, the three Phillips policy rules may only be described as optimal in certain special cases. Nevertheless, the merit of Phillips' analysis is mainly that of drawing our attention to the problem of stabilisation policy in a dynamic setting and of providing some analytically tractable examples of such policy-making.

9.2.2. *Optimal Control and Optimal Policy*

The techniques applied in this field of economics were initially pioneered in applied mathematics, physics and control engineering. The similarities between these subjects and economics become apparent when discussing dynamic macroeconomic systems. As we have seen so far, the presence of structural dynamics (so-called *system dynamics*) within the economic system (e.g. our expenditure–income lag in (9.1d)), means that the economic model can be described by a set of differential equations, also known as *equations of motion*. The problem facing the economic policy-maker, therefore, is to use the instruments of policy at his disposal (also known as *control variables*) to guide the economy so as to satisfy particular objectives, which in general are represented by some objective or cost function. Thus the problem facing the economist is not dissimilar to that facing a scientist attempting to guide a missile to a particular objective by using the missile's thrust vectors as control variables while taking into account the external forces (e.g. gravity, friction, wind velocity) impinging upon the missile. The solution to the problem is then found by deriving the optimal path for the control variables (instruments) at the disposal of the authorities.

An *optimal control* problem can be set up either in discrete or continuous time. In what follows we briefly survey both methods to enable us to interpret the current literature which has employed both techniques (for a more detailed treatment of these methods see Intriligator 1971, Astrom 1970, Kushner 1971, and Hadley and Kemp 1971).

In general, it is assumed that the policy-maker attempts to maximise or minimise over time an objective function which depends on a number of state variables (which may be seen as the policy objectives), the controls (or instruments), and may be a function of time. The control variables enter the objective function as it is assumed that the authorities cannot costlessly vary their policy instruments over time. This is a sensible assumption to make, and precludes the choice of optimal strategies which involve extreme policy settings, e.g. massive fiscal and monetary expansions or deflations. The form of objective function chosen is generally quadratic, to facilitate algebraic manipulation. Thus, for example, in discrete time we have the following representative cost function to be minimised:

$$V = \left(\frac{1}{2}\right)\Sigma_{t=1}^{T} \; x'_{t-1}Qx_{t-1} + u'_tRu_t \qquad (9.9)$$

where the two matrices Q and R are weighting matrices and are assumed to be positive semi-definite. The vector u is a vector of control variables (instruments), and x is a vector of state variables (final objectives), both measured as *deviations from the authorities' target values*. Thus, if income, Y is a target variable, it enters vector x as $(Y - Y^*)$, where Y^* is the policy-makers' desired objective for income. Similarly, if the interest rate r is a control variable it enters u as $(r - r^*)$ where r^* is that value of the interest rate consistent with obtaining the desired target values for x. (This is analogous to the definition of G and Y in deviation form in the Phillips' policy rules, see (9.2').)

The fact that the weighting matrices are positive semi-definite implies that not all variations in policy instruments or deviations of policy objectives from equilibrium are penalised. Thus (9.9) states that the authorities wish to minimise deviations from desired target values of certain economic variables over the time period $t = 1, \ldots T$ and have controls at their disposal to ensure this, where the latter are costly to operate. The same problem may be restated in a continuous time form as follows:

$$V = \left(\frac{1}{2}\right)\int_{t_0}^{T}[x'(\tau)Qx(\tau) + u'(\tau)Ru(\tau)]d\tau \qquad (9.9')$$

where we now seek to minimise the integral over the time period t_0 to T. The minimisation in both cases is carried out with respect to the state equations, or equations of motion, which represent the dynamic system which the policy-maker faces.

The difference between discrete and continuous time formulations may be seen from the appearance of x_{t-1} in the objective function. This derives from the fact that in discrete time, policies only impinge on the state variables in the next period, and thus it is the previous period's value of the state variables which enter the objective function. The choice between representing an economic problem as a discrete or continuous time control problem is mainly dictated by the lag with which the policy-maker is assumed to observe the state variable. In some cases, accurate data on policy objectives are available only at infrequent intervals, and a continuous time formulation would appear unduly restrictive in these circumstances. Thus, both formulations may be of interest to economic modellers, but it should be observed in passing that if the policy-maker is able to observe current rather than just lagged values of x his ability to stabilise the economy is enhanced (see Karenken, Muench and Wallace 1973).

The structural model may be represented either by a set of difference equations in discrete time, or by a set of differential equations in continuous time. Thus, we have, in discrete time:

$$x_t = Ax_{t-1} + Bu_t \qquad (9.10)$$

and in continuous time:

$$\frac{dx(t)}{dt} = Ax + Bu \qquad (9.10')$$

The solution to the problem may be found either using Bellman's principle of dynamic programming, or Pontryagin's maximum principle. Here we follow the latter course, which first involves the construction of a *Hamiltonian* function. For both discrete and continuous time cases we may write:

$$H_t = x_{t-1}Qx_{t-1} + u'_tRu_t + \lambda'_t(Ax_{t-1} + Bu_t) \tag{9.11}$$

$$H = x'Qx + u'Ru + \lambda'(Ax + Bu) \tag{9.11'}$$

where the λ are called the Euler–Lagrange multipliers or *costate* variables, and fulfil a similar role to the Lagrangean multiplier in static constrained optimisation. The problem is solved by the application of the following first-order conditions, which yield equations of motion for the state variables and the policy instruments, as well as for the costate variables. This, therefore, solves the problem of optimal policy by prescribing the authorities' best choice of policy setting over the chosen time horizon (for further details on the solution procedure, see Intriligator 1971, Hadley and Kemp 1971):

Discrete time	*Continuous time*
(i) $\dfrac{\partial H}{\partial u_t} = 0$	$\dfrac{\partial H}{\partial u} = 0$
(ii) $x_t = \dfrac{\partial H}{\partial \lambda_t}$	$\dfrac{dx(t)}{dt} = \dfrac{\partial H}{\partial \lambda}$
(iii) $\lambda_{t-1} = \dfrac{\partial H}{\partial x_{t-1}}$	$\dfrac{d\lambda(t)}{dt} = \dfrac{\partial H}{\partial x}$

$$\tag{9.12}$$

The application of these three first-order conditions enables us to find the optimal policy setting which the authorities should adopt for their policy instruments (controls), u, over the specified time horizon, and the resulting movements in the state and costate variables, x and λ. The former are the economic variables of interest, while the latter may be treated as shadow prices, as a direct analogy with the static Lagrangean maximisation. It is possible, through the application of the conditions in (9.12), to relate the optimal setting for the control variables to the final objectives (see Intriligator 1971, for a detailed outline):

Discrete time	*Continuous time*
$u_t = F_t x_{t-1}$	$u(t) = F(t)x(t)$

$$\tag{9.13}$$

where the F matrices are obtained from the coefficient matrices Q, R, A, and B, and vary over time. The most significant result yielded by (9.13) is that the authorities' optimal policy is to relate *all* their instruments to past values of *all* the state variables in the discrete time case, and to contemporaneous values of *all* these objectives for the continuous time case. Thus, optimal control theory suggests that the optimal policy rule is a *contingent* one, depending upon the evolution of the state variables. In the discrete time case, such *contingent* rules are also known as *feedback* rules, as we have already seen in Chapters 3 and 4. Given that the policy objectives enter the vector x in the form of deviations from the policy-maker's desired values for these variables, such a feedback rule may be seen as a variant of Phillips' proportional rule (see (9.2')).

Thus, in general, contingent rules are optimal, and this proposition extends to stochastic economic systems with additive and multiplicative disturbances, though the methods required to derive the optimal rules are obviously more complex (see, for example, Theil 1957, Chow 1970, Prescott 1972, Turnovsky 1977). In the special case where additive disturbances are present, the policy-maker is assumed to minimise the *expected value* of the cost function (equations (9.9) or (9.9')) in steady state (see Levine and Currie 1984, Currie and Levine, 1984b, 1985a).

The proposition that contingent (or feedback) rules dominate 'fixed' rules, where the latter refers to policies in which the policy-maker sets his instruments irrespective of the evolution of his final objectives, has been a matter of some contention in the macroeconomics literature since the 1960s when monetarists, and in particular Friedman (1961, 1968), suggested that it would be more appropriate to adopt a fixed monetary growth rule to stabilise the economy. This argument has been taken further by the new classical school in the so-called 'policy neutrality' debate.

How can the result in (9.13) be reconciled with this preference for *fixed rules*? At the outset it should be noted that though, in general, the optimal policy rule is a 'contingent' one, a fixed rule is a special case of a contingent rule, where the coefficients of the F matrices in (9.13) are equal to zero. Thus, in some cases, the optimal policy rule may be a 'fixed' one. We now examine the factors which may affect the choice of a policy rule, and which have implications for the 'fixed' versus 'contingent' rule debate between monetarists and Keynesians. To do this, it is appropriate to apply the optimal control techniques surveyed above to actual macroeconomic models. In particular, in the next subsection we will focus our attention on those models which incorporate the rational expectations hypothesis (REH). While in Chapters 3 and 4 we concentrated our attention on the result that, in market-clearing models which incorporated the REH, monetary policy could not affect real variables (i.e. it was neutral), we now turn to the implications which such models have for the choice between a fixed money growth rule and a feedback (contingent) rule. In other words, while our analysis in Chapters 3 and 4 examined whether anticipated (feedback) policy rules are at all *effective*, we now turn to the question of whether they are to be *preferred* or not to fixed rules.

9.2.3. Fixed versus Feedback Rules in the Stabilisation of a Closed Economy

Sargent and Wallace (1975) consider the arguments for choosing either a fixed or a contingent rule when stabilising an economy at full employment in the presence of rational expectations. To begin with, they show that feedback rules are generally optimal in the absence of rational expectations, using a simple economic model, which consists of one single difference equation describing the dynamics of the policy objective, y_t, and relating this to the policy instrument m_t:

$$y_t = \lambda y_{t-1} + \beta m_t + u_t \tag{9.14}$$

where y_t denotes the deviation of income from its 'potential', 'full employment', or 'natural' level, m_t denotes the money stock, u_t represents a white noise disturbance with variance σ_u^2, and all variables appear in logarithms.

Equation (9.14) is essentially a 'Keynesian' macroeconomic model, as it allows changes in the money stock to affect the deviation of output from its 'natural' level, and represents the macroeconomic model on which the optimal policy exercise is to be conducted (corresponding to (9.10) in our overview of optimal control theory). However, in designing an objective function (corresponding to (9.9)) for this model we are faced with an additional difficulty, due to the presence of an additive disturbance, u_t. Suppose that the government wishes to minimise the deviations of the income level from its steady state, i.e. at any given point in time their costs C_t (corresponding to (9.9)) are given by:

$$C_t = y_t^2$$

Note that, for simplicity, we assume that the authorities do not find it costly to operate their monetary policy, and hence m_t does not appear in the above cost function.

As we saw in subsection 9.2.2, with a stochastic model the proper procedure is to assume that the authorities minimise the *expected value* of their intertemporal cost function over their time horizon (see Turnovsky 1977, Taylor 1979, Levine and Currie 1984, Currie and Levine 1985a):

$$V = \Sigma_{t=1}^{T} C_t$$

If we make the simplifying assumption that the authorities have an infinite time horizon ($T=\infty$), then the optimal policy problem may be set up as one where the authorities seek to minimise the steady-state (asymptotic) variance of income around its equilibrium value (see Chow 1975, Taylor 1979):

$$V = \text{var}(y) \tag{9.15}$$

where var(.) denotes the variance of a variable. As we saw in subsection 9.2.2, the optimal policy problem in general leads to a feedback rule of the type:

$$m_t = gy_{t-1} \tag{9.16}$$

where the optimal policy problem faced by the authorities is to find that value of g in (9.16) which minimises the cost function (9.15). If the optimal value of g is zero, then it follows that a fixed rule is to be preferred to a feedback rule. The converse obviously holds when the optimal value of g is non-zero.

Following Sargent and Wallace, we may show that a feedback policy rule is optimal in the case where the reduced form of the underlying economic model (9.14) is Keynesian in character. Substituting for m_t from (9.16) into (9.14):

$$y_t = (\lambda + \beta g)y_{t-1} + u_t \tag{9.17}$$

From (9.17) we can find the steady-state level of income by setting $y_t = y_{t-1} = \bar{y}$, solving for $\bar{y}$, and its (asymptotic) variance:

$$\text{var}\,(\bar{y}) = \frac{\sigma_u^2}{1 - (\lambda + \beta g)^2} \tag{9.18}$$

The value of g which minimises var($\bar{y}$) in (9.18) is $\bar{g} = -(\lambda/\beta)$, and the resulting optimal rule is the following:

$$m_t = -\left(\frac{\lambda}{\beta}\right)y_{t-1} \tag{9.19}$$

There are two important things which one may note about this optimal policy rule. First, a feedback (contingent) policy rule will generally dominate a fixed rule in this Keynesian model. Only in the special case where $\lambda = 0$ will fixed rules perform as well as the contingent rule, which implies that the 'monetarist' policy prescription only holds when there are no business cycles in the economy. As long as there are structural lags of adjustment in this Keynesian model, contingent rules will be preferable.

Second, we may note that the optimal rule is of the same type as the Phillips proportional rule, in (9.2'), where $y^* = m^* = 0$ in this case, as the variables are written in deviation form. This shows that Phillips' feasible policies may have the same structure as optimal policy rules, and that the optimal policy problem is, as we have seen, to find that value of the proportional policy parameter which minimises some government cost function.

However, as Sargent and Wallace point out, this finding in favour of feedback rules does not apply if we modify the above structural model to one which displays the 'invariance' properties of new classical models (see Chapters 3 and 4). We now turn to analyse such a model. If we modify (9.14) to a reduced form which may be derived from a model with a Lucas 'surprise' aggregate supply function, and the quantity theory of money:

$$y_t = \lambda y_{t-1} + \beta(m_t - E_{t-1}m_t) + u_t \qquad (9.14')$$

where E_{t-1} denotes the (rational) expectation of a variable conditional on information at time $t - 1$. Note that (9.14') displays the invariance proposition since it only allows *unanticipated* changes in the money stock to affect real income. Taking conditional expectations of (9.16), it follows that the expected value of the money stock is equal to its actual value:

$$E_{t-1}m_t = gy_{t-1} \qquad (9.20)$$

Substituting for m_t and $E_{t-1}m_t$ into (9.14'), we obtain:

$$y_t = \lambda y_{t-1} + u_t \qquad (9.17')$$

By comparing (9.17') with (9.17) we note that the level of income in (9.17') is independent of the policy parameter g, which is the policy neutrality result obtained in Chapter 3. Furthermore, the steady-state (asymptotic) variance of income for (9.17') can be found to be:

$$\text{var }(\bar{y}) = \frac{\sigma_u^2}{(1 - \lambda^2)} \qquad (9.18')$$

Thus the variance of income is independent of the policy parameter in the presence of rational expectations, and it appears that any value of g will yield the same result in terms of carrying out the authorities' optimal policy (minimising V in (9.15)). Hence the fixed rule $g = 0$ is as good as the feedback rule $g \neq 0$ in this instance.

In fact, we may extend Sargent and Wallace's argument in favour of fixed rules by modifying the authorities' objective function in (9.15) to take into account price level fluctuations. So far, employing reduced forms in our argument, we have left implicit the determination of the price level in the Keynesian and new classical models set out in (9.14) and (9.14′). Let us assume, in line with the new classical model outlined in Chapter 3, that the aggregate demand side of (9.14′) is accurately described by a simple quantity theory relation:

$$p_t = m_t + \bar{v} - y_t \qquad (9.21)$$

where p is the logarithm of the price level, and $\bar{v}$ is a constant. Substituting for m_t in (9.21) from (9.16):

$$p_t = gy_{t-1} - y_t + \bar{v}$$

It then follows that the steady-state variance of p is related to the steady-state variance of real income as follows:

$$\mathrm{var}(p) = (g^2 + 1)\mathrm{var}(y) \qquad (9.22)$$

In other words, fluctuations in real income have implications for price level fluctuations. Suppose next that the policy-makers not only have real income as a final objective, but also the price level, so that the cost function now becomes:

$$V' = \mathrm{var}\,(y) + \mathrm{var}\,(p) \qquad (9.15')$$

where we assume for simplicity that the authorities attach equal weights to the variance of income and the variance of the price level. If we replace (9.15) with (9.15′), and substitute (9.22) and (9.18′) into (9.15′), we obtain:

$$V' = \frac{(g^2 + 1)\sigma_u^2}{(1 - \lambda^2)}$$

From this it follows that, if the policy-maker wishes to minimise the new objective function, V', the optimal policy is to set $g = 0$. While in the case where the authorities were exclusively concerned with the variance of income (equation (9.15)), fixed and feedback rules performed equally well, fixed rules are definitely superior if price variability is also one of the authorities' objectives. This is because, when the economy embodies the neutrality position, it is essentially self-stabilising, and feedback policies at best have no role to play in stabilising income, and may actually be counter-productive in that they destabilise the price level. The reason why feedback rules destabilise the price level is that, in targeting monetary policy on past real income, the authorities are reacting to purely random aggregate supply shocks u_t, thus further increasing the variability of the price level. This is of some importance, as it suggests another factor, in addition to the presence of rational expectations, which will influence our choice between fixed and feedback rules: that is, whether the stochastic disturbances impinging on the economy are totally random, or whether they contain systematic elements.

This last point may be demonstrated with the aid of the Fischer contract model outlined in Chapter 4. We should recall from our previous analysis of this model that the presence of multiperiod contracts ensures that monetary policy is *not* neutral, and we now examine whether contingent or fixed rules are to be preferred given particular assumptions regarding the nature of the stochastic disturbances impinging on this model. To simplify our analysis, we once again assume that the authorities wish to minimise the steady-state variance of real income (see (9.15)).

The Fischer model yields (4.11) as the equation determining output in a rational expectations model with multiperiod contracts:

$$y_t = \left(\frac{1}{2}\right)(u_t - v_t) + \left(\frac{1}{3}\right)(a_1 u_{t-1} + b_1 v_{t-1}) \qquad (4.11)$$

where the v_i and u_i are stochastic disturbances reflecting aggregate demand and supply shocks respectively. We initially assume that these are white noise disturbances with variances σ_v^2 and σ_u^2 respectively. Note that a_1 and b_1 are policy parameters, from the following feedback policy rule:

$$m_t = a_1 u_{t-1} + b_1 v_{t-1} \qquad (9.23)$$

where it will be recalled that in the Fischer model the feedback rule is designed to offset past stochastic shocks to the system. (This may be seen as a special case of the optimal control feedback rule (9.16) where the authorities target the u_{t-1} and v_{t-1} as proxies for the past level of income, y_{t-1}). As in the case of the Sargent and Wallace (1975) model outlined above, the optimal policy problem is to find the values of a_1 and b_1 which minimise the steady-state variance of income. From (4.11) it follows that this steady-state variance of y is given by:

$$\text{var}(y) = \left(\frac{1}{4}\right)(\sigma_u^2 + \sigma_v^2) + \left(\frac{1}{9}\right)(a_1^2 \sigma_u^2 + b_1^2 \sigma_v^2) \qquad (9.24)$$

Thus, the optimal policy in this instance is to set $a_1 = b_1 = 0$, which in terms of equation (9.23) implies the adoption of a fixed money supply rule in preference to a contingent rule, despite the presence of non-neutralities. This result derives from our assumption that all disturbances hitting the economy are purely random. Under these circumstances, we would obviously not expect counter-cyclical policy to be effective, given that such shocks cannot be offset. In fact, as in the Sargent and Wallace model, where feedback policies increased the variability of the price level, here feedback policies make matters worse by making real income more volatile around its steady state. This is because, in attempting to offset purely random shocks, counter-cyclical policy 'amplifies' the effects of this random noise impinging on the system. To put this matter another way, feedback policies have been shown, in general, to be the solution to the optimal policy problem in subsection 9.2.2 but this presumes that past values of the state variables contain significant information which current policy may exploit in stabilising the economy. We have shown that when the economy is fully self-stabilising in the short run (a 'new classical' world), or where the economy is disturbed by purely random shocks, past state variables contain no useful information for the setting of policy instruments, and fixed rules are to be preferred.

This result may be illustrated further by introducing lag patterns in the additive disturbance terms (error dynamics) in the Fischer model, through the use of autocorrelated disturbances. Once such sustained disturbances are introduced contingent rules once again dominate fixed rules. (This result is analogous to the amendment of the Poole procedure by B. M. Friedman, which we examined in section 1.) We therefore drop our assumption that u_t and v_t are white noise errors and we follow Fischer (1977a) in postulating the following simple autoregressive scheme for these additive disturbances:

$$u_t = \rho_1 u_{t-1} + \epsilon_t \qquad |\rho_1| < 1$$

$$v_t = \rho_2 v_{t-1} + \eta_t \qquad |\rho_2| < 1 \tag{9.25}$$

where ϵ_t and η_t are white noise disturbances with variances of σ_ϵ^2 and σ_η^2 respectively. Using (9.25), it can be shown that equation (4.11) becomes:

$$y_t = \left(\frac{1}{2}\right)(\epsilon_t - \eta_t) + \left(\frac{1}{3}\right)[\epsilon_{t-1}(a_1 + 2\rho_1) + \eta_{t-1}(b_1 - \rho_2)] + \rho_1^2 u_{t-2}$$

It then follows from this that the steady state (asymptotic) variance of y_t is given by:

$$\text{var}(\bar{y}) = \sigma_\epsilon^2\left[\left(\frac{1}{4}\right) + \left(\frac{4}{9}\right)\rho_1^2 + \left(\frac{\rho_1^4}{1 - \rho_1^2}\right) + \frac{a_1(4\rho_1 + a_1)}{9}\right]$$

$$+ \sigma_\eta^2\left[\left(\frac{1}{4}\right) + \left(\frac{1}{9}\right)\rho_2^2 - \left(\frac{b_1}{9}\right)(2\rho_2 - b_1)\right]$$

If we wish to minimise the variance of income, it is apparent from this expression that choosing a fixed money supply rule by setting $a_1 = b_1 = 0$ is now suboptimal. The optimal state-contingent rule is now one which sets $a_1 = -2\rho_1$ and $b_1 = \rho_2$:

$$m_t = -2\rho_1 u_{t-1} + \rho_2 v_{t-1}$$

This reiterates our point that, while in the absence of error dynamics there is no scope for feedback stabilisation policies, this is not the case in the presence of autocorrelated disturbances.

Thus, to summarise our above analysis, the debate between those who advocate fixed policy rules and those who see feedback (or contingent) rules as optimal hinges on a number of considerations. First, as we saw in the case of the Sargent and Wallace (1975) model, a choice between these general policy strategies may be dictated by the exact nature of the authorities' objective (or cost) function. Turnovsky (1977) provides a useful summary of these factors. He shows that the scope for feedback policies increases, the larger the costs associated with the variability of the final objectives (i.e. the larger the elements in weight matrix Q in (9.9)), and the smaller the costs of varying the policy instruments (i.e. the smaller the elements of weight matrix R in (9.9)).

Second, given RE, the economy may be fully self-stabilising in the short run (the strong policy invariance result), and this will lead to fixed rules being preferred over contingent rules. A corollary of this is that, the more complex are the structural lags in the economic model, the more likely it is that feedback rules are to be preferred to fixed rules. Models with higher order dynamics will be particularly amenable to stabilisation via contingent rules, but the need for such stabilisation policies are removed by new classical models, which eliminate the business cycle altogether.

Third, in the absence of error dynamics, fixed rules tend to dominate contingent rules. This result is quite intuitive, when viewed as an optimal control problem. In the steady state, in the absence of error dynamics, the economy converges to its equilibrium with an asymptotic variance which is as small as possible, and is purely the result of unavoidable noise in the system (caused by white noise stochastic processes impinging on the economy in equilibrium). In these circumstances policy has no role, as there is no unused information in the system for it to exploit.

Fourth, a relevant consideration in choosing an optimal policy strategy is the possible presence of *policy implementation lags*, which we have so far ignored, but on which Friedman (1961, 1968) and other monetarists (e.g. Laidler 1978) have placed considerable emphasis. Thus far we have assumed that policy can be implemented with no lags (current values of u appear in (9.10) and (9.10′)), and that the government has full knowledge of both the structure of the economy, and the structure of the disturbances impinging on the economy. In general, the presence of policy lags will tend to favour the adoption of fixed rather than feedback rules.

Lastly, we have ignored the distinction, introduced in section 1, between intermediate and final objectives. As we saw in the context of the debate on intermediate objectives, some variables (e.g. the money stock) may be observed more accurately and more frequently than some final objectives (e.g. income, the price level), thus implying that some variables contain more useful policy information in the short run. Furthermore, we have not allowed directly for the possibility of 'instrumental uncertainty', which we mentioned in the static models of section 1. Overall, these practical policy considerations may cause some instruments and intermediate objectives to be preferred to others, so that if a proper optimal control exercise is to be performed, it must take all these factors into account. This is clearly unrealistic, given the uncertain world in which economic policy is carried out, and we will return to these issues in section 3, when we examine some of the difficulties in using our theoretical optimal policy exercise as a framework for practical policy-making.

However, before turning to these matters, we briefly examine an alternative application of optimal policy theory, namely the issue of optimal exchange market intervention in open economy models.

9.2.4. Stabilisation Policy in an Open Economy: Optimal Exchange Market Intervention

In our analysis of the open economy in Chapters 7 and 8 we adopted the conventional polarisation of fixed and flexible exchange rate regimes. As we noted in these chapters, both these scenarios are oversimplified. In particular, since the breakdown of the Bretton Woods system in the early 1970s, exchange rates have experienced a prolonged period of 'dirty floating', during which governments' intervention in the foreign exchange market has varied over time.

In this subsection, we show that the determination of the optimal degree of intervention in the foreign exchange market may be framed as an optimal policy problem, enabling us to apply the techniques outlined in subsection 9.2.2. In the interests of simplicity, we focus our attention on a small model, which may be regarded as a simple version of Turnovsky (1983). The model is essentially a modified version of the monetary approach to exchange rate determination, and is summarised in the following equations:

$$m_t^d - p_t = \alpha_1 \bar{y} - \alpha_2 r_t + \epsilon_t \tag{9.26a}$$

$$p_t = \bar{p}^* + e_t \tag{9.26b}$$

$$r_t = \bar{r}^* + (e_{t+1}^e - e_t) + \eta_t \tag{9.26c}$$

$$e_{t+1}^e = e_{t+1} \tag{9.26d}$$

where all exogenous variables are denoted by $-$, and all the equations are in log-linear form. Equation (9.26a) is a demand for money (m^d) function, where income, y, is fixed at full employment, and p and r denote the price level and the interest rate respectively. Equation (9.26b) is a purchasing power parity relation, where p^* denotes the foreign price level. Equation (9.26c) is an uncovered interest parity (UIP) condition, where r^* represents the foreign interest rate, and e_t and e_{t+1}^e the current exchange rate and the exchange rate expected to prevail in the next time period. Note furthermore that equation (9.26d) represents the assumption of perfect foresight in forming exchange rate expectations.

To these equations we add an additional monetary policy equation, which includes a policy parameter μ, determining the degree of exchange rate market intervention:

$$m^s = \bar{m} - \mu(e_t - \bar{e} + \xi_t) \tag{9.26e}$$

where $\bar{m}$ and $\bar{e}$ represent respectively an exogenous component of the money supply (m^s), and the steady state value of the exchange rate, which the authorities know. Furthermore, ξ_t is a white noise disturbance with variance σ_ξ^2 which may be interpreted as a policy error term, or a foreign shock affecting the equilibrium exchange rate $\bar{e}$ independently of the domestic money stock. Thus, the degree of exchange rate market intervention clearly depends on μ. When $\mu = 0$, the money supply is exogenously determined without reference to the exchange rate, and the country pursues a monetary policy independently of the rest of the world. This therefore corresponds to a perfectly floating exchange rate regime. On the other hand, when $\mu = \infty$, the money stock is entirely endogenous to the model, and linked to any incipient movements in the exchange rate. Any deviation of e from its fixed parity $\bar{e}$, brings forth a sufficiently large degree of monetary intervention to offset pressure on the exchange rate. This therefore corresponds to the fixed exchange rate case, as monetary conditions in a country are totally dictated by external factors.

To further simplify this model, we may write it in terms of deviations from full equilibrium, where the exogenous variables are normalised to zero. The model of equations (9.26a)–(9.26e) can be reduced to a single first-order stochastic difference equation by substituting for m_t, r_t and p_t from (9.26e), (9.26a), (9.26b) into (9.26c):

$$\alpha_2 e_{t+1} - (\alpha_2 + \mu + 1)e_t = -\alpha_2\eta_t + \epsilon_t + \mu\xi_t \tag{9.27}$$

We can then evaluate the optimal policy choice for μ, assuming that the authorities wish to minimise price fluctuations in the economy, i.e. they wish to minimise var(p), the steady-state variance of the price level. In steady state equilibrium:

$$\bar{e} = \frac{(-\alpha_2 \eta_t + \epsilon_t + \mu \xi_t)}{-(\mu + 1)}$$

Evaluating the variance of the exchange rate:

$$\text{var}(\bar{e}) = \sigma_\eta^2 \left(\frac{\alpha_2}{\mu + 1} \right)^2 + \sigma_\epsilon^2 \left(\frac{1}{\mu + 1} \right)^2 + \sigma_\xi^2 \left(\frac{\mu}{1 + \mu} \right)^2 \qquad (9.28)$$

From the purchasing power parity equation, it follows that:

$$\text{var}(\bar{p}) = \text{var}(\bar{e})$$

given that the foreign price level is assumed to be constant. This implies that to minimise price level fluctuations, the authorities have to minimise exchange rate fluctuations. Let us assume for the moment that there are no policy errors, or foreign shocks, so that $\sigma_\xi^2 = 0$. From (9.28), it follows that the optimal policy would then be to make the absolute value of μ as large as possible, which in the limit implies that the authorities should adopt a regime of fixed exchange rates. However, this conclusion does not carry over to the case where we reintroduce ξ_t as a stochastic disturbance in (9.28). To reduce the value of the coefficient on σ_ξ^2 one must make the absolute size of μ as small as possible. Thus, in general, we can conclude that, to the extent that shocks are of a domestic origin (a large value of σ_η^2 and σ_ϵ^2), the authorities should increase the degree of intervention, while, to the extent that shocks are of a foreign origin, or due to policy errors (a large value of σ_ξ^2), the authorities should refrain from intervening in the exchange market. This is not a new result (see for instance Artis and Currie 1981), and follows quite naturally from the debate on the relative merits of fixed and flexible exchange rates, where the former are usually favoured by those who argue that fixed rates impart some discipline on domestic policy-makers in the face of domestic inflationary pressures, while the latter are favoured by those who argue that flexible rates insulate the domestic economy from foreign inflationary shocks.

However, the model of optimal intervention as presented here is too limited in scope to answer some of the more interesting questions regarding stabilisation policy in an open economy. Other models have been developed which relax some of the restrictive assumptions of the above model (see, for instance, Boyer 1978, Roper and Turnovsky 1980, and Turnovsky 1983). The work of Boyer and of Roper and Turnovsky is set in a fixed-price world, while Turnovsky (1983) allows both prices and income to vary, with a short-run surprise aggregate supply function, in contrast to the assumption of perfectly flexible prices in our simplified model of (9.25). Turnovsky also provides a fuller specification of the disturbances likely to impinge on the model, and the conclusions on the choice of optimal policy, not surprisingly, again depend on the origin of the stochastic shocks under consideration. If shocks originate mainly from the domestic monetary sector, intervention should be pursued as vigorously as possible. If the shocks originate mainly from the domestic aggregate supply sector, there is a trade-off between income and price stability with less intervention favouring the former, and more intervention the latter. This is because with a fixed exchange rate, domestic prices are pegged, given the law of one price, and hence all supply shocks are reflected in output variations, while the converse is true with fixed rates. In the case of foreign shocks the effects are ambiguous, and depend on the relative features of the domestic and foreign economy. As a result, the relative wage and price behaviour in the two economies will influence each other's preferences for a regime of relatively fixed or relatively flexible exchange rates. We will return to this question in Chapter 10, when addressing the question of coordination between economies.

As we have seen, therefore, the formulation of a policy of optimal intervention will involve a trade-off between different final objectives, and one also needs to consider the source of all the possible shocks which may affect the economy. Given a government objective function, is it then possible to find a single optimal value for μ, using optimal control techniques? As should be apparent from (9.28), such an exercise would require knowledge of the values of σ_η^2, σ_ϵ^2, σ_ξ^2. In general, optimal policy problems involving stochastic disturbances may be solved only with accurate knowledge of the variance–covariance matrix for the vector of disturbances. In reality, it is unlikely that governments will have accurate knowledge of the possible source of future shocks, and this criticism also applies to the closed economy models of subsection 9.2.3. Bearing this problem in mind, it is reasonable to ask whether optimal control is really a feasible approach to practical policy-making. We turn to this question in the next section, where we also examine some further problems which may arise when carrying out optimal policy exercises with models which incorporate rational expectations.

9.3. Rational Expectations and Other Problems in Optimal Policy Formulation

9.3.1. Is Optimal Control a Practical Approach to Policy?

Despite the existence of a large volume of literature which applies optimal control concepts to macroeconomics, many economists have shifted the emphasis away from the search for a *single fully optimal* policy rule. There are several reasons for abandoning a strict optimal control approach to policy. First of all, the derivation of optimal rules using the maximum principle requires a large amount of computational effort. As a result, there have been proposals for alternative policy strategies, one of which is the adoption of *simple* contingent rules which, though not fully optimal in the sense of being a solution to the full optimal control problem, are optimal within a single instrument-objective framework (see Currie and Levine 1985a).

To illustrate an example of such a simple rule, consider an economic model where the authorities have three policy instruments: the interest rate, r, government expenditure, g, and the tax rate, s:

$$u = [r\ g\ s]$$

and where there are four state variables: prices, p, real income, y, the money stock, m, and the exchange rate, e:

$$x = [p\ y\ m\ e]$$

Consider, then, a simple contingent rule for the interest rate where the target is only one of the state variables, say, the money supply:

$$r(t) = \alpha m(t) \tag{9.29}$$

where α is chosen so as to minimise the authorities' cost function. Equation (9.29) is unlikely to represent the fully optimal rule, as it is unlikely that the F matrix in (9.13) will contain a zero coefficient on each of the other state variables, p, y, and e. In other words, in general a fully optimal rule is a rule contingent on *all* final objectives. 'Looking at everything' is in general a better policy than focusing exclusively on some of the state variables. However, advocates of simple rules argue that it is easier to target policy instruments on individual state variables, as in the case of the money supply rule in (9.29), and then find the value of the policy parameter α which minimises the authorities' cost function.

Apart from the question of computational efficiency, what are the other advantages of simple rules when compared to fully optimal policy rules? First, simple policy rules are better understood by the private sector, which may explain why they prove so attractive to governments (see Currie 1985, Currie and Levine 1985a). In fact, there is a body of opinion which would argue that the widespread adoption of monetarist policies in OECD countries since the 1970s is primarily due to the attractiveness of their simple policy prescriptions (see, for instance, Fforde 1983). In any case, it is generally true that the public at large is more likely to trust simple policy rules and objectives rather than complicated fully optimal feedback rules whose derivation is only familiar to a few mortals (most of them engineers and economists).

Second, the solution of optimal control problems is generally limited to simple linear economic models, which excludes the majority of the currently popular econometric models of national economies and the international economy. Given the complex non-linearities involved in some econometric models, the direct application of our techniques to the original models becomes difficult (for an exception see Taylor 1979). Though linearisation of these models is possible, the approximations involved in this may render the resulting policy rules worthless for practical policy purposes. At the very least, the optimal control rules derived from such econometric models would have to be re-evaluated in the light of new evidence, given that many macroeconometric models show rather peculiar behaviour in the long run.

Third, optimal control techniques were initially applied to the world of engineering, where the dynamic features of the systems to be stabilised are known with certainty, as such systems obey physical laws and are generally invariant over time. In contrast, in economics, we do not have an accurate knowledge of the underlying economic model. Furthermore, even if we were to agree on the specification of a model of the economy, we are still likely to be partially ignorant regarding the values of the model's structural parameters and the likely covariance structure of the shocks impinging on the economy. In addition, these factors are unlikely to remain the same over long periods of time. Perhaps one of the few truths about the theory of economic policy is that it evolves with the economic environment. For example, while monetary targets were emphasised in the 1970s, they have become less fashionable in many countries in the 1980s.

Given this degree of structural uncertainty, it is not clear whether optimal control rules may really be feasible in the 'real world'. Currie and Levine (1985a) argue that while complex rules dominate simple rules in a world of perfect knowledge because they allow the authorities to exploit fully the information on the model's dynamic and stochastic structure, in a world of imperfect knowledge some simple rules may perform better, i.e. simple rules may be more robust in the case where the wrong structural parameter values are used in computing the policy rule, or where the model is subject to structural changes, than fully optimal rules which are designed specifically for a given model structure. In other words, they advocate that policy-makers should look for 'a horse for all courses' instead of the 'best horse for a particular course' in formulating policy rules. We should note in passing that this argument in favour of 'simplicity' in policy-making is analogous to arguments presented by monetarists against discretionary policy in the presence of imperfect information.

In the light of these comments we now briefly examine some of the recent work on ways of adapting optimal control techniques by designing robust simple rules (see Currie and Levine 1984a, 1985a), and forms of so-called 'decoupled control' (see Vines, Maciejowski and Meade 1983).

Currie and Levine compared the performance of alternative simple contingent monetary policy rules in a small open economy model, with parameters imposed *a priori*, and not estimated. The interest rate was targeted on four alternative state variables: the exchange rate, the price level, nominal income, and the money stock:

$$r = \alpha e, r = \alpha p, r = \alpha(p + y), r = \alpha m$$

For each policy rule, the parameter α was chosen with respect to a particular expected disturbance, and the performance of the rule was then assessed against a number of alternative actual perturbations. Thus, for example the α's could be chosen so as to minimise the effects of a domestic demand disturbance. The performance of these policies, designed for aggregate demand shocks, would then be evaluated when shocks of other types perturbed the model, so as to test the robustness of these rules.

Currie and Levine found that no single type of rule performed better than the others at all times, and that (as in subsection 9.2.4) the perceived source of shocks impinging on the economy was the major factor in assessing the suitability of a policy rule. Similarly, as in the choice of an optimal policy rule, Currie and Levine show that also in the case of simple rules the weights attached to the state variables in the cost function are important.

Vines *et al.* (1983) follow a rather different route to the problem of optimal policy formulation, arguing that there is no guarantee that the theoretical formulation of the objective function or the dynamic economic system will offer a good approximation to the real economic problem faced by the policy-maker. Nevertheless, in a manner similar to Currie and Levine, they advocate and evaluate simple policy rules. In particular, they test the performance of so-called 'new Keynesian' policies which advocate the adoption of 'decoupled control' rules, which involve the assignment of particular instruments to particular targets. Thus one may have:

$$s = f_1(p + y), r = f_2(e), w = f_3(U)$$

where fiscal policy in the form of the tax rate is assigned to target nominal income, monetary policy is assigned to pursuing the external objective (in this case the exchange rate), and the wage rate (through the use of a wage fixing policy) is assigned to target unemployment. To test the performance of these rules, given that they choose not to use cost functions such as (9.9) or (9.9′) as a criterion of performance, they propose the use of *frequency response* control methods. These methods basically consist of first transforming the dynamic system (including policy rules) into transfer function form, and then examining its properties in the frequency domain (for further details see Vines *et al.* 1983). The essence of this approach is therefore not to minimise some arbitrary cost function, but to examine whether the proposed policy rules improve the stability properties of the economy. Thus, the approach is more in the spirit of Phillips' (1954, 1957) *feasible* stabilisation policies, in that one discriminates between different policies by comparing the general stability of the system once the respective policies have been adopted.

The most interesting aspect of this work is its comparison of the 'new Keynesian' approach to decoupled control set out above with what Vines *et al.* call the 'orthodox Keynesian' approach to policy, which traditionally used wage control (incomes policy) to control inflationary pressures, and aggregate demand policy to target unemployment and the level of real activity. In general, the former approach is shown to be preferable. (For a detailed comparison of these alternative strategies the reader is referred to Meade 1982, Vines *et al.* 1983, and Christodoulakis, Vines and Weale 1986.)

We conclude this subsection by confirming that the major weakness of the optimal control approach to policy is its assumption that policy-makers possess full knowledge of the underlying economic structure they seek to stabilise, so that optimal control in its pure form seems to have only limited application in the field of economic policy. However, as we have seen, there are alternative, related, approaches to optimal control which may be used to evaluate the performance of contingent rules. Nevertheless, the 'monetarist' criticism that contingent rules assume too much prior knowledge on the part of policy-makers may still have some force.

9.3.2. *Rational Expectations and the Problem of Time Consistency*

Another line of research in stabilisation policy which has received increasing attention is the problem caused to optimal policy plans by the presence of rational agents in the economy. This problem, known as 'time inconsistency', was initially formalised by Kydland and Prescott (1977), and can be briefly stated in the following way: even supposing that policy-makers have a cost function to minimise (e.g. equation (9.9′)) subject to some dynamic economic system (e.g. equations (9.10′)) and they have perfect knowledge of the economic system, in the presence of rational forward looking agents the optimal policy plan does not minimise the desired cost function *ex post*. Kydland and Prescott (1977) presented this as a powerful argument against the adoption of contingent rules and in favour of fixed rules.

The reason for this result is that an economic system is not simply a 'black box' with a given dynamic structure, unlike the dynamic systems analysed in engineering, where control methods may be applied without these difficulties. Current decisions by private agents are conditional on future expectations. As a result, if a government formulates an optimal policy plan ignoring this fact, it will, *ex post*, find that the optimal policy plan should be changed as economic agents have reacted to it. In a sense, this problem may be seen as akin to the Lucas (1976) policy critique, and in some ways as a dynamic analogue of it. In general, a *time-consistent* policy may be formally defined as a policy which maximises the policy-maker's objective function, subject to the economic structure *including economic agents' possible reaction to the optimal policy itself*. By contrast, a *time-inconsistent* policy ignores possible reactions by private agents. As we shall subsequently see through an example, while *time-consistent* policies are credible to rational agents, *time-inconsistent* policies are not.

Kydland and Prescott consider a government's choice of an optimal policy in a simple closed economy model. Suppose that the inflation–unemployment trade-off is accurately described by an expectations-augmented Phillips curve:

$$U_t = U^* + \lambda(\dot{P}^e_t - \dot{P}_t) \tag{9.30}$$

where U_t is the unemployment rate, U^* the natural rate of unemployment, and $\dot{P}$ and $\dot{P}^e$ the actual and expected rate of inflation respectively. Further, assume that inflationary expectations are formed rationally:

$$\dot{P}^e_t = E_{t-1}\dot{P}_t \tag{9.31}$$

Suppose that the policy-maker has an objective function defined over unemployment and inflation, which penalises deviations from some unemployment target (which we assume is below the 'natural' unemployment rate) and a non-zero inflation rate:

$$V = V(\dot{P}_t, u_t), V_{|\dot{p}|} < 0, V_{|u|} < 0 \tag{9.32}$$

where $u_t = U_t - \tilde{U}$, where $\tilde{U}$ is the authorities' unemployment target, and where $\tilde{U} < U^*$. The contours of this objective function can be represented as 'indifference curves' in $(\dot{P}, U-U^*)$ space, with the 'bliss point' to the left of the origin, at $\tilde{U}$, as in Figure 9.4.

The *XX* line represents the Phillips curve relationship mentioned above,

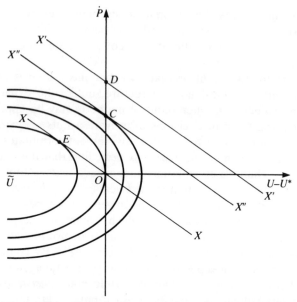

Figure 9.4 The Problem of Time Consistency and the Kydland–Prescott Model

drawn on the assumption that inflationary expectations $\dot{P}^e$ are zero, and from (9.30) it will have a slope of $-(1/\lambda)$. The $X'X'$ line is another short-run Phillips curve, drawn for a positive level of inflationary expectations. Lastly, $X''X''$ is a Phillips curve drawn for a lower level of inflationary expectations than $X'X'$. The exact position of the short-run Phillips curve in the diagram at any given time depends on inflationary expectations, and hence is entirely determined by economic agents. Governments, on the other hand, may expand or contract aggregate demand, so as to attempt to move *along* a short-run Phillips curve. Given that the underlying structural model incorporates the 'natural rate hypothesis', the government's objective function reflects the fact that even temporary reductions in unemployment below U^* represent welfare gains to the government.

Suppose that the economy is initially at point D on the Phillips curve $X'X'$ and is suffering a positive inflation rate. Consider the strategies available to the policy-maker and the public in the next time period. The policy-maker wishes to achieve the highest possible indifference curve knowing that if agents adjust their inflationary expectations accordingly, the economy will reach an equilibrium along the y-axis, since economic agents will only be in equilibrium at the 'natural' rate of unemployment U^*, at point O. Thus, the policy-maker announces that he will deflate the economy so as to achieve zero inflation in the next time period, hoping that agents will revise their inflationary expectations, shifting the Phillips curve from $X'X'$ to XX, thereby taking the economy to point O.

How should economic agents respond to this announcement of a deflationary policy designed to eliminate inflation? If we assume that they have perfect knowledge of the authorities' objective function, they will realise that if the government keeps to its promised policy in the next time period, it will have an incentive in the time period after that to renege on its anti-inflation policy, and expand the economy along XX, to reach point E, which is tangential to a higher government indifference curve. That is, once the government has obtained the gains from lower inflation (the shift from point D to point O), it has an incentive to renege on its previous policy. *Ex post*, the announcement of a policy of zero inflation is not optimal, and hence this policy is time-inconsistent. One feature of a time-inconsistent policy is that it is obviously not *credible* in the eyes of economic agents. Knowing that the government has the incentive to abandon a zero-inflation policy, they will not believe it, and hence they will not reduce their inflationary expectations to zero. What will rational economic agents' optimal strategy then be with regard to inflationary expectations? They will observe that point C, where the short-run Phillips curve $X''X''$ is tangent to a government indifference curve on the y-axis is the only point at which the government has no incentive to deviate from the natural rate (the agents' desired objective). At point C the government has no incentive to expand the economy by moving along $X''X''$, since it cannot reach a higher indifference curve by doing so. Thus, the only credible anti-inflation policy which the authorities may implement is one which partially reduces inflation, to point C.

These strategic actions by the authorities and economic agents may be described in game-theoretic terms (for a guide to the basic principles of game theory, and some applications, see Chapter 10, section 2). These two parties are behaving as if they were players in a multiperiod static game. This is illustrated in Figure 9.5. Economic agents have a preferred equilibrium along the y-axis (at the 'natural' rate of unemployment), and for any given government aggregate demand policy, their *best reply* is to adjust their inflationary expectations so as to return to the 'natural' rate of unemployment. Thus, the y-axis may be seen as economic agents' *reaction function*, in game theory terminology. The authorities, on the other hand, seek to move along the short-run Phillips curve so as to achieve their highest indifference curve. Thus, for any given short-run Phillips curve, the authorities' *best reply* is to move to the point of tangency between it and the highest indifference curve. The schedule AA is the locus of points of tangency of successive short-run Phillips curves (for different inflationary expectations) with the authorities' contour map. It represents the government's reaction function, showing the best outcome it can achieve for any given move by economic agents.

Using this game-theoretic framework, we may now see that the time-consistent equilibrium, C, is in fact the Nash non-cooperative equilibrium

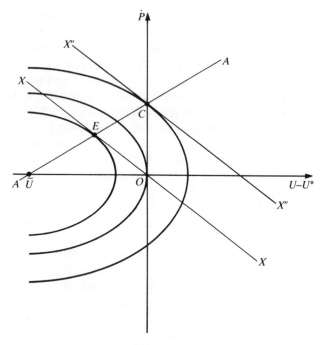

Figure 9.5

point, at which no player can do better, given the other's strategy. On the other hand, point O at which the agents' reaction function (the y-axis) is tangential to the highest indifference curve is a Stackelberg equilibrium, where the authorities act as leader. The problem illustrated by Kydland and Prescott is that, as in this case, such Stackelberg equilibria may be time-inconsistent in a non-cooperative game, because the government has an incentive to 'cheat'. On the other hand, the Nash equilibrium C is believable, but less optimal for the government (and the agents too, if we choose to assume that economic agents do not particularly value high inflation, and seek to be as close as possible to point O, on the y-axis). The reader should note the similarity between this result and the Cournot and Stackelberg models of oligopoly.

Given this problem of time consistency, is there any way in which the economy may achieve an outcome which is Pareto-superior to the Nash equilibrium? One way would be to turn this non-cooperative game into one where the two players cooperate, and seek to achieve an alternative outcome which both prefer to point C. However, as we shall see in Chapter 10, full cooperation of this type is a feasible proposition only when the negotiations take place among a small number of players. Given the atomistic nature of the private sector, it cannot be assumed to engage in cooperative behaviour, and hence this does not resolve the problem posed by time consistency. Of course if the government had an informational advantage over the private sector, then it could hope to establish a position of Stackelberg leader (see Chapter 10). Unfortunately, the assumption of rational expectations implies that this game is one of full information and thus rules out such a solution.

Another way in which the government may establish a position of Stackelberg leader is by a 'pre-commitment' to what appears to be a time-inconsistent policy. In the above example, if the authorities can persuade economic agents that they will 'pre-commit' themselves to a zero-inflation strategy, then the time-inconsistent equilibrium O could be achieved. Effectively, this is another cooperative solution, but is potentially more feasible than the full cooperative solution as it does not require the government and economic agents actually to negotiate. However, in the absence of binding legislation to govern aggregate demand policies, it is doubtful whether such pledges to stick to policies may *by themselves* carry much weight. This is merely another way of stating the fact that, as in the theory of collusive oligopoly, cooperative agreements imposed by the 'leader' will only hold if they are binding.

A more promising escape route from the problem of time inconsistency in achieving optimal policy is to recognise that, while a simple pledge by a government that it will not renege on its policies will initially not be believed by the suspicious public, economic agents may accept the authorities' leadership if *ex post* they have been seen to stick by their policies. For instance, one may argue that the post-1979 Conservative government in the UK built up a reputation for controlling inflation over its first few years in power. This observation has led some authors to investigate the way in which governments gain and lose reputations (see for instance Barro and Gordon 1983, Backus and Driffill 1985, 1986). Governments will gain reputations by sticking for a number of time periods to a zero-inflation policy, but will lose them if they at any time renege on this policy stance. Thus, it is arguable that while a time-inconsistent equilibrium such as point O in Figure 9.5 is not attainable in a non-cooperative situation where the game is only played for a small number of periods, if the game is repeated for a large number of periods then eventually both players will learn that it is in their interests to reach an equilibrium such as O. In other words, in repeated non-cooperative games, players may attain some of the benefits normally associated with cooperation (see J. W. Friedman 1986).

An appropriate question at this juncture is whether the problem of time inconsistency arises in all models which incorporate rational expectations, as this will determine the importance of the problem raised by Kydland and Prescott. As Borio (1986) points out, whether the time consistency problem is relevant depends on whether a proper 'game situation' arises.

For instance, the problem in the Kydland and Prescott model arises because there is a conflict of objectives between the authorities and economic agents, and there is a degree of interdependence between the two parties in the sense that one player's actions affect the other's pay-off. The problem analysed above disappears if, for instance, the authorities' objectives switch to one of stabilising the economy at the natural rate, U^*, as the conflict of objectives is then removed. To put this matter another way, the time consistency problem arises because 'economic planning is not a game against nature but, rather, a game against rational economic agents' (Kydland and Prescott 1977, p.473). Thus the problem may arise when two optimisers are engaged in a multiperiod *static* game like the one described in this subsection, and also when they both engage in an optimal control exercise when their state variables are linked by a common *dynamic* economic structure. One example of this is the case where two separate countries are attempting to formulate optimal policies and their economies are linked through their balance of payments. The action of each country obviously acts as a constraint on the other through the common linkages in the dynamic economic system. Thus if one country acts as a 'leader' in forming and announcing economic policies first, the reactions of the other country (the follower) may *ex post* cause the leader to revise his initial optimal plan, thus rendering the original plan time-inconsistent. These *dynamic games* will be briefly re-examined in Chapter 10 (for further details see Miller and Salmon 1983, 1985a, 1985b).

Kydland and Prescott saw the importance of time inconsistency (whether applied to repeated static games or to dynamic games) as a major flaw in the application of optimal control methods to economic problems. However, this critique has merely emphasised that optimal control techniques cannot be applied indiscriminately in economics by assuming that economic models are simple invariant physical systems. In the presence of rational economic agents, optimal control techniques have to be modified to find time-consistent solutions (see Miller and Salmon 1983, 1985a, 1985b), or, alternatively, the problem of reputation and credibility raised by time consistency has to be carefully studied.

9.4. Conclusion

In this chapter we have applied some of the recent developments in policy design to some of the current debates in the theory of economic policy. Unfortunately the pace of technique development in this area has by far outstripped the practical application of these techniques to real economic problems (on this see, for example, Currie 1985). Nevertheless, much has been learned about the strong and weak spots of particular targets and instruments, through the use of optimal control and frequency response techniques on small to medium size macroeconomic models. At the analytical level, we have also found out more about the factors which are likely to affect a government's choice of optimal policy instrument, target, or type of policy rule.

Though very few economists would seek to treat the problem of proper economic policy design as akin to the quest for the Holy Grail of fully optimal policy, the techniques developed in this theoretical quest have been applied to test the robustness of particular policy rules, targets and instruments and these findings will undoubtedly affect the conduct of real economic policy-making in the years to come. Furthermore, the introduction of rational expectations, despite its complications, has pointed to the need to make policies congruent with, and not diametrically opposed to, the behaviour of the private sector. The outcomes of policies, we are constantly reminded, are not the output from a mechanical, time invariant 'black box', but are closely dependent on the forward looking behaviour of the private sector.

10
INTERNATIONAL INTERDEPENDENCE AND POLICY COORDINATION

Up to now in this book, we have been concerned with the role and conduct of macroeconomic policy either in a closed economy, or, when dealing with an open economy, we have assumed that the individual country has been sufficiently small for world economic conditions to be exogenous and unaffected by domestic macroeconomic policies. In this chapter, we relax both these assumptions to focus on two general questions. First, in a context where individual economies are sufficiently large to affect economic conditions in their trading partner countries, what are the channels through which such spill-over effects will be transmitted, and will these effects be positive or negative? These questions refer to what Cooper (1985) calls *structural interdependence*, and they form the subject of section 1 of this chapter.

The second question arises directly out of such interdependence. In the same way that interdependence, and the possible recognition of it, gives rise to questions of pricing and marketing strategy in the theory of the firm under conditions of oligopoly, so structural interdependence raises issues of strategy in macroeconomic policy-making in an open economy. As a further parallel with the theory of oligopoly, the use of game theory has proved to be a fruitful approach to the analysis of these questions, and in section 2 we have set out the general features of game theory, with specific reference to international interdependence. In so doing, we distinguish between *static* games, where the countries choose policies whose impact is immediate, and *dynamic* games, where the impact of policies varies over time, and as a result governments implement their optimal strategy over a period of time. Finally, in section 3, we examine in greater detail some of the models which apply game theory to problems of interdependence, focusing for the greater part on static games (in the interests of simplicity).

10.1. The International Transmission of Economic Policies

In this section, we extend the Fleming–Mundell model, outlined in Chapters 7 and 8, to a two-country context. The emphasis on the

334

Fleming–Mundell model, together with all its shortcomings, is justifiable principally on the grounds that the other mainstream approaches are inappropriate. On the one hand, the monetary model largely generates results which run counter to the very notion of interdependence. Under flexible exchange rates, the economy is insulated from foreign shocks, while under fixed rates, with real income tied to its 'natural' level and the balance of payments automatically self-correcting (given the authorities' inability to sterilise), there is little for policy to achieve. On the other hand, portfolio models of the open economy, with the dynamics inherent in their stock–flow interactions, generate considerable complexities in a two-country setting and such models are rare in the literature. (One example is provided by Branson and Henderson 1985.)

In focusing on the Fleming–Mundell two-country model, we follow Mundell (1968) and Mussa (1979), and the following assumptions should be noted. First, while the bonds issued by both countries are perfect substitutes, neither country is small, so that although each country's interest rate is pegged to the interest rate of the other country, each country can affect this common interest rate by its domestic policies. Second, we assume that the two countries are similar in their economic structures. This is an assumption which is relaxed later.

We now proceed to examine the international transmission of monetary and fiscal policies in such a model under both fixed and flexible exchange rates, beginning in the following subsection with the fixed rates case.

10.1.1. International Policy Transmission under Fixed Exchange Rates

Let us assume two countries, 1 and 2, in the Fleming–Mundell model as set out in Figure 10.1. Consider initially a monetary expansion in country 1, and its effects on country 2, as shown in Figure 10.1(a). The monetary expansion in country 1 will cause the LM_1 curve to shift rightward, to LM_1', pushing that country's balance of payments towards deficit on both the current and capital accounts. In a small open economy with perfect capital mobility this position would be unsustainable, as the resulting fall in the money supply would shift LM_1' back to LM_1. However, in a two-country model, given that country 1 determines part of the world money stock, a domestic credit expansion originating there will cause the world interest rate to fall. In determining the new world (and domestic) interest rate, however, account must be taken of the change in economic conditions in country 2, following country 1's monetary expansion. In the event, both the IS curve and the LM curve in country 2 will shift to the right, reflecting an increase in exports to country 1 generated by increased income in country 1, and an increase in the money stock due to country 2's balance of payments surplus. The net outcome is that the world interest rate settles at a point like r_2, and income at y_2.

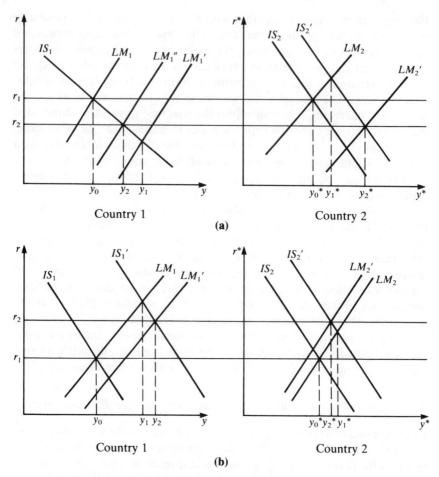

Figure 10.1 The Two-Country Fleming–Mundell Model under
Fixed Exchange Rates

These results are in important contrast to those of the small country
case. In the first place, domestic monetary policy can affect domestic
income because an individual country can affect the world interest rate. In
addition, the spill-over effects are positive, as income in country 2 is
increased by monetary expansion in country 1. As noted above, this spill-
over effect works through two channels. First, the rise in income in country
1 will tend to increase country 2's exports, thus pushing IS_2 outwards to
IS_2', and increasing income from y_0^* to y_1^*. Second, country 1 will run a
(temporary) balance of payments deficit, losing foreign currency to country
2, and therefore increasing the money stock in country 2. This shifts LM_2
to LM_2' (in the absence of sterilisation policies). The net outcome is an
increase in income to y_2^*. These adjustments to income and interest rate

levels also serve to bring the balance of payments back into equilibrium.

To sum up the results so far, the multiplier effects of an increase in domestic credit (D) in country 1 on its domestic income (y), foreign income (y^*), domestic reserves, (R), and foreign reserves (R^*) are:

$$\partial y/\partial D > 0,\ \partial y^*/\partial D > 0,\ \partial R/\partial D < 0,\ \partial R^*/\partial D > 0$$

and similarly for a domestic credit expansion in country 2:

$$\partial y/\partial D^* > 0,\ \partial y^*/\partial D^* > 0,\ \partial R/\partial D^* > 0,\ \partial R^*/\partial D^* < 0$$

Next, we briefly turn to the effects of a fiscal expansion in country 1 on the variables of interest. This is illustrated on Figure 10.1(b). A fiscal expansion in country 1 will shift IS_1 to IS_1', thus causing income to increase from y_0 to y_1. However, since total expenditure in the world economy has increased while the total world money stock has remained constant, world interest rates will rise from r_1 to r_2. In country 2 exports will increase as the increase in income in country 1 will cause an increase in imports there. Thus IS_2 will shift to IS_2', and income will rise from y_0^* to y_1^*. Note, however, that the shift of IS_1 to IS_1' is greater than the shift of IS_2 to IS_2', as this second effect is diluted due to the marginal import propensity of country 1. Therefore, in general, country 1 will have an overall balance of payments surplus (due to a capital account surplus), as the intersection of IS_1' and LM_1 is above the new world interest rate r_2. Similarly, country 2 will have an overall balance of payments deficit as the intersection of IS_2' and LM_2 lies below r_2. Thus there will be a capital outflow from country 2 to country 1, with a corresponding transfer of foreign exchange reserves. This will shift LM_1 to LM_1' and LM_2 to LM_2', thus finally causing income in the two countries to finally settle at y_2 and y_2^* respectively. The effect of an increase in government expenditure (g) in country 1 on domestic income and on income in country 2 will be positive, although the spill-over effects in this case are weaker than in the monetary policy case. In addition, there will be a fall in foreign exchange reserves for country 2, and a rise in country 1's reserves. We summarise these results as follows:

$$\partial y/\partial g > 0,\ \partial y^*/\partial g > 0,\ \partial R/\partial g > 0,\ \partial R^*/\partial g < 0$$

and similarly for an increase in government expenditure in country 2 (g^*):

$$\partial y/\partial g^* > 0,\ \partial y^*/\partial g^* > 0,\ \partial R/\partial g^* < 0,\ \partial R^*/\partial g^* > 0$$

As the above discussion shows, in a simple fixed exchange rate Fleming–Mundell model there are two basic channels of economic interdependence. The first is through the current account of the balance of payments, as changes in income in one country affect the second country's exports. The second is through the effect of domestic policies on the world interest rate, and thus on the capital account of the other country. In the case of both fiscal policy and monetary policy, these channels serve to generate positive spill-over effects in the second country.

These particular results are dependent on the assumption of perfect capital mobility. However, the opposite assumption (of complete capital immobility) does not change the general conclusion that under fixed exchange rates, both monetary and fiscal policies are transmitted positively to the foreign country. However, capital immobility does tend to weaken the spill-over effects of monetary policy relative to those of fiscal policy. With respect to monetary policy, there are now no interest rate effects on the foreign country, while the balance of payments deficit (and therefore its expansionary monetary consequences in country 2) is smaller than under perfect capital mobility. With respect to fiscal expansion, the interest rate effects in country 2 (which were contractionary under perfect capital mobility) are now absent, while the balance of payments in country 2 will now be in surplus (rather than deficit in the perfect mobility case), with a consequent monetary expansion in country 2. (A useful discussion of the role of capital mobility in economic interdependence is provided by Mussa 1979.)

10.1.2.   The Flexible Exchange Rates Case

As we now move from the fixed to the flexible exchange rate version of the Fleming–Mundell model, one channel of transmission is replaced. The effect on the exchange rate (and hence terms of trade) of each country's domestic monetary and fiscal policies is now included, while the monetary consequences of the balance of payments (which is set at zero under flexible exchange rates) are removed.

The effects of monetary expansion in a two-country flexible exchange rate Fleming–Mundell model is shown in Figure 10.2(a). Consider an increase of the money stock in country 1, i.e. a shift of LM_1 to LM_1'. This tends to have two effects. First, income in country 1 adjusts from y_0 to y_1, and second, the world interest rate tends to fall from r_1 to r_2. Notice, however, that the interest rate does not fall by enough to restore overall balance of payments equilibrium at the prevailing exchange rate, as the world interest rate is determined jointly across two countries, and *not* at the intersection of the IS_1 and LM_1 curves. Country 1 will therefore move into incipient balance of payments deficit. In country 2, the increase in country 1's income will increase country 2's net exports through the export multiplier, thus shifting IS_2 rightward to IS_2' (but by less than the rise in

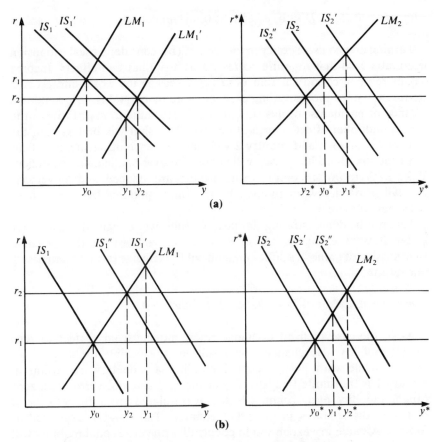

Figure 10.2 The Two-Country Fleming–Mundell Model under
Flexible Exchange Rates

income from y_0 to y_1), while the fall in the world interest rate will generate an incipient balance of payments surplus for country 2. Neither y_1 nor y_1^* are points of equilibrium, as the balance of payments of the two countries is non-zero and country 1's exchange rate will depreciate, increasing its net exports, and shifting IS_1 further to IS_1', so as to intersect LM_1' at the new world interest rate. The converse happens in country 2, where the appreciation of its exchange rate will lead to an equivalent fall in net exports, shifting IS_2' to IS_2''. The key result is that while income in country 1 increases to y_2 income in country 2 will fall back to y_2^*. This negative transmission abroad of domestic monetary policy under flexible exchange rates with perfect capital mobility is a feature of the model which Mundell (1968) recognised, and as a result this type of policy has often been dubbed a 'beggar-thy-neighbour' policy. We summarise the effects of monetary expansions in the two countries on their respective incomes as follows:

$\partial y / \partial D > 0, \ \partial y^* / \partial D < 0, \ \partial y / \partial D^* < 0, \ \partial y^* / \partial D^* > 0$

Turning now to fiscal policy in Figure 10.2(b), consider a fiscal expansion in country 1 so that IS_1 shifts to IS_1'. This again has two effects. Income will increase in country 1 from y_0 to y_1, increasing the world interest rate from r_1 to r_2. At the prevailing exchange rate, country 1 is now running a balance of payments surplus. In country 2, IS_2 shifts to IS_2', through the export multiplier effect referred to above. This shift will be less than the shift of IS_1 to IS_1', and country 2 will run a balance of payments deficit. Thus country 1's exchange rate will appreciate so as to eliminate the deficit, shifting IS_1' to IS_1'' as country 1's net exports are reduced, and conversely, IS_2' will shift rightward to IS_2'', by the same amount. Income in both countries will rise.

This result, demonstrating the positive spill-over effects of fiscal policy under flexible exchange rates, is in direct contrast to the negative transmission of monetary policy under flexible exchange rates. Summarising our results:

$$\partial y / \partial g > 0, \ \partial y^* / \partial g > 0, \ \partial y / \partial g^* > 0, \ \partial y^* / \partial g^* > 0$$

As in the case of fixed exchange rates, moving from perfect to zero capital mobility also changes the results of the flexible exchange rates model. While with perfect capital mobility a monetary expansion in country 1 is transmitted negatively to country 2 and vice versa, with zero capital mobility each country is totally insulated from the effects of monetary disturbances in the other country. This may be explained as follows. A monetary expansion in country 1 with zero capital mobility will cause the interest rate in country 1 to fall, but leaves the interest rate in country 2 unaffected. Thus, this channel of transmission is eliminated. The only remaining channel of transmission is through net exports, and under floating rates and capital immobility net exports are necessarily zero, thus removing the second channel of transmission. Clearly, exactly the same line of reasoning may be applied to the case of fiscal expansion. It is only when capital is mobile that each country can affect the level of desired expenditure of the other by either changing the world rate of interest (i.e. the interest rate in the other country), or by causing the exchange rate to settle at a point where the balance of payments is zero, and the non-zero current account is matched by ongoing capital flows. It will be recalled from Chapter 8 that this result is peculiar to models which assume *perfect* capital mobility, or which adopt *flow* theories of the capital account, and as we shall discuss below, these results would contrast with those obtained in long-run equilibrium in a two-country portfolio model of the exchange rate.

To summarise the results of this section so far, it is apparent that some of the insulating properties of flexible exchange rates are dependent upon the assumption that individual country actions cannot affect the world interest rate. This cannot be true in the case of an economic expansion by a large country, or a coordinated expansion by a group of smaller countries. Nevertheless, it remains true that in a Fleming–Mundell world with flexible exchange rates each country is free to determine its own level of real income, by an appropriate setting of fiscal and monetary policy. We will return to this issue below, as it is of great importance when discussing the strategic aspects of economic interdependence. For the moment it is sufficient to note that, even under flexible exchange rates, individual countries' policy actions will affect economic conditions in other countries, and that both positive and negative spill-over effects may occur (provided that capital is not totally immobile). However, these results are specific to the simple Fleming–Mundell model, and we now examine the implications of relaxing some of its characteristic assumptions.

Following Obstfeld (1985), let us now assume that prices and wages are entirely flexible. That is, the aggregate supply curve is vertical in both countries even in the short run. To avoid a multiplicity of cases, we will restrict our attention to a log-linear flexible exchange rate model with perfect capital mobility, assuming static exchange rate expectations. It is apparent that in this model any economic interdependence between the two countries will be reflected entirely in changes in price levels, rather than real income.

Equations (10.1) and (10.2) below represent goods market equilibrium conditions in country 1 and country 2 respectively (where the variables relating to country 2 are marked by asterisks):

$$d = \delta q - \sigma r + \gamma y^* + g \tag{10.1}$$

$$d^* = -\delta q - \sigma r^* + \gamma y + g^* \tag{10.2}$$

where q, d, y, r, and g represent the real exchange rate, aggregate demand, real income, the real interest rate, and a fiscal shock respectively. We define the real exchange rate q as:

$$q = e + p^* - p \tag{10.3}$$

where e is the nominal exchange rate (defined as the price of country 2's currency in terms of country 1's currency), and p is the price level. Aggregate income in each country is assumed to be fixed at a natural rate, given that prices and wages are totally flexible:

$$y = y^* = k \tag{10.4}$$

The money market in each country is characterised by a conventional demand for money function:

$$m - p = \phi y - \lambda r \tag{10.5}$$

$$m^* - p^* = \phi y^* - \lambda r^* \tag{10.6}$$

Assuming perfect capital mobility, and static exchange rate expectations, we may write:

$$r = r^* \tag{10.7}$$

The above model can be solved to determine the equilibrium values of the endogenous variables. We may then see how shocks in the exogenous variables g, g^*, m, and m^* (i.e. fiscal and monetary shocks in the two countries) affect prices and interest rates in the other country, and the exchange rate. The equilibrium values for these endogenous variables are:

$$r = r^* = (g + g^*)/2\sigma \tag{10.8}$$

$$q = (g^* - g)/2\delta \tag{10.9}$$

$$p = m + \lambda r \tag{10.10}$$

$$p^* = m^* + \lambda r^* \tag{10.11}$$

$$e = (m - m^*) + q \tag{10.12}$$

Let us first examine the effects of a monetary expansion in country 1. As we would expect, from (10.10) and (10.12), this raises the price level in country 1, and causes an equivalent depreciation in its currency. However, from (10.11) we see that the monetary expansion in country 1 has no effect on the price level in country 2. This result, of *zero* monetary spill-over, is in contrast to that of the fix-price Fleming–Mundell model, and may be explained as follows. In a fixed-price model, monetary shocks are transmitted through three main channels. First, through an adjustment of the real exchange rate, which here cannot take place, as both countries are at full employment. Second, through the Keynesian export multiplier, as a country's increased income leads to increased exports for the second country. Again, here income is treated as fixed at full employment, and therefore this channel of transmission is eliminated. Third, through a lower real world interest rate, which again is not applicable here, as both countries are at full employment. It therefore follows that the assumption of full employment restores the insulation property of flexible exchange rates in the face of foreign monetary shocks, even if capital is perfectly mobile. In this sense, this model parallels the results of the monetary approach.

This insulation property does not, however, carry over to fiscal shocks. From (10.8) and (10.9) we may note that a fiscal expansion in country 1 will lead to an increase in the world rate of interest, and will lead to a real appreciation of country 1's exchange rate. The latter effect is in line with the standard fix-price Fleming–Mundell result, but in this case it is associated with upward pressure on interest rates due to a rising price level. The net result is an expansion in demand in country 1, and as a consequence some of the increase in domestic demand is transmitted abroad, and causes a rise in the price level in country 2. Therefore, flexible exchange rates cannot insulate the domestic economy from *real* shocks originating abroad, while they can insulate it from foreign *monetary* shocks, *provided* that prices are perfectly flexible in both countries. Another way of making this point is that, as in a simple closed economy IS–LM model with flexible wages and prices, an increase in the money stock is neutral, since the price level will rise to reverse the rightward shift in the LM curve. On the other hand, a fiscal expansion is seen as an increase in *real* expenditure, which permanently shifts the IS curve to the right, thus permanently raising interest rates since a rise in the price level cannot offset this.

Thus far, we have examined a number of models under different assumptions of price flexibility and capital mobility. However, all of these models share the common feature that they are essentially *static* in nature. As we have seen in Chapter 8, however, exchange rate theory has developed a range of models which are more *dynamic* in nature, involving differential speeds of adjustment in different markets (see, for example, Dornbusch 1976), wealth effects with consequent stock–flow interactions (see Branson 1977, 1979, Kouri 1976, Dornbusch and Fischer 1980), and information and expectations effects (see Mussa 1976, Wilson 1979). Such dynamic models, however, are difficult to incorporate into a two-country setting, especially when considering issues of policy coordination. The inclusion of dynamic elements involves the application of dynamic game theory, which is an extension of the optimal control techniques outlined in Chapter 9, with all its attendant complexities. In contrast, the static models outlined so far provide a more tractable framework within which policy coordination may be analysed.

However, before turning to these issues, we may examine some of the general implications for spill-over effects of extending these simple models to take account of recent developments in exchange rate theory. In particular, we examine the implications of incorporating exchange rate expectations and the short-run inflexibility of wages and prices, as in Dornbusch (1976), in a two-country context.

First, let us change the simple perfect capital mobility condition adopted so far (equation (10.7)), to include exchange rate expectations, thereby obtaining a conventional uncovered interest parity equation (see Chapter 8):

$$r = r^* + \dot{e}^e \tag{10.13}$$

Second, we may adopt an intermediate position with regard to wage and price flexibility between the original fix-price Fleming–Mundell model and the model illustrated in (10.1)–(10.7). In Obstfeld (1985), prices and wages are assumed to adjust gradually until output returns to its 'natural' level. So while this assumes an upward sloping aggregate supply curve in the short run, in the long run the aggregate supply curve is vertical. Such amendments give the model short-run dynamics while (10.8)–(10.12) still give the long-run solution of the model once the price and exchange rate dynamics have worked themselves out. As a result, these innovations do not alter the channels through which monetary and fiscal shocks are transmitted between countries, but they oblige us to distinguish between short- and long-run effects. The impact effects will differ from the results obtained in the fix-price Fleming–Mundell model because of the presence of exchange rate expectations. As explained in Dornbusch (1976), sticky goods prices lead to the phenomenon of 'real exchange rate overshooting' in response to monetary shocks in models which incorporate (rational) exchange rate expectations. As a result, the transmission of monetary policies across the terms of trade will be exaggerated in the short run with respect to the final long-run equilibrium. The results obtained in subsection 10.1.2 will therefore underestimate the short-run impact effects of monetary policy in the presence of exchange rate expectations. In contrast, fiscal expansions will cause the real exchange rate to move directly to its new equilibrium. Hence, as Dornbusch (1983) points out, while flexible exchange rates may insulate a country from monetary disturbances in the long run, this will not be the case in the short run. Furthermore, real disturbances cause permanent spill-over effects.

Another development in exchange rate theory, surveyed in Chapter 8, has been the introduction of portfolio models and wealth effects (see Branson 1977, 1979, Kouri 1976, Dornbusch and Fischer 1980). The long-run solution of these models requires the current account to be in balance, and in the short run current account imbalances cause wealth transfers, and therefore wealth effects, between economies. Such wealth effects would affect the transmission mechanism in our fix-price flexible exchange rate model illustrated in Figure 10.2. Starting from current account equilibrium, a fiscal expansion in country 1 is transmitted positively to country 2 (see Figure 10.2(b)). At the equilibrium income levels y_2 and y_2^*, country 1 is running a current account deficit, and country 2 an equivalent surplus. This current account deficit is financed by an outflow of assets from country 1 to country 2, and over time this is likely to cause an increase in expenditure in country 2 and a corresponding fall in country 1. Thus the effect of asset flows over time is to amplify the initial effect of fiscal policy on country 2, while diminishing the effect on country 1.

Turning now to monetary policy, Figure 10.2(a) illustrates the 'beggar-thy-neighbour' case whereby a monetary expansion in country 1 has a negative effect on foreign income. At income levels y_2 and y_2^*, however, country 1 is now running a current account surplus, while country 2 has an equivalent deficit, with the resulting asset flows further reducing expenditure and output in country 2, and further increasing expenditure in country 1. Thus, in both the cases of domestic fiscal and monetary expansions in fix-price exchange rate models, the incorporation of wealth effects tends to amplify the transmission of these policies to the foreign country.

It will be clear from this section that the nature of the transmission of monetary and fiscal policies between countries is very model-specific. The modification of any of the underlying assumptions of the simple Fleming–Mundell model has been shown to lead to different results. Consequently, models of economic interdependence have increasingly come to be based on stylised facts regarding the asset, goods, or labour market structure of the countries under scrutiny. This tends to lead to departures from the assumption that countries are identical in every respect. A familiar approach is to recognise that wage-setting behaviour may differ between countries (e.g. see Branson and Rotemberg 1980, Corden and Turnovsky 1983). Another possibility is that put forward by Canzoneri and Gray (1983), that some factors of production (typically raw materials) may have a price fixed in one country's currency, and that this will introduce interesting asymmetries in the transmission of economic policies. Canzoneri and Gray analyse the case of oil, whose price is typically set in US dollars. This example is of considerable interest, not least given the importance of oil as an intermediate good in the more developed economies, and we examine it in some detail in the next subsection.

10.1.3. *Economic Interdependence: a Case Study Approach*

The model proposed by Canzoneri and Gray (1983) is a three-country model, with one oil producer (OPEC), and two oil importers (the USA, and the rest of the world (ROW)). The basic model of the oil-importing economies consists of a conventional aggregate demand and supply model under flexible exchange rates and with perfect capital mobility. The aggregate demand side of the basic model is therefore closely related to the Fleming–Mundell model of subsection 10.1.2. The aggregate supply side of the model includes another factor of production (oil), in addition to labour, and both the USA and the ROW produce their own particular consumption good. However, both regions are assumed to consume a mix of home-produced and imported goods, so that the relevant price index for workers in assessing their real wage is the consumer price index, which includes imports. Firms, on the other hand, in making their supply decision will look at the real product wage, and the real product price of oil. As a result, the level of real income in each oil-importing country is a function not only of the real product wage, but also of the real price of oil relative to a country's own price level. Because of the presence of the real product price of oil in these aggregate supply functions, the oil producer, OPEC, can cause aggregate supply shocks in the US and the ROW by changing the nominal price of oil. These aggregate supply relationships and real factor price definitions may be set out as follows. We can write down the aggregate supply functions in the USA and ROW in the following functional form:

$$y^{us} = f(w^{us}, c^{us}) \qquad\qquad f_w < 0, f_c < 0 \qquad\qquad (10.14)$$

$$y^{row} = f(w^{row}, c^{row}) \qquad\qquad f_w < 0, f_c < 0 \qquad\qquad (10.15)$$

where the y denotes output, w the real product wage, and c the real product price of oil respectively, and the superscripts identify the country to which the variables refer. The variables w and c are defined as follows:

$$w^{us} = W^{us}/P^{us} \qquad\qquad\qquad\qquad\qquad\qquad (10.16)$$

$$w^{row} = W^{row}/P^{row} \qquad\qquad\qquad\qquad\qquad\qquad (10.17)$$

$$c^{us} = C/P^{us} \qquad\qquad\qquad\qquad\qquad\qquad (10.18)$$

$$c^{row} = Ce/P^{row} \qquad\qquad\qquad\qquad\qquad\qquad (10.19)$$

where W denotes the nominal wage, P the price of the product produced in the country, e the exchange rate the price of one dollar in ROW currency), and C is the US dollar price of oil. On the other hand, the real consumer wage, R, which is relevant to workers in the US and the ROW in making their labour supply decision is defined as follows:

$$R^{us} = W^{us}/I^{us} \qquad\qquad\qquad\qquad\qquad\qquad (10.20)$$

$$R^{row} = W^{row}/I^{row} \qquad\qquad\qquad\qquad\qquad\qquad (10.21)$$

where I denotes the consumer price index, which is calculated as follows:

$$I^{us} = (P^{us})^{\delta}(P^{row})^{1-\delta} \tag{10.22}$$

$$I^{row} = (P^{row})^{\varepsilon}(P^{row})^{1-\varepsilon} \tag{10.23}$$

where δ is the share of domestic goods in the total consumption basket in the US, and ε is the equivalent measure for the ROW.

OPEC is assumed to produce only oil, and to consume goods from both the US and the ROW. It is assumed that OPEC fixes the nominal price of oil in US dollar terms, while it may or may not decide to index-link this price to its consumption price index, which will be similar in form to (10.22) and (10.23).

Canzoneri and Gray examine the interdependence of monetary policies between the two oil-importing countries in three different versions of this basic model. In the first version, they assume that wages are fixed in nominal terms in the US and the ROW, but that OPEC fully indexes the price of oil to its consumption price index. As a result the aggregate supply curve in both countries will be upward sloping, due to fixed nominal wages. This version of the model is a simple variant of the Fleming–Mundell model of subsection 10.1.2, and similar results are obtained. The transmission of monetary policies between the US and the ROW will be negative, as analysed in 10.1.2. This is therefore a 'beggar-thy-neighbour' policy world.

The second version assumes that there is a high degree of real wage resistance in both oil-importing countries, as well as full indexing by OPEC of the oil price. A monetary expansion in this case will initially cause a depreciation of the domestic currency, and hence real wage resistance, as the domestic real consumer wage has fallen. This raises the price of the domestic product, and hence lowers the real product wage abroad, increasing foreign output. The interesting feature of this version is that this positive spill-over effect modifies the negative transmission properties of the Fleming–Mundell model. When there is a high degree of wage indexation, the net spill–over effects of monetary policies may become positive, and this case is labelled a 'locomotive' policy world. It is usually suggested that this second version of the model may be of greater relevance in describing the world economy in the 1970s than the first, given the high degree of real wage resistance present in the advanced economies over that period.

In both these versions of the basic model the effects of monetary policy between the US and ROW are symmetric. That is, in each version of the model, the spill-over effects are of the same sign, irrespective of which economy is carrying out the policy. However, the third version of the model introduces the possibility that asymmetries may exist in spill-over effects, by appealing to some 'real world' features of oil pricing by OPEC. The vital assumption made here is that the nominal price of oil is fixed, i.e. it is not indexed to any price or basket of prices in the period under consideration. This assumption implies that movements in prices in the USA or the ROW do not in turn affect the price of oil. Let us also assume, for simplicity, that nominal wages are also fixed in both the ROW and the US, but that prices are flexible, so that we have an upward sloping aggregate supply curve because a rise in the price level, P, will lead to a fall in the real product price of both factors of production, i.e. the real product wage, w, and the real product price of oil, c. We may now examine the effects of monetary policy in each of the oil-importing countries in turn.

This version of the model retains the channels of interdependence present in the Fleming–Mundell model of subsection 10.1.2, and in addition the real product price of oil provides an additional channel of transmission. An increase in the real price of oil (for any given level of a country's product price, P), will cause output to fall in the country in question, and may be interpreted as a leftward shift in the aggregate supply curve. The real price of oil may be changed in either country by an exogenous change in OPEC's nominal price of oil, C (see (10.18) and (10.19)). In addition, from (10.19), we can see that a change in the exchange rate between the US and ROW will alter the nominal price of oil in terms of ROW currency, eC, and, for a given ROW price level, P^{row}, will alter the real product price of oil in the ROW. However, from (10.18) we can see that such an exchange rate change will leave the real product price of oil in the US, c^{us}, unchanged. This is the key source of the asymmetry in this model.

Using this framework, consider an expansionary monetary policy in the US. In an aggregate supply-extended Fleming–Mundell model, output in the US will rise to the extent that the real product wage falls. However, in the model presented by Canzoneri and Gray, the aggregate supply curve now depends not only on the real wage, but also on the real price of oil. Given that the US price level, P^{us}, rises following an expansion, the real price of oil will fall, thus causing the effect of a monetary expansion to be stronger compared to a model where oil plays no part (still assuming, of course, that OPEC does not react to raise the US dollar price of oil so as to keep its real produce price constant, in the face of expansionary policies in oil-importing countries). Thus the effect of an expansionary monetary policy on output in the US is positive. Its effect on ROW output depends in part on the conventional Fleming–Mundell mechanism which imparts a negative effect to ROW output, and on an additional effect working through the real product price of oil in the ROW (see (10.19)). Given that a monetary expansion in the US tends to depreciate the US dollar with respect to the ROW currency (a fall in e), it will cause a reduction in the real product price of oil in the ROW. This positive effect on the ROW output may well outweigh the negative Fleming–Mundell transmission effect.

On the other hand, a monetary expansion in the ROW will have a negative effect on US output, working through conventional Fleming–Mundell channels. It will also cause the ROW currency to depreciate (a rise in e); but the key point here is that the exchange rate change will leave the price of oil in dollar terms unchanged (see (10.18)). Thus, the transmission of monetary policy may be asymmetric between the two countries: a ROW monetary expansion will have unambiguously negative spill-over effects on US output, while a US monetary expansion may well have a positive total spill-over effect on ROW output.

This model is important because it demonstrates that one can obtain asymmetric results; but this asymmetry hinges on the rather questionable assumption that OPEC will choose to keep the nominal price of oil (in US dollars) fixed in the face of a rise in the price of US and ROW consumption goods, despite the fact that the real consumption value of its oil exports is being eroded. However, it may be argued that such a model retains some validity in a world where OPEC does not have full power to manipulate the oil price. Furthermore, there are other potential sources of asymmetry between countries. For instance, if wage-setting behaviour differed between the US and the ROW, such that there was a high degree of real wage resistance in the ROW, and a low degree of real wage resistance in the US, a similar result to that of the above fix-oil-price model would be obtained (see Canzoneri and Gray 1983, Branson and Rotemberg 1980).

10.1.4. Conclusions

It is clear from this section that the degree, channels, and nature of international interdependence are determined by a host of model-specific considerations, and correspondingly a range of possible results can be obtained. This range of results generates a degree of uncertainty regarding interdependence, and leads to a variety of possible macroeconomic strategies on the part of an individual country or groups of countries. The types of questions which we may wish to address, using our above models, are the following: what are the strategies which individual governments are likely to adopt in the face of economic interdependence? What scope and incentives are there for cooperation between countries in designing economic policies? What outcomes for the world economy as a whole will result from the actions of individual countries? It is to these questions that we turn in the remaining sections of this chapter.

10.2. An Introduction to Static Game Theory

10.2.1. Basic Definitions and Assumptions

The recognition by governments that their economies are structurally interdependent with the rest of the world can lead to strategic behaviour in the setting of economic policies, as each country considers the effects of its own policies on other countries, and their possible policy responses. Before proceeding to analyse the strategic aspects of our models in detail, it is necessary to survey some basic features of static game theory (for further details see Harsanyi 1977, J. W. Friedman 1977, 1986).

Every game has a finite number of rational decision-makers (players). In the special case of our two-country models the players involved are two, namely the governments of the two countries. Players are assumed to have a number of courses of action (strategies) at their disposal, and the choice of strategies by all the players in the game determines the pay-off (utility) to each player. Each player is aware that any other player's actions may affect his pay-off. For simplicity we assume that each player possesses *complete information*. That is, each player knows who the other players are, what actions are available to all the players, and the potential outcomes for all players. The timing of each player's moves is governed by the rules of the game. In practice we assume that both players must declare their moves simultaneously so that neither has a strategic advantage, although this assumption may be relaxed, as we shall see below.

Let us examine the concept of a strategy more closely. In a game, a player's *move* consists of an action taken at a particular moment while, in contrast, a *strategy* is a player's plan with regard to all the moves which he may wish to make at any future stage of the game. Thus, in general, games are made up of a series of moves by the players involved, and their strategies must specify what moves are to be made in any contingency which may arise. In certain games (e.g. chess), it is clearly inconceivable that all strategies can be considered by the players; but it is usual to assume in economic models that players know all the strategies open to them, and that they select one from this set. In fact, the static games we consider in this chapter are one-off, or single-period games, so that the terms 'strategy' and 'move' coincide.

Games can be subdivided into various categories. One such subdivision is between *cooperative* and *non-cooperative* games. In games of the latter type agents are precluded from making binding agreements to their mutual benefit, while in the former such agreements are possible. However, cooperation is only beneficial in certain games with a particular pay-off structure, and these are known as *variable sum* games. Games can also be subdivided between those possessing a *constant sum* (or Pareto-optimal) pay-off structure, and those with a variable sum pay-off structure. An

Table 10.1   A Constant Sum Game

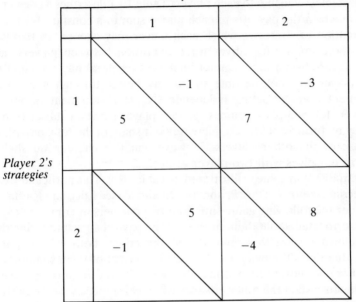

Player 1's strategies

		1	2
Player 2's strategies	1	5 / −1	7 / −3
	2	−1 / 5	−4 / 8

Table 10.2   A Variable Sum Game

Player 1's strategies

		Confess	Do not confess
Player 2's strategies	Confess	−5 / −5	0 / −10
	Do not confess	−10 / 0	−2 / −2

example of each type of game is given in Tables 10.1 and 10.2. Each table enumerates the pay-off accruing to each player for any combination of the two strategies available to each player. Table 10.1 describes a constant sum game in which the pay-offs to each player sum to a constant (4) for every combination of strategies which each player may choose. In this type of game there are no incentives for cooperation between players, as any agreement between them cannot increase their total pay-offs, and hence each player will not be able to do any better through a cooperative agreement than by acting independently. This statement is only true, however, for two-player games, as in *n*-player games a subset of players can always form a coalition to increase their share of the total pay-off at the expense of the other players. However, in this chapter we shall only concern ourselves with two-player games.

A variable sum game is illustrated in Table 10.2. This particular example has become famous as the 'Prisoners' Dilemma' (see Luce and Raiffa 1957). Consider the following game situation: two partners in crime are captured and interrogated about their misdeeds. The pay-off structure facing them is the following: if neither confesses to the crime, both will be punished lightly due to lack of evidence. However, if either of them confesses while the other does not, the one who cooperates with the authorities will escape punishment, while the other prisoner will receive the severest punishment. If both confess, they will be punished severely, but neither will receive the severest punishment. Note that the sum of the pay-offs to each player is not constant for all pairs of strategies. If the prisoners are able to consult each other and enter an agreement, they will probably both agree to cooperate to avoid severe punishment. However, there are incentives for each player to 'cheat' by repudiating any agreement and confessing. The fragile nature of cooperative behaviour will be discussed further below.

One question which is relevant to this classification is whether *constant sum* games (sometimes called zero sum games) or *variable sum* games are more likely to occur in practice in economics. While some games are obviously constant sum in nature (e.g. in gambling, one player's *money* loss is inevitably another's gain), in economics the 'pay-off' described above is generally identified with *utility* accruing to a player, and there is no reason to believe that in such circumstances a game will be of a constant sum type. In the examples described below the players are governments whose utility functions are defined in terms of different macroeconomic objectives. In this case, it is difficult to conceive why different outcomes in terms of macroeconomic indicators should yield a constant sum pay-off structure.

10.2.2. An Application of Game Theory

We now employ the concepts of game theory to analyse the strategic aspects of international interdependence. Following the work of Hamada (1976, 1979, 1985), we again adopt the fixed exchange rate Fleming–Mundell model. The economic interdependence which occurs in this model ensures that each country's strategy with regard to its policy instrument will affect the final objectives and therefore the pay-off of the other country. Each country is assumed to have only one policy instrument at its disposal (monetary policy), and the strategy it needs to choose is the setting of this policy instrument. The pay-off structure of the game depends on two factors: first, on the relationship between each government's policy instruments and the final objectives of policy, and second on the utility or welfare attached by each country to each policy objective. The first element is fully described by the multipliers of the structural model adopted, and the second is described by the particular utility function of each government.

The two countries are assumed to have utility (national welfare) functions which depend on each country's own level of income and level of international reserves:

$$U = U(y, R) \tag{10.24}$$

The exact signs and magnitudes of the partial derivatives of this utility function will vary from country to country. However, the following general assumptions may be made about the shape of this utility function, following Hamada's analysis. Each country desires a reasonably high level of income at any given time, but fears that too high a level of income may trigger off inflationary pressures. Thus the second partial derivative with respect to y is negative. This interpretation is clearly problematic in a fix-price model, but it is only intended as an approximation of reality. Similarly, the presence of R in (10.24) implies that a country's welfare depends in part on the country's recent balance of payments history. A country's preference at any given point in time with regard to its level of reserves will have implications for its preference with regard to its balance of payments in the period of the game. In practice, if a country has a utility function such that it reaches an absolute maximum when $R > R_0$, and where R_0 represents a country's level of reserves before the game commences, the country in question desires a balance of payments surplus over the period of the game. The reverse applies if the utility function is maximised at some level of reserves $R < R_0$. However, whatever a country's preference for a surplus or deficit, we assume that the second partial derivative with respect to R is negative, so that when the balance of payments surplus/deficit and the consequent gain/loss in reserves is large, there will be a deterioration in national welfare. The reason for this is that a large loss in reserves would impose a future constraint on the country's ability to expand, while an excessive accumulation of reserves may be seen as a waste of resources. In what follows we shall initially assume that both countries have a preference for a balance of payments surplus over the period of the game, and that both have identical national welfare functions. Thus, assuming that each country starts off with a level of international reserves R_0, we may represent each country's preferences by means of indifference curves in (y, R) space in Figure 10.3. The indifference curves represent lower levels of utility as we move outward from the centre.

To carry out our analysis we require to know how each country's policy instrument, domestic credit expansion, D, affects the governments' objectives, namely the incomes and levels of reserves in the two countries. Let us recall the revelant multipliers from subsection 10.1.1:

$$\partial y/\partial D > 0, \ \partial y^*/\partial D > 0, \ \partial y/\partial D^* > 0, \ \partial y^*/\partial D^* > 0$$

$$\partial R/\partial D < 0, \ \partial R^*/\partial D > 0, \ \partial R/\partial D^* > 0, \ \partial R^*/\partial D^* < 0$$

It is useful to represent the utility functions for the two countries in (D, D^*) space instead of (y, R) space as in Figure 10.3, by adopting the following argument. Equation (10.20) shows the relationship between the government's utility and their final objectives, R and y, and the above multipliers illustrate the relationship between the two countries' policy instruments and their final objectives. By combining these two relations, it follows that we may relate the two countries' utility levels directly to their

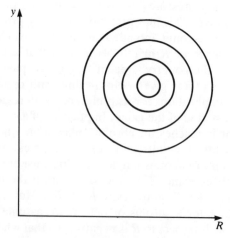

Figure 10.3

monetary policy settings. Figure 10.4 then shows each country's preference ordering with regard to different combinations of the two countries' monetary policies. The $BP = 0$ line shows those combinations of D and D^* which keep the balance of payments in equilibrium, and it will be at a 45° angle to the horizontal axis, because the two countries are assumed to have an identical economic structure. To the right (left) of the BP line country 1 has a balance of payments deficit (surplus), and country 2 has an equivalent surplus (deficit). Also, as domestic credit expands in either country, income increases in both countries. P and P^* represent the maxima (or 'bliss points') of the utility functions for country 1 and 2 respectively.

We may now examine some of the strategic aspects of the policy decisions facing the two countries. As we pointed out in subsection 10.2.1, the static games we consider in detail in this chapter are single-period games in which each country is only allowed to make a single move. That is, both countries will simultaneously decide on their setting of D and D^*, with the intersection of these two coordinates providing the outcome of the game. The pay-off to each country can then be gauged by looking at the position of the outcome with respect to the indifference map for each country.

Let us initially assume that the two countries do not cooperate, and that

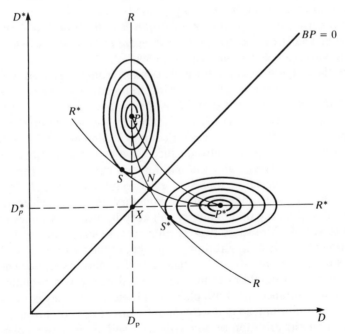

Figure 10.4 The Fixed-Exchange Rate Game When Both Countries Desire Surpluses

both have full information regarding the game. Clearly under these circumstances the set of strategies available to each country is vast, excluding only negative values of D, which are impossible, and very large values of D which are not feasible because of the low pay-off resulting from such a move. Under these circumstances, unless we make prior assumptions about agents' maximisation behaviour, we do not know which strategy will actually be chosen. One possible assumption is that each country attempts to achieve its very best outcome, P, thus setting their monetary policies at D_p and D_p^*. The net outcome of this game would be point X (with coordinates (D_p, D_p^*)), which would be suboptimal for both countries. Note that point X will be on the $BP = 0$ line because the two countries are assumed identical in terms of their economic structure and policy preferences, and hence they will adopt an identical monetary policy $(D_p = D_p^*)$.

If the two countries have complete information, it is unlikely that they will attempt this (maximax) strategy, as they will predict that the other country is likely to attempt a similar move. Thus, a point such as X is not generally considered to be an *equilibrium* in a non-cooperative game, because if either country were to be given the option to choose its strategy again, *given* the strategy choice of the other player, they would not choose D_p or D_p^*. For this reason, it is generally assumed that players in a non-cooperative game will act so as to reach the *Nash non-cooperative* equilibrium, which can be formally defined as follows:

A point (D, D^*) is a Nash equilibrium if both D and D^* are feasible strategies, and if each player finds it impossible to obtain a better pay-off treating the other player's strategy as given.

This Nash equilibrium point can be derived from the pay-off structure in Figure 10.4 by considering the following argument. The *reaction curves RR* and R^*R^* are drawn such that RR is the locus of the points of tangency between successive values of D^* (measured by a series of horizontal lines), and the set of indifference curves for country 1. Similarly, R^*R^* is the locus of the points of tangency between successive values of D (measured by a series of vertical lines), and the indifference curves of country 2. These reaction curves therefore represent each country's *best reply* for various given values of the other country's monetary policy, provided of course that it thinks that the other country will keep its monetary policy constant. The intersection N of these two reaction curves clearly corresponds to our definition of the Nash equilibrium, as neither of the two players will be able to obtain a better pay-off (if they take the other player's strategy as given).

The notion of equilibrium in single-period games is a peculiar one, as there is no assurance that both players will select a strategy consistent with the Nash equilibrium, so that we cannot be sure if this equilibrium provides a correct characterisation of how countries will act if they recognise their interdependence and do not cooperate. However, there are certain attractions in assuming that each player will select a monetary policy consistent with the Nash equilibrium, given that each player knows the pay-off functions and available strategies for both players. If both select a Nash equilibrium strategy, then *ex post* both will realise that they would not have been able to choose a strategy which would have obtained a better pay-off. If we assume that both players approach the game in a similar fashion and believe that the other player will act consistently, a Nash equilibrium will be reached. This does require the players to possess a large amount of information pertaining to the game, but it should be noted that the Nash equilibrium may also be reached in an alternative way. If we assume that the rules of the game are modified so that each player makes a move in turn, and that players do not have complete information regarding the structure of the game, a feasible strategy for each to adopt is to assume that the other country will not change its monetary policy in the next move. In this case, each player will respond to the other's move according to his reaction curve until the equilibrium N is reached. (Readers familiar with the oligopoly theory will note the similarity between this modified game and the Cournot model.)

Let us now allow countries to cooperate. We note that this game is a variable sum game, given the gains available to both players if they cooperate. The locus of the points of tangency between the two sets of indifference curves is the 'contract' curve PP^*. Note that along this contract curve, each country cannot improve its welfare without decreasing the welfare of the other country. Thus, this constitutes a locus of Pareto-efficient points, and a cooperative game will involve countries in selecting a strategy such that a point on this curve is chosen. Notice the similarity with the Prisoners' Dilemma outlined above. The Nash solution is not generally on the contract curve, and hence countries would benefit from cooperating. In a two-player cooperative game, an equilibrium is reached only if the outcome is Pareto-optimal, and if this outcome is superior to the non-cooperative outcome for each player. The exact location of the equilibrium on the PP^* curve depends on the relative bargaining strengths of the two countries. As discussed in the case of the Prisoners' Dilemma, however, each country has an incentive to cheat under a cooperative agreement to attempt to achieve an outcome closer to its 'bliss point'.

Finally we may examine the concept of equilibrium arising from the Stackelberg leader solution to a two-player game. This occurs if one player (the leader) is permitted by the rules of the game to make his move first. In this case, the leader will choose his monetary policy knowing that the other player (the follower) will choose his monetary policy according to the latter's reaction curve. In this case, it is clear that if country 1 is the leader, it will choose D at the point where R^*R^* is tangent to its highest possible indifference curve, i.e. at point S. (Similarly, if country 2 were the leader, it would set its monetary policy so as to achieve S^*.)

In reality it is questionable whether any one country possesses such an advantage. As J. W. Friedman (1983) points out, there is no *a priori* reason for one player to be nominated a leader from the very outset of a game, unless one country has the informational advantage of being able to observe its opponent's reaction curve, while the other does not. A Stackelberg equilibrium, though not Pareto-optimal, will leave the leader better off in terms of welfare, and may or may not leave the follower better off, depending on the structure of the model and on the two countries' welfare functions. Therefore, it may be rational for some countries to allow others to become policy-leaders in that the outcome would be Pareto-superior to the Nash equilibrium. The relevance of these different equilibria to actual policy-making will be described below, once the concepts of game theory have been applied to some of the two-country models discussed in the earlier part of the chapter.

We conclude this section by noting some of the shortcomings of the simple static game described so far. In particular, in concentrating on single-period static games, we have excluded dynamic considerations. There are two ways to introduce time as a factor in game theory. First, *strategic time dependence* may be adopted, where countries are likely to engage in sequences of static games over a period of time, during which information is gained about the other player's behaviour. Countries gain or lose 'reputations', and learn from 'experience'. These multiperiod games, also called supergames, will not be discussed further in this chapter, but they may form a fruitful area for further research for economists, as it may be shown (see J. W. Friedman 1986) that non-cooperative strategies in supergames may dominate one-off Nash equilibria. In certain supergames players may be able to reap pay-offs normally associated with cooperative equilibria without the difficulties associated with the latter. A good example of this is the Kydland and Prescott (1977) inflation–unemployment game analysed in the previous chapter, where the government may build up a reputation for controlling inflation, thus achieving a Stackelberg equilibrium in a non-cooperative situation which is Pareto-superior to the Nash equilibrium. This is an important consideration since cooperative agreements are only effective if they are binding. Unfortunately this is rarely the case in the field of international economic interdependence.

Second, *structural time dependence* may be introduced where the pay-off in any one period is not totally dependent upon actions taken in that period. As we saw above, many models which incorporate exchange rate expectations or wealth effects are dynamic in nature, and hence the structure of the game varies over time. Some of these models will be briefly discussed at the end of the chapter.

10.2.3. Targets and Instruments in Static Games

The static game described in Figures 10.3 and 10.4 is set in a regime of fixed exchange rates. Each country has two final targets (real income and its level of international reserves) and a single policy instrument (monetary policy). If we move to a flexible exchange rate regime, one of these targets is dropped, as reserves do not change under flexible rates. The flexible exchange rate Fleming–Mundell model shows us that a country can achieve its desired income level through monetary policy. Consequently, the simple game described above becomes redundant in the case where each country possesses an equal number of targets and instruments. Each country can achieve its optimal income and hence its 'bliss point'. Therefore, a game situation requires not only a degree of economic interdependence to be present, but also the number of independent policy instruments available to each country to be less than the number of policy targets it pursues, as is the case under fixed exchange rates.

Thus, the application of static game theory to the case of economic interdependence restricts its attention to cases where countries attempt to optimise in the face of conflicting objectives. However, it should be pointed out that this general rule is only applicable to static games. As we shall see below, when dealing with dynamic games, this simple instrument–targets rule breaks down.

10.3. The Application of Static Games to Fixed and Flexible Exchange Rate Models

10.3.1. The Case of Fixed Exchange Rates

Models of the type illustrated in Figure 10.4 have been analysed at length by Hamada (1979, 1985), concentrating on the international aspects of monetary policy. It is important to recognise at the outset that the results obtained from these models are heavily dependent upon the assumptions we choose to make regarding the national welfare functions, and the sign of monetary spill-over effects between the two countries. Throughout this subsection we employ the Fleming–Mundell model where spill-over effects are unambiguously positive under fixed exchange rates. Hamada's work focuses mainly on the effects of changing the form of the national welfare functions on the outcomes of the game.

If we consider the economic implications of Figure 10.4 we see that, if both countries desire a surplus, the result of Nash non-cooperative behaviour would be point N. However, point N is inferior to any outcome on the PP^* curve which could have been achieved through cooperation. Note also that the Nash equilibrium involves a more contractionary policy on the part of both countries compared to a Pareto-optimal policy. Thus the result of Nash non-cooperative behaviour is to cause excessive recession in the world economy, as compared with the alternative cooperative solution. However, if we modify Figure 10.4 such that both countries desire a balance of payments *deficit*, then the indifference maps for the two countries will be centred on the opposite side of the $BP = 0$ line compared to Figure 10.4 (see Figure 10.5). As a result, the reaction curves will slope in the opposite direction, resulting in a Nash equilibrium with an expansionary bias. Again, note that the Nash solution is inferior to a solution on the PP^* curve which could be obtained through cooperation.

A third possibility is that the two countries have asymmetric preferences. Suppose, for example, that country 1 desires a balance of payments deficit, while country 2 desires a small balance of payments surplus, so that both P and P^* lie to the right of the $BP = 0$ line (see Figure 10.6). Notice that in this case non-cooperative behaviour results in a larger surplus than country 2 had hoped for. In Figure 10.6, in fact, the non-cooperative solution N is better in terms of national welfare from the point of view of country 1, than for country 2. We would therefore expect country 1 to be less prepared to negotiate a cooperative solution in this situation, unless this was closer to P

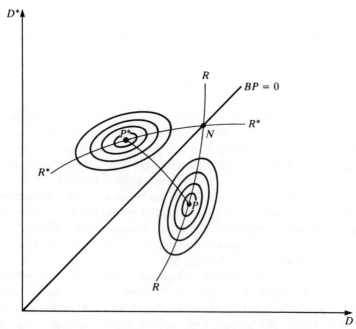

Figure 10.5   The Fixed Exchange Rate Game when both Countries Desire Deficits

than point *N*. In any case, the incentive for cooperation in this case is stronger for country 2.

Hamada interprets the situation prevailing in the world economy in the late 1960s up to the emergence of floating exchange rates in the early 1970s in terms of Figure 10.6. If we cast the US as country 1 and West Germany and Japan as country 2, this explains why a non-cooperative solution will lead to larger surpluses than West Germany and Japan had wished. Furthermore, it shows that the US will apparently have less of an incentive than the other countries to cooperate in this situation. However, this model cannot tell us the whole story. One objection is that any position off the *BP* = 0 line is unsustainable in the long run, especially for the deficit country. However, under a dollar standard, the US had an additional reason for neglecting its large deficit, in that it had a less severe reserve constraint (except, of course, to the extent that US dollars were convertible to gold under the Bretton Woods agreement, and that US gold reserves were limited).

Thus, we can expect the non-cooperative solution in Figure 10.6 to lead to greater international tensions under a fixed exchange rate regime than the Nash equilibria in Figures 10.4 and 10.5. This is because, while the latter cases lead to suboptimal solutions in that there will be an

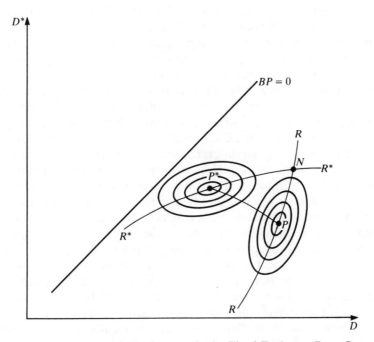

Figure 10.6 Asymmetric Preferences in the Fixed Exchange Rate Game

overexpansion or overcontraction of the world economy as a whole, the balance of payments of the two countries will not experience massive deficits or surpluses. In contrast, with asymmetric preferences, countries may experience undesirable and intolerable balance of payments imbalances under the Nash solution. This result also generalises to the case where there are more than two countries, each with widely differing preferences. It is at this juncture that the self-regulating properties of the fixed exchange regime are put to the test. In the absence of precise rules governing the attainment of a jointly agreeable long-run equilibrium on the $BP = 0$ line, the system of fixed exchange rates may well break down.

Hamada suggests that the situations depicted in Figures 10.4 and 10.5 may be cured by the issuing or withdrawing of Special Drawing Rights (SDRs) by the International Monetary Fund (IMF), so as to reconcile both countries' objectives in terms of their desired holdings of foreign reserves. However, this solution is not plausible if, as we assumed in this chapter, countries' welfares depend on their balance of payments situation rather than their levels of reserves *per se*. If both countries desire balance of payments surpluses, these objectives are fundamentally conflicting, and we will not approach a Pareto-optimal solution by issuing both countries with SDRs. As Cooper (1985) points out, countries' welfares are more likely to be functions of reserves obtained through a good past balance of payments record, because of the resulting implications for economic growth, rather than of reserves obtained through the IMF. However, the issue of additional SDRs *will* reconcile conflicting objectives if countries desire higher levels of reserves as a 'buffer' against possible future deficits.

Another solution to the problems posed by a fixed exchange rate regime would seem to be a move to flexible exchange rates. As we noted in subsection 10.2.3, under a flexible exchange rates regime each country can independently determine its own level of real income, thus apparently removing the problem of conflicting objectives. For example, in the period subsequent to the first OPEC oil shock in 1973–74, different countries in the OECD block adopted different monetary policies, according to their own particular national objectives. It is argued that these circumstances made a quick return to a world of fixed exchange rates impossible.

However, a move to flexible exchange rates in itself does not solve the problem of international interdependence. It is arguable that we have presented an oversimplified picture of the problem of economic inter-dependence in this chapter by assuming that each country has only one policy instrument and two policy objectives. In practice, however, each country is likely to have a larger number of economic objectives (e.g. output growth, inflation, components of the overall balance of payments, etc.), and it is unlikely that in practice each will have sufficient policy instruments to reach its 'bliss point' independently of other countries' actions.

In the next section, therefore, we discuss the problem of policy coordination under flexible exchange rates by replacing the reserves objective, which becomes redundant, with a price level objective. Thus we assume that both countries have a welfare function dependent upon the level of real output and the price level. This ensures that the number of government objectives still exceeds the number of its policy instruments, and hence a game situation still prevails.

10.3.2. The Case of Flexible Exchange Rates

In this section we will review a class of models analysed by Canzoneri and Gray (1983), Cooper (1985), and Turnovsky and D'Orey (1986). The model by Canzoneri and Gray has already been briefly described in subsection 10.1.3, and we recall that in that model, the international transmission of monetary policies under flexible exchange rates may be positive, negative or asymmetric. We will analyse these three cases in turn, thus demonstrating that the outcomes of the resulting games differ substantially between these three scenarios. While in the previous subsection we showed that the nature of the resulting equilibria were crucially dependent upon governments' preferences, we now focus on the way in which the outcome of the games is affected by our assumptions regarding the underlying structural model, and the signs of the spill-over effects between countries. In any case, there is little scope in this section for varying the form of the government welfare functions, as most countries will prefer full employment output and low inflation.

In describing the policy game under flexible exchange rates, we follow Canzoneri and Gray in assuming that the authorities' policy instrument is monetary *growth* (m and m^*), so that *inflation* is introduced into the model of subsection 10.1.3. We assume that the utility function for both countries takes the following form:

$$U = U(\tilde{y}^2, \pi^2), \text{ where } U_{y^2} < 0 \text{ and } U_{\pi^2} < 0 \tag{10.25}$$

where $\tilde{y}$ is the deviation of output from its natural rate, and π is the steady-state inflation rate. The signs of the partial derivatives indicate that each country dislikes inflation and deviations of output from its 'natural' level. In addition, the spill-over effects of monetary policy may take the following signs:

(a) Negative Spill-Over Effects

$$\delta\tilde{y}/\delta m > 0, \ \delta\tilde{y}^*/\delta m < 0, \ \delta\pi/\delta m > 0$$

$$\partial\tilde{y}/\partial m^* < 0, \ \partial\tilde{y}^*/\partial m^* > 0, \ \partial\pi^*/\partial m^* > 0$$

(b) Positive Spill-Over Effects

$\partial \bar{y}/\partial m > 0,\ \partial \bar{y}^*/\partial m > 0,\ \partial \pi/\partial m > 0$

$\partial \bar{y}/\partial m^* > 0,\ \partial \bar{y}^*/\partial m^* > 0,\ \partial \pi^*/\partial m^* > 0$

(c) Asymmetric Spill-Over Effects

$\partial \bar{y}/\partial m > 0,\ \partial \bar{y}^*/\partial m > 0,\ \partial \pi/\partial m > 0$

$\partial \bar{y}/\partial m^* < 0,\ \partial \bar{y}^*/\partial m^* > 0,\ \partial \pi^*/\partial m^* > 0$

The game described by Canzoneri and Gray analyses the two oil-importing countries' reactions following an oil price shock by OPEC. We illustrate case (a) in Figure 10.7(a), using an identical framework to that described in the case of fixed exchange rates. As we noted in subsection 10.1.3, this scenario has been labelled a 'beggar-thy-neighbour' world by Canzoneri and Gray. Note that the Nash non-cooperative equilibrium, N, has an expansionary bias compared to a Pareto-optimal policy. Note also that we have drawn the utility functions in this diagram such that both Stackelberg equilibria S and S^* involve a larger gain for the follower than for the leader. This particular situation may encourage either country to avoid cooperation hoping that the other country will act as a leader by overcontracting compared to the Nash equilibrium. This policy of 'benign neglect' by either country is likely to be resented by the other party. It should be noted, though, that the conclusions of Figure 10.7(a) regarding the nature of the Stackelberg solution follow directly from the way in which the indifference curves have been drawn. As an alternative, consider a 'beggar-thy-neighbour' world where the indifference curves have the shape illustrated in Figure 10.7(b), due, say, to a slightly different shape in the utility functions, or to different magnitudes of monetary multipliers in the two countries. In this case a Stackelberg solution favours the leader, and both countries will attempt to establish a position of leadership. It should also be noted that in Figure 10.7(b) the gains from cooperation are greater than in Figure 10.7(a), given the smaller distance between points N and C. This emphasises the fact that estimates of the gains from cooperation are likely to be model-specific, dependent upon the structural parameters of the model, and government preferences.

A solution to the problem of over expansion via competitive deprecia-tions in this case would be to move to a fixed exchange rate regime. If the exchange rate were fixed, this would equalise the money stocks in both countries if they are assumed to be identical, and point C would be reached on the 45° line. Thus, fixed exchange rates are presented as one particular Pareto-optimal solution to this particular model. However, it should be

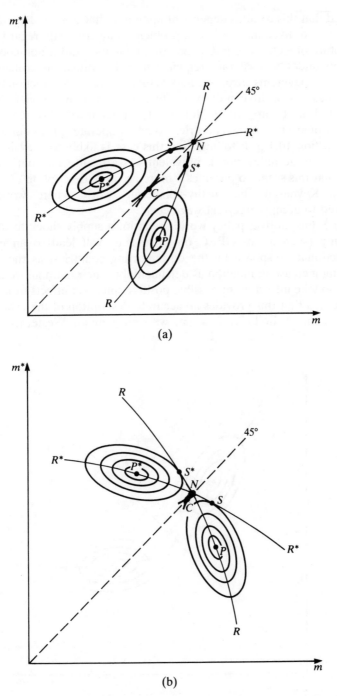

(a)

(b)

Figure 10.7 Negative Spill-Over Effects in the Flexible Exchange Rate Game

stressed that this result is dependent upon our choice of model. As we saw in the case of fixed interest rates, problems may arise with regard to other conflicting objectives (e.g. balance of payments), and a non-cooperative solution under a fixed rate regime where individual governments seek balance of payments surpluses may actually imply a contractionary bias.

The case of positive spill-over effects (a 'locomotive policy' world) is illustrated in Figure 10.8. Note that, in contrast, this model has a contractionary bias if the countries do not cooperate. From our argument in subsection 10.1.3, it follows that this case is likely to prevail if a high degree of wage indexation is prevalent. As a result Canzoneri and Gray argue that this scenario provides a more accurate description of the 1970s than a Keynesian 'beggar-thy-neighbour' world where workers are prepared to accept large real wage cuts.

In the 'locomotive' policy world scenario, a supply shock to the world economy (such as an OPEC oil price rise) will lead to an excessive contractionary response by the oil-importing countries, as they see the resulting increase in inflation as detrimental to their national welfare, and they also take into account possible positive spill-over effects from abroad. It is argued that this provides an accurate description of the events in the world economy in 1979–82 when, with most major Western economies

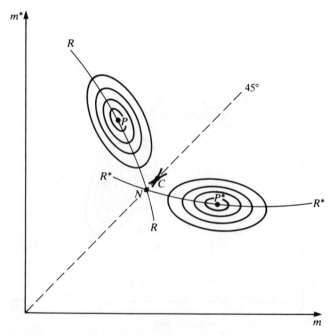

Figure 10.8   Positive Spill-Over Effects in the Flexible Exchange Rate Game

committed to a fight against inflation, the second OPEC oil shock led to a world recession.

Case (c) which is depicted in Figure 10.9 shows an asymmetric world. This could be explained by the fixing of the price of oil in terms of country 1's currency, as explained in subsection 10.1.3. Alternatively, it may be explained by asymmetries in the determination of wages and prices in the two countries. For example, there may be a greater degree of wage indexation in country 2 than in country 1 (see Canzoneri and Gray 1983). Both these cases may be of relevance to recent events in the world economy, if in what follows we make the US correspond to country 1 and Europe to country 2. The main interest of this scenario is that the fixed exchange rate solution is not a Pareto-optimal cooperative outcome. As explained above, the fixed exchange rate solution must lie along the 45° line, given our assumption that countries have identical aggregate demand sectors. However, the locus PP^* of Pareto-efficient points does not now intersect the 45° line, given the asymmetry in the two countries' aggregate supplies. Thus, the fixed exchange rate solution C cannot be preferred in the case depicted in Figure 10.9. Furthermore, Canzoneri and Gray show that Europe would not prefer solution C under any circumstances, while the US may do so depending on the values of the model's parameters. In any case, given that C is *at best* only preferred by one country, it could not

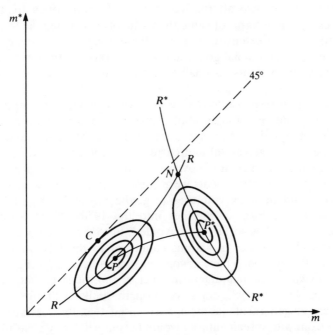

Figure 10.9   Asymmetric Spill-Over Effects in the Flexible Exchange Rate Game

be an equilibrium to the asymmetric game. Arguably this may explain why in a period like the 1970s the large differences between various countries' aggregate supply responses led to a definite movement away from fixed exchange rates. As we noted above (see Figure 10.6), divergences between countries' preferences with regard to their aggregate demand strategies may also play a part in straining a system of fixed exchange rates. However, the contribution of Canzoneri and Gray has been to show that asymmetries in countries' economic structures may also lead to a movement away from fixed exchange rates.

10.3.3. *Practical Policy Responses to Economic Interdependence*

In the above subsections we have examined various (simplified) scenarios in which one may discuss the problem of economic interdependence. Implicitly, we have assumed that countries' strategies were limited to a simple decision on whether or not to cooperate with other countries in resolving their conflicting policy objectives. We also noted that in these simple models cooperation generally leads to welfare gains for both countries. This raises a number of further issues, to which we now turn.

The first question is whether policy coordination provides the only way to achieve welfare gains in the presence of economic interdependence. There are in fact two alternative courses of action open to individual countries, which in terms of game theory involve changing the 'rules of the game' to a certain extent. In practice, these involve either changes in the operation of international goods and asset markets or the development of new policy instruments to enable governments to reconcile conflicting objectives.

One common response to the problem of economic interdependence is to reduce the degree of integration between a country and the rest of the world in both goods and asset markets. It is possible that a country faced with persistent large capital and current account deficits will respond by imposing controls on capital movements and some form of protectionism. Controls on capital movements were common in the post-war period until the 1960s, and in some countries (e.g. the US and UK) such policies persisted in one form or another into the 1970s. Protectionism on a widespread scale has so far been avoided, but there have been recurring calls for such measures in various countries. In the UK the Cambridge Economic Policy Group have advocated such policies as part of a package for the revival of the manufacturing sector, and the large trade deficits in the US in the post-1983 era have brought similar calls for protection. However, in general it has been recognised that the losses in national welfare from widespread autarky would far outweigh any gains in terms of achieving domestic policy goals.

A second response which became popular during the 1970s was the adoption of new instruments of domestic economic policy to pursue the goal of economic stabilisation (see Cooper 1974, Lindbeck 1973). 'Supply-side' fiscal policies have been introduced to attempt to stimulate economic growth, and there have been attempts at making labour markets more flexible to reconcile the objectives of real growth and lower inflation. However, while some of these measures may be useful as part of a total programme for stabilisation, they cannot totally remove the problems caused by economic interdependence. As a result, the need for a greater international coordination of macroeconomic policies remains.

Given that alternative policies may not be entirely successful in removing the conflict of objectives, economic cooperation remains the only way to achieve welfare gains for interdependent economies. The models presented in this chapter have shown that, in general, there are benefits to be reaped from cooperation in two-country games. However, due to the simple structure of these models, this conclusion must be interpreted with care.

One problem is that our analysis has concentrated on examining the strategies of policy-making bodies, thereby ignoring the possible strategic role of wage-setters in individual economies. The degree of wage flexibility has been treated as a datum in the models presented here, but it has been pointed out (see Rogoff 1983) that it may be an important factor in determining the gains from cooperation. The argument here is that while under a non-cooperative regime governments are less likely to engage in unanticipated money supply shocks because real depreciation will lower employment gains and raise inflation costs, a coordinated expansion will remove the problem of depreciation in both countries. The removal of this constraint to government expansionary policies may be perceived by rational agents, who may then strategically raise the level of wage inflation, along the lines of the Kydland–Prescott inflation game outlined in Chapter 9.

A second issue is whether the costs incurred in coordinating economic policies outweigh any gains. It has been shown above that the gains from cooperation vary widely between different scenarios, depending on our assumptions regarding national welfare functions and the underlying economic structure. There have been only a few attempts so far to evaluate empirically the gains from cooperation by applying game theory techniques to multicountry econometric models. Oudiz and Sachs (1984) use policy multipliers from a number of multicountry econometric models to show that the gains from policy coordination may be small. Similarly, Hughes Hallett (1984) finds small gains from cooperation from a study of US–Europe interdependence. However, to some extent these results may be due to the small spill-over effects in the models analysed by these authors. This is confirmed by Canzoneri and Minford (1986) who analyse the problem using the Liverpool World Model which has large spill-over effects (see also Minford 1984, Minford *et al.* 1983). Another interesting point raised by Canzoneri and Minford is that the gains from cooperation may also depend on the origin of the shocks impinging on the world economy. Recalling the results from Chapter 9, where we showed that the optimal exchange rate policy for a single country depends critically on the origin of the disturbances affecting the economy, it is apparent that any gains from cooperation will also depend on such factors.

This shows that there are severe difficulties in assessing the likely gains from cooperation, and it follows that different countries will have different views on how to react to interdependence and the prospect of cooperation (see Hughes Hallett 1986). Thus, in practice, countries are unlikely to know *a priori* what the gains from cooperation are likely to be. This is in sharp contrast to our above assumption that the problem of policy coordination may be approximated by a game with *complete* information, in which each player solves the entire model for himself to assess the gains from cooperation. In practice there are likely to be conflicting views between countries regarding the appropriate cooperative strategy. For example, in 1977–78 there was continuous disagreement between the US on one hand and Germany and Japan on the other, as to whether the optimal solution to the large US balance of payments deficit was a US demand reduction, or an expansion by the surplus countries. A similar argument has arisen during 1986. To some extent, these conflicting views may reflect bargaining tricks on the part of each side in order to obtain a cooperative solution closer to their respective 'bliss points'. To a larger extent, though, they reflect differences in opinion on the underlying economic structure.

A third question is whether the whole issue of economic interdependence can be meaningfully separated from the political environment in which cooperation is supposed to take place. Kindleberger (1973), Whitman (1979), and Cooper (1985) argue that questions of trust, political leadership, and public sentiment have important roles to play in deciding whether policy coordination is feasible. This, however, is a question outwith the scope of economic analysis. Nevertheless, there are good economic reasons for doubting the feasibility of widespread policy coordination between countries. As we saw in the case of the Prisoners' Dilemma, where there are gains from cooperation, there are often gains from reneging on an agreed common policy. These problems are compounded if we move to models with more than two countries. In these cases the 'free rider' problem common to the analysis of public goods becomes relevant. To put this matter another way, in general it is difficult to envisage long lasting cooperative equilibria without some form of binding agreement between the countries involved in the game. As we showed in the case of the Kydland–Prescott inflation game in Chapter 9,

Pareto-preferred outcomes such as the time-inconsistent Stackelberg solution are not credible in the absence of pre-commitment. Thus, it is arguable that there is unlikely to be much progress in the sphere of international policy coordination in the absence of a new formal and institutionalised international agreement, in the style of (if not the substance of) the Bretton Woods system. Informal economic summits may only have a limited efficacy in advancing the cause of international cooperation.

Finally, however, it is arguable that if we are to study the problem of cooperation, our single-period static games are not an appropriate vehicle. As we have pointed out in section 2, if countries are allowed to play repeated (multiperiod) games, then countries may eventually learn that there are gains to be made in moving away from a Nash equilibrium, and cooperative behaviour may emerge without the explicit need for formal binding agreements. In fact, as we saw in Chapter 9, the problem of credibility is more usefully studied in multiperiod games, by allowing players to perceive their *strategic time dependence*. This, therefore, is a counter-argument to the above claim that only formal agreements may lead countries to experience the benefits of policy coordination: countries may eventually recognise their interdependence and deploy their policies in the pursuit of the common good rather than narrow national interests. Such an argument of course carries less force if the players are many, since the 'free rider' problem then becomes more acute.

10.3.4. Dynamic Games and International Interdependence

Conceptually, the extension of simple static games to games where macroeconomic policies will vary through time, because of lags in the adjustment of prices, wages, and the current account, is not a major step. Each player still has a choice of strategies, where strategies now dictate the players' actions throughout their time horizons, and again players may either pursue non-cooperative strategies or attempt to cooperate. The main difference is that our analysis typically requires us to employ an *intertemporal* utility function, so that each player does not maximise a function such as (10.21) but its intertemporal equivalent:

$$V = \Sigma_{t=0}^{\infty} \delta^t U(\bar{y}^2, \pi^2) \tag{10.26}$$

where δ represents a subjective discount factor. In effect, each country conducts an optimal control exercise, along the lines described in Chapter 9. As in the case of static games, we may consider a variety of solutions, namely the Nash non-cooperative game, the Stackelberg game, and Pareto-optimal cooperative solutions. However, as in the case of strategic time dependence, the existence of structural time dependence introduces the issue of time consistency. As Miller and Salmon (1985a, 1985b) and Oudiz and Sachs (1985) point out, some Stackelberg solutions may be time-inconsistent, and hence may not be credible in the absence of pre-commitment. One country may announce that it will pursue a particular policy strategy, thus evoking a reaction from the other 'forward looking' players which, *ex post*, causes it to re-evaluate its optimal policy (see Chapter 9 for a further analysis of the problem of time consistency).

One interesting aspect of such models is that they lead to a modification of the simple 'targets and instruments' rule discussed in subsection 10.2.3. In static models a game situation only emerges if each country does not possess sufficient policy instruments to achieve all its policy objectives. In contrast, some of these models (e.g. Miller and Salmon 1985b) do not involve a *long-run* conflict of objectives, in that exchange rates are floating, and the long-run aggregate supply curve is vertical. Thus each country can set its monetary policy so as to obtain its desired long-run level of inflation without any need for cooperation. However, even if a game situation appears to 'vanish' in the long run, there are still short-run gains to be made from cooperation. As we saw in section 1, most modern exchange rate models involve some degree of gradual price and/or exchange rate adjustment in the short run (see, for instance, Dornbusch 1976), so that while flexible exchange rates may insulate the domestic economy from foreign shocks in the long run, in the short run there will still be spill-over effects (see Dornbusch 1983a). Therefore the choice of monetary strategy on the part of each country will still be vital in determining the path to long-run equilibrium, thus affecting the welfare gains through an inter-temporal utility function such as (10.26). This further emphasises the need for economic cooperation since, even if we believe that in the long run exchange rates perform their insulating function in the case of monetary policy, there may still be scope for countries to choose a path to long-run equilibrium for the world economy which minimises welfare losses to both sides.

However, these dynamic considerations also add another dimension to the problems of implementing policy coordination. In contrast to static games, the *timing* of policy actions is of relevance in determining welfare outcomes for each country. Given the difficulties encountered by countries in reconciling conflicting long-run objectives, one must be even more pessimistic with regard to their ability to coordinate the timing of their short-run policies. This is an extension of the problems which arise in the application of optimal control techniques to policy-making in single economies. As we saw in Chapter 9, it is doubtful whether optimal control is really a feasible approach to policy design, and these problems are compounded when we have a number of optimal controllers. Nevertheless, game theory may still prove useful as a heuristic device in studying the problem of policy coordination.

In general dynamic games lead to similar conclusions regarding the benefits of economic cooperation, in the sense that the benefits from cooperation depend crucially on the assumptions made about the structure of the model, and the welfare functions of the countries involved. In addition, though, these types of models introduce additional problems of coordination of short-run policies, and the time consistency of such policies.

10.4. Conclusion

Despite the fact that many of the results regarding the nature of economic interdependence and the gains from policy coordination are model-specific, the literature surveyed in this chapter has an important contribution to make to the theory of stabilisation policies. We have shown that some of the stabilisation policy debates outlined in the chapters dealing with a closed economy or a small open economy have to be modified if we recognise that all major economies will react similarly to shocks in the world economy. What may be an optimal policy for a single country may not be beneficial for the whole world economy, if every major country adopts a similar strategy. Similarly, it has been shown that the recurring debates regarding the appropriateness of different exchange regimes cannot ignore the nature of countries' policy objectives and the underlying structure of the world economy. What may be an appropriate exchange rate regime in the 1970s will not necessarily be ideal in the 1980s. Finally, it should be noted that, despite our pessimism regarding the feasibility of economic cooperation between the major economies, there has been an increasing awareness among these economies in the 1970s and 1980s of the way in which each individual country's actions have implications for the world economy as a whole.

BIBLIOGRAPHY

Abel, A. and Mishkin, F.S. (1983) 'An integrated view of tests of rationality, market efficiency and the short-run neutrality of monetary policy', *Journal of Monetary Economics*, 11, pp. 3–24.

Akerlof, G.A. and Yellen, J. (eds) (1987) *Efficiency Wage Models of the Labour Market*, Cambridge University Press, Cambridge.

Allen, P.R. and Kenen, P.B. (1980) *Asset Markets, Exchange Rates and Economic Integration*, Cambridge University Press, Cambridge.

Andersen, L.C. and Carlson, K.M. (1970) 'A monetarist model for economic stabilisation', *Federal Reserve Bank of St Louis Review*, 52, April, pp. 7–25.

Andersen, L.C. and Jordan, J.L. (1968) 'Monetary and fiscal actions: a test of their relative importance in economic stabilisation', *Federal Reserve Bank of St Louis Review*, 50, November, pp. 11–24.

Andrews, M. and Nickell, S. (1982) 'Unemployment in the UK since the war', *Review of Economic Studies*, 49, pp. 731–759.

Ando, A. and Modigliani, F. (1976) 'Impacts of fiscal actions on aggregate income and the monetarist controversy: theory and evidence', in J.L. Stein (ed.) *Monetarism*, North-Holland, Amsterdam

Argy, V. (1981) *The Post-War International Money Crisis*, Allen and Unwin, London.

Argy, V. and Kouri, P.J.K. (1974) 'Sterilisation policies and the volatility of international reserves', in R.Z. Aliber (ed.) *National Monetary Policies and the International Financial System*, University of Chicago Press, Chicago.

Arrow, K.J. (1959) 'Toward a theory of price adjustment', in M. Abramovitz *et al.*, *The Allocation of Economic Resources: Essays in Honour of Bernard Francis Haley*, Stanford University Press, Stanford.

Arrow, K.J. (1962) 'The economic implications of learning by doing', *Review of Economic Studies*, 29, p. 159.

Artis, M.J. (1979) 'Recent developments in the theory of fiscal policy — a survey', in S.T. Cook and P.M. Jackson (eds) *Current Issues in Fiscal Policy*, Martin Robertson, London.

Arrow, K.J. (1964) 'The role of securities in the optimal allocation of risk bearing', *Review of Economic Studies,* 31, pp. 91–96.

Artis, M.J. and Currie, D.A. (1981) 'Monetary targets and the exchange rate. A case for conditional targets', in W.A. Eltis and P.J.N. Sinclair (eds) *The Money Supply and the Exchange Rate,* Oxford University Press, Oxford.

Artis, M.J. and Lewis, M.K. (1976) 'The demand for money in the UK, 1963–1973', *The Manchester School,* 44, pp. 147–181.

Astrom, K.J. (1970) *Introduction to Stochastic Control Theory,* Academic Press, New York.

Attfield, C.J., Demery, D. and Duck, N.W. (1981a) 'Unanticipated monetary growth, output, and the price level: UK 1946–77', *European Economic Review,* 16, pp. 367–385.

Attfield, C.J., Demery, D. and Duck, N.W. (1981b) 'A quarterly model of unanticipated monetary growth and output in the UK, 1963–78', *Journal of Monetary Economics,* 8, pp. 331–350.

Azariadis, C. (1975) 'Implicit contracts and underemployment equilibria', *Journal of Political Economy,* 83, pp. 1183–1202.

Azariadis, C. (1976) 'On the incidence of unemployment', *Review of Economic Studies,* 43, pp. 115–125.

Azariadis, C. (1983) 'Employment with asymmetric information', *Quarterly Journal of Economics,* 98 (Supplement), pp. 157–172.

Backus, D. and Driffill, J. (1985) 'Inflation and reputation', *American Economic Review,* 75, pp. 530–538.

Backus, D. and Driffill, J. (1986) 'Policy credibility and unemployment in the UK', in D.A. Currie (ed.) *Advances in Monetary Economics,* Croom Helm, London.

Balassa, B. (1963) 'Some observations on Mr Beckerman's "export-propelled" growth model', *Economic Journal,* 73, pp. 781–785.

Barratt, C.R. and Walters, A.A. (1966) 'The stability of Keynesian and money multipliers in the UK', *Review of Economics and Statistics,* 48, pp. 395–405.

Barro, R.J. (1974) 'Are government bonds net wealth?', *Journal of Political Economy,* 82, pp. 1095–1118.

Barro, R.J. (1977a) 'Long-term contracting, sticky prices and monetary policy', *Journal of Monetary Economics,* 3, pp. 305–316.

Barro, R.J. (1977b) 'Unanticipated money growth and unemployment in the United States', *American Economic Review,* 67, pp. 101–115.

Barro, R.J. (1978) 'Unanticipated money, output, and the price level in the United States', *Journal of Political Economy,* 86, pp. 549–581.

Barro, R.J. (1979) 'Unanticipated money growth and unemployment in the United States: reply', *American Economic Review,* 69, pp. 1004–1009.

Barro, R.J. and Gordon, D.B. (1983) 'Rules, discretion, and reputation in a model of monetary policy', *Journal of Monetary Economics*, 12, pp. 101–121.

Barro, R.J. and Grossman, H.I. (1971) 'A general disequilibrium model of income and employment', *American Economic Review*, 61, pp. 82–93.

Barro, R.J. and Rush, M. (1980) 'Unanticipated money and economic activity', in S. Fischer (ed.) *Rational Expectations and Economic Policy*, Chicago University Press, Chicago.

Baumol, W.J. (1952) 'The transactions demand for cash: an inventory–theoretic approach', *Quarterly Journal of Economics*, 66, pp. 545–556.

Beckerman, W. (1962) 'Projecting Europe's growth', *Economic Journal*, 72, pp. 912–925.

Begg, D.K.H. (1982) *The Rational Expectations Revolution in Macro-economics*, Philip Allan, Deddington.

Benassy, J.-P. (1975) 'Neo-Keynesian disequilibrium theory in a monetary economy', *Review of Economic Studies*, 42, pp. 503–524.

Bhattacharyya, D.K. (1979) 'On the validity of the quadratic utility approach in mean–variance portfolio analysis: an empirical test', *De Economist*, 127, pp. 422–425.

Blanchard, O.J. (1976) *The Non-Transition to Rational Expectations*, MIT mimeo.

Blanchard, O.J. (1979) 'Speculative bubbles, crashes and rational expectations', *Economic Letters, 3*, pp. 387–389.

Blanchard, O.J. (1981) 'Output, the stock market and interest rates', *American Economic Review*, 71, pp. 132–143.

Blanchard, O.J. (1985) 'Debts, deficits, and finite horizons', *Journal of Political Economy*, 93, pp. 223–247.

Blanchard, O.J. and Kahn, C.M. (1980) 'The solution of linear difference models under rational expectations', *Econometrica*, 48, pp. 1305–1309.

Blinder, A.S. and Solow, R.M. (1973) 'Does fiscal policy matter?', *Journal of Public Economics*, 2, pp. 319–337.

Blume, L.E. and Easley, D. (1982) 'Learning to be rational', *Journal of Economic Theory*, 26, pp. 340–351.

Blundell, R. and Walker, I. (1982) 'Modelling the joint determination of household labour supplies and commodity demands', *Economic Journal*, 92, pp. 351–364.

Bodkin, R.G. (1969) 'Real wages and cyclical variation in employment: a re-examination of the evidence', *The Canadian Journal of Economics*, 2, pp. 353–374.

Borio, C.E.V. (1986) 'Do contingent rules really dominate fixed rules?', *Economic Journal*, 96, pp. 1000–1010.

Boyer, R. (1978) 'Optimal foreign exchange market intervention', *Journal of Political Economy*, 86, pp. 1045–1056.

Branson, W.H. (1974) 'Stocks and flows in international monetary analysis', in A. Ando, R.J. Herring and R.C. Marston (eds) *International*

Aspects of Stabilisation Policies, Federal Reserve Bank of Boston, Boston.

Branson, W.H. (1975) 'Portfolio equilibrium and monetary policy with foreign and non-traded assets', in F. Claasen and P. Salin (eds) *Recent Issues in International Monetary Economics*, North-Holland, Amsterdam.

Branson, W.H. (1976) 'The dual roles of the government budget and the balance of payments in the movement from short-run to long-run equilibrium', *Quarterly Journal of Economics*, 90, August.

Branson, W.H. (1977) 'Asset markets and relative prices in exchange rate determination', *Sozialwissenschaftliche Annalen*, 1, pp. 69–89.

Branson, W.H. (1979) 'Exchange rate dynamics and monetary policy', in A. Lindbeck (ed.) *Inflation and Unemployment in Open Economies*, North-Holland, Amsterdam.

Branson, W.H. (1981) *Macroeconomic Determinants of Real Exchange Rates*, NBER Working Paper No. 801, November.

Branson, W.H and Buiter, W.H. (1983) 'Monetary and fiscal policy with flexible exchange rates', in J.S. Bhandari and B.H. Putnam (eds) *Economic Interdependence and Flexible Exchange Rates*, MIT Press, Cambridge, Mass.

Branson, W.H., Haltunnen, H. and Masson, P. (1977) 'Exchange rates in the short run', *European Economic Review*, 10, pp. 303–324.

Branson, W.H. and Henderson, D.W. (1985) 'The specification of asset markets', in R.W. Jones and P.B. Kenen (eds) *Handbook of International Economics*, Vol. 2, Elsevier, Amsterdam.

Branson, W.H. and Rotemberg, J. (1980) 'International adjustment with wage rigidity', *European Economic Review*, 13, pp. 309–332.

Bray, M. (1982) 'Learning, estimation, and the stability of rational expectations', *Journal of Economic Theory*, 26, pp. 318–339.

Bray, M. and Savin, N.E. (1984) *Rational Expectations Equilibria, Learning and Model Specification*, University of Cambridge Discussion Paper No. 79.

Brock, W.A. (1975) 'A simple perfect foresight monetary model', *Journal of Monetary Economics*, 1, pp. 133–150.

Brown, E.C. (1956) 'Fiscal policy in the thirties: a re-appraisal', *American Economic Review*, 46, pp. 857–879.

Bruce, N. and Purvis, D.D. (1985) 'The specification and influence of goods and factor markets in open-economy macroeconomic models', in R.W. Jones and P.B. Kenen (eds) *Handbook of International Economics*, Vol. 2, Elsevier, Amsterdam.

Brunner, K. and Meltzer, A.H. (1963) 'The place of financial intermediaries in the transmission of monetary policy', *American Economic Review*, 53, pp. 372–382.

Brunner, K. and Meltzer, A.H. (1964) 'Some further evidence on supply and demand functions for money', *Journal of Finance*, 19, pp. 240–283.

Brunner, K. and Meltzer, A.H. (1972) 'Money, debt, and economic activity', *Journal of Political Economy*, 80, pp. 951–977.

Brunner, K. and Meltzer, A.H. (1976) 'An aggregate theory for a closed economy', in J. Stein (ed.) *Monetarism*, North-Holland, Amsterdam.

Buchanan, J.M. (1976) 'Barro on the Ricardian equivalence theorem', *Journal of Political Economy*, 84, pp. 337–342.

Buiter, W.H. (1977) 'Crowding out and the effectiveness of fiscal policy', *Journal of Public Economics*, 7, pp. 309–328.

Buiter, W.H. (1980) 'The macroeconomics of Dr Pangloss: a critical survey of the new classical macroeconomics', *Economic Journal*, 90, pp. 34–50.

Buiter, W.H. (1983) 'Real effects of anticipated and unanticipated money: some problems of estimation and hypothesis testing', *Journal of Monetary Economics*, 11, pp. 207–224.

Buiter, W.H. (1985) 'A guide to public sector debt and deficits', *Economic Policy*, 1, pp. 13–60.

Cagan, P. (1956) 'The monetary dynamics of hyperinflation', in M. Friedman (ed.) *Studies in the Quantity Theory of Money*, Chicago University Press, Chicago.

Calvo, G. and Phelps, E.S. (1977) 'Indexation issues: appendix', *Journal of Monetary Economics* (Supplementary Series), 5, pp. 160–168.

Canzoneri, M.B. and Gray, J. (1983) *Two Essays on Monetary Policy in an Interdependent World*, International Finance Discussion Papers, Federal Reserve Board, No. 219.

Canzoneri, M.B. and Minford, P. (1986) *When International Policy Co-ordination Matters: An Empirical Analysis*, CEPR Discussion Paper No. 119, July.

Carr, J. and Darby, M.R. (1981) 'The role of money supply shocks in the short-run demand for money', *Journal of Monetary Economics*, 8, pp. 183–200.

Chiang, A.C. (1984) *Fundamentals of Mathematical Economics*, 3rd edn, McGraw-Hill, New York.

Chick, V. (1977) *The Theory of Monetary Policy* (revised edition), Basil Blackwell, Oxford.

Chow, G.C. (1970) 'Optimal stochastic control of linear economic systems', *Journal of Money, Credit, and Banking*, 2, pp. 291–302.

Chow, G.C. (1975) *Analysis and Control of Dynamical Systems*, J. Wiley and Sons, New York.

Chow, G.C. (1979) 'Optimal control of stochastic differential equation systems', *Journal of Economic Dynamics and Control*, 1, pp. 143–175.

Chow, G.C. (1981) *Econometric Analysis by Control Methods*, J. Wiley and Sons, New York.

Christ, C. (1968) 'A simple macroeconomic model with a government budget restraint', *Journal of Political Economy*, 76, pp. 53–67.

Christ, C. (1969) 'A model of monetary and fiscal policy effects on the money stock, price level and real output', *Journal of Money, Credit, and Banking*, 1, pp. 683–705.

Christodoulakis, N., Vines, D.A. and Weale, M. (1986) *Policy Design and Operation in a Macroeconomic Model with a Managed Exchange Rate Under Different Expectational Regimes*, University of Cambridge, mimeo.

Clower, R. (1965) 'The Keynesian counterrevolution: a theoretical appraisal', in F.H. Hahn and F.P.R. Brechling (eds) *Theory of Interest Rates*, Macmillan, London.

Cooper, R.N. (1974) 'Worldwide versus regional integration: is there an optimal size of the integrated area?', in F. Machlup (ed.) *Economic Integration: Worldwide, Regional, Sectional*, St Martin's Press, New York.

Cooper, R.N. (1985) 'Economic interdependence and coordination of economic policies', in R.W. Jones and P.B. Kenen (eds) *Handbook of International Economics*, Vol. 2, Elsevier, Amsterdam.

Corden, W.M. and Turnovsky, S.J. (1983) 'Negative international transmission of economic expansion', *European Economic Review*, 16, pp. 291–310.

Courakis, A.S. (1978) 'Serial correlation and a Bank of England study of the demand for money: an exercise in measurement without theory', *Economic Journal*, 88, pp. 537–548.

Courakis, A.S. (1981) 'Monetary targets: conceptual antecedents and recent policies in the US, UK, and West Germany', in A.S. Courakis (ed.) *Inflation, Depression, and Economic Policy in the West*, Alexandrine Press, Oxford.

Cumby, R. and Obstfeld, M. (1981) 'A note on exchange rate expectations and nominal interest difficulties: a test of the Fischer hypothesis', *Journal of Finance*, 36, pp. 697–704.

Currie, D.A. (1976) 'Some criticisms of the monetary analysis of balance of payments correction', *Economic Journal*, 43, pp. 508–522.

Currie, D.A. (1985) 'Macroeconomic policy design and control theory: a failed partnership?', *Economic Journal*, 95, pp. 285–306.

Currie, D.A. and Levine, P.L. (1984a) *Optimal Feedback Rules in an Open Economy Macromodel with Rational Expectations*, PRISM Discussion Paper No. 5.

Currie, D.A. and Levine, P.L. (1984b) 'Stochastic macroeconomic policy simulations for a small open economy', in F. van der Ploeg (ed.) *Mathematical Methods in Economics*, J. Wiley and Sons, New York.

Currie, D.A. and Levine, P.L. (1985a) 'Simple macropolicy rules for the open economy', *Economic Journal* (Supplement), 95, pp. 60–70.

Currie, D.A. and Levine, P.L. (1985b) 'Macroeconomic policy design in an interdependent world', in W.H. Buiter and R.C. Marston (eds) *International Economic Policy Coordination*, Cambridge University Press, Cambridge.

Cuthbertson, K. (1985a) *The Supply and Demand for Money*, Basil Blackwell, Oxford.

Cuthbertson, K. (1985b) *The demand for M1: A Forward-Looking Buffer-Stock Model*, National Institute of Economic and Social Research, Discussion Paper.

Cuthbertson, K. and Taylor, M.P. (1986) 'Buffer stock money: an assessment', in D.A. Currie, C.A.E. Goodhart and D.T. Llewellyn (eds) *The Operation and Regulation of Financial Markets*, Macmillan, London.

Cuthbertson, K. and Taylor, M.P. (1987) 'The demand for money: a dynamic rational expectations model', *Economic Journal*, (Supplement) 97, pp. 65–76.

David, P.A. and Scadding, J.L. (1974) 'Private savings: "ultrarationality", aggregation and Denison's Law', *Journal of Political Economy*, 82, pp. 225–249.

Davidson, J.E.H. (1985) *Monetary Disequilibrium: An Approach to Modelling Monetary Phenomena in the UK?*, London School of Economics, mimeo.

Davidson, J.E.H. and Hendry, D.F. (1981) 'Interpreting econometric evidence: the behaviour of consumers' expenditure in the UK', *European Economic Review*, 15, pp. 177–192.

Davis, M.H.A. (1977) *Linear Estimation and Stochastic Control*, Chapman and Hall, London.

Deaton, A. and Muellbauer, J. (1980) *Economics and Consumer Behaviour*, Cambridge University Press, Cambridge.

DeCanio, S.J. (1979) 'Rational expectations and learning from experience', *Quarterly Journal of Economics*, 93, pp. 47–57.

Desai, M. (1975) *The Phillips Curve: A Revisionist Interpretation*, London School of Economics, mimeo.

Desai, M. (1981) *Testing Monetarism*, Frances Pinter, London.

Dixit, A.K. (1980) *A Solution Technique for Rational Expectations Models with Applications to Exchange Rate and Interest Rate Determination*, University of Warwick, mimeo.

Dornbusch, R. (1973) 'Devaluation, money, and non-traded goods', *The American Economic Review*, 63, pp. 871–880.

Dornbusch, R. (1976) 'Expectations and exchange rate dynamics', *Journal of Political Economy*, 84, pp. 1161–1176.

Dornbusch, R. (1980) 'Exchange rate economics: where do we stand?', *Brookings Papers on Economic Activity*, Issue 1, pp. 143–185.

Dornbush, R. (1983a) 'Flexible exchange rates and interdependence', *IMF Staff Papers*, 30, pp. 3–30.

Dornbusch, R. (1983b) 'Exchange rate risk and the macroeconomics of exchange rate determination', in R.G. Hawkins, R.M. Levich and C. Wihlborg (eds) *The Internationalisation of Financial Markets and National Economic Policy*, JAI Press, Greenwich.

Dornbusch, R. and Fischer, S. (1980) 'Exchange rates and the current account', *American Economic Review*, 70, pp. 960–971.

Driffill, J. (1982) 'Optimal money and exchange rate policies', *Greek Economic Review*, 4, December.

Driskill, R.A. (1981) 'Exchange rate overshooting, the trade balance, and rational expectations', *Journal of International Economics*, 11, pp. 361–377.

Driskill, R.A. and Sheffrin, S.M. (1981) 'On the mark: comment', *American Economic Review*, 71, pp. 1068–1074.

Dunlop, J.T. (1938) 'The movement of real and money wage rates', *Economic Journal*, 48, pp. 413–434.

Eastwood, R.K. and Venables, A.J. (1982) 'The macroeconomic implications of a resource discovery in an open economy', *Economic Journal*, 92, pp. 285–299.

Eaton, J. and Turnovsky, S.J. (1983) 'Covered interest parity, uncovered interest parity, and exchange rate dynamics', *Economic Journal*, 93, pp. 555–575.

Edgren, G., Faxen, K.-O. and Odhmer, C.-E. (1969) 'Wages growth and the distribution of income', *Swedish Journal of Economics*, 3.

Edwards, S. (1983) 'Floating exchange rates, expectations and new information', *Journal of Monetary Economics*, 11, pp. 321–336.

Evans, G. (1985) 'Bottlenecks and the Phillips curve: a disaggregated Keynesian model of inflation, output, and unemployment', *Economic Journal*, 95, pp. 345–357.

Evans, G.W. (1986) 'A test for speculative bubbles and the sterling–dollar exchange rate: 1981–1984', *American Economic Review*, 76, pp. 621–636.

Feige, E. (1967) 'Expectations and adjustments in the monetary sector', *American Economic Review*, 57, pp. 462–473.

Feldstein, M.S. (1975) 'The importance of temporary layoffs: an empirical analysis', *Brookings Papers on Economic Activity*, Issue 3, pp. 725–744.

Fforde, J. (1983) 'Setting monetary objectives', *Bank of England Quarterly Bulletin*, 23, pp. 200–208.

Fischer, S. (1977a) 'Long-term contracts, rational expectations, and the optimal money supply rule', *Journal of Political Economy*, 85, pp. 191–206.

Fischer, S. (1977b) 'Long-term contracting, sticky prices and monetary policy: a comment', *Journal of Monetary Economics*, 3, pp. 317–323.

Flavin, M.A. (1981) 'The adjustment of consumption to changing expectations about future income', *Journal of Political Economy*, 89, pp. 974–1009.

Fleming, J.M. (1962) 'Domestic financial policies under fixed and floating exchange rates', *IMF Staff Papers*, 9, pp. 369–379.

Flood, R.P. and Garber, P.M. (1983) 'Market fundamentals versus price-level bubbles: the first tests', *Journal of Political Economy*, 88, pp. 745–770.

Frankel, J.A. (1979) 'On the mark: a theory of floating exchange rates based on real interest differentials', *American Economic Review*, 69, pp. 610–622.

Frenkel, J.A. (1978) 'Purchasing power parity: doctrinal perspective and evidence from the 1970s', *Journal of International Economics*, 8, pp. 169–191.

Frenkel, J.A. (1981a) 'The collapse of purchasing power parities during the 1970s', *European Economic Review*, 16, pp. 145–165.

Frenkel, J.A. (1981b) 'Flexible exchange rates, prices, and the role of news: lessons from the 1970s', *Journal of Political Economy*, 89, pp. 665–705.

Frenkel, J.A., Gylfason, T. and Helliwell, J.F. (1980) 'A synthesis of monetary and Keynesian approaches to short-run balance-of-payments theories', *Economic Journal*, 90, pp. 582–592.

Frenkel, J.A. and Johnson, H.G. (1976) *The Monetary Approach to the Balance of Payments*, Allen and Unwin, London.

Frenkel, J.A. and Johnson, H.G. (1978) *The Economics of Exchange Rates: Selected Studies*, Addison Wesley, Reading, Mass.

Frenkel, J.A. and Levich, R.M. (1975) 'Covered interest arbitrage: exploited profits?', *Journal of Political Economy*, 83, pp. 325–338.

Frenkel, J.A. and Levich, R.M. (1977) 'Transactions costs and interest arbitrage: tranquil versus turbulent periods', *Journal of Political Economy*, 85, pp. 1209–1226.

Friedman, B.M. (1975) 'Targets, instruments and indicators of monetary policy', *Journal of Monetary Economics*, 1, pp. 443–473.

Friedman, B.M. (1977) 'The inefficiency of short-run monetary targets for monetary policy', *Brookings Papers on Economic Activity*, Issue 2, pp. 293–335.

Friedman, B.M. (1978a) 'The theoretical non-debate about monetarism', in T. Mayer (ed.) *The Structure of Monetarism*, Norton, New York.

Friedman, B.M. (1978b) 'Crowding out or crowding in? Economic consequences of financing government deficits', *Brookings Papers in Economic Activity*, Issue 3, pp. 593–641.

Friedman, B.M. (1979) 'Optimal expectations and the extreme informational assumptions of rational expectations macromodels', *Journal of Monetary Economics*, 5, pp. 23–41.

Friedman, J.W. (1977) *Oligopoly and the Theory of Games*, North-Holland, Amsterdam.

Friedman, J.W. (1983) *Oligopoly Theory*, Cambridge University Press, Cambridge.

Friedman, J.W. (1986) *Game Theory with Applications to Economics*, Oxford University Press, New York.

Friedman, M. (1953) 'The case for flexible rates', in *Essays in Positive Economics*, Chicago University Press, Chicago.

Friedman, M. (1956) 'The quantity theory of money: a restatement', in M. Friedman (ed.) *Studies in the Quantity Theory of Money*, Chicago University Press, Chicago.

Friedman, M. (1957) *A Theory of the Consumption Function*, Princeton University Press, New Jersey.

Friedman, M. (1961) 'The lag in effect of monetary policy', *The American Economic Review*, 69, pp. 447–466.

Friedman, M. (1968) 'The role of monetary policy', *The American Economic Review*, 58, pp. 1–17.

Friedman, M. and Meiselman, D. (1963) 'The relative stability of monetary velocity and the investment multiplier in the United States, 1897–1958', in Commission on Money and Credit, *Stabilisation Policies*, Prentice-Hall, Englewood Cliffs, NJ.

Frydman, R. and Phelps, E.S. (1983), *Individual Forecasting and Aggregate Outcomes*, Cambridge University Press, Cambridge.

Gandolfo, G. (1972) *Mathematical Methods and Models in Economic Dynamics*, North-Holland, Amsterdam.

Gapinski, J.H. (1982) *Macroeconomic Theory: Statics, Dynamics and Policy*, McGraw-Hill, New York.

Goldfeld, S.M. (1976) 'The case of the missing money', *Brookings Papers on Economic Activity*, Issue 3, pp. 683–730.

Goodhart, C.A.E. (1975) *Money, Information, and Uncertainty*, Macmillan, London.

Goodhart, C.A.E. (1984) *Monetary Theory and Practice: the UK Experience*, Macmillan, London.

Goodhart, C.A.E. and Crockett, A.D. (1970) 'The importance of money', *Bank of England Quarterly Bulletin*, June.

Gordon, R.J. (1970) 'The recent acceleration of inflation and its lessons for the future', *Brookings Papers on Economic Activity*, Issue 1, pp. 8–47.

Gordon, R.J. (ed.) (1974) *Milton Friedman's Monetary Framework: A Debate With His Critics*, University of Chicago Press, Chicago.

Gordon, R.J. (1976) 'Recent developments in the theory of inflation and unemployment', *Journal of Monetary Economics*, 2, pp. 185–219.

Gordon, R.J. (1984) 'The Short-run demand for money: a reconsideration, *Journal of Money, Credit and Banking*, 16, pp. 403–434.

Grandmont, J.-M. and Laroque, G. (1974) 'On temporary Keynesian equilibria', CEPREMAP, Paris.

Granger, C.W.J. (1969) 'Investigating causal relations by econometric models and cross-spectral methods', *Econometrica*, 37, pp. 424–438.

Green, J. and Kahn, C.N. (1983) 'Wage employment contracts', *Quarterly*

Journal of Economics, 98 (Supplement), pp. 173–187.

Grice, J.W. and Bennett, A. (1984) 'Wealth and the demand for Sterling M3 in the United Kingdom, 1963–1978', *The Manchester School*, 52, pp. 239–271.

Grossman, H. (1977) 'Risk shifting and reliability in labour markets', *Scandinavian Journal of Economics*, 2, pp. 187–209.

Grossman, H. (1978) 'Risk shifting, layoffs, and seniority', *Journal of Monetary Economics*, 4, pp. 661–686.

Grossman, S.J. and Hart, O.D. (1983) 'Implicit contracts under asymmetrical information', *Quarterly Journal of Economics*, 98 (Supplement), pp. 123–156.

Gurley, J.G. and Shaw, E.S. (1960) *Money in a Theory of Finance*, The Brookings Institution, Washington D.C.

Gylfason, T. and Helliwell, J.F. (1983) 'A synthesis of Keynesian, monetary, and portfolio approaches to flexible exchange rates', *Economic Journal*, 93, pp. 820–831.

Haberler, G. (1941) *Prosperity and Depression*, Allen and Unwin, London (reprinted 1964).

Hacche, G. (1974) 'The demand for money in the UK: experience since 1971', *Bank of England Quarterly Bulletin*, 14, pp. 284–305.

Hacche, G. and Townend J. (1981) 'Exchange rates and monetary policy: modelling sterling's effective exchange rate, 1972–1980', in W. Eltis & P.J.N. Sinclair (eds) '*The Money Supply and the Exchange Rate*', Oxford University Press, Oxford.

Hadley, G. and Kemp, M.C. (1971) *Variational Methods in Economics*, North-Holland, Amsterdam.

Hall, R.E. (1976) 'The Phillips curve and macroeconomic policy', in K. Brunner and A.H. Meltzer (eds) *The Phillips Curves and Labor Markets*, Carnegie-Rochester Conference Series on Public Policy, North-Holland, Amsterdam.

Hall, R.E. (1978) 'Stochastic implications of the life cycle–permanent income hypothesis: theory and evidence', *Journal of Political Economy*, 86, pp. 971–988.

Hall, R.E. (1980) 'Employment fluctuations and wage rigidity', *Brookings Papers on Economic Activity*, 1, pp. 91–123.

Hall, R.E. (1982) 'The importance of lifetime jobs in the US economy', *American Economic Review*, 72, pp. 716–724.

Hall, R.E. and Lillien, D.M. (1979) 'Efficient wage bargains under uncertain supply and demand', *American Economic Review*, 69, pp. 868–879.

Hall, S.G., Henry, S.G.B. and Wren-Lewis, S. (1984) *Manufacturing Stocks and Forward-Looking Expectations in the UK*, National Institute of Economic and Social Research, Discussion Paper No. 64.

Hamada, K. (1976) 'A strategic analysis of monetary interdependence',

Journal of Political Economy, 84, pp. 677–700.

Hamada, K. (1979) 'Macroeconomic strategy and coordination under alternative exchange rates', in R. Dornbusch and J.A. Frenkel (eds) *International Economic Policy*, John Hopkins University Press, Baltimore.

Hamada, K. (1985) *The Political Economy of International Monetary Interdependence*, MIT Press, Cambridge, Mass.

Hansen, B. (1970) 'Excess demand, unemployment, vacancies and wages', *Quarterly Journal of Economics*, 84, pp. 1–23.

Hansen, L.P. and Hodrick, R.J. (1980) 'Forward exchange rates as optimal predictors of future spot rates: an econometric analysis', *Journal of Political Economy*, 88, pp. 829–853.

Harris, L. (1981) *Monetary Theory*, McGraw-Hill, New York.

Harsanyi, J. (1977) *Rational Behaviour and Bargaining Equilibrium in Games and Social Situations*, Cambridge University Press, Cambridge.

Harvey, A.C. (1981) *The Econometric Analysis of Time Series*, Philip Allan, Deddington.

Hendry, D.F. (1979) 'Predictive failure and econometric modelling in macroeconomics: the transactions demand for money', in P. Ormerod (ed.) *Economic Modelling*, Heinemann, London.

Hendry, D.F. (1985) 'Monetary economic myth and econometric reality', *Oxford Review of Economic Policy*, 1, Spring, pp. 72–84.

Hendry, D.F. and Mizon, G.E. (1978) 'Serial correlation as a convenient simplification, not a nuisance: a comment on a study of the demand for money by the Bank of England', *Economic Journal*, 88, pp. 549–563.

Hendry, D.F., Pagan, A.R. and Sargan, J.D. (1984) 'Dynamic specification', in Z. Griliches and M.D. Intriligator (eds) *Handbook of Econometrics*, Vol. 2, Elsevier, Amsterdam.

Herring, R.J. and Marston, R.C. (1977) 'Sterilisation policy: the trade-off between monetary autonomy and control over foreign exchange reserves', *European Economic Review*, 10, pp. 325–343.

Hicks, J.R. (1967) 'The "classics" again', in *Critical Essays in Monetary Theory*, Clarendon Press, Oxford.

Hughes Hallett, A.J. (1984) *Policy Design in Interdependent Economies: the Case for Co-ordinating EEC and US Policies*, Paper delivered at CEPR conference on EMS.

Hughes Hallett, A.J. (1986) *The Impact of Interdependence on Economic Policy Design: the Case of the US, EEC, Japan*, CEPR Discussion Paper No. 108, May.

Hume, D. (1752) 'Of the balance of trade', reprinted in R.N. Cooper (ed.) *International Finance*, Penguin, London, 1969.

Intriligator, M.D. (1971) *Mathematical Optimisation and Economic Theory*, Prentice-Hall, Englewood Cliffs, NJ.

Iwai, K. (1981) *Disequilibrium Dynamics: A Theoretical Analysis of*

Inflation and Unemployment, Yale University Press, New Haven.

Johnson, H.G. (1961) 'The general theory after Keynes', *American Economic Review* 51, pp. 1–17.

Johnson, H.G. (1967) 'Money in a neoclassical one-sector growth model', in H.G. Johnson (ed.) *Essays in Monetary Economics*, Allen and Unwin, London.

Johnson, H.G. (1969) 'Inside money, outside money, income, wealth and welfare in monetary theory', *Journal of Money, Credit, and Banking*, 1, pp. 30–46.

Johnson, H.G. (1972) 'Monetary approach to balance of payments theory', in H.G. Johnson (ed.) *Further Essays in Monetary Theory*, Allen and Unwin, London.

Johnston, J. (1984) *Econometric Methods*, 3rd edn, McGraw-Hill, New York.

Jones, R.W. and Kenen, P.B. (1985) *Handbook of International Economics*, Vol. 2, Elsevier, Amsterdam.

Judd, J.P. and Scadding, J.L. (1982) 'The search for a stable demand for money function: a survey of the post-1973 literature', *Journal of Economic Literature*, 20, pp. 992–1023.

Kaldor, N. (1966) *Causes of the Slow Rate of Growth in the United Kingdom: An Inaugural Lecture*, Cambridge University Press, Cambridge.

Karenken, J.A., Muench, T. and Wallace, N. (1973) 'Optimal open market strategy: the use of information variables', *The American Economic Review*, 63, pp. 156–172.

Keynes, J.M. (1936) *The General Theory of Employment, Interest and Money*, Macmillan, London.

Keynes, J.M. (1937) 'The general theory of employment', *Quarterly Journal of Economics*, 51, pp. 209–223.

Keynes, J.M. (1986) *The Collected Writings of J.M. Keynes*, edited by Sir A. Robinson and D.E. Moggridge, Volumes XIII, XIV, and XXIX, Macmillan, London.

Kindleberger, C. (1967) *Europe's Postwar Growth: the Role of Labor Supply*, Harvard University Press, Cambridge, Mass.

Kindleberger, C. (1973) *The World in Depression 1929–1939*, University of California Press, Berkeley.

Kouri, P.J.K. (1976) 'The exchange rate and the balance of payments in the short run and in the long run', *Scandinavian Journal of Economics*, 78, pp. 255–275.

Kouri, P.J.K. and Porter, M.G. (1974) 'International capital flows and portfolio equilibrium', *Journal of Political Economy*, 82, pp. 443–468.

Kuh, E. (1966) 'Unemployment, production functions and effective demand', *Journal of Political Economy*, 74, pp. 238–249.

Kushner, H.J. (1971) *Introduction to Stochastic Control*, Rinehart and Winston, New York.

Kydland, F. and Prescott, E.C. (1977) 'Rules rather than discretion: the inconsistency of optimal plans', *Journal of Political Economy*, 84, pp. 473–491.

Laidler, D.E.W. (1966) 'The role of interest rates and the demand for money: some empirical evidence', *Journal of Political Economy*, 74, pp. 545–555.

Laidler, D.E.W. (1971) 'The influence of money on economic activity: a survey of some current problems', in G. Clayton, J.C. Gilbert and R. Sedgwick (eds) *Monetary Theory and Policy in the 1970s*, Oxford University Press, Oxford.

Laidler, D.E.W. (1978) 'Inflation in Britain: a monetarist perspective: reply', *American Economic Review*, 68, pp. 726–729.

Laidler, D.E.W. (1980) 'The demand for money in the United States — yet again', in K. Brunner and A.H. Meltzer (eds) *On the State of Macroeconomics*, Carnegie-Rochester Conference Series on Public Policy, No. 12.

Laidler, D.E.W. (1982) *Monetarist Perspectives*, Philip Allan, Deddington.

Laidler, D.E.W. (1984) 'The buffer stock notion in macroeconomics', *Economic Journal* (Supplement), 94, pp. 17–33.

Laidler, D.E.W. and Parkin, J.M. (1970), 'The demand for money in the United Kingdom, 1956–1967: some preliminary estimates', *The Manchester School*, 38, pp. 187–208.

Lamfalussy, A. (1963) 'Contribution à une théorie de la croissance en économie ouverte', *Recherches Economiques de Louvain*.

Leijonhufvud, A. (1968) *On Keynesian Economics and the Economics of Keynes*, Oxford University Press, London and New York.

Levine, P.L. and Currie, D.A. (1984) *The Design of Feedback Rules in Stochastic Rational Expectations Models*, PRISM Discussion Paper No. 20.

Lillien, D.M. (1980) 'The cyclical pattern of temporary layoffs in US manufacturing', *Review of Economic Statistics*, 62, pp. 24–31.

Lindbeck, A. (1973) *The National State in an Internationalized World Economy*, Conjunto Universitario Candido Mendes, Rio de Janeiro.

Lipsey, R.G. (1960) 'The relationship between unemployment and the rate of change of money wages in the UK, 1861–1957: a further analysis', *Economica*, 27, pp. 1–31.

Lucas, R.E. (1972a) 'Expectations and the neutrality of money', *Journal of Economic Theory*, 4, pp. 103–124.

Lucas, R.E. (1972b) 'Econometric testing of the natural rate hypothesis', in O. Eckstein (ed.) *The Econometrics of Price Determination*, Federal Reserve Bank, Washington D.C.

Lucas, R.E. (1973) 'Some international evidence on output–inflation trade-offs', *American Economic Review*, 63, pp. 326–334.

Lucas, R.E. (1975) 'An equilibrium model of the business cycle', *Journal of Political Economy*, 83, pp. 1113–1144.

Lucas, R.E. (1976) 'Econometric policy evaluation: a critique', in K. Brunner and A.H. Meltzer (eds) *The Phillips Curve and Labor Markets*, North-Holland, Amsterdam.

Lucas, R.E. (1977) 'Understanding business cycles', in K. Brunner and A.H. Meltzer (eds) *Stabilisation of the Domestic and International Economy*, North-Holland, Amsterdam.

Lucas, R.E. (1980) 'Methods and problems in business cycle theory', *Journal of Money, Credit, and Banking*, 12, pp. 696–715.

Lucas, R.E. and Prescott, E.C. (1971) 'Investment under uncertainty', *Econometrica*, 39, pp. 659–681.

Lucas, R.E. and Rapping, L. (1969) 'Real wages, employment and inflation', *Journal of Political Economy*, 77, pp. 721–754.

Luce, R.D. and Raiffa, H. (1957) *Games and Decisions*, J. Wiley and Sons, New York.

Main, B.G.M. (1982) 'The length of a job in Great Britain', *Economica*, 49, pp. 325–332.

Malinvaud, E. (1977) *The Theory of Unemployment Reconsidered*, Basil Blackwell, Oxford.

Markowitz, H.M. (1959) *Portfolio Selection: Efficient Diversification of Investments*, J. Wiley and Sons, New York.

McCallum, B.T. (1979a) 'On the observational inequivalence of classical and Keynesian models', *Journal of Political Economy*, 87, pp. 395–409.

McCallum, B.T. (1979b) 'The Current State of the Policy — ineffectiveness debate', in R.E. Lucas and T. Sargent (eds) *Rational Expectations*, Allen and Unwin, London.

McCallum, B.T. (1983) 'On non-uniqueness in rational expectations models: an attempt at perspective', *Journal of Monetary Economics*, 11, pp. 139–168.

MacDonald, I.M. and Solow, R.M. (1981) 'Wage bargaining and employment', *American Economic Review*, 71, pp. 896–908.

MacKinnon, J.G. and Milbourne, R.D. (1984) 'Monetary anticipations and the demand for money', *Journal of Monetary Economics*, 13, pp. 263–274.

McKinnon, R.I. (1969) 'Portfolio balance and international payments adjustment', in R.A. Mundell and A.K. Swoboda (eds) *Monetary Problems of the International Economy*, University of Chicago Press, Chicago.

Meade, J.E. (1951) *The Theory of International Economic Policy, Vol. 1: The Balance of Payments*, Oxford University Press, Oxford.

Meade, J.E (1982) *Wage Fixing*, Allen and Unwin, London.

Meese, R.A. and Rogoff, K. (1983a) 'Empirical exchange rate models of the seventies: are any fit to survive?', *Journal of International Economics*, 14, pp. 3–24.

Meese, R.A. and Rogoff, K. (1983b) 'The out-of-sample failure of empirical exchange rate models: sampling error or misspecification?', in J.A. Frenkel (ed.) *Exchange Rates and International Economics*, Chicago University Press, Chicago.

Meltzer, A.H. (1963) 'The demand for money: the evidence from the time series', *Journal of Political Economy*, 71, pp. 219–246.

Metzler, L.A. (1951) 'Wealth, saving and the rate of interest', *Journal of Political Economy*, 59, pp. 93–116.

Miller, M.H. (1985) 'Monetary stabilisation policy in an open economy', *Scottish Journal of Political Economy*, 32, pp. 220–233.

Miller, M.H. and Salmon, M.H. (1983) *Dynamic Games and the Time Inconsistency of Optimal Policy in Open Economies*, Working Paper No. 232, Department of Economics, University of Warwick.

Miller, M.H. and Salmon, M.H. (1985a) 'Dynamic games and the time inconsistency of optimal policy in open economies', *Economic Journal* (Supplement), 95, pp. 124–137.

Miller, M.H. and Salmon, M.H. (1985b) 'Policy coordination and dynamic games', in W.H. Buiter and R.C. Marston (eds) *International Economic Policy Coordination*, Cambridge University Press, Cambridge.

Minford, A.P.L. (1984) 'The effects of American policies — a new classical interpretation' in W.H. Buiter and R.C. Marston (eds) *International Economic Policy Coordination*, Cambridge University Press, Cambridge.

Minford, A.P.L., Ioannides, C. and Marwaha, S. (1983) 'Rational expectations in a multilateral macro-model', in P. deGrauwe and T. Peeters (eds) *Exchange Rates in Multi-Country Econometric Models*, Macmillan, London.

Minsky, H. (1963) 'Can "it" happen again?', in D. Carson (ed.) *Banking and Monetary Studies*, Irwin, Homewood, Ill.

Minsky, H. (1972) 'An evaluation of recent monetary policy, monetary control and economic stability', *The Bankers Magazine*, Vol. 214, No. 1544.

Mishkin, F.S. (1982) 'Does anticipated monetary policy matter? An econometric investigation', *Journal of Political Economy*, 90, pp. 22–51.

Mishkin, F.S. (1983) *A Rational Expectations Approach to Macroeconometrics*, Chicago University Press, Chicago.

Modigliani, F. (1977) 'The monetarist controversy, or should we forsake stabilisation policies?', *American Economic Review*, 67, pp. 1–19.

Modigliani, F. and Brumberg, R. (1954) 'Utility analysis and the consumption function: an interpretation of cross-section data', in K.K. Kurihara (ed.) *Post-Keynesian Economics*, Rutgers University Press, New Brunswick.

Mortensen, D.T. (1970a) 'A theory of wage and employment dynamics', in E.S. Phelps (ed.) *Microeconomic Foundations of Employment and Inflation Theory*, Norton, New York.

Mortensen, D.T. (1970b) 'Job search, the duration of unemployment and the Phillips curve', *American Economic Review*, 60, pp. 847–867.

Muellbauer, J. and Portes, R. (1978) 'Macroeconomic models with quantity rationing', *Economic Journal*, 88, pp. 788–821.

Mundell, R.A. (1962) 'The appropriate use of monetary and fiscal policy for internal and external stability', *IMF Staff Papers*, 9, pp. 70–79.

Mundell, R.A. (1963) 'Capital mobility and stabilisation policy under fixed and flexible exchange rates', *Canadian Journal of Economics and Political Science*, 29, pp. 475–485.

Mundell, R.A. (1968) *International Economics*, Macmillan, New York.

Muscatelli, V.A. (1986) 'Alternative models of buffer stock money: an empirical investigation', *Scottish Journal of Political Economy* (forthcoming).

Mussa, M. (1976) 'The exchange rate, the balance of payments and monetary and fiscal policy under a regime of controlled floating', in J. Herin, A. Lindbeck and J. Nyhrman (eds) *Flexible Exchange Rates and Stabilisation Policy*, Macmillan, London.

Mussa, M. (1979) 'Macroeconomic interdependence and the exchange rate regime', in R. Dornbusch and J.A. Frenkel (eds) *International Economic Policy*, Johns Hopkins University Press, Baltimore.

Muth, J.F. (1961) 'Rational expectations and the theory of price movements', *Econometrica*, 29, pp. 315–335.

Neary, J.P. and Purvis, D.D. (1983) 'Real adjustment and exchange rate dynamics', in J.A. Frenkel (ed.) *Exchange Rates and International Macroeconomics*, University of Chicago Press, Chicago.

Nickell, S.J. (1985) 'Error correction, partial adjustment and all that: an expository note', *Oxford Bulletin of Economics and Statistics*, 47, pp. 119–130.

Oates, W.E. (1966) 'Budget balance and equilibrium income: a comment on the efficiency of fiscal and monetary policy in an open economy', *Journal of Finance*, 21, pp. 489–498.

Obstfeld, M. (1982) 'Can we sterilise? theory and evidence', *American Economic Review*, 72, pp. 45–50.

Obstfeld, M. (1984) 'Balance-of-payments crises and devaluation', *Journal of Money, Credit, and Banking*, 16, pp. 208–217.

Obstfeld, M. (1985) 'Floating exchange rates: experience and prospects', *Brookings Papers on Economic Activity*, Issue 2, pp. 369–450.

OECD (1979) 'The demand for money in major OECD countries', *OECD Economic Outlook* (Occasional Studies), January.

Officer, L. (1976) 'The purchasing power parity theory of exchange rates: a review article', *IMF Staff Papers*, 23, pp. 1–60.

Okun, A. (1975) 'Inflation: its mechanics and welfare costs', *Brookings Papers on Economic Activity*, Issue 2, pp. 351–390.

Okun, A. (1981) *Prices and Quantities*, The Brookings Institution, Washington D.C.

Ott, D.J. and Ott, A. (1965) 'Budget balance and equilibrium income', *Journal of Finance*, 20, pp. 71–77.

Oudiz, G. and Sachs, J. (1984) 'Macroeconomic policy coordination among industrial nations', *Brookings Papers on Economic Activity*, No. 2, pp. 1–64.

Oudiz, G. and Sachs, J. (1985) 'International policy coordination in dynamic macroeconomic models', in W.H. Buiter and R.C. Marston (eds) *International Economic Policy Coordination*, Cambridge University Press, Cambridge.

Pagan, A.R. (1984) 'Econometric issues in the analysis of regressions with generated regressors', *International Economic Review*, 25, pp. 221–247.

Patinkin, D. (1965) *Money, Interest and Prices*, 2nd edn, Harper and Row, New York.

Pesaran, M.H. (1984) 'The new classical macroeconomics: a critical exposition', in F. van der Ploeg (ed.) *Mathematical Methods in Economics*, J. Wiley and Sons, New York.

Pesek, B.P. and Saving, T.R. (1967) *Money, Wealth, and Economic Theory*, Macmillan, New York.

Phelps, E.S. (1969) 'A note on short-run employment and real wage rates under competitive commodity markets', *International Economic Review*, 10, pp. 220–232.

Phelps, E.S. (1970a) 'The new microeconomics', in E.S. Phelps (ed.) *Microeconomic Foundations of Employment and Inflation Theory*, Norton, New York.

Phelps, E.S (1970b) 'Money wage dynamics and labor market equilibrium', in E.S. Phelps (ed.) *Microeconomic Foundations of Employment and Inflation Theory*, Norton, New York.

Phelps, E.S (1972) *Inflation Policy and Unemployment Theory: the Cost-Benefit Approach to Monetary Planning*, Norton, New York.

Phillips, A.W. (1954) 'Stabilisation policies in a closed economy', *Economic Journal*, 64, pp. 290–323.

Phillips, A.W. (1957) 'Stabilisation policies and the time form of lagged responses', *Economic Journal*, 67, pp. 265–277.

Phillips, A.W. (1958) 'The relation between unemployment and the rate of change of money wage rates in the United Kingdom, 1861–1957', *Economica*, 25, pp. 283–299.

Pierce, J.L. and Thomson, T.D. (1972) *Controlling Monetary Aggregates II: The Implementation*, pp. 115–136, Federal Reserve Bank of Boston.

Pigou, A.C. (1941) *Employment and Equilibrium*, Macmillan, London.

Pigou, A.C. (1943) 'The classical stationary state', *Economic Journal*, 53, pp. 343–351.

Pigou, A.C. (1947) 'Economic progress in a stable environment', *Economica*, 14, pp. 180–188.

Poole, W. (1970) 'Optimal choice of monetary policy instruments in a simple stochastic macro model', *Quarterly Journal of Economics*, 84, pp. 197–216.

Popper, K. (1959) *The Logic of Scientific Discovery*, Oxford University Press, Oxford.

Prescott, E.C. (1972) 'The multi-period control problem under uncertainty', *Econometrica*, 40, pp. 1043–1058.

Price, L.D. (1972) 'The demand for money in the UK: a further investigation', *Bank of England Quarterly Bulletin*, 12, pp. 43–55.

Radcliffe Report (1959) *Committee on the Working of the Monetary System: Report*, Cmnd 827, HMSO.

Rogoff, K. (1983) *Productive and Counterproductive Monetary Policies*, International Finance Discussion Paper No. 223, Board of Governors of the Federal Reserve.

Roper, D.E. and Turnovsky, S.J. (1980) 'Optimal exchange market intervention in a simple stochastic macro model', *Canadian Journal of Economics*, 13, pp. 296–309.

Rose, H. (1966) 'Unemployment in a theory of growth', *International Economic Review*, 7, pp. 260–282.

Rosen, S. (1983) 'Unemployment and insurance', *Carnegie–Rochester Conference Series on Public Policy*, No. 20, pp. 5–49.

Rosen, S. (1985) 'Implicit contracts: a survey', *Journal of Economic Literature*, 23, pp. 1144–1175.

Sachs, J. (1983) *International Policy Coordination in a Dynamic Macroeconomic Model*, NBER Working Paper No. 1166.

Salter, W. (1959) 'Internal and external balance: the role of price and expenditure effects', *Economic Record*, 35, pp. 226–238.

Samuelson, P.A. (1967a) 'General proof that diversification pays', *Journal of Financial and Quantitative Analysis*, 2, pp. 1–13.

Samuelson, P.A. (1967b) 'Efficient portfolio selection for Pareto-Levy investments', *Journal of Financial and Quantitative Analysis*, 2, pp. 107–122.

Samuelson, P.A. (1983) *Foundations of Economic Analysis* (enlarged edition), Harvard University Press, Cambridge, Mass.

Samuelson, P.A. and Solow, R.M. (1960) 'Analytical aspects of anti-inflation policy', *American Economic Review*, 50 (Papers and Proceedings), pp. 177–194.

Sargan, J.D. (1986) *Montecarlo Studies of the Properties of Some Estimators of a Simple Rational Expectations Model*, Paper delivered at the RES/AUTE Conference, Cambridge.

Sargent, T.J. (1973) 'Rational expectations, the real rate of interest, and the natural rate of unemployment', *Brookings Papers on Economic Activity*, Issue 2, pp. 429–480.

Sargent, T.J. (1976a) 'A classical macroeconometric model for the United States', *Journal of Political Economy*, 84, pp. 207–237.

Sargent, T.J. (1976b) 'The observational equivalence of natural and unnatural theories of macroeconomics', *Journal of Political Economy*, 84, pp. 631–640.

Sargent, T.J. (1977) 'The demand for money during hyperinflations under rational expectations', *International Economic Review*, 18, pp. 59–82.

Sargent, T.J. (1978a) 'Estimation of dynamic labour demand schedules under rational expectations', *Journal of Political Economy*, 86, pp. 1009–1044.

Sargent, T.J. (1978b) 'Rational expectations, econometric exogeneity and consumption', *Journal of Political Economy*, 86, pp. 673–700.

Sargent, T.J. (1979) *Macroeconomic Theory*, Academic Press, New York.

Sargent, T.J. (1981) 'The ends of four big inflations', in R.E. Hall (ed.) *Inflation*, Chicago University Press, Chicago.

Sargent, T.J. and Wallace, N. (1975) '"Rational" expectations, the optimal monetary instrument, and the optimal money supply rule', *Journal of Political Economy*, 83, pp. 241–254.

Sargent, T.J. and Wallace, N. (1976) 'Rational expectations and the theory of economic policy', *Journal of Monetary Economics*, 2, pp. 169–184.

Scarth, W.M. (1985) 'A note on non-uniqueness in rational expectations models', *Journal of Monetary Economics*, 15, pp. 247–254.

Scarth, W.M. and Myatt, A. (1980) 'The real wage–employment relationship', *Economic Journal*, 90, pp. 85–94.

Sharpe, W.F. (1964) 'Capital asset prices: a theory of market equilibrium under conditions of risk', *Journal of Finance*, 19, pp. 425–442.

Shaw, G.K. (1979) 'The measurement of fiscal influence', in S.T. Cook and P.M. Jackson (eds) *Current Issues in Fiscal Policy*, Martin Robertson, London.

Sidrauski, M. (1967) 'Rational choice and patterns of growth in a monetary economy', *American Economic Review* (Papers and Proceedings), 57, pp. 534–544.

Silber, W. (1970) 'Fiscal policy in IS–LM analysis: a correction', *Journal of Money, Credit, and Banking*, 2, November.

Sims, C.A. (1972) 'Money, income, and causality', *American Economic Review*, 62, pp. 540–552.

Sims, C.A. (1980) 'Macroeconomics and reality', *Econometrica*, 48, pp. 1–48.

Smith, P.N. and Wickens, M.R. (1986) 'An empirical investigation into the causes of failure of the monetary approach of the exchange rate', *Journal of Applied Econometrics*, 1, pp. 143–162.

Snower, D.J. (1981) *Rational Expectations, Stochastic Coefficients and Monetary Stabilisation Policy*, Birbeck College Discussion Paper No. 95.

Solow, R.M. (1980) 'On theories of unemployment', *American Economic Review*, 70, pp. 1–11.

Solow, R.M. (1984) 'Mr. Hicks and the classics', *Oxford Economic Papers*, 36, Supplement, pp. 13–25.

Solow, R.M. and Stiglitz, J.E. (1968) 'Output, employment and wages in the short run', *Quarterly Journal of Economics*, 82, pp. 537–560.

Stein, J.L. (1970) Monetary growth in perspective', *American Economic Review*, 60, pp. 85–106.

Stein, J.L. (1976) 'Inside the monetarist black box', in J. Stein (ed.) *Monetarism*, North-Holland, Amsterdam.

Stern, R.M., Francis, J. and Schumaker, B. (1976) *Price Statistics in International Trade: An Annotated Bibliography*, Macmillan, London.

Stiglitz, J.E. (1984) *Theories of Wage Rigidity*, Princeton University, mimeo.

Swan, T. (1960) 'Economic control in a dependent economy', *Economic Record*, 36, pp. 51–66.

Swoboda, A.K. (1973) 'Monetary policy under fixed exchange rates: effectiveness, the speed of adjustment, and proper use', *Economica*, 40, pp. 136–154.

Tarshis, L. (1939) 'Changes in real and money wage rates', *Economic Journal*, 49, pp. 150–154.

Taylor, J.B. (1975) 'Monetary policy during a transition to rational expectations', *Journal of Political Economy*, 83, pp. 1009–1021.

Taylor, J.B. (1979) 'Estimation and control of a macroeconomic model with rational expectations', *Econometrica*, 47, pp. 1267–1286.

Taylor, J.B. (1980) 'Aggregate dynamics and staggered contracts', *Journal of Political Economy*, 88, pp. 1–23.

Taylor, J.B. (1983) 'Rational expectations and the invisible handshake', in J. Tobin (ed.) *Macroeconomics, Prices and Quantities*, The Brookings Institution, Washington D.C.

Teigen, R. (1964) 'Demand and supply functions of money in the United States', *Econometrica*, 32, pp. 477–509.

Theil, H. (1957) 'A note on certainty equivalence in dynamic planning', *Econometrica*, 25, pp. 346–349.

Tinbergen, J. (1952) *On the Theory of Economic Policy*, North-Holland, Amsterdam.

Tobin, J. (1956) 'The interest-elasticity of transactions demand for cash', *Review of Economics and Statistics*, 38, pp. 241–247.

Tobin, J. (1958) 'Liquidity preference as behaviour towards risk', *The Review of Economic Studies*, 25, pp. 65–86.

Tobin, J. (1961) 'Money, capital and other stores of value', *American Economic Review*, 51, pp. 26–37.

Tobin, J. (1965) 'Money and economic growth', *Econometrica*, 33, pp. 671–684.

Tobin, J. (1969) 'A general equilibrium approach to monetary theory', *Journal of Money, Credit, and Banking*, 1, pp. 15–29.

Tobin, J. (1972) 'Inflation and unemployment', *American Economic Review*, 62, pp. 1–18.

Tobin, J. (1977) 'How dead is Keynes?', *Economic Inquiry*, 15, pp. 459–468.

Tobin, J. (1978) 'Monetary policy and the economy: the transmission mechanism', *Southern Economic Journal*, January.

Tobin, J. (1980) *Asset Accumulation and Economic Activity*, Basil Blackwell, Oxford.

Tobin, J. (1982) 'Money and finance in the macroeconomic process', *Journal of Money, Credit, and Banking*, 14, pp. 171–204.

Tobin, J. and Brainard, W.C. (1963) 'Financial intermediaries and the effectiveness of monetary controls', *American Economic Review*, 53, pp. 383–400.

Tobin, J. and Buiter, W.H. (1980) 'Fiscal and monetary policies, capital formation, and economic activity', in C.M. von Furstenberg (ed.) *The Government and Capital Formation*, Ballinger, Cambridge, Mass., pp. 73–151.

Tobin, J. and de Macedo, J.B. (1981) 'The short-run macroeconomics of floating exchange rates: an exposition', in J. Chipman and C. Kindleberger (eds) *Flexible Exchange Rates and the Balance of Payments: Essays in Memory of E. Sohmen*, North-Holland, New York.

Turnovsky, S.J. (1976) 'The dynamics of fiscal policy in an open economy', *Journal of International Economics*, 6, pp. 115–142.

Turnovsky, S.J. (1977) *Macroeconomic Analysis and Stabilisation Policy*, Cambridge University Press, Cambridge.

Turnovsky, S.J. (1983) 'Exchange market intervention in a small open economy', in J.S. Bhandari and B.H. Putnam (eds) *Economic Interdependence and Flexible Exchange Rates*, MIT Press, Cambridge, Mass.

Turnovsky, S.J. and D'Orey, V. (1986) 'Monetary policies in interdependent economies with stochastic disturbances: a strategic approach', *Economic Journal*, 96, pp. 696–721.

Vines, D.A. and Moutos, T. (1987) *Macroeconomics in an Open Economy*, Allen and Unwin, London (forthcoming).

Vines, D.A., Maciejowski, J. and Meade, J.E. (1983) *Demand Management*, Allen and Unwin, London.

Von Neumann, J. and Morgenstern, O. (1947) *Theory of Games and Economic Behaviour*, Princeton University Press, Princeton.

Wallis, K.F. (1980), 'Econometric implications of the rational expectations hypothesis', *Econometrica*, 48, pp. 49–72.

Whitman, M. v-N. (1975) 'Global monetarism and the monetary approach to the balance of payments', *Brookings Papers on Economic Activity*, pp. 491–536.

Whitman, M. v-N. (1979) *Reflections on Interdependence*, University of Pittsburgh Press, Pittsburgh.

Wickens, M.R. (1982) 'The efficient estimation of econometric models

with rational expectations', *Review of Economic Studies*, 49, pp. 55–67.
Wilson, C.A. (1979) 'Anticipated shocks and exchange rate dynamics',
Journal of Political Economy, 87, pp. 639–647.

AUTHOR INDEX

Also consult the Bibliography for references and names designating models in the Subject Index.

SUBJECT INDEX